Isidore of Seville and the *Liber Iudiciorum*

The Medieval and
Early Modern Iberian World

Edited by

Larry J. Simon (*Western Michigan University*)
Gerard Wiegers (*University of Amsterdam*)
Isidro J. Rivera (*University of Kansas*)
Mercedes García-Arenal (*CCHS/CSIC*)
Montserrat Piera (*Temple University*)
Sabine Panzram (*Universität Hamburg*)

VOLUME 80

The titles published in this series are listed at *brill.com/memi*

Isidore of Seville and the *Liber Iudiciorum*

The Struggle for the Past in the Visigothic Kingdom

By

Michael J. Kelly

BRILL

LEIDEN | BOSTON

Cover illustration: MS Bayerische Staatsbibliothek München, Clm 13031, fol. 1r. (http://daten.digitale-sammlungen.de/bsb00072196/image_5). With kind permission of the Bayerische Staatsbibliothek München.

Library of Congress Cataloging-in-Publication Data

Names: Kelly, Michael J. (Historian), author.
Title: Isidore of Seville and the Liber Ludiciorum : the struggle for the past in the Visigothic Kingdom / by Michael J. Kelly.
Description: Leiden ; Boston : Brill, [2021] | Series: The Medieval and early modern Iberian world, 1569-1934 ; volume 80 | Based on author's thesis (doctoral - University of Leeds, School of History, 2014) issued under title: Writing history, narrating fulfillment : the 'Isidore-moment' and the struggle for the 'before now' in late antique and early medieval Hispania. | Includes bibliographical references and index.
Identifiers: LCCN 2021001103 (print) | LCCN 2021001104 (ebook) | ISBN 9789004343986 (hardback) | ISBN 9789004450011 (ebook)
Subjects: LCSH: Liber judiciorum. | Law, Visigothic. | Spain–History–Gothic period, 414-711. | Isidore, of Seville, Saint, -636–Influence.
Classification: LCC KJ252 .K45 2021 (print) | LCC KJ252 (ebook) | DDC 349.4609/021–dc23
LC record available at https://lccn.loc.gov/2021001103
LC ebook record available at https://lccn.loc.gov/2021001104

All royalties earned from the sale of this book go directly into running the international open-access project Networks and Neighbours (https://networksandneighbours.org/) and its associated no-fees, non-profit, open-access research activities.

Typeface for the Latin, Greek, and Cyrillic scripts: "Brill". See and download: brill.com/brill-typeface.

ISSN 1569-1934
ISBN 978-90-04-34398-6 (hardback)
ISBN 978-90-04-45001-1 (e-book)

Copyright 2021 by Koninklijke Brill NV, Leiden, The Netherlands.
Koninklijke Brill NV incorporates the imprints Brill, Brill Hes & De Graaf, Brill Nijhoff, Brill Rodopi, Brill Sense, Hotei Publishing, mentis Verlag, Verlag Ferdinand Schöningh and Wilhelm Fink Verlag.
All rights reserved. No part of this publication may be reproduced, translated, stored in a retrieval system, or transmitted in any form or by any means, electronic, mechanical, photocopying, recording or otherwise, without prior written permission from the publisher. Requests for re-use and/or translations must be addressed to Koninklijke Brill NV via brill.com or copyright.com.

This book is printed on acid-free paper and produced in a sustainable manner.

For Mutz

Too many echoes, not enough voices.
CORNEL WEST

Contents

1 **Introduction: the Isidore-Moment, the *Liber Iudiciorum*, and the Schools Thesis** 1
   1 A Brief History and Introduction to Seventh-Century Hispania 1
   2 The Isidore-Moment and the *Liber Iudiciorum* 13
   3 The "Schools" – *Hasta Siempre*, Bishop Isidore 22

2 **In the Beginning: The History of the Historiography of Isidore** 43
   1 Introduction 43
   2 The Historiography of Isidore 44
   3 The Representations 45
   4 Other Contemporary Historical Representations of Isidore 59
   5 Conclusion 63

3 **Origins and Histories: Creating New Chains of Signification** 64
   1 Introduction 64
   2 Isidore's Literature of the Past 68
   3 Isidore's [Use, Abuse and Philosophy of] History 87
   4 Conversion and the Locating of Seville 97
   5 The Goths in Isidore-Seville's Historical Representations 105
   6 Conclusion 117

4 **The Historical *Lacunae* and *Damnatio*[*nes*] *Memoriae* of the *Hispana*** 119
   1 Introduction 119
   2 The *Hispana* 120
   3 The Example of Gundemar and his Council (610) 136
   4 The Example of the Third Council of Seville (624) 159

5 **Pinnacle and Twilight: The *Liber Iudiciorum* and the "Historical" Fulfillment of the Isidore-Moment** 175
   1 Introduction 175
   2 What Is the *Liber Iudiciorum*? 177
   3 Interlude: Short Historical Background 184
   4 The Structure of the *Liber Iudiciorum*, and Its Meaning 188
   5 Constituent Influence of the School of Isidore-Seville 192
   6 Conclusion 206

Conclusion 209

Appendix: Julian of Toledo Not an Agalian 213
Bibliography 216
Index 248

CHAPTER 1

Introduction: the Isidore-Moment, the *Liber Iudiciorum*, and the Schools Thesis

> What a contrast, at the end of the sixth century, between the ruins of Italy and the rebuilding of Spain!
> JACQUES FONTAINE[1]

∴

> No early medieval writer set pen to papyrus or parchment without good reason: the reasons usually involved power or land.
> IAN WOOD[2]

∴

1 A Brief History and Introduction to Seventh-Century Hispania

The setting of this book is seventh-century Hispania, a place politically dominated by the Visigothic kingdom. The kingdom was administratively centered in Toledo, from where its kings enforced control over most of the peninsula and parts of southeastern Gaul.[3] The kingdom's territory ranged from the south of the Iberian Peninsula to the northwestern edge of Galicia, to Narbonensis in the northeast. This area contained the five formerly Roman imperial provinces of Baetica, Carthaginensis, Galicia, Lusitania, and Tarraconensis, broken up at times into other units, such as the province of Carpetania. The Balearics

---

1 Jacques Fontaine, "Education and Learning," in *Cambridge Medieval History, 500–700*, vol. 1, ed. Paul Fouracre (Cambridge: Cambridge University Press, 2008), 735–59 (738).
2 Ian Wood, *The Merovingian kingdoms 450–751* (New York: Longman, 1994), 3.
3 The Visigoths controlled Septimania, only a part of the Roman province of Narbonensis, but the Visigothic texts refer to the area as Narbonensis. For maps and a general introduction to Visigothic Hispania and its extra-peninsular territory see Roger Collins, *Visigothic Spain: 409–711* (Malden, MA: Blackwell Publishing, 2004). For helpful regional and local maps see Jesús Vico Monteoliva, María Cruz Cores Gomendio and Gonzalo Cores Uría, *Corpus Nummorum Visigothorum Ca. 575–714: Leovigildus-Achila* (Madrid: Real Academia de la Historia, 2006).

were in the hands of the Byzantines, who also controlled pockets of the southeastern peninsula, an area which they called "Spania" (in contrast to Visigothic "Hispania"), from the 550s to the 620s.[4]

The core structure of the Visigothic kingdom of Toledo, as the political entity it became in the seventh century, was forged in the late sixth century by the Arian king Liuvigild's (r. 567/8–586) vigorous campaigns and desire to build a functioning monarchy centered in Toledo. Liuvigild's son and royal successor Reccared (r. 586–601) attempted to stabilize the kingdom by converting it from Arianism to Catholicism (Nicene Orthodoxy) in 589 at the Third Council of Toledo (III Toledo).[5] This move deflated the political authority and propaganda of the Byzantines in the peninsula, whose claim for authority relied on a righteous religious argument. It also led to a boom in the construction of landscapes of Catholic authority, especially in the southern province of Baetica, the frontier with Spania.[6] The conversion of the kingdom was intended to soothe violent rifts between factions of nobles dedicated culturally or religiously to Arianism or Catholicism. As will be shown, this worked to some degree, but at the turn of the seventh century new and old antagonisms and competitions (re-)emerged despite shared religious identities.

The Visigothic kingdom of Toledo, as a strong and permanent royal site, was a development of the late sixth century. However, the Visigothic kings, armies and people had been part of the fabric of the peninsula's life since the turn of the fifth century. After the Gothic sack of Rome in 410, and the untimely death of the Gothic leader Alaric I in 410, his second successor, the Visigothic king Wallia (r. 416–419), was sent into the Iberian Peninsula to fight against barbarians in the name of the Western Roman Empire. The Visigothic armies were exceptionally successful, as well as loyal. After their victories, they were recalled from the peninsula and were granted a region and capital of their

---

4   For a review of the Byzantines in sixth- and seventh-century Hispania see Jamie Wood, "Defending Byzantine Spain: frontiers and diplomacy," in *Early Medieval Europe* 18 (2010): 292–319; Margarita Vallejo Girvés, *Bizancio y la España tardoantigua (ss. V–VIII): un capitulo de historia mediterránea* (Alcalá de Henares: Universidad de Alcalá, 1993); and, Cynthia María Valente, "As Relações Políticas entre o Império Bizantino e o Reino Visigodo de Toledo durante o século VI," *Revista Mosaico* 11 (2018): 123–30. NB, although occasionally reiterated for clarification, all dates in the text should be presumed to be AD, unless noted.

5   From this point on in the book councils normally will be abbreviated by citing the location of the council, preceded by a Roman numeral indicating its accepted number as council there, and, when relevant, followed by the number of the canon, for example, III Toledo 1, VIII Toledo 2, or II Seville 4.

6   See Javier Arce and Xavier Barral i Altet, eds., *Art and Architecture of Spain* (Boston: Little, Brown, 1998), 64ff.

own, Aquitaine and the city of Toulouse in south/southwestern Gaul.[7] The birth in Toulouse of a proper Visigothic monarchy should be dated to about 439.[8] The Iberian Peninsula, the part of it that was still the old Roman province of Hispania, remained in the Western Roman Empire until 476, when Odoacer deposed the last Western Roman Emperor, Romulus Augustulus. Almost immediately, the Visigothic king Euric (r. 466–483) declared full independence for the kingdom based in Toulouse. Visigoths had, however, been steadily settling in Hispania since at least the time of Athaulf in Barcelona.[9]

After the Visigothic Toulousan kingdom was destroyed in 507 by Clovis and the Franks, the Ostrogothic kingdom led by king Theoderic the Great became, in 511, guardian of the Visigothic treasury and remaining armies. Theoderic set up a proxy government in Hispania, led first by him and then by his nephew Amalaric. The regency lasted technically until 526 when Amalaric, firmly in Hispania, regained independence of the Visigothic treasure and ended Visigothic tribute to the Ostrogothic government in Italy. However, an Ostrogoth would remain on the throne until the end of the brief reign of Theudisculus in 549.[10] While the Ostrogoths were on the throne in Hispania, and for the

7   Isidore of Seville, *De Origine Gothorum*, 21–22 and Jordanes, *Getica*, 31–35. All quotes from and references to Isidore's *De Origine Gothorum* are from the edition in *Las Historias de los Godos, los Vandalos y los suevos de Isidoro de Sevilla*, ed. Cristóbal Rodríguez Alonso (León: Centro de Estudios e Investigación "San Isidoro," 1975), 167–321, or, when appropriate, *Historia Gothorum Vandalorum Sueborum* in *Chronica Minora, saec. IV–VII*, ed. Theodor Mommsen, Monumenta Germaniae Historica, Auctores Antiquissimi 11 (Berlin: Weidemann, 1894), 267–303. References to Jordanes's *Getica* are to the edition in *Jordanes: "Getica,"* ed. Antonio Grillone, Auters Latins du Moyen Âge (Paris: Les Belles Lettres, 2017), 3–263, or, when appropriate, *Romana et Getica*, ed. Theodor Mommsen, Monumenta Germaniae Historica, Auctores Antiquissimi 5.1 (Berlin: Weidemann, 1882), 53–138 or *The Gothic History of Jordanes: In English with an Introduction and a Commentary*, trans. Charles C. Mierow (Princeton: Princeton University Press, 1915).
8   For the early history of the Goths and their development of a kingdom in Aquitaine see Herwig Wolfram, *History of the Goths*, trans. Thomas J. Dunlap (Berkeley: University of California Press, 1979); Peter Heather, "The Creation of the Visigoths," in *The Visigoths from the Migration Age to the Seventh Century: An Ethnographic Perspective*, ed. Peter Heather (Woodbridge: Boydell Press, 1999), 43–68; Ana María Jiménez Garnica, "Settlement of the Visigoths in the Fifth Century," in *The Visigoths from the Migration Age*, 93–109; and, Ralph Mathisen and Hagith Sivan, "Forging a New Identity: The kingdom of Toulouse and the Frontiers of Visigothic Aquitania (418–507)," in *The Visigoths: Studies in Culture & Society*, ed. Alberto Ferreiro (Boston and Leiden: Brill, 1999), 1–63.
9   Jordanes, *Getica*, 31.
10 On the moving of Visigoths into Hispania around the turn of the sixth century, and for relations between Visigoths and Ostrogoths in the peninsula, see Edward A. Thompson, *Goths in Spain* (Oxford: Oxford University Press, 1969), esp. ch. 1, and Pablo C. Díaz and María del Rosario Valverde Castro, "Goths Confronting Goths: Ostrogothic Political Rela-

period beyond, areas of the peninsula were variously under the control of the Suevic kingdom, as well as residual Roman forces, slave armies of the elite, and regional and urban authorities, and then the Byzantines from the 550s.[11]

In the first half of the sixth century, the Visigothic king was stationed around the peninsula, from Barcelona to Seville, until king Athanagild (r. 551/555–568) established Toledo as the *de facto* royal capital, and died there, on the throne, of natural causes. Liuvigild granted Toledo official royal status in the 580s.[12] Toledo was chosen as the royal city for its geographical position in the center of the peninsula, its position on top of a hill surrounded on three sides by the Tagus River, but also because it was a site minimally hampered by pre-existing, powerful factions that could challenge the king's authority.[13] The Visigothic king preferred to construct authority more or less *ex novo* and away from the old Roman centers like Seville, Mérida or Tarragona. The growth of a Toledan aristocracy loyal to the king would become a powerful factor in seventh-century politics.[14]

Seventh-century Hispania was remarkably diverse and varied. In recent years, scholars have been piecing together various forms of newly found and re-interpreted evidence, from texts to rocks, coins to aqueducts, to slates with writing.[15] From this activity, scholars are increasingly painting a picture of

---

tions in Hispania," in *The Ostrogoths from the Migration Period to the Sixth Century: An Ethnographic Perspective*, ed. Sam J. Barnish and Federico Marazzi (San Marino, 2007), 353–76.

11   On the slave armies of Spain see Procopius, *History of the Wars*, trans. H. B. Dewing, vol. 3, *Loeb Classical Library* 107 (Cambridge: Harvard University Press, 1916), 130–31 (5.12.50–52).

12   Athanagild reigned from the death of his rival Agila in 555, but dated his reign to the beginning of the revolt against Agila. For a discussion of this rebellion see Chapter 3, § 4.4, as well as Otto Fiebiger and Ludwig Schmidt, *Inschriftensammlung zur Geschichte der Ostgermanen* (Vienna: Hölder, 1917), 256–57.

13   See Roger Collins, "Mérida and Toledo: 550–585," in *Visigothic Spain. New Approaches*, ed. Edward James (Oxford: Oxford University Press, 1980), 218.

14   Daniel Osland, "Urban Change in Late Antique Hispania: The Case of Augusta Emerita" (Ph.D. diss., University of Cincinnati, 2011), 275ff.

15   See Sam Koon and Jamie Wood, "Unity from disunity: law, rhetoric and power in the Visigothic kingdom," *European Review of History* 16 (2009): 793–808; Santiago Castellanos, "The Political Nature of Taxation in Visigothic Spain," *Early Medieval Europe* 12 (2003): 214; Santiago Castellanos and Iñaki Martín Viso, "The local articulation of central power in the north of the Iberian Peninsula (500–1000)," *Early Medieval Europe* 13 (2005): 1–42; Michael Kulikowski, *Late Roman Spain and Its Cities* (Baltimore: The Johns Hopkins University Press, 2004); Javier Martínez Jiménez, "Aqueducts and Water Supply in the Towns of Post-Roman Spain (AD 400–1000), Volume I" (Ph.D. diss., Oxford University, 2014); Isabel Velázquez Soriano, *Las Pizarras Visigodas: Entre el latín y su disgregación. La lengua hablada en Hispania, siglos VI–VIII* (Madrid: Real Academia Española, 2004); Christian Cuello, "Visigothic coins in the Gale collection of the Australian Centre for Ancient Numismatic Studies," *Journal of the Numismatic Association of Australia* 28 (2017): 19–33;

seventh-century Hispania as categorized by differences and dominated by local interests and localisms, as well as regional competitions and friendships.[16]

In contrast to interpretations that have seen in the evidence, and praised, the social and political centrality and "unity" in the period, the new materials and increasingly critical readings of previously known texts and manuscripts elicit the persistence and growth of regional identities and autonomies.[17] Jamie Wood and Sam Koon have convincingly argued that the rhetoric about unity was a symptomatic response to the very opposite situation on the ground: a peninsula widely diverse in beliefs, languages, cultural backgrounds and loyalties, a peninsula disparate in its political allegiances, fragmented by violent and persistent struggles of local networks of authority, secular and ecclesiastical, against Toledo and against themselves, intra-regional and inter-urban.[18]

Diversity here means a collection of identities, but also varying political opinions, social beliefs and situations, and, of course, conditions of existence. Such heterogeneity led to beautiful results, for example, Christians protecting their Jewish neighbors from kings and bishops trying to score political points, or groups of Britons fleeing other barbarian groups being welcomed into a community, or North African immigrants being embraced around the south. Whereas, in other stories, bigotries were revealed, based along classist, linguistic or other differences. This is the complex constellation of life in early medieval Hispania.[19]

---

and, Andrew Kurt, *Minting, State and Economy in the Visigothic Kingdom: From Settlement in Aquitaine through the First Decade of the Muslim Conquest of Spain* (Amsterdam: Amsterdam University Press, 2020).

16   For an overview see Jamie Wood and Javier Martínez Jiménez, "New Directions in the Study of Visigothic Spain," *History Compass* 14, no. 1 (2016): 29–38.

17   For discussion see Peter Linehan, *History and the Historians of Medieval Spain* (Oxford: Oxford University Press, 1993), 73ff.

18   On unity and consensus as a response to disaster in late antiquity see Peter Brown, *Through the Eye of a Needle: Wealth, the Fall of Rome, and the Making of Christianity in the West, 350–550 AD* (Princeton: Princeton University Press, 2012), 396; and, Renan Frighetto, "When confrontation generates collaboration: Goths, Romans and the emergence of the Hispano-Visigothic Kingdom of Toledo (5th–6th centuries)," *Vínculos de Historia* 7 (2018): 157–72.

19   The groups and identities known to have been living in seventh-century Hispania include: Africans, Asturians, Basques, Berbers, Britons, Burgundians, Byzantines, Carpetanians, Celtiberians, Franks, Greeks, "Hispano-Romans," Jews, Ostrogoths, Ruccones, Syrians, and Visigoths. This list is simply illustrative of the diversities of socio-religious identities, not by any means comprehensive: to the list could be added the residual pockets of Arians and Acephali, general paganism and heresy, peasants, farmers, slaves, freedpersons, generations-old communities with local, shared identities, "woman," "man," and so on. On these diversities see Gisela Ripoll López, "The Arrival of the Visigoths in Hispania: Population Problems and the Process of Acculturation," in *Strategies of Distinction: the Construction of Ethnic Communities, 300–800*, ed. Walter Pohl and Helmut Reimitz (Boston

Seventh-century Hispania was a variegated society, where one could find wonderful displays of communal activities and parades, love for fellow human beings, and deep familial bonds. It was also a violent, dangerous and volatile society full of antagonisms and contradictions. It was a society in which one could find religious leaders of all types physically confronting one another, even in the royal capital. One could find bishops taking up arms against kings, raising rebellions, and rival bishops in the same cities. One could find would-be assassins of Catholic bishops later becoming kings of the Catholic kingdom. One could find virulently anti-Jewish laws on the books, and community protection of Jews on the ground. One could find slaves fleeing captivity in mass numbers and being protected by ordinary people and elites around the peninsula. There were also waves of plagues across the kingdom, year after year, decade after decade, causing unknown levels of devastation to the populations.[20] The middle and later seventh-century was a socio-economic disaster,

and Leiden: Brill, 1998), 155–56; Alice Rio, "Self-sale and Voluntary Entry into Unfreedom, 300–1000," *Journal of Social History* 45 (2012): 661–85; Joaquin Martínez Pizarro, "Ethnic and National History ca. 500–1000," in *Historiography in the Middle Ages*, ed. Deborah Mauskopf Deliyannis (Boston and Leiden: Brill, 2003), 43–87; Paul Reynolds, *Hispania and the Roman Mediterranean, AD 100–700: Ceramics and Trade* (London: Duckworth, 2010), 120ff.; Gisela Ripoll, "The archaeological characterisation of the Visigothic kingdom of Toledo: the question of the Visigothic cemeteries," in *Völker, Reiche und Namen im frühen Mittelalter, 65 Geburtstag Prof. Dr. Jörg Jarnut (Mittelalter Studien* 22), ed. Matthias Becher and Stefanie Dick (Munich: W. Fink, 2010), 161–80; and, Peter Heather, *The Goths* (Oxford: Oxford University Press, 1996), 284–87. On Christians helping Jews, Wolfram Drews, "Jews as Pagans? Polemical definitions of identity in Visigothic Spain," *Early Medieval Europe* 11 (2002): 189–207. On Britons in Iberia, Simon Young, "The Bishops of the Early Medieval Spanish Diocese of Britonia," *Cambrian Medieval Celtic Studies* 45 (2003): 1–19, and Antonio Tovar, "Un obispo con nombre británico y los orígines de la diócesis de Mondoñedo," *Habis* 3 (1972): 155–58. Furthermore, Alberto Ferreiro suggests that king Chindaswinth's (642–649) son and successor Recceswinth (649/653–672) spoke Gothic, as was related by the *Chronicon* of Pseudo-Isidore, thus establishing a royal use of Gothic into the late seventh century. In addition to Gothic, Celtic languages and Basque, other local tongues persisted in diverse regions, on which see Alberto Ferreiro, "Saint Martin of Braga and the Germanic Languages: An Addendum to Recent Research," *Perita* 6 (1987): 298–306. On liturgy and identity see Molly Lester, "Mapping Liturgical Identity in Early Medieval Iberia and Beyond," *Visigothic Symposia* 2 (2017): 114–30, and Kati Ihnat, "Liturgy against apostasy: Marian commemoration and the Jews in Visigothic Iberia," *Early Medieval Europe* 25, no. 4 (2017): 443–65.

20   For discussion see Henry Gruber, "Indirect Evidence for the Social Impact of the Justinianic Pandemic: Episcopal Burial and Conciliar Legislation in Visigothic Hispania," *Journal of Late Antiquity* 11, no. 1 (2018): 193–215; Michael Kulikowski, "Plague in Spanish Late Antiquity," in *Plague and the End of Antiquity*, ed. Lester K. Little (Cambridge: Cambridge University Press, 2007), 150–70; and, Kyle Harper, *The Fate of Rome: Climate, Disease, and the End of an Empire* (Princeton: Princeton University Press, 2017).

in which, in a span of only a couple of decades, the value of the primary Visigothic coinage (the tremiss) fell drastically.[21] Moreover, this period saw a steady increase in the killing of children by their own parents, to the extent that already in the 640s a law was passed against this activity.[22] With the peninsula seemingly facing a demographic crisis, the penalties for abortion were severe: death for both would-have-been parents, a law made not for religious reasons since the canon laws were not as strict.

Fredric Jameson argues that in historiography "the decision about continuity or discontinuity is not an empirical one [...] it is taken in advance, as a kind of absolute presupposition, which then determines your subsequent reading and interpretation of the materials (sometimes called 'the facts')."[23] One could describe the events and historiographies of seventh-century Hispania as signs of a collapsing kingdom or society, in the face of diversities, localisms, regional affiliations, and political fragmentation, but one could also read them as evidence of vibrant transition or transformation, and the forced attempts at centralization as the catalyst for the destruction of entire communities. Regardless of what historiographical tradition one wants to use to define and explain them, the diversities of life and experience were paramount in seventh-century Hispania, where at least twenty different "ethnicities" and identities, regional dialects and languages could be found.[24]

The peninsula had constituted the Roman imperial province of Hispania since the first century. Seventh-century Hispania lived in the shadow of the legacy of Rome, despite the post-Roman autonomies, Byzantine occupation, Suevic and Vandal conquests, Visigothic settlements and kingdoms, and the Western Empire's political collapse centuries earlier. The peninsula was an occupied territory whose people had been colonized, their languages, topographies of life and customs suppressed in favor of imperial ones. After centuries

---

21 The same item rose in price from six *solidi* in the time of Recceswinth to twelve by the time of king Ervig (680–687) (*Liber Iudiciorum* 5.4.22 [on the *Liber Iudiciorum* (*LI*), see Chapter 5, § 2]). On the impact of the recent growth in coin finds on this image of the late Visigothic coinage and its circulation see Manuel Castro Priego, "Absent Coinage: Archaeological Contexts and Tremisses on the Central Iberian Peninsula in the 7th and 8th Centuries AD," *Medieval Archaeology* 60, no. 1 (2016): 27–56.

22 *LI*, 6.3.7.

23 Fredric Jameson, *Late Marxism: Adorno or the Persistence of the Dialectic* (London: Verso, 2007, orig. 1990), 3.

24 On identity in late antique Iberia see Jacques Fontaine, "Romanité et hispanité dans la littérature hispano-romaine des IVe et Ve siècles," in *Assimilation et résistance à la culture gréco-romaine dans le monde ancien. Actes du VIe Congrès, International d'Études Classiques*, ed. Dionis M. Pippidi (Paris: Société d'édition "Les Belles Lettres," 1976), 301–22, and Erica Buchberger, *Shifting Ethnic Identities in Spain and Gaul, 500–700* (Amsterdam: Amsterdam University Press, 2017).

of settlements and colonization, when, as a collection of cities, farms, provinces and other localities, the peninsula became a sort of independent (and post- or really neo-colonial) political, social and cultural body in the wake of the Empire's political fracturing, the legacy of Rome, and its aftermath prevailed.

Despite its exceptional breadth, at a meta-level, seventh-century Hispania was "arguably the most Romanised" society in post-Roman Europe.[25] Visigothic kings were late Roman in mindset, which is not to say that they entirely emulated the Empire and its forms (although emulation of the Byzantines was a permanent feature of Visigothic society), but rather, that they had been conditioned by a wider Euro-Mediterranean culture of domination and empire, adjusted to and born from an epistemological world in which massive state structures were the norm, and the aim of aspiring individuals.

The Visigothic kings re-confirmed late Roman forms of authority, suppressed local languages and identities, used councils for canonical regulations, late Roman laws as the basis of their legal system, Latin as their official language, and even associated the Visigothic monarchy with the emperors.[26] Their actualizations of power and authority depended upon military might, but also on the expectation that cities were centers for regional authority, from which countrysides should be controlled. The Visigothic kings, alone of their post-Roman contemporaries, built *ex novo* cities, such as Reccopolis, Ologitis and Victoriacum, as well as bishoprics like El Tolmo de Minateda and the church of Sts. Peter and Paul, to develop territorial authority by means of settlement directed from the center.[27]

---

25   Ian Wood, *The Modern Origins of the Early Middle Ages* (Oxford: Oxford University Press, 2013), ch. 15. "Romanised" here refers to the lasting presence in Iberia (Roman Hispania) of social frameworks and life that developed during the period there of the late Roman Empire.

26   This will be discussed further below in the context of the law, but the phenomenon is also particularly evident in the numismatic evidence, on which see the work of Ruth Pliego, as well as Kurt, *Minting, State and Economy*. For a recent problematization of the matter see Ruth Pliego, "Kings' Names on Visigothic Coins: A New Minimus from Ispali in the Name of Leovigild," *American Journal of Numismatics*, Second Series 30 (2018): 245–57.

27   Victoriacum was founded by Liuvigild and Ologicus was founded by Swinthila (621–631) (see John of Biclar, *Chron.*, a. 581, Isid., *De Orig. Goth.*, 63). For relevant archaeological research on the north see Augustín Azkárate Garai-Oraun, "El País Vasco en los siglos inmediatos a la desparación del Impero Romano," in *Historia del País Vasco* (San Sebastian: Hiria, 2004), 34–35. For an overview of landscape changes in the peninsula during the period see Pilar Diarte-Blasco, *Late Antique and Early Medieval Hispania* (Philadelphia: Oxbow Books, 2018). On the economy that facilitated the building of towns see Jaime Vizcaíno, *La presencia bizantina en Hispania (siglos vi–viii)*, 2nd edn. (Murcia: Universidad de Murcia Press, 2009). On the archaeological changes to the region around Toledo and Reccopolis, and on the symbolic value of Roman urban sites within, see Rafael Barroso Cabrera, *De la provincia Celtiberia a la qūrā de*

With such an urban, imperial mindset, it is no wonder that Visigothic kings struggled to adapt to the rise of agricultural patronage networks. Only very late into the kingdom, after the period covered by this book, from the 670s on, did the monarchy begin incorporating rural networks into the orbit of Toledo.[28] The policy of collectivizing power into Toledo could not deal effectively with alternative agricultural networks, although it embraced the power of cities. This policy struggled to satisfy the non-Toledan urban powers, i.e. the established elite, the provincial cities like Seville, Mérida, and Tarragona. The

---

Santabariyya: Arqueología de la Antigüedad tardía en la provincia de Cuenca (siglos v–viii d.C.) (Oxford: Archaeopress, 2019). On Reccopolis see Lauro Olmo, "Recópolis: una cuidad en época de transformaciones," in *Recópolis y la ciudad en la época visigoda*, ed. Lauro Olmo Enciso (Alcalá de Henares: Museo Arqueológico Regional, 2008), 40–63; Javier Martínez Jiménez, "Engineering, Aqueducts, and the Rupture of Knowledge Transmission in the Visigothic Period," *Visigothic Symposia* 3 (2018): 37–57; and, Javier Martínez Jiménez, "Reccopolitani and Other Town Dwellers in the Southern Meseta during the Visigothic Period of State Formation," in *Urban Interactions: Communication and Competition in Late Antiquity and the Early Middle Ages*, ed. Michael Burrows and Michael J. Kelly (Binghamton: Gracchi Books, 2020), 183–204. On El Tolmo de Minateda see Sonia Gutiérrez Lloret, Lorenzo Abad Casal, and Blanca Gamo Parras, "La Iglesia Visigoda de el Tolmo de Minateda (Hellín, Albacete)," in *Sacralidad y Arqueología: homenaje al Prof. Thilo Ulbert al cumplir 65 años, Antigüedad y cristianismo* 21, ed. Thilo Ulbert, José María Blázquez, and Antonino González Blanco (Murcia: Universidad de Murcia, 2004), 137–69; and, Victoria Amorós Ruiz, Julia Sarabia Bautista, Carolina Doménech Belda, and Sonia Gutiérrez Lloret, "The Buildings of the Visigothic Elite: Function and Material Culture in Spaces of Power," *Visigothic Symposia* 2 (2017): 34–59. On the Alicante region see Javier Martínez Jiménez and José María Moreno Narganes, "*Nunc autem a Gothis subversa*: the province of Alicante and the Spanish Mediterranean towns between the Byzantine and Visigothic periods," *Early Medieval Europe* 23, no. 3 (2015): 263–89. On new churches in Seville see Concepción Fernández Martínez and Joan Goméz Pallarès, "¿Hermenegildo, para siempre en Sevilla? Una nueva interpretación de *IHC*, n. 76 = *ILCV*, n. 50," *Gerión* 19 (2001), 629–58, and in Toledo, Luis J. Balmaseda, "En busca de las iglesias toledanas de época visigoda," in *Hispania Gothorum: San Ildefonso y el reino visigodo de Toledo*, ed. Rafael García Serrano (Toledo: Don Quijote, 2006), 194–214, and in Córdoba, Pedro Marfil, "La sede episcopal cordobesa en época bizantina: evidencia arqueológia," in *V Reunió d'arqueologia cristiana hispànica*, ed. Josep M. Gurt and Núria Tena (Barcelona: Institut d'Estudis Catalans, 2000), 157–75. For John of Biclar's *Chronicles* see *Iohannes abbatis Biclarensis chronica, chron. min. ii.*, ed. Theodor Mommsen, Monumenta Germaniae Historica, Auctorum Antiquissimorum 11 (Berlin: Weidmann, 1894), 211–20, and *Victoris Tunnunensis Chronicon cum reliquiis ex Consularibus Caesaraugustanis et Iohannis Biclarensis Chronicon*, ed. Carmen Cardelle de Hartmann and Roger Collins, Corpus Christianorum Series Latina 173A (Turnhout: Brepols, 2001). On Isidore's *De Origine Gothorum* see Chapter 3, § 2.5.

28 On the growth and definition of agricultural networks see Castellanos and Martín Viso, "The local articulation of central power." For further discussion about the relationship between the Visigothic monarchy and these networks see Castellanos, "The Political Nature of Taxation" and Damian Fernández, "Property, Social Status, and Church Building in Visigothic Iberia," *Journal of Late Antiquity* 9, no. 2 (2016): 512–41.

conversion of the kingdom to Catholicism in 589 hardly unified it. Even the dramatic rise of the cults of saints was an expression of local authority and autonomy. Toledo itself, from about 620, in order to compete in this assemblage of local powers, felt the need to construct and advertise its own saintly cult tradition and began earnestly promoting its own saints, specifically Leocadia. The connection between the urban and rural churches, and the Church, remained competitively close, especially compared to elsewhere in the former Empire.[29]

Seventh-century Hispania was a well-educated, functionally literate society, and a legalist one. Not long before the turn of the seventh century, Gregory of Tours (538–594), who loathed his Visigothic neighbors, was frustrated and slightly infuriated by the fact that a couple of Visigothic ambassadors – laymen, not clerics – were able to engage in serious theological arguments, in proper Latin.[30] The legacies of Roman education in Hispania are impossible to discern, but throughout the seventh century there was a palace school in Toledo and an episcopal school in every major see, if not all moderately wealthy bishoprics.[31] A collection of slates from the period even contains what appear to be homework exercises of some sort.[32] The foundation for episcopal schools was established at II Toledo in 527,[33] and a program for education promoted by

---

29 See Manuel Sotomayor, "Las Relaciones Iglesia Urbana-Iglesia Rural en los Concilios Hispano-Romanos y Visigodos," in *Sacralidad y Arqueología*, ed. Thilo Ulbert et al., 525–39, and Neil Allies, "The Monastic Rules of Visigothic Iberia: A Study of Their Text and Language" (Ph.D. diss., University of Birmingham, 2009).

30 Greg. Tours, *Lib. Hist.*, 5.43 and 6.40. Raymond Van Dam argues that Gregory purposely misrepresented the articulate Visigoths as less skillful than they really were. Raymond Van Dam, *Saints and Their Miracles in Late Antique Gaul* (Princeton: Princeton University Press, 1993), 107. For the text of Gregory see *Historiarum Libri x*, ed. Bruno Krusch and Wilhelm Levison, Monumenta Germaniae Historica, Scriptores Rerum Merovingicarum 1.1 (Hanover: Hahn, 1951).

31 Jamie Wood and Javier Martínez Jiménez, "New Directions in the Study of Visigothic Spain," *History Compass* 14, no. 1 (2016): 29–38.

32 See slate 128 in Velázquez Soriano, *Las Pizarras Visigodas*, 426–32.

33 On education in seventh-century Hispania see Pierre Riché, "La pastorale populaire en Occident, VIe–XIe siècles," in *Histoire vécue du peuple chrétien*, ed. Jean Delumeau (Toulouse: Privat, 1979), 195–221; Michel Banniard, *Viva Voce. Communication écrite et communication orale du IVe au IXe siècle Occident latin* (Paris: Institut des Études Augustiniennes, 1992); and, Marc Reydellet, "La signification du Livre IX des *Etymologies*: érudition et actualité," in *Los Visigodos, Historia y Civilización, Actas de la Semana Internacional de Estudios Visigóticos, Antigüedad y cristianismo* 3 (Murcia: Universidad de Murcia, 1986), 337–50. On the palace school of Toledo see María del Rosario Valverde Castro, *Ideología, simbolismo y ejercicio del poder real en la monarquía visigoda: un proceso de cambio* (Salamanca: Universidad de Salamanca, 2000), 186; Pierre Riché, "Les écoles, l'église et état en Occident du Ve au XIe siècle," in *Église et enseignement. Actes du Colloque du Xe anniversaire de l'Institut d'Histoire du Christianisme de l'Université Libre de Bruxelles* (Brussels:

bishop Leander of Seville (before 579–600) and then by his brother and episcopal successor Isidore (600–636).[34] Jacques Fontaine argues that there was a surprising coherence in pedagogy, material means and purposes, combined with a *une grande indécision institutionelle*.[35] He maintained that education was diverse in its forms and applications, and depended on local applications: every town, villa, bishopric, and rural site had it owns traditions. Educational traditions and pedagogies were influenced by the personality of the ruling bishops and abbots, who could adapt the curricula to their own sentiments. The lector and the *sous-diacre* were the main people that ran studies in the episcopal schools. In the monasteries, the teaching situation is less clear.[36]

Despite the evidence for education, scholars disagree on the extent of literacy in the seventh century, and, perhaps a more meaningful inquiry, what it meant to be literate. Neil Allies has argued convincingly that a literate person was one that could participate in a community whose ontological existence was based on an axiomatic belief in a book. This definition of early medieval literacy helps Allies show that the monastic rules represent significant evidence for literacy in the period. This makes sense, in that Gregory the Great defines an author as the person who inspires texts and who dictates to the scribes, opening up literacy then to anyone that could grasp the inspiration of the authors. However, this working definition for early medieval literacy also suggests a paramount link between literacy and memory.[37] Anna Grotans claims that reading in the early middle ages "was a process whereby memory deferred in sound was reactivated [...], readers saw in a written text a [musical] score – letters that needed to be interpreted and vocalized before any meaning could be made of them."[38] Complementary to this is the contemporary

---

Editions de l'Université de Bruxelles, 1977), 35–36; and, Thompson, *Goths in Spain*, 3–4 and 17–18.

34 On the school see Carlos Cañal, *Sevilla prehistorica* (Seville, 1894).

35 Jacques Fontaine, "Fins et Moyens de l'Enseignement Ecclésiastique," in Jacques Fontaine, *Culture et spiritualité en Espagna du IVᵉ au VIIᵉ siècle* (London: Variorum Reprints, 1986), IV, 200.

36 See Fontaine, "Fins et Moyens," in Fontaine, *Culture et spiritualité*, IV, 202.

37 On the relationship between texts, literacy and memory in seventh-century Hispania see Allies, "Monastic Rules;" Iñaki Martín, "The Memory of the 'Holy Men' in Hispanic Monasticism: The Case of the Bierzo Region," *Imago Temporis* 6 (2012): 165–90; and, Claudia di Sciacca, *Finding the Right Words: Isidore's Synonyma in Anglo-Saxon England* (Toronto: University of Toronto Press, 2008), 33–34. For a general theoretical discussion see Paul Ricoeur, *Memory, History and Forgetting*, trans. Kathleen Blamey and David Pellauer (Chicago: University of Chicago Press, 2004, orig. 2000).

38 Anna Grotans, *Reading in Medieval St. Gall* (Cambridge: University of Cambridge Press, 2006), 28.

opinion of Isidore of Seville who believed that words are special because they have the ability to communicate without sound (*sine voce*).[39] Vocalization and memorization were essential for the act of learning the inspirations present in books, and so for literacy: yet the words themselves allowed for silent, solemn devotion to the meaning of those texts.

Legal literacy, meaning the awareness and employment of written and other legally enforceable forms of law, seems to have been extensive in seventh-century Hispania, although the evidence is relatively thin. The records of legal activities, such as testament charters, for example, hardly compares to Merovingian Francia. This may be the result simply of different historical circumstances that led to the loss or destruction of these materials in Spain, and not in France. It could also have to do with the differences in approaches to law. The *Liber Iudiciorum* (*LI*) is a twelve-book law-code, with a remarkable constitution and hundreds of well-organized and detailed laws, promulgated in Toledo in 653.[40] The contemporary legal evidence from Francia includes a charter of 653, by Landeric, bishop of Paris and two charters from 660, by Emmo, bishop of Sens.[41] The difference in Visigothic and Frankish evidence may only indicate complementary approaches to law. Nevertheless, seventh-century Hispania was a society of *lex scripta*, in which law was known and applied, and which has also left, to a smaller degree, charters and other evidence of the application of law. At some points in the seventh century, the law actually may have functioned too well. For instance, Ervig in XII Toledo 7 asks the bishops to ease the law banning those who do not immediately go to war to protect their locales and neighbors against usurpers and invaders, since apparently half the country had lost legal status and the system was collapsing.[42] Seventh-century Hispania, despite its collection of social and political

---

39 Isid., *Orig.*, 1.3.1. For details about the *Origines*, or *Etymologies*, including the editions and discussion about naming see Chapter 3, § 2.4.

40 For a full introduction to the *Liber Iudiciorum*, with information about the edition, manuscripts and naming, see Chapter 5, § 2.

41 For Landeric's charter see *Archives de l'Empire – Inventaires et Documents. Monuments Historiques*, ed. Jules Tardiff (Paris, 1886), no. 10, p. 8, and Léon Levillain, "Etudes sur l'abbaye de Saint-Denis à l'époque mérovingienne," *Bibliothèque de l'école des chartes* 87 (1926): 35–48. For the charter of Emmo and Berthefrid see *Diplomata Chartae, Epistolae, Leges Aliaque Instrumenta ad res Gallo-Francicas Spectantia: Instrumenta ab anno 628 ad annum 751*, vol. 2, ed. Jean-Marie Pardessus, Louis Georges Oudart-Feudrix de Bréquigny, and François Jean Gabriel de la Portu du Thiel (Charleston: Nabu Press, 2011, orig. 1849), nos. 333, 335, 345.

42 Roger Collins, "Literacy and the laity in early medieval Spain," in *The Uses of Literacy in the Early Middle Ages*, ed. Rosamond McKitterick (Cambridge: University of Cambridge Press, 1990), 109–33 (117); Ian Wood, "Social Relations in the Visigothic kingdom from the Fifth to the Seventh Century: The Example of Mérida," in *The Visigoths*, ed. Heather, 191–207 (201); Thompson, *Goths in Spain*, 263. On Visigothic administration see Rafael

troubles, its violence, struggles, and competing networks of authority, was not a chaotic, uneducated or illiterate society. In fact, this self-sufficiency and functioning of the peninsula's people, communities and local institutions may have been a primary factor in the struggles against larger, centralizing, and alternative powers.

2   The Isidore-Moment and the *Liber Iudiciorum*

In this midst of such a social, political and cultural context, seventh-century Hispania produced a collection of impressive writers and texts. The collective authorship and editorial labors of these writers, as well as their networks, students and detractors form an impressive body of Visigothic literature, which is interesting in itself. It also provides a window into the multifaceted historical situation of seventh-century Hispania. This book critically interrogates major texts produced within this historical milieu, as a way to expose new insights about, and chart a new historiography for, the history of seventh-century

---

Gibert, *Enseñanza del derecho en Hispania durante los siglos VI a XI, Ius Romanum medii aevi* 1.5b (Milan: Giuffrè, 1967). For evidence of the application of law in seventh-century Hispania see the discussion of the *Liber Iudiciorum* in Yolanda García López, *Estudios Críticos y Literarios de la "Lex Wisigothorum"* (Alcalá: Universidad de Alcalá, 1996), and the Visigothic charters in *Diplomática Hispano-Visigoda*, ed. Ángel Canellas López (Zaragoza: Institución Fernando el Católico, 1979), nos. 119, 119a, 178, 192, and 229, including the *Exemplum Legis* from Cartagena, which cites Justinian's *Novella* and *Digest* (*Diplomática*, ed. Canellas López, 176). See also the Visigothic formularies in *Las "Formulae Wisigothicae": Aproximación a la práctica jurídica visigoda* (Lecce, Italy: Edizioni Grifio, 2010), ed. Edorta Córcoles Olaitz, and *Miscellanea Wisigothica*, ed. Juan Gil (Seville: Universidad de Sevilla, 1972), 71–112. For the origin of the formularies see Edorta Córcoles Olaitz, "About the Origin of the *Formulae Wisigothicae*," *Anuario Facultad de Derecho, Universidade de Coruña* 12 (2008), 199–221, and on the use of formularies as historical see Ian Wood, "The Bloodfeud of the Franks: A Historiographical Legend," *Early Medieval Europe* 14 (2006): 489–504, and Alice Rio, *Legal Practice and the Written Word in the Early Middle Ages: Frankish Formulae c. 500–1000* (Cambridge: Cambridge University Press, 2009), 165–240. For further primary evidence see II Seville 1, 3 and 8, IV Toledo 46, the *Exemplar iudicii* (see Chapter 4, n. 137); Isidore's, *De Viris Illustribus*, 1.31 (see Chapter 2); Velázquez Soriano, *Las Pizarras Visigodas*, esp. no. 39; Julian of Toledo, *Historia Wambae* (for the edition see *Historia Wambae regis*, ed. Wilhelm Levison, Corpus Christianorum Series Latina 115 [Turnhout: Brepols, 1976], 217–55, and for the English translation see Joaquin Martínez Pizarro, intro. and trans., *The Story of Wamba: Julian of Toledo's "Historia Wambae regis"* [Washington, D.C.: Catholic University Press, 2005]); *Vita Fructuosi* (see Chapter 1, note 101); and, king Sisebut (612–619), *De Defectione Lunae*, in John R. C. Martyn, *King Sisebut and the Culture of Visigothic Spain* (Lewiston: The Edwin Mellen Press, 2008), 111–17. Finally, it should be noted that although laws were known and used, and judges appointed and performed their duties, this does not mean that the legal rulings or laws were always followed or followed as prescribed.

Hispania. The primary purpose of this research is to develop a novel framework for re-interpreting the *Liber Iudiciorum*, the law-code issued by the Visigothic king Recceswinth (649/653–672) in early 654.[43]

The *Liber Iudiciorum* (*LI*) was not a shallow or superficial attempt to appease parties upset with the monarchy by way of affirming the laws, nor singularly a book of laws meant for courts and confirming symbolic, prior-existent political and legal authority. The *LI* was a smartly designed historical construction imbued with layers of political and spiritual significance that narrated a story of specific historical legitimacy for a reigning monarch. The *LI* constructs an imagined past to confirm the authority of the current dynasty, as well as the monarchy as a politically and religiously totalizing institution, and, in so doing, ends a vibrant literary and historical situation, the Isidore-moment, and the competition between its schools.

The *LI* spoke, had meaning as a voice within, the discourses and dialectics of the Isidore-moment: it was a manifestation of the moment's sustained and productive competitive dialectics, running from the early 600s to the promulgation and issuance of the *LI*, which represents both its fulfillment and its collapse. The significance and purposes of the *LI* are the products of this literary-political competition, and the *LI* must be interpreted by way of an acute awareness of its surrounding discursive culture. "What permits us," Foucault argues, "to individualize a discourse such as political economy or general grammar, is not the unity of an object; it is not a formal structure; nor is it a conceptual coherent architecture; it is not a fundamental philosophical choice; it is rather the existence of rules of formation for all its objects (however scattered they may be), for all its operations (which often can neither be superimposed nor linked together in succession), for all its concepts (which may very well be incompatible), for all its theoretical options (which are often mutually exclusive). There is an individualized discursive formation every time one can define a similar set of rules."[44]

The current investigation, then, in order to chart an alternative historiography for the *LI*, sets out to develop the theory of the Isidore-moment. It does this through a series of four case-studies of texts and collections of texts from the period, read within the context of the central feature of it, the competitive dialectics between the two schools, or networks, which I refer to respectively as Isidore-Seville and Toledo-Agali. The competitive dialectics between them

---

43   Recceswinth was co-ruler with his father Chindaswinth from 649 to 653.
44   Michel Foucault, *Foucault Live (Interviews, 1961–1984)*, ed. Sylvère Lotringer, trans. Lysa Hochroth and John Johnston (New York: Semiotext[e], 1996), "History, Discourse, and Discontinuity," 34–35.

is a primary characteristic of the moment and one which colors the entire fabric of writing in seventh-century Hispania.

The historical category "Isidore-moment" is a revised version of Jacques Fontaine's categorization of the seventh century in Hispania as the period of the "Isidorian Renaissance."[45] Fontaine argued that the extensive pedagogical writings, educational reforms, and ecclesiastical activities of Isidore, bishop of Seville for almost forty years, inaugurated a veritable re-birth of culture in the peninsula. The Isidorian Renaissance, he argued, "had as its aim nothing less than the reconstruction of the civil and religious life of Visigothic Spain."[46] This interpretation requires that such learning and writing had, to a measurable extent, disappeared in the peninsula, and that Isidore was the father of a new era, a re-birth of the classical world into a now [early] medieval one.

Fontaine's thesis was written as part of a historiographical debate with Henri-Irénée Marrou over the timing and nature of the end of the classical world, and Marrou's commitment, in this debate, to Augustine of Hippo. Fontaine's *Isidore de Séville et la culture classique dans l'Espagne* was published, in 1959, by the Études Augustiniennes. The renowned Visigothic historian Jocelyn Hillgarth calls Fontaine's book "a work of the first importance, one that marks an epoch in the study of Isidore of Seville and of Visigothic Spain. It can be compared to Professor H-I. Marrou's *St. Augustin et la fin de la culture antique* (Paris, 1938), in that it brings to life the whole culture of an age in the person of its principal representative."[47] Marrou was not the only scholar of his time stressing the significance of Augustine, but it was Marrou that Fontaine was engaging when he was developing his thesis about the Isidorian Renaissance.[48] Augustine represented a mediating point between classical brilliance and new Christian piety. In his second edition of *St. Augustin*, Marrou presented an Augustine that was the pillar of a new culture, a historical situation neither ancient nor medieval, but functional according to its own cultural logic, the culture of *antiquité tardive*.[49]

---

45   See Jacques Fontaine, *Isidore de Séville et la Culture Classique dans l'Espagne Wisigothique*, 2 vols. (Paris: Études Augustiniennes, 1959), II, 863–66.
46   Jacques Fontaine, "King Sisebut's *Vita Desiderii* and the Political Function of Visigothic Hagiography," in *Visigothic Spain,* ed. James, 97.
47   Jocelyn N. Hillgarth, "Review, J. Fontaine, *Isidore de Séville et la Culture Classique dans l'Espagne Wisigothique*, Vols. I, II: Paris: Études Augustiniennes, 1959," *Journal of Roman Studies* 51 (1961), 273–75 (273).
48   See for example, Charles Cochrane, *Christianity and Classical Culture: A Study of Thought and Action from Augustus to Augustine* (Oxford: Oxford University Press, 1940).
49   Henri-Irénée Marrou, *St. Augustin et la fin de la culture antique* (Paris: E. Boccard, 1958), *Retractio*, 689. For an extended discussion see Mark Vessey's article, dedicated to Jacques Fontaine, "The Demise of the Christian Writer and the Remaking of 'Late Antiquity'," *Journal of Early Christian Studies* 6 (1998), 386–87, and especially the detailed historio-

However, this culture, the "civilization of the Theopolis," could not survive the final, later collapse of Roman civic structures.[50] For Fontaine, Isidore not only inaugurated a new historical period, but he was also an individual genius, a Renaissance-man who would forge the culture of the Latin middle ages.[51]

Fontaine historicizes Isidore's texts and remains a firm believer in the need to reconstruct and understand the world in which a text was born in order to grasp its contemporary significance, meaning, and the historical actors involved in its authorship, editorship, transmission, and general discourse of the time. Although his contextualization may hint at the social-historical method of the Annales scholars, Fontaine's approach and the Isidorian Renaissance itself are grounded, as a phenomenon, on chance historical conditions, to contemporary events.[52] This attitude reflects a broader shift in historical scholarship at the time that Fontaine was forging his ideas. Fontaine was writing during a moment when theories about the Fall of Rome were beginning to change, from seeing the disappearance of the Roman Empire as collapse related to late Roman decadence, to envisioning post-Roman Europe as a collection of local changes and transformations.[53]

The theory of the Isidore-moment developed here is not a direct challenge to Fontaine, "the greatest expert on Visigothic culture,"[54] and his imagination of an Isidorian Renaissance defined by a rebirth of literary forms, pedagogical tools, and historical structures and methods. Instead, what is proposed is a sustained critical reflection upon the oeuvre of diverse texts produced within a certain discourse. In so doing, I qualify the meaning of the expression "Isidorian Renaissance" and replace it with "Isidore-moment," which ascribes increased and competitive political agency to Isidore, and those contemporaries employing his literary models and styles. Isidore dedicated texts not to

---

graphical discussion in Wood, *Modern Origins*, chapters 14 and 15. On Marrou's objectives see the work by his student, Pierre Riché, *Henri Irénée Marrou, historien engagé* (Paris: Les Éditions du Cerf, 2003).

50 Marrou, *Retractio*, 692.
51 Fontaine, "Education and Learning," 738: Amidst "the period when the debate between the antique past and new future of Christian Europe was its most lively. Great writers – and men of action – [such as Isidore] then began, to intervene in this cultural debate, by producing the works upon which rests their reputation as 'the founders of the Middle Ages'."
52 See Fontaine, "Education and Learning," 750.
53 The first major shift in the historiography of Spain came with Pierre Riché's *Éducation et culture dans l'occident barbare, VIe–VIIIe siècle* (Paris: Éditions du Seuil, 1962). The transformation interpretation has been firmly established by the Transformation of the Roman World Series published by Brill, 1997–2004.
54 Wood, *Modern Origins*, ch. 15.

transmit a new culture *per se*, but to promote the interests of his family, his network, his see, his province, and his theology. The literary output of Isidore introduced into the historical situation of his time alternative and varied ways of communicating and promoting agendas. Isidore's concern was not with rebuilding classical culture or learning for the sake of it, or even solely for a Christian universalism, although salvation was a paramount concern in all of his writing. What mattered to Isidore was delivering messages, "speaking," within the discourses in Iberia at the time, discourses that were largely products of his writings. He used existing knowledges, motifs, images, language and historical awarenesses to create Christian narratives that promoted his network's authority in the peninsula. This is one reason why "Isidore a donc ignoré, et sans doute délibérément, la Gaule franque et sa culture appauvrie."[55]

Fontaine sees in the uses of Isidore's texts, models and ideas after him, emulation of Isidore by writers in Toledo and elsewhere in Hispania. This allows Fontaine to craft a story in which Isidore is massively significant as the father of a renaissance of writing and literature. Although I agree that Isidore influenced the writing of contemporaries in meaningful ways, the use of Isidorian forms by other writers in this historical moment was not due to a passive emulation or objective, shared interest in classical learning and education. They were negotiated and deployed in order to sustain a supportive or antagonistic dialogue with Isidore and his school. The literary forms he introduced were copied later in order to challenge Isidore-Seville, not to emulate it. This is why I prefer to label this the "Isidore-moment" as opposed to Fontaine's "Isidorian Renaissance." In the historiographical search for the appearance of a new or renewed culture, what can be lost are the social antagonisms, debates and competitions that drove cultural production and the politics behind it.[56] The Isidore-moment is a broader flourishing of writing activities that does not represent a "renaissance," but rather an accelerated use of literary and historical forms for spiritual and political promotion initiated by Isidore and

---

55   Fontaine, *Isidore de Séville*, II, 841.
56   As Peter Brown has shown, the link between inner-ecclesiastical competition and impressive literary output is evident in fourth-century Africa, a product of the Donatists vs. the Catholics (335) and in fifth-century Marseilles, Arles, and Lérins (Brown, *Through the Eye of a Needle*, 335 and 411). Generally speaking, competition was at times a significant motor driving the advancement of the Church, e.g. in the competition within a social circle in Rome to build the best church (Brown, *Through the Eye of a Needle*, 249). On the use of the past in Christian literary argumentation and competition, a useful article is Averil Cameron, "Remaking the Past," in *Interpreting Late Antiquity*, ed. Glen W. Bowersock, Peter Brown, and Oleg Grabar (Cambridge: Harvard University Press, 2001), 1–20. For more on the Donatists see Paola Marone, *Donatism. Online Dynamic Bibliography* (Rome: Sapienz, Università di Roma, 2018).

subsequently built upon his legacy. It is a competitive moment, a real struggle through texts, with Isidore pushing his school's agenda by issuing texts for multiple audiences, and the school of Toledo-Agali doing the same, in similar forms but with competing messages.

The Isidore-moment should be considered a historical event representing a chronological period from roughly the beginning of the seventh century to the middle of the 650s, and, in ossified form, into the late 660s. It transcends the life of Isidore because the competitive dialectic inaugurated by him was embraced by his school, challenged by the school of Toledo-Agali, closing with the *Liber Iudiciorum*, and put to a crushing end by the bishop of Toledo, Ildefonsus (657–667). This Isidorian event was one in which a cadre of people participated, including those constituting the schools, and many whose names or specific contributions are unknown: from anonymous editors and redactors, to supporters of rival bishops in Toledo, to editors of the canonical collection (the *Hispana*), to those who hung plaques showing public support for defaced bishops.[57] However, in addition to representing measurable existences, or beings-in-time, by the term "Isidore-moment" should also be understood the dialectics of the literary competition between the schools, the competitive dialectics itself. In this sense, it is an abstract figuration of the historical symbolic and imaginary of the earlier part of the seventh century, on the one hand, and, on the other hand, the discourses of power and authority that were endemic to it. The specific manifestation of the discourse under discussion in this book is that between the schools of Isidore-Seville and Toledo-Agali.[58]

The contemporary meaning and purpose of the *LI* was determined by the literary and cultural expectations of the Isidore-moment, whose competitive

---

57 For a detailed discussion of the *Hispana* see Chapter 4, § 2, and for reference to public support for defaced bishops see Chapter 4, § 4. Citations from and references directly to the collection of Spanish councils known as the *Hispana* are all from, unless otherwise noted, the authoritative edition, *La Colección Canónica Hispana,* ed. Gonzalo Martínez Díez and (from 1982 forward as co-editor) Félix Rodríguez, 6 vols. (Madrid, 1966–2002), referred to hereafter simply as CCH with respective volume and year of publication noted. The Spanish councils have never been translated into English, but for a translation into Spanish (and slightly earlier edition based on fewer manuscripts) see *Concilios Visigóticos e Hispano-Romanos,* ed. and trans. José Vives (Barcelona and Madrid: Consejo Superior de Investigaciones Científicas, Instituto Enrique Flórez, 1963).

58 For a theoretical discussion of the concept of the imaginary versus symbolic see Jacques Lacan, *Écrits,* trans. Bruce Fink (New York: W. W. Norton, 2006), particularly the articles, "Seminar on the Purloined Letter," 6–50, "On an *Ex Post Facto* Syllabary," 602–09, and "Subversion of the Subject and the Dialectics of Desire in the Freudian Unconscious," 671–702. See also Slavoj Žižek and Simon Critchley, *How to Read Lacan (How to Read)* (New York: W.W. Norton, 2007), esp. 4–8.

dialectics were the symbolic order through which the *LI* spoke, and the historical conditions for its being. The *LI*, deeply integrated into local disputes and competing historiographies about the peninsula and its people, reconfigured the dynamics of the period, making it its final product and both its fulfillment and destruction. The *LI*, as the end of this Isidorian event, was not a dialectical synthesis of the competition between the schools, in the sense of how Hegel's theory of dialectic is often read – thesis, anti-thesis, synthesis. The event was a master-servant dialectic, in which each contributor struggled for mastery, and in which each required the other for existence.[59] The *LI* absolutely depended for its meaning upon this dialectics, yet it pulled the carpet out from under both the metaphorical master and servant, and so the entire historical moment, by silencing the servant and destroying the master in turn: by Toledo-Agali fully sublimating Isidore-Seville to it. The *LI* fulfilled the dialectics of the Isidore-moment, while simultaneously destroying its basis.

Late antique and early medieval writers of history, origins, and other "past-related" narratives wrote rhetorically, with expressed purpose. This is as true about Augustine, Cassiodorus, Gregory, Procopius and Jordanes, as it is about Isidore. Numerous studies in recent decades have demonstrated how such writers constructed texts with exceptional subjective sophistication, and sensitivity to it.[60] In the specific case of Isidore and seventh-century Hispan-

---

59 See Georg Wilhem Friedrich Hegel, *Phenomenology of Spirit*, trans. Arnold V. Miller (Oxford: Oxford University Press, 1976), ch. "Self-Consciousness." For a general reading of Hegel's dialectics see Alexandre Kojève, *Introduction to the Reading of Hegel: Lectures on the Phenomenology of Spirit*, trans. James H. Nichols, Jr. (Ithaca: Cornell University Press, 1980). For discussion of the master-servant dialectic in particular, see Slavoj Žižek, *Less Than Nothing: Hegel and the Shadow of Dialectical Materialism* (London: Verso, 2012), esp. 196–99, and on the master in the dialectic as future, see 507, n. 2. In general, also see Frederic Jameson, *The Hegel Variations* (London: Verso, 2010). One might argue that Hegel's dialectics of consciousness and power, in which the one who fears death in the dialectical struggle becomes the servant, is fundamentally a working-through of the thoughts of a more ancient Spaniard than Isidore, the Hispano-Roman Seneca who, thinking of Epicurus, said "Meditare mortem: qui hoc dicit meditari libertatem iubet. Qui mori didicit servire dedidicit (Sen., *Ep. Mor. ad Luc.*, 26 [see the Loeb edition of 1917])." For the relationship to Christian thought, the master-servant dialectic being embodied miraculously in Jesus, as a continuous historical process in life and between the dead and living see John Milbank and Slavoj Žižek, *The Monstrosity of Christ: Paradox or Dialectic?* (Cambridge: MIT Press, 2009), and Peter Brown, *The Cult of the Saints: Its Rise and Function in Latin Christianity* (Chicago: University of Chicago, 1981).
60 See Walter Goffart, *The Narrators of the Barbarian History* (Princeton: Princeton University Press, 1988); Andrew H. Merrills, *History and Geography in Late Antiquity* (Cambridge: University of Cambridge Press, 2005), 170–85; James O'Donnell, *Cassiodorus* (Berkeley: University of California Press, 1979); James O'Donnell, "The Aims of Jordanes," *Historia* 31 (1982): 233–40; and, Brian Croke, "Jordanes and the Immediate Past," *Historia* 54 (2005): 473–94.

ian writers, the exposing of the schools-competition helps scholars re-imagine the Isidorian Renaissance and grasp the historical situation and meaning of the period's texts, such as the *LI*. Furthermore, it exposes other longstanding historiographical problems. Important examples of this are the "quest for unity" and consensus narratives, and the centrality of historiography in late antiquity and the early middle ages.

The "quest for unity" and consensus narratives claim that the religious and secular elite of seventh-century Hispania put the centralization of the Church and the kingdom's administrative functioning in Toledo above all other personal, local, regional or other agendas. The "quest for unity" narrative dominates historiography about early medieval Hispania, but it is based upon a veneer within the textual evidence and the interpretation of it. The reality of the historical situation, and also the consensus literature, was more complicated, if not wholly other. Expressions of unity and consensus appeared throughout the seventh century, but it is a period characterized by various sites and schools competing with one another for authority and autonomy. The consensus narrative, as a history of the period, although visible on the literary surface in the seventh century, is the development of later generations and, indeed, centuries within Hispania, and, from there, was carried into modern historiography.[61] This is not to say that there was no desire for cooperation between various parties in seventh-century Hispania, for there certainly was. However, while the whole area of Hispania was a Christian polity, or collection of polities, Christians felt safe competing for authority against one another. It was only after the Christian communities in Toledo, Seville, Mérida, Córdoba and elsewhere in the peninsula became diasporic or political minorities that a true and urgent desire for unity arose, and the old literary constructions taken seriously as such – the birth of what I call "Gothstalgie," the nostalgia for a

---

On how Carolingian writers constructed their texts in such a way as to deliver particular understandings about the past to their audiences, see Rosamond McKitterick, *Perceptions of the Past in the Early Middle Ages* (Notre Dame: University of Notre Dame Press, 2006).

61   On the political uses of the unity idea in modern Spain see the excellent article by Francisco J. Moreno Martín ("Visigoths, Crowns, Crosses, and the Construction of Spain," *Memoirs of the American Academy of Rome* 62 [2017]: 41–64), which contains a disturbing picture of Heinrich Himmler in Madrid in 1940 inspecting Visigothic artifacts with Julio Martínez Santa-Olalla. In general, see also Tomás Pérez Vejo, *España imaginada. Historia de la invención de una nación* (Barcelona: Galaxia Gutenberg, 2015); Jocelyn N. Hillgarth, "Spanish Historiography and Iberian Reality," *History and Theory* 24 (1985): 23–43; and, James F. O'Callaghan, *A History of Medieval Spain* (Ithaca: Cornell University Press, 1975).

unified Christian, Visigothic past.[62] In addition to laying the groundwork to challenge the early historiography of the consensus narrative, this book shows that one must also re-think Isidore as the voice of the monarchy in Toledo, which he categorically was not. The texts of Isidore-Seville, despite the veneer of collegiality and unity – itself a response to competition – are full of damning criticisms of the monarchy and Church officials in Toledo, in a specific fight that ends with the *LI*. A critical interrogation of these texts, with others of the Isidore-moment, illustrates the centrality of historiography to the politics and culture of the period.

This book is important because it will assist scholars in better grasping the intensity, complexity and cultural scope of historical writing in the period. Through that, this book will also help elucidate the purpose of the *Liber Iudiciorum* and the language of Visigothic writing and literature in the Isidore-moment, and why it should not be framed within a discourse of "Isidorian Renaissance." This research will also suggest alternative ways for reading early medieval texts, promote the urgent need for critical revisions of the historiography and manuscripts of early medieval Hispania, and encourage alternative interpretations of and methods for interpreting the collapse of the Visigothic kingdom. The ideas developed in this book and the conclusions elicited from them have larger implications, then, for the history of the Visigothic kingdom and our constructions about late antique and early medieval Hispania beyond the time and space of its Visigothic period.

Finally, one of the underlying metahistorical aims of this book is to encourage new, "post-historical" ways of dealing with the diversity of methods in late antiquity and the early middle ages for representing the past. This diversity needs to be matched, in kind, by flexible, pluralistic methodologies for interpreting and communicating the past in the present. In short, new philosophies of history should be developed for engaging this material, methodologies that can reach for the past beyond the singularizing search for *the* past by History.[63] Hence, the work of philosophers, literary and cultural theorists and other thinkers, although always supplemental to the apparent internal logic of the primary, historical source material and only part of the theoretical and methodological frameworks underlying the author's thinking, provide fundamental conceptual tools for the literary analyses of this book.

---

62 I am currently elaborating on this idea in a forthcoming article and for the *Visigothic Symposia* postscript.

63 For elaboration on "*the* past" as a totalizing historical methodology see Zachary Sayre Schiffmann, *The Birth of the Past* (Baltimore: The Johns Hopkins University Press, 2011).

3 The "Schools" – *Hasta Siempre*, Bishop Isidore

The underlying antagonisms in the texts of the first half of the seventh century are defined by the dialectical competition referred to in this book as the Isidore-moment and categorized by two schools of thought: Isidore-Seville and Toledo-Agali. Although episcopal, monastic and other physical schools existed, the schools referred to here should not be taken as tangible entities. They represent a collection of individuals, texts, bishoprics, cities and communities tied by their connections to each other in diverse ways. The "schools" here are not material places, but rather schools of thought, networks of people and texts, for example, the Frankfurt School, as opposed to Boston Latin School. Moreover, despite the discursive presence of two schools, the schools thesis should not be imagined as dichotomous, binary or reductive. There are figures of and texts produced within the Isidore-moment, including by these two schools, that are not definable as prescriptions wholly of one school or the other. Indeed, the final product of the competitive dialectics of the period, the-*Liber Iudiciorum*, and the bishop that oversaw its promulgation, Eugenius II of Toledo (646–657), are examples of overlapping themes and interests.

Isidore-Seville vs. Toledo-Agali is not a single socio-cultural category that demands interpretation of all Iberian authors and texts from the early 600s to the 660s down one school of thought or the other. Rather, the schools thesis is a historiographical model for reflecting upon the complex nature of the texts produced during those years. There were other struggles for authority and smart uses of literary and historical expressions happening at the time: for example, in the competitive constellations of Toledo vs. Tarragona vs. Seville, Toledo vs. Cartagena, Mérida vs. Seville, Zaragoza vs. Barcelona vs. Tarragona, Narbonne vs. Lusitania-Galicia; also between new aristocratic networks and old urban centers, and between the old conventus of Baetica, as once laid out by Augustus – Astigi (Ecija), Gades (Cadiz), Córdoba, and Seville – and so on. However, the dialectical competition between Isidore-Seville and Toledo-Agali was not only one of the most intense and sustained, but it also produced a significant amount of material by which to understand it and which defined the history and memory of the seventh century of Hispania, for contemporaries and for those in the centuries to follow.

3.1 *School of Isidore-Seville (600–657)*

Since the development of the Toledo-Agali school was a reaction to the threat posed by the authority of Isidore, his school and city, it is fair to maintain this order. The school of Isidore-Seville consists of Isidore, of course, as well as his living family and friends, the clerics working in and around Seville, Isidore's former students and those trained by or who networked with them, such as Braulio and Eugenius II.[64] The school's dates of existence, so far as the specific competitive dialectics of the moment goes, are from circa 600, when Isidore began his bishopric, through to the end of the episcopacy of Eugenius II in 657. The following introduces the key figures, the literarily active members, more or less, of the school of Isidore-Seville.[65] The short biographies presented in the sections below are to help the reader understand why each person is considered a member of the respective schools, and to what degree they are.

3.1.1 Leander

All bishops of Toledo during the Isidore-moment, and not a single one thereafter, were first monks, all but one at the monastery of Agali. In this basic professional structure, they emulated the career of bishop Leander of Seville. His younger brother and successor as bishop, Isidore, relates that Leander was a monk by profession before he became bishop.[66] Born in the middle or late-540s, he was consecrated as bishop of Seville before 579, a position he held until his death about 600.[67] Leander and his family were from Cartagena, and his father Severian was, perhaps, the governor. It is not clear how long his family had been in Cartagena, but it is possible that they arrived with the Byzantines in the 550s.[68] Whatever the case, in 563, Leander left Cartagena

---

64 On the intimate relationship between Isidore and Braulio, and that Braulio was at some point with Isidore, see note 71 below.
65 For general prosopographies of seventh-century figures see Luis A. García Moreno, *Prosopografía del Reino Visigoda de Toledo* (Salamanca: Universidad de Salamanca, 1974); John R. Martindale, *The Prosopography of the Later Roman Empire*, 3 vols. (Cambridge: Cambridge University Press, 1992), and *The Prosopography of the Visigothic Period in Gaul and Iberia, c. 400–750*, ed. Michael J. Kelly, Javier Martínez Jiménez et al. (Binghamton: Gracchi Books, forthcoming 2021).
66 Isid., *DVI*, 55.
67 In 521, only several years before Montanus's II Toledo (527) (and a single generation before Isidore's family arrived in Seville), the Papacy appointed an independent vicar of the metropolitan see of Seville, covering both Baetica and Lusitania. On this see Patrologia Latina 84, ed. Jacques-Paul Migne (Paris, 1862), 827f.; Jocelyn N. Hillgarth, "Coins and Chronicles: Propaganda in Sixth-Century Spain and the Byzantine Background," *Historia: Zeitschrift für Alte Geschichte* 15 (1966): 483–508 (495); Louis Duchesne, *L'Église au VI siècle* (Paris: E. de Boccard, 1925), 553–55; and, Ramón d'Abadal y de Vinyals, *Del Reino de Tolosa al Reino de Toledo* (Madrid: Real Academia de la Historia, 1960), 57ff.
68 On the family's connection to Cartagena see chapter twenty-one of Leander's *Liber de institutione virginum*, written for his sister Florentina. For edition and translation see *Saint Leander, Archbishop of Seville: A Book on the Teaching of Nuns and a Homily in Praise of the Church*, ed. and trans. John C. Martyn (Lanham: Lexington Books, 2009). For secondary material on the family see Fontaine, *Isidore de Seville*; Jacques Fontaine and Pierre Cazier, "Qui a chassé de Cathaginoise Severianus et les siens? Observations sur l'histoire familiale

for Seville, with his two younger brothers, Fulgentius and Isidore, for reasons having to do with the fighting in the city between Goths and Byzantines. His mother and father also left Cartagena, with Leander's young sister, Florentina, and headed for old Cartagena, that is, Carthage.⁶⁹

Leander is most famous in history for his role in converting the rebel Hermenegild, and then his brother Reccared, both sons of the last Arian king of the Visigoths, Liuvigild. In 589, at the Third Council of Toledo, Leander led the formal conversion of king Reccared and the kingdom. Leander wrote anti-Arian treatises, letters, a body of liturgical texts and even music, as well as the sermon at the end of III Toledo and a treatise on monastic life for his sister. Only the latter two texts survive.⁷⁰

Leander, despite being the older brother and educator of Isidore, is not a member of the Isidore-Seville school. The school begins with the antagonistic discourse developed by Isidore in response to actions by Toledo in the early 600s and which lead to the competitive dialectics of the Isidore-moment. That said, the memory, or memory industry, of Leander, was very much part of this event. Despite his foundational role in establishing Catholicism in the kingdom, Leander is never mentioned in any texts, including specifically religious ones, in seventh-century Hispania, except for those produced by this school, specifically by Isidore and his "student" Braulio.⁷¹ This is quite surprising if

---

d'Isidore de Séville," in *Estudios de Homenaje a Don Claudio Sánchez Albornoz en sus 90 años*, vol. 1 (Ávila: Instituto de España, 1983), 349–400; and, Gerd Kampers, "Isidor von Sevilla und seine Familie. Überlegungen zu 'De institutione virginum et de contemptu mundi' c. 31," *Frühmittelalterliche Studien* 52 (2018): 43–58.

69   On Leander's life see Isidore, *DVI*, 57–59, and Martyn, *Leander*, 4–13 and 28–34.

70   For a detailed analysis of Leander's sermon, how he viewed the spiritual significance of III Toledo, and his role in the kingdom's conversion, see Alberto Ferreiro, "*Quia pax et caritas facta est*: Unity and Peace in Leander's Homily at the Third Council of Toledo (589)," *Annuarium Historiae Conciliorum* 48 (2016/2017): 87–108.

71   For more on Braulio, see the short biographical bit below and references throughout the book. As for his having been a student of Isidore in Seville and studying in person with him, see the letters between the two men, which indicate such a situation, and the arguments by Charles H. Lynch (Charles H. Lynch, *Saint Braulio, Bishop of Saragossa [631–651]: His Life and Writings* [Washington, D.C.: The Catholic University of America, 1938], 19–27). José Carlos Martín-Iglesias has argued against this reading (see *Scripta de Vita Isidori Hispalensis Episcopi*, ed. José Carlos Martín-Iglesias, Corpus Christianorum Series Latina 113B [Turnhout: Brepols, 2006], 74–91). For a recent reconsideration of the relationship between Isidore and Braulio, including when they may have first met, see the introductory discussion in *Braulio de Zaragoza: Epístolas*, ed. Ruth Miguel Franco (Madrid: Ediciones Akal, S. A., 2015); and, *Braulionis Caesaraugustani Epistulae et Isidori Hispalensis Epistulae ad Braulionem*, ed. Ruth Miguel Franco, Corpus Christianorum Series Latina 114B (Turnhout: Brepols, 2018), 22–23. Braulio is referred to in this book as Isidore's "student" at the very least because of the clear tutorial, personal and mutually supportive relationship between the two.

one adheres to the narrative about the drive for Catholic consensus and unity, since Leander did as much, if not more, than anyone else to convert the kingdom to Catholicism.[72] As shown in Chapter 2, not only is Leander ignored in the Isidore-moment by those outside of the Isidore-Seville network, but also, when opportunities arose in texts to discuss him, he was excluded and sometimes purposely cut from the existing narratives. There was, effectively, a *damnatio memoriae* of Leander by those wanting to elevate and promote sites of power outside the affiliations of Seville. The reasons for this astonishing *damnatio memoriae* are wrapped up in the antagonisms of the moment. The situation of Leander's legacy was different before the 600s, in the generation of euphoria for the conversion, in which John of Biclar, Licinianus, the bishop of Cartagena and, outside of Hispania, Pope Gregory the Great, celebrated Leander. The Isidore-moment was defined by a different approach to the history of Hispania, to the rhetoric and propaganda of its memory.

3.1.2 Isidore

Isidore, the younger brother of Leander, was the bishop of Seville from about 600 to his death on 4 April 636. Fontaine suggests that Isidore was born in Cartagena, around the year 559. This is because he was consecrated as bishop circa 600, an event which could not have happened before he was forty years old according to canonical legislation and custom.[73] Isidore was educated by his brother in Seville and could have been a monk, like his brother, but there is no direct evidence for him having been one.

According to the late 12th or early 13th-century *Vita Sancti Isidori*, Isidore's family was related to the Ostrogothic king Theoderic, whose first wife was Sanctia, the sister of Isidore's father Severian.[74] If so, Isidore would have had kinship ties with the Visigothic king Sisebut (612–619), himself kin with Theodoric

---

72 For more on Leander's and III Toledo's attempt at unity, and the idea of unity as a core Biblical fulfillment, see Ferreiro, *"Quia pax et caritas facta est."*
73 Fontaine, *Isidore de Séville*, 6.
74 *Vita Sancti Isidori* 2, ls. 57–67 (Martín-Iglesias, ed., pp. 24–25 [see later in this note]). For more on the authorship and dating of the *Vita sancti Isidori*, attributed by Jacques-Paul Migne to Lucas de Tuy, and on the medieval hagiography of Isidore, see David Thomas and Alex Mallett, *"Vita Sancti Isidori,"* in *Christian-Muslim Relations: A Bibliographical History*, vol. 3 (1050–1200) (Boston and Leiden: Brill, 2011): 708–14, and *Scripta medii aevi de vita Isidori Hispalensis episcopi*, ed. José Carlos Martín-Iglesias, Corpus Christianorum Continuatio Mediaevalis 281 (Turnhout: Brepols, 2016), 6–45, esp. 19–25 (with the critical edition in the second part of the book, pp. 23–105). On the Ostrogothic king Theoderic's possible marriage to Isidore's aunt Sanctia (his father Severian's sister) see *Anonymi Valesiani pars posterior*, in *Chronica Minora Saeculi*, ed. Theodor Mommsen, Monumenta Germaniae Historica, Auctores Antiquissimi 9 (Berlin: Weidmann, 1894), 306–29.

the Amal.⁷⁵ Such later medieval claims that Isidore's family was connected to Theoderic the Great, however, were meant to have served rhetorical purposes that were engrossed in the events of the time, including the use of historical memory for the promotion of contemporary agendas. These rhetorical claims further served a medieval desire to entrench the connection between Isidore and Sisebut, for a variety of reasons, including finding legitimization for conquest and for anti-Semitic activities, and are unlikely to reflect real kinship connections.

Isidore was a powerful ecclesiastic, defender against heresy, famed teacher and promoter of education. Isidore is said to have been beautiful physically, as well as intellectually. He was a gifted orator and prolific writer, author of at least seventeen texts. Isidore was also responsible for the development and proliferation of the Isidore-moment, and the school of Isidore-Seville. The story of Isidore's life has been repeated extensively in modern historiography. The details of the early historiography on Isidore, as well as his career and writing, will be covered in the following chapters. It is imperative to remember that Isidore's family was powerful and well-resourced in Baetica, along the coasts of Carthaginensis in the southeast of the peninsula, and to some extent connected with Constantinople.⁷⁶

3.1.3   Redemptus

Redemptus was a cleric in Seville who wrote the first posthumous account of Isidore, in 636, in his eulogy, the *Obitus Beati Isidori*. He may also have contributed to the editing of the history of the Iberian church councils, the *Hispana*, and perhaps also the canons of IV Toledo. He was certainly one of Isidore's "network of clerical disciples," and his text represents the first historical account of Isidore.⁷⁷ Redemptus is firmly a member of Isidore-Seville.

---

75   The assertion about Sisebut is based on the kinship claims made by Sisebut in a letter to the Lombard king Adaloaldo, son of Agiulf and descendant of Theoderic. However, these kinship ties were likely rhetorical or metaphorical. For discussion see Luis A. García Moreno, "La sucesión al trono en el Reino Godo: La perspectiva prosopográfica," in *Doctrina a magistro discipulis tradita. Estudios en homenaje al Prof. Dr. Luis García Iglesias*, ed. Adolfo Jerónimo Domínguez Monedero and Gloria Mora Rodríguez (Madrid: Ediciones de la Universidad Autónoma de Madrid, 2010), 409–10.

76   For an overview of Isidore's life and the historical background to it see *The "Etymologies" of Isidore of Seville*, trans. Stephen A. Barney, W. J. Lewish, J. A Beach, and Oliver Berghof (Cambridge: Cambridge University Press, 2006), 4–10. For bibliography, see Jocelyn N. Hillgarth, *The Visigoths in History and Legend* (Toronto: PIMS, 2009), 31 n. 21.

77   Rachel Stocking, "Martianus, Aventius and Isidore: Provincial Councils in Seventh-Century Spain," *Early Medieval Europe* 6 (1997): 172.

3.1.4 Braulio

A former student of Isidore in Seville, Braulio was, after Isidore, the most significant figure of the school.[78] At one point, Braulio even wrote a letter to Pope Honorius in which he criticized the Pope's lack of Scriptural knowledge and defended the relatively restrained Isidore-Seville position towards Jews and Judaism.[79] After his years as a student in Seville, in the 610s, Braulio was a cleric in Zaragoza until succeeding his brother to the bishopric of Zaragoza, which he then held from 631 to his death in 651.[80] Braulio and his brother John shared the bishopric of Zaragoza between them for more than thirty years; their father Gregory was the bishop of Osma.[81] Braulio, a member of a well-established and powerful family of the Ebro valley, advanced the interests of his family and their affiliations, and also promoted Zaragoza over other bishoprics in the valley and around Tarraconensis, particularly challenging the metropolitan authority of Tarragona.[82] The connection, then, between Isidore's family and their Baetican influence with Braulio's Tarraconensian was an exceptional network dangerous to the centralizing interests of Toledo-Agali. The addition to the network of exceptional families of Galicia and Narbonne, as would be the case with Fructuosus, helped forge its strength. Braulio is said to have excelled and impressed at both the Fourth and Fifth Councils of Toledo. It was in the middle of the 630s, at IV Toledo, that leadership of the school was formally passed on to Braulio, as discussed below in Chapter 4.

Braulio was renowned for his wit, charm, oratory, and especially epistolary skills. He wrote a variety of texts, including a series of letters that may or may not have been collected by him into a single work, as Cassiodorus had done (for very different purposes) with his *Variae*.[83] The letters of Braulio reveal a

---

78 On this, see note 71 above.
79 Braulio, *Ep.*, 21. On Braulio's letters see Chapter 2, § 3.2.
80 On the date of Braulio's death see José Carlos Martín-Iglesias, *La "Renotatio Librorum Domini Isidori" de Braulio de Zaragoza* (Logroño: Fundación San Millán de la Cogolla, 2002), 18–19.
81 On Braulio's family see Vitalino Valcárcel Martínez, "Sobre el origen geográfico de la familia de Braulio, obispo de Zaragoza," in *Mnemosynum C. Codoñer a discipulis oblatum*, ed. Augustín Ramos Guerreira (Salamanca: Universidad de Salamanca, 1991), 333–40.
82 Meritxell Pérez Martínez sees the rise in the importance of the bishopric of Zaragoza as attributable also to the urban growth of the city. See Meritxell Pérez Martínez, *Tarraco en la Antigüedad tardía. Cristianización y organización eclesiástica (III a VIII siglos)* (Tarragona: Arola Editors, 2012), 355–61.
83 On Braulio's construction of the letter collection see Ruth Miguel Franco, "Braulio de Zaragoza, el rey Chindasvinto y Eugenio de Toledo: imagen y opinión en el *Epistularium* de Braulio de Zaragoza," *Emerita, Revista de Lingüística y Filología Clásica*, 79 (2011), 155–76. For Cassiodorus's construction of the *Variae* see Otávio Luiz Vieira Pinto, "O Mais Belo Ornamento de Roma" (M.A. thesis, Universidade Federal do Paraná, 2012), and M. Shane

lot about his life, including his close connections with Isidore, about whose life and works he wrote the first posthumous account.[84] Braulio also edited into its final form Isidore's *Etymologies*, or as it will be referred in this book, the *Origines*. At IV Toledo, Isidore transferred the school to Braulio, and Braulio subsequently re-dedicated the *Origines* from Sisebut to himself. This clarification helps clear the confusion found in later manuscripts, which introduce the *Origines* as a text initiated by Sisebut and/or Braulio, and, in so doing, miss the struggle that was going on in seventh-century Hispania for the rights over the *Origines* and the historical record.[85] Later writers and scribes were less interested in the historical discourses and fights between Catholic powers in Visigothic Hispania than with representing the impressive collective output of them.

In addition to the *Origines*, Braulio edited the laws for what would become the *Liber Iudiciorum* and could have contributed to the editing of the canonical collection known as the *Hispana*. Moreover, aside from this important literary activity, Braulio also wrote the *Vita Aemeliani*, which extols proper monastic life, as rural not urban.[86] The text may have been written at the request of king Chindaswinth, who was raised to the throne somewhere between Burgos and Pamplona, the two cities constituting the edges of La Rioja, the region where Aemelian had had his monastery. The text, with its elevation of rural monasticism, could also have been a subtle criticism of the monastery of Agali, located just outside the walls of Toledo. Indeed, it was during Chindaswinth's reign that the only non-Agalian bishop of Toledo of the Isidore-moment, Eugenius II, held the bishopric. However, the *Vita Aemeliani* also certainly promoted Fronimian, a relative of Braulio and abbot of the monastery around the sepulcher of St. Aemelian. The relationship with Chindaswinth will be discussed below. Suffice it to note here, Chindaswinth forced Braulio's archdeacon Eugenius to return from Zaragoza to Toledo against the wishes of Braulio and Eugenius (whose bond will be discussed shortly).[87]

Bjornlie, *Politics and Tradition Between Rome, Ravenna and Constantinople: A Study of Cassiodorus and the Variae, 527–554* (Cambridge: Cambridge University Press, 2013), chs. 7, 8 and 11.

84 Braulio's *Renotatio*, about which see Chapter 2, note 3.

85 For example, see the British Library's ninth-century MS Harley 2686, f. 5ʳ "Incipit liber Isidori iunioris spalensis episcopi ad Bruionem [sic] / Cesar Agustanum episcopum vel ad sesebutum regem."

86 See Francisco Javier Lomas Salmonte, "Análisis Funcionalidad de la *Vita Aemiliani* (BHL 100)," *Studia Historica. Historia Antigua* 16 (1998): 247–66.

87 Braulio, *Ep.*, 31–3.

3.1.5   Taio

Taio was consecrated as bishop of Zaragoza in late 651, after the death of Braulio. He was Braulio's successor, and while he was bishop the bishopric of Toledo had at least three bishops. It is unclear exactly when Taio died, although it could have been before 681 since Taio was not present at the Twelfth Council of Toledo in that year. However, no bishops of any of the major bishoprics of Tarragona signed XII Toledo, or, in fact, the following council of Toledo. Taio's death must have been before 683, since that is when Fredebado signed XIII Toledo as the representative of Valderedo, bishop of Zaragoza. Prior to Taio's episcopacy he was an abbot, possibly in the monastery associated with the sepulcher of the Eighteen Martyrs in Zaragoza, where Braulio's brother or close relative Fronimian was previously abbot. On the orders of Chindaswinth, Taio went to Rome to collect Gregorian texts.[88]

While still abbot, Taio exchanged letters with Eugenius II discussing his trip to Rome. He also had an epistolary conversation with Braulio. In one letter, Taio asked Braulio for theological advice, for proof that the blood of Christ, from the Resurrection, could have become a relic. Braulio responded by telling Taio that it was impossible, since only the good parts of nature were resurrected, and blood was corrupting and superfluous.[89] Taio's primary literary

---

[88] *Chronicle of 754*, 28–33, and the letter from Taio to Eugenius II, in *Eugenii Toletani Episcopi Carmina et Epistulae*, ed. Frideric Vollmer, Monumenta Germaniae Historica, Auctorum Antiquissimorum 14 (Berlin: Weidmann, 1905), 287–90. On the *Chronicle of 754* see Chapter 2, § 4.3.

[89] Braulio, *Ep.*, 41–42. To be precise, Braulio maintains that the historical blood of the body will not remain with the corpse. Rather, a new set of blood will be provided to the arisen body at the time of the Parousia. The parable presented in 1 Corinthians 15:35–38 would seem to support this conclusion. However, Visigothic theology presented fluctuating or even competing opinions on this. Following Scripture, for instance 2 Corinthians 5:17, Isidore implies a transformation of bodies at the resurrection into ones at perfect maturity (Isid., *Sent.*, 1.27). Julian of Toledo echoes and elaborates on this maturity contention, doing so, however, not through Isidore but by way of the Scriptures, Augustine, and the fifth-century Gallic priest Julian Pomerius (Julian, *Progn.*, 3.19). Julian also suggests, arguably in contrast to Braulio, and by citing Eugenius II, that the same body in which one lived will be the one risen (Julian, *Progn.* 3.17). All references to Isidore's *Sententiae* are to the Cazier edition: *Isidorus Hispalensis Sententiae*, ed. Pierre Cazier, Corpus Christianorum Series Latina 111 (Turnhout: Brepols, 1998); and the Knoebel translation: Isidore of Seville, *Sententiae*, intro. and trans. Thomas L. Knoebel, Ancient Christian Writers 73 (New York: Newman Press, 2018). All references to Julian of Toledo's *Prognosticum futuri saeculi* are to the Hillgarth edition: Julian of Toledo, *Opera 1: Idalii Barcelonis Episcopi epistulae, Prognosticum futuri saeculi libri tres, Apologeticum de tribus capitulis, De comprobatione sextae aetatis libri tres*, ed. Jocelyn N. Hillgarth, Corpus Christianorum Series Latina 115 (Turnhout: Brepols, 1976), 11–126; and, the Stancati translation: Julian of Toledo, *Prognosticum saeculi futuri: Foreknowledge of the world to come*, intro. and trans. Tommaso Stancati,

activity was after the collapse of the Isidore-moment. This includes his *Sententiae*, written per the request of Quiricius, bishop of Toledo (667–680), and in which Isidore and his *Sententiae* are not mentioned, despite reliance on Isidorian innovations.[90] In addition, Taio may also have helped edit the *Liber Iudiciorum*.[91] Direct contributor to the school or not, Taio's connections to it and its key figures are evident.

3.1.6 Eugenius II

Eugenius began his career as a cleric in the church of Toledo. However, his calling was to the monastic life. Early during his time as a Toledan cleric, he abandoned the church of Toledo in favor of the monastery in Zaragoza at the site of the Eighteen Martyrs, where Fronimian and Taio would be abbots.[92] While in Zaragoza he became a close friend, confidant and protégé of Braulio, and also archdeacon. Eugenius was born before the year 606, since he became bishop in 646, and died in 657.

In the midst of a monastic life in Zaragoza, Eugenius was ordered by Chindaswinth back to Toledo, to become its next bishop, after the death of Eugenius I, bishop of Toledo from 636 to 646. Braulio desperately wanted his friend Eugenius to stay, and he expressed this desire clearly in an epistolary exchange with the king. Braulio was also writing on behalf of Eugenius, who had no wish to return to the church that he had abandoned years before. If Eugenius, a Toledan, had longed to become bishop of Toledo at some point in his life, the natural choice would have been to enter the monastery of Agali: Helladius, decades before, had left his public life specifically to enter the monastery of Agali, and not long afterwards was appointed bishop of Toledo. However, Eugenius had

---

Ancient Christian Writers 63 (New York: Newman Press, 2010). But see also Jocelyn N. Hillgarth, "A Critical Edition of the *Prognosticum* of Saint Julian of Toledo" (Ph.D. diss., Cambridge University, 1956).

90 Taio was influenced by Isidorian innovations, but his *Sententiae* would be more eschatological than Isidore's and updated to deal with the circumstances of the later seventh century. On this and on Isidore's influence generally see Laureano Robles Carcedo, "Tajón de Zaragoza, continuador de Isidoro," *Saitabi* 21 (1971): 19–25, and, Joel Varela Rodríguez, "Las *Sententiae* de Tajón de Zaragoza. Sus modelos literarios y su aproximación a la teología de Gregorio Magno," *e-Spania* (2018): 1–15. On the prologue to Taio's *Sententiae* see Julia Aguilar Miquel, "El *Epigramma operis subsequentis* de Tajón de Zaragoza en los mss. Aug. Perg. 255, Clm 14854 y Ott. lat. 2546," *Revista de Estudios Latinos* 18 (2018): 73–88.

91 On the former see Patrologia Latina 80, cols. 731–990, and, for the latter, see Chapter 5, § 2.3.

92 Eugenius II is sometimes referred to erroneously as Eugenius III. This is the result either of the growth of a later cult about a mythic first-century bishop of Toledo, or a fourth-century bishop and martyr that would make Eugenius I and II in the seventh century actually Eugenius II and III in Iberian history. For discussion on this see García Moreno, *Prosopografía*, no. 247 n. 1, and *Lives of the Visigothic Fathers*, ed. and trans. Andy Fear (Liverpool: Liverpool University Press, 1997), 118, n. 54.

specifically chosen not to do so. As a non-Agalian, Eugenius became the first bishop of Toledo, since Gundemar's council in 610, not to have been previously a monk at Agali. He represents the only non-Agalian bishop of Toledo during the entire Isidore-moment, from the early 600s to 667. Eugenius was also the first bishop appointed to the Catholic *sedes regia*, in that Chindaswinth was the first Catholic king to declare Toledo as such.[93] Chindaswinth's move to break the local Agalian tradition may have been related to his own anxieties as a non-Toledan usurper of the Crown, with questionable or rather poor connections with the local aristocracy, evidenced by his slaughtering of the Gothic nobility. Another recent usurper, Sisenand (r. 631–636), who had to fight off at least one major revolt and one minor, likewise tried to appoint a non-Agalian as bishop of the royal see, but, in that instance, was not successful in getting his appointment through.[94]

Early in Chindaswinth's reign, in 646, Eugenius held the Seventh Council of Toledo, and later, during the sole reign of Chindaswinth's son Recceswinth, he oversaw three consecutive councils (VIII in 653, IX in 655, and X Toledo in 656), checking the power of the monarch and ensuring the king's commitments made in the *Liber Iudiciorum*. Eugenius led more councils of Toledo than any other bishop in the entirety of the Visigothic kingdom, three of which were convened by the longest reigning king in the Toledan kingdom's history. As such, Eugenius's influence, during his life, should not be underestimated. After Eugenius's death in 657, Recceswinth appointed an Agalian as bishop of Toledo, and from that point on was never forced to hold another council, or return to the *Liber Iudiciorum*, during the rest of his long reign ending in 672. The next Toledan council was not held until 675, by king Wamba (672–680) and Eugenius's second successor, Quiricius.[95]

Despite the forced removal from Zaragoza to Toledo, if not also fueled by it, the intimate relationship between Eugenius II and Braulio remained tight. This is evidenced in the construction of Braulio's letter collection, and the form and content of the letters between he and Eugenius.[96] In addition to the epistolary exchange, and his involvement in councils, Eugenius wrote a harsh epitaph against Chindaswinth, and more significantly he edited the works of the North African poet, Dracontius.[97] Eugenius may also have edited the *Liber*

---

93   Chindaswinth was the first Catholic monarch to declare Toledo the *sedes regia*, a move he announced formally at VII Toledo in 646. On Chindaswinth see Chapter 5, § 3.
94   On the Gerontius affair see Chapter 4, § 3.5.1.
95   The Third Council of Braga was held in the same year.
96   Braulio, *Ep.*, 35 and 36.
97   Eug., *carm.*, 25, *Epitaphion Chindasuintho Regi Conscriptum*. On the epitaph and for a discussion of its historical significance in the period see Chapter 5 below, as well as David Ungvary, "The voice of the dead king Chindasuinth: poetry, politics, and the discourse of

Iudiciorum, and definitely led the Eighth Council of Toledo by which the *Liber Iudiciorum* was promulgated.

As an intimate associate, friend and advisee of Braulio, heir to Isidore in Isidore-Seville, it has been said that Eugenius II was the "intellectual grandchild of Isidore," who oversaw Isidore's being declared a doctor of the church.[98] Eugenius is firmly in the orbit of the school, not only because of this friendship with Braulio and the student-teacher relationship between them, but also because he was by choice a non-member of the Agali monastery and its network. Eugenius represents a very important mediating voice on behalf of the school within Toledo. Despite his ties to Isidore-Seville, being an outsider to the traditions of the Toledan bishopric and having been forced into it by the king, Eugenius had a working relationship with both Chindaswinth and Recceswinth. It is this position that is ultimately expressed in VIII Toledo and its promulgation of the *Liber Iudiciorum* – serious attempts by the *sedes regia* at reconciliation with local networks of power – but most especially between the two schools and their respective networks of influence.

---

penance in Visigothic Spain," *Early Medieval Europe* 26, no. 3 (2018): 327–54. Ungvary challenges the traditional reading of the epitaph as critical of the king, while doing so within the frame of a traditional historiographical argument of royal versus ecclesiastical power. Ungvary argues, essentially, that the king in this instance maintains his ultimate authority over the church. Chindaswinth does so by subverting any chance of genuine criticism against him and his audacious reign, and his son as successor, through forcing this public act of penance. Yet, Ungvary pleads with his readers to reconsider the prevailing negative image of Chindaswinth as a forceful and violent leader. The article is a welcome intervention on the subject with an insightful discussion of penance in mid-seventh-century Hispania, but the harsh tone and intention of the epitaph, even if forced upon Eugenius by Chindaswinth as a political stunt (penance), remains reflective of attitudes towards Chindaswinth and his reign. What is arguable is the extent to which Eugenius's criticism is two-sided, meant as both a genuine act of penance for the king – which Eugenius as bishop and following Isidore's theology likely did mean to do – and a cathartic way for him to expose, in writing for the court and those reading his poetry, the deeds of Chindaswinth and the reparative acts Recceswinth would need to accomplish if he were to stay in power. In fact, Ungvary's discussion on Recceswinth's law (*LI*, 2.1.19) subsequently reinforcing regulation against slander could confirm this reading. Ungvary's article is helpful in reminding scholars that we should remember to keep in mind the former when considering the epitaph. For a recent study of Eugenius's engagement with Dracontius see Mark Tizzoni, "The Poems of Dracontius in Their Vandalic and Visigothic Contexts" (Ph.D. diss., University of Leeds, 2012), as well as the authoritative edition of Eugenius's work: *Eugenius Toletani*, Corpus Christianorum Series Latina 114, ed. Paulo Farmhouse Alberto (Turnhout: Brepols, 2005).

98   See Mayke de Jong, "Adding Insult to Injury: Julian of Toledo and His *Historia Wambae*," in *The Visigoths*, ed. Heather, 376.

3.1.7   Fructuosus

The final member, or rather, sympathetic associate, of the school of Isidore-Seville was Fructuosus, born prior to 610 and died before 675, since he was no longer present at the councils from that point. Fructuosus was the wealthy son of a Spanish duke, and was related to the Visigothic usurper Sisenand, as well as the bishop of Narbonne, Sclua, who was, after Isidore, the primary signatory of IV Toledo held by Sisenand.[99] Fructuosus was also related to Peter, the bishop of the Narbonnensian bishopric of Betteris. Fructuosus was the "intellectual grandchild" of Murila, an Arian bishop that formally converted at III Toledo. Fructuosus's teacher in Palentia was Conantius, bishop of Palentia for thirty years, from 609 to 639. Contanius had been trained by Murila, before going on to educate Fructuosus, and was a man that Ildefonsus praised for his lyrical and musical skills, and fidelity to church ritual.[100] Conantius was the second-ranking signatory of V Toledo in 636, next only to Eugenius I of Toledo.

Fructuosus became a monk by 640 and, in that decade, fulfilling what is said to have been his boyhood dream, built a monastery at Compludo.[101] Fructuosus composed a rule for Compludo and appointed an abbot, and after a period of time of being bothered by people, he fled into the woods to live quietly with his servant Baldarius.[102] Nevertheless, he was the authority behind the founding of countless monasteries in the north of the peninsula. In the early or

---

99   See the anonymous, *Versiculi editi a beatissimo Fructuoso, vv.* 5, ed. Manuel C. Díaz y Díaz, in *Hispania Sacra* 4 (1954), 142–44.

100   Ildef., *DVI*, 10. For edition and further information about Ildefonsus's *DVI* see Chapter 2, § 3.3.

101   *Vita Fructuosi*, 2–3. The *Vita Fructuosi* was written by an anonymous disciple of Fructuosus after his death in 665. The oldest extant manuscript is the tenth-century MS 10.007 (formerly, MS Toletanus 10.25) in the Biblioteca Nacional de Madrid. For a critical edition of the *Vita Fructuosi* see *La Vida de San Fructuoso de Braga*, ed. Manuel C. Díaz y Díaz (Braga: Diário do Minho, 1974). For discussion of the text see Roger Collins, "The Autobiographical Works of Valerius of Bierzo: their structure and purpose," in *Los Visigodos: Historia y Civilización* 3, 425–42.

102   For the latter points see *Vita Fruct.* 4, and Valerius of Bierzo, *De Coelesti Revelatione*, Patrologia Latina 87, cols. 435–36. For an edition, translation, and discussion of the monastic rule of Fructuosus see Patrologia Latina 87, cols. 1099–1130; Claude Barlow, *Fructuosus of Braga* (Washington, D.C.: The Catholic University Press, 1969); Allies, "Monastic Rules;" and, Iñaki Martín, "The Memory of the 'Holy Men' in Hispanic Monasticism: The Case of the Bierzo Region," in *Imago Temporis. Medium Aevum* 6 (2012): 165–90. For an account of life in the region during the period see Pablo C. Díaz, "Sociability and Sense of Belonging: Community Interaction in the World of Valerius of Bierzo," *Visigothic Symposia* 3 (2018): 112–29 and Céline Martin, "The Asturia of Valerius: Bierzo at the End of the Seventh Century," *Visigothic Symposia* 2 (2017): 60–78. For more of Valerius and his works see Manuel C. Díaz y Díaz, *Valerio del Bierzo. Su persona. Su obra* (León: Centro de Estudios e Investigación San Isidoro, 2006).

mid-650s, Fructuosus was forced by Recceswinth into the bishopric of the see of Dumio, near Braga. He was appointed probably to deal with a serious dispute concerning the previous bishop's manumission of slaves.[103] He was formally elevated to the bishopric of Braga at x Toledo in December 656, thereby making him metropolitan of Galicia, the northwest of the peninsula.

Fructuosus is not considered here a member of the school of Isidore-Seville, and his writings should not be interpreted as part of the competitive dialectics between the schools. However, as an exceptionally powerful figure in the north of the peninsula and in Narbonensis with connections to members of Isidore-Seville, he is an important example of a person and network sympathetic to it and what this could mean to officials and the establishment in Toledo. Fructuosus's affiliation with the school is apparent from diverse evidence. For example, the anonymous *Vita Fructuosi*, written after 675, starts by praising Isidore.[104] One might suspect that such praise was standard in later seventh-century Hispania given Isidore's historical fame, but, as Chapter 2 below shows, this was hardly the case; representations of Isidore in the period were rare. Writing after the Isidore-moment, the anonymous disciple of Fructuosus, instead of promoting either the contemplative or the active, literary life as support for a particular bishop over another, used Isidore and Fructuosus as complementary figures for the proper Christian life.[105] Furthermore, in the *Vita Fructuosi*, the bishop of Seville, Antoninus (c. 641–654), pleads with Fructuosus to remain with him in Seville, establishing a connection between the two figures and their respective sees.[106] In fact, Fructuosus visited Seville at least twice, although Fructuosus traveled widely throughout the peninsula.[107]

In addition to the evidence from the *Vita* of Fructuosus's relationship with Isidore-Seville, there are extant letters exchanged between Fructuosus and Braulio at the turn of the 650s. The content of the letters is not mundane: in his initial letter to Braulio, Fructuosus, author of his own rule and founder by then of multiple monasteries, entrusts Braulio with answering crucial theological questions. Braulio's response is a serious and detailed one in which he elicits several key explanations of biblical narratives and truths. In his response to Fructuosus, Braulio mentions Isidore as a great and learned man and cites the

---

103   See the second decretal of x Toledo: "Item aliud decretum eorundem prafatorum pontificum editum."
104   Isidore is praised for his divine love, brilliance, eloquent speech, personal charm, the reintroduction, it is said, of Roman education, as well as his productivity. This is a description reminiscent of Braulio's.
105   *Vita Fruct.*, 1.
106   *Vita Fruct.*, 14.
107   *Vita Fruct.*, 11–14.

latter's *Origines* (*Etymologies*). This implies that Fructuosus knew the *Origines* and that he trusted Isidore's opinion, not a given by contemporaries.[108]

Another issue that may have bonded Fructuosus to Braulio, as well as to Eugenius II, was Fructuosus's early discontent with Recceswinth's Toledo, a conclusion made possible on several grounds. First, Fructuosus's family was an important one in the north, with close connections to Narbonne, Gaul and the Gallic-backed usurper, Sisenand. Given the anti-Gallic, semantically pro-Gothic response to Sisenand, it may have been that Fructuosus, by family relation, had a problematic relationship with Toledo. Second, as seen in his letter to Recceswinth on the topic, Fructuosus wanted the king to release political prisoners that had been held since the reign of king Chintila (r. 636–639).[109] Third, Fructuosus, desiring to experience the East, was prevented by Recceswinth from leaving the kingdom without his permission.[110] Fourth, Fructuosus was initially made bishop against his will, by Recceswinth.[111] Fifth, after Fructuosus used his inheritance to found and lavishly supply the monastery of Compludo, his sister's husband successfully pleaded with the king that part of the family inheritance should be given instead to him for the purposes, we are told, of a *publica expeditione*.[112]

3.2   School of Toledo-Agali (600s–660s)

In competition with Isidore and his school of Seville are the Toledan aristocracy and their monastery of Agali, labeled here the school of Toledo-Agali; the monarchy in Toledo is associated directly with the school. The primary members of Toledo-Agali are the bishops of Toledo, from Helladius to Ildefonsus. The dates of the school are from early in the 600s, when the monastery of Agali

---

108   Braulio, *Ep.*, 43 and 44.
109   For Fructuosus's letter to Recceswinth see *Epistolae Wisigothicae*, Ep. 19, in *Epistolae Merovingici et Karolini aevi*, ed. Wilhem Gundlach, Monumenta Germaniae Historica, Epistolarum III (Berlin: Weidmann, 1892), 658–90 (688–89), and Wilhelm Gundlach, *Neues Archiv* 16 (1891): 45–46. The letter survives in the eighth-century manuscript of the *Ep. Wis.*, the MS Escurialensis I. 14.
110   For the account, see the *Vita Fruct.*, 17. The story draws a parallel to the betrayal story of the New Testament, but regardless, appears to have been a real incident. Why someone from Fructuosus's inner-circle betrayed him to the king's authorities may have to do with the clause in the law, as seen in the preface to Chindaswinth's VII Toledo of 646, in which it is said that even accomplices of a cleric planning to leave the country without permission would be instantly deprived of their rank, destined to live the rest of their temporal life out of Communion with the Church.
111   *Vita Fruct.*, 18, and X Toledo 2.
112   *Vita Fruct.*, 3. P. D. King interprets this as some sort of "feudal" service, since all were already subject to military duty. See P. D. King, *Law and Society in the Visigothic kingdom* (Cambridge: University of Cambridge Press, 1972), 62.

was founded (and when Isidore became bishop), until the death, in 667, of the last bishop of Toledo from Agali, Ildefonsus. In correlation with the Isidore-moment, every bishop of Toledo, from the founding of Agali and the elevation of Toledo as the metropolitan of Carthaginensis was elevated from the ranks of Agali. The only exception was, as explained, Eugenius II. The monastic rule used by Agali is uncertain, but may have been the rule of Donatus, if this is why Ildefonsus includes him in his *De Viris Illustribus*.[113] The monastery of Agali was located just outside the walls of Toledo, in the southeastern plateau, close to the Tagus River. At the time, there were also four abbeys, two cathedrals and a basilica, perhaps even a functioning *palatium* and a palace goldsmith's workshop outside the walls of Toledo. This area was a vibrant part of the urban life of the city.[114]

---

113 Ildef., *DVI* 3. The name Agali is considered to have been derived from its location on the road up through Zaragoza to Gallia, and so *ad Galiense iter*, which presumably was pronounced as "Agali." The monastery is also figured to have been dedicated to the Eastern martyrs Sts. Cosmas and Damian, as noted in the *Vita vel Gesta Sancti Ildephonsi,* the hagiography to Ildefonsus, once considered written by the eighth-century bishop of Toledo, Cixila, and more recently an eleventh-century Cluniac monk. The signature list at the end of XI Toledo (675) contains reference to an abbot named Gratinidus at the monastery of "Cosme et Damiani," yet also lists another, Anila, at Agali, suggesting they were different places. However, this is found in the quite late MS Paris BN lat. 3846, and may reflect the erroneous medieval tradition of Julian as abbot of Agali. In any case, whether or not Agali was dedicated to Cosmas and Damian is an open question. For more on the naming, dedication and foundation of Agali, see Valeriano Yarza Urquiola, "*La Vita vel Gesta Sancti Ildephonsi, de ps. Eladio*: Estudio, Edición Crítica y Traducción," *Veleia* 23 (2006): 279–325; Ramón González Ruiz, "Agali: Historia del Monasterio de San Ildefonso," *Toletum: boletín de la Real Academia de Bellas Artes y Ciencias Históricas de Toledo* (2007): 99–145; Collins, *Visigothic Spain*, 153. Collins agrees with García Moreno that the establishment of Agali was around the year 600 (Luis A. García Moreno, "Los monjes y monasterios en las cuidades de las Españas Tardorromanas y visigodas," *Habis* 24 [1993]: 179–92). On the seventh-century inscription placing the relics of Cosmas and Damian in Toledo, see Mark Handley, *Death, Society and Culture: Inscriptions and Epitaphs in Gaul and Spain, AD 300–750* (Oxford: BAR Series, 2003), 151–52.

114 See Javier Martínez Jiménez, "The Rural hinterland of the Visigothic capitals of Toledo and Reccopolis, between the years 400–800 CE," in *Authority and Control in the Countryside: Continuity and Change in the Mediterranean, 6th–10th century CE*, ed. Alain Delattre, Marie Legendre and Petra Sijpesteijn (Boston and Leiden: Brill, 2018), 97–127; Rafael Barroso Cabrera, Jesús Carrobles Santos, Jorge Morín de Pablos and Isabel Sánchez Ramos, "El Paisaje Urbano de Toledo en la Antigüedad Tardía," *AnTard* 23 (2015): 55–78; Rafael Barroso Cabrera, Jesús Carrobles Santos, Jorge Morín de Pablos and Isabel Sánchez Ramos, "Ciudad y territorio toledano entre la Antigüedad tardía y el reino visigodo: la construcción de una *Civitas regia* (ss. IV–VIII d.C.)," *Erytheia* 36 (2015): 9–61; and, Felix Retamero, "As Coins go Home: Towns, Merchants, Bishops and Kings in Visigothic Hispania," in *The Visigoths*, ed. Heather, 273.

3.2.1 Helladius

Helladius was Isidore's contemporary rival. He was the bishop of Toledo from 615 to his death in 633. Prior to his episcopacy he was *rector rerum publicarum* of Carthaginensis, until giving up public life to become the second abbot of Agali. Shortly thereafter, he was appointed by Sisebut as the first bishop of Toledo after the city's elevation to metropolitan status by Gundemar in 610.[115] That he had left public life specifically to enter Agali, likely at the request of Sisebut, suggests political intentions for himself and also Agali. Sisebut's appointment tied Agali intimately to the bishopric of Toledo by solidifying Toledo's recent elevation as metropolitan of Carthaginensis with the promotion of its own, local monastery, and public officials. Helladius was the first bishop of Toledo since it had become primatial see of Carthaginensis, and, along with this, came the wealth and growth of Agali, and the growth of the Toledo-Agali tradition.[116] Rising from public position to abbot of Agali, in 619, four years after Helladius's elevation to bishop of Toledo, Isidore held a council in Seville. The council began by promoting Baetica's own public officials, including its *rector rerum publicarum*, Sisisclo, but also significantly demonstrating Seville's strict separation of secular from religious officials, a clear insult aimed at Sisebut and Helladius.

The anonymous author of the *Vita Fructuosus* in the 670s praised Isidore and Fructuosus as complementary models of piety, citing the significance both of living well and writing holy texts. In his chapter on Helladius and Isidore, the anonymous chronicler of 754, writing in Toledo, provides a similar sort of complementary praise of Helladius and Isidore, although he places Helladius first. He commemorated Helladius for his outstanding sanctity, and celebrated Isidore as a teacher and defender against heresy through writing and canonical texts. In contrast, Ildefonsus, committed representative of Toledo-Agali and made deacon at Agali by Helladius, praised Isidore's writing in a back-handed way and promoted Helladius's holiness through reference to his lifestyle. Ildefonsus not only elevated actions over writing, he also justified the praise of Helladius against Isidore by saying that Helladius actively chose not to write, demonstrating virtue by the way he lived.

Helladius was at various points in his life the governor of Carthaginensis, bishop of the primatial see in the royal see, and head of the most politically significant monastery in the kingdom. He was powerful and well-connected, and

---

115 Aurasius was the bishop of Toledo when the bishopric was promoted. As such, he had also served in Toledo when it was not the leading bishopric of Carthaginensis, a situation that neither Helladius nor any bishop of Toledo after him would experience.
116 Ildef., *DVI*, 6.

remained throughout his life integral to the political, administrative functioning of Toledo, as well as to the growth and promotion of the city, its offices, and aristocracy.[117] In terms of religious affairs alone, Helladius allowed no councils in Toledo during his long eighteen years in office. This means that there were no councils in Toledo between that of Gundemar's in 610 and IV Toledo in late 633, after the death of Helladius. Isidore led both of the councils in Toledo, in 610 and 633, but attended not a single one in Toledo, it would appear, while Helladius was its bishop. Helladius, in preventing five kings from holding councils, also effectively blocked Isidore from Toledo.[118]

The only known correspondence between Isidore and Helladius is a letter from the former to the latter. In it, Isidore hints at Helladius's school, or network, and its competition with Isidore-Seville. In fact, the letter begins, "Dominis meis et Dei servis Helladio caeterisque qui cum eo sunt coadunati episcopis Isidorus." This could refer to the bishops of Carthaginensis in a broad sense, but even so, it is a weird phrase in an epistolary exchange. It implies that these bishops, this circle of Helladius, are particularly united with each other in contrast to Isidore-Seville, in some capacity. The tone of the letter, in which Isidore speaks to the royally granted authority of the clerics in Toledo, suggests that the school of Helladius, noted in the opening, was firmly in Toledo only. There is no record of a response by Helladius.[119]

3.2.2 Justus

Helladius's successor, Justus, had been a child oblate of Agali. He not only owed his life to Agali, and Helladius, he was educated by them both and spent his life in Agali, eventually becoming Helladius's successor as abbot.[120] After Helladius's death in 633, Justus was consecrated as bishop of Toledo. His term as bishop was brief and troubled, due to serious political events happening in Toledo in the early 630s. In 631 a Gallic-backed Goth, Sisenand, usurped the throne from Swinthila (621–631), the king who had, it is said, finally driven the Byzantines from Hispania. That he had done so may have contributed to his being overthrown by a Gallic-sponsored and Narbonnian-supported rebellion. Whatever the reasons for it, Sisenand's usurpation in 631 led to serious

---

117 Ildef., *DVI*, 6.
118 The five kings were Sisebut, Reccared II, Swinthila, Riccimir, and early into Sisenand's reign.
119 For an edition of the letter see Patrologia Latina 83, vol. 6, ed. Faustino Arévalo (Paris, 1862), col. 566. The only medieval manuscript containing the letter to Helladius is MS Escurialensis R. II. 18 (*Codex Ovetensis*), a miscellaneous codex produced between the seventh and ninth centuries.
120 Ildef., *DVI*, 7.

political disturbances. He spent two years fighting rebellions until eventually holding a council in Toledo that was led by Isidore, Braulio, and Sclua, the bishop of Narbonne and relative of Fructuosus. During the rebellions, Sisenand also seems to have supported the usurpation of the bishopric in Toledo, from the Agalian Justus, in favor of the non-Agalian, Gerontius. This was part of the attempt to break the power of the local Toledan aristocracy, good reasons for bringing in Isidore, Braulio, and Sclua to run the council, and waiting to hold it until just after Helladius, conveniently, died. The attack on the local aristocracy, and Agali in particular, seems to have been so significant that Justus even wrote a letter to Rechila, the abbot of Agali, pleading with him not to abandon his flock. Justus died only three years into his bishopric, in February 636, only several weeks before the end of Sisenand's reign.

3.2.3 Eugenius I

Like his predecessor Justus, Eugenius I entered the care of Agali as an infant. He was also a student of Helladius and worked with him running the bishopric of Toledo until he eventually became the second successor of Helladius as abbot of Agali. After the death of Justus in 636, Eugenius I became bishop of Toledo, Helladius's second successor in that position as well. Eugenius I entered the bishopric under more stable conditions than Justus had done and, likely because of that, maintained the position for eleven years covering the reigns of three kings – Chintila, Tulga (r. 639–642), and Chindaswinth – until his death in March 646. Helladius and his Agali students held the bishopric of Toledo for thirty-one consecutive years, from 615 to 646.

3.2.4 Ildefonsus

After Eugenius I, the non-Agalian Eugenius II was consecrated and held the bishopric until 657. The successor to Eugenius II was Ildefonsus, bishop of Toledo from 657 to 667. In contrast to Eugenius II, who was made bishop against his will, having earlier fled from Toledo, and who was the intellectual and ecclesiastical grandchild of Isidore, Ildefonsus was an Agalian and Toledan through and through. Prior to his appointment as bishop of Toledo, Ildefonsus was a deacon and abbot of Agali. He was also a member of a very powerful local, Toledan family.[121] In his *De Viris Illustribus*, Ildefonsus ascribes high praise to Agali, and explains how the bishopric of Toledo and abbacy of Agali

---

121 On Ildefonsus's career and family see Julian of Toledo, *Beati Hildefonsi Elogium*, Patrologia Latina 96, cols. 43–44; Felix of Toledo, *Vita sancti Juliani Toletani episcopi*, ed. in *España Sagrada. Theatro geographico-histórico de la Iglesia de España* v (Madrid, 1747), 484–87; and, Quiricius of Toledo, *Epistolae*, Patrologia Latina 96, col. 193–94, *Chron. 754*, 48.

were not only intimately tied to one another, but were positions of patrimony.[122] After the attempted overthrow of the Agalians from the bishopric of Toledo, by the Frankish-backed usurper Sisenand in the 630s, and, in the 640s, the traumatic reign of Chindaswinth, who killed hundreds of Gothic nobles and temporarily broke the Agali tradition, Ildefonsus was appointed by Recceswinth to re-build cooperation within Toledo.[123] He would, however, be the last bishop of Toledo raised through Agali.

Recceswinth's royal successor, Wamba, established a new royal see by investing with a bishop the church of Sts. Peter and Paul, outside the walls of Toledo, perhaps not far from Agali, and meant as a rival. This see was eliminated promptly by bishop Julian of Toledo (ep. 680–690) and king Ervig (r. 680–687), before they re-introduced important centralizing texts, decretals and laws from earlier in the century, such as Gundemar's decretal, and re-worked major texts from the Isidore-moment in their favor.[124]

Ildefonsus was not only the last Agalian to become bishop of Toledo, but he also represents the very end of the Isidore-moment. The closing of the dialectical competition of Isidore-Seville and Toledo-Agali happened with the promulgation of the *Liber Iudiciorum* at the Eighth Council of Toledo in 653 and its issuance in early 654. Ildefonsus's appointment from Agali and subsequent career allowed him to institutionalize the closing of the period and the sublimation of Isidore-Seville by Toledan power more broadly. From his bishopric forward, Toledo actively and successfully brought Seville into its orbit. Julian, the next bishop of Seville following Ildefonsus's bishopric in Toledo, was possibly a native Toledan, appointed to be the metropolitan of Baetica by Julian, bishop of Toledo and friend of Julian of Seville.[125] Felix, Julian's second successor as bishop of Seville, was transferred to Toledo to run the royal see, and then wrote about the life of Julian. His very next successor as bishop of Toledo, Faustinus, was transferred from Toledo to Seville, and is the last recorded bishop of Seville during the Visigothic kingdom of Toledo. From the time of Ildefonsus onwards, Isidore-Seville was not only no longer part of a competitive dialectic with Toledo-Agali, but was sublimated to, integrated with and silenced by Toledo.

---

122 Ildef., *DVI*, 6–7.
123 On Sisenand's support for the non-Agalian Gerontius against Justus see Chapter 4, § 3.5.1
124 XII Toledo 4.
125 For further discussion of this possibility see Appendix: Julian of Toledo Not an Agalian.

3.2.5 Julian of Toledo

The final figure that needs to be addressed is Julian, the bishop of Toledo from 680–690. From his impressive re-editing of the Isidore-Seville material, and virtual conquest of Seville through these revisions, he may seem to be a perfect candidate for the school of Toledo-Agali. Born in Chindaswinth's dynamic Toledo c. 642–645 to parents who were native Toledans as well as Catholics converted from Judaism, Julian was educated at the episcopal school of Toledo.[126] Despite being a Toledan, he was speaking after the Isidore-moment and the closing of the competitive dialectics between the former schools. Moreover, although he may have spent a short "residency" at the monastery, Julian was not an Agalian, and this is a significant point. That it has been long-rumored that Julian served as abbot of Agali, despite evidence to the contrary, is proof of how intimately connected Agali and the bishopric of Toledo became in the historiographical tradition about seventh-century Hispania, and of the problems of this tradition.[127]

There is good reason for concluding that Julian of Toledo was never the abbot of Agali. Julian himself claims that he was educated at the episcopal school in Toledo, by Eugenius II, *praeceptor noster*.[128] This is confirmed in the *Vita Iuliani*, written by Felix, Julian's second successor as bishop of Toledo.[129] In addition to this evidence, Julian, according to Felix, was never an abbot at all, let alone abbot of Agali; Julian was a deacon, priest (presbyter), and then bishop.[130] The combination of literary and classical training that Julian received, with the specific knowledge of Isidore-Seville via Eugenius, and loyalty to Toledan centralizing interests, manifested in a dynamic individual who

---

126 According to Felix of Toledo (*Vita*, 4), he was ordained as deacon in the seventeenth year of Recceswinth, at which point he needed to be twenty-five years old, according to IV Toledo 2. It is uncertain, though, whether Felix was referring to the beginning of Recceswinth's joint or sole reign. On Julian's Jewish heritage see *Chron. 754*, 50. On the place of Jewish converts in the late Visigothic kingdom see Liubov Chernin, "Visigothic Jewish Converts: A Life in Between," *Visigothic Symposia* 3 (2018): 1–18, and on the early period from Sisebut, Rodrigo Laham Cohen and Carolina Pecznik, "Iudaei et Iudaei baptizati en ley de los visigodos," *Anuario de Historia* de la Universidad Nacional de Rosario (2016): 141–69.

127 It is a long-standing rumor that Julian was abbot of Agali, which I refute below in Appendix: Julian of Toledo Not an Agalian. For more on the topic, see Ramón Gonzálvez Ruiz, "San Julián de Toledo en el Contexto de su Tiempo," *Análes Toledanos* 32 (1996): 7–21.

128 Julian of Toledo, *Prognosticum futuri saeculi*, 3.24.

129 *Vita Iuliani*, 1. References are to the edition: *Vita sancti Juliani Toletani episcopi*, Corpus Christianorum Series Latina 115B, ed. Valeriano Yarza Urquiola, 9–14 (Turnhout: Brepols, 2014).

130 *Vita Iuliani*, 4. For further discussion of Julian's supposed connection to Agali see Appendix: Julian of Toledo Not an Agalian.

redacted the major works of that school, introduced Gundemar's council into the *Hispana*, and appointed a friend of his as bishop of Seville.

3.3 *Schools Conclusion*

Finally, it must be reiterated that the respective entries in the schools section represent only those figures whose works and activities are known specifically to have contributed, or could be believed by historians to have been related, to the Isidore-moment, a dynamic dialogue constituted by more than those named above, but about whose individual ideas and actions little or nothing is known. Many of the conversations, written and oral, that must have contributed to the period have been lost. From those that remain, this book argues that their meanings and functions were products of the competitive dialectics between the schools. They spoke and had significance within a dialectics of power that oscillated between the networks of authority Isidore-Seville and Toledo-Agali.

CHAPTER 2

In the Beginning: The History of the Historiography of Isidore

1   Introduction

This chapter[1] serves as a case-study on the development, meaning, importance and impact of the schools-competition on the texts produced during the Isidore-moment. The argument is put forth in this chapter through a critical exploration of the competing constellations for the memory of Isidore of Seville. Immediately after the illustrious bishop's death in 636, the fight for his memory began, revealing that, from its inception, the history and historiography on Isidore was characterized by opposing representations. These competing accounts demonstrate the vigor that history-writing played in the fierce regional and personal struggles for authority.

The texts that follow can be constituted as historical in that each is an act or object of the past as well as a representation of individuals, ideas or events of the past, or rather, pasts. These historical representations reflect interpretations of Isidore and the associated past that differ depending on the context, content and form of the text, but also because of deliberate reconstructions of the author, tied, it is argued, to one of the schools. As such, this chapter is an exploration of the initial historical representations of Isidore and the development of a competitive discourse about him, but it also reflects the historiographical work that must have been done by seventh-century authors to construct their accounts.

The intention of this exploration into the origins of the written memory of Isidore is two-fold. The primary aim is to show that such activity, encapsulated in the historical texts and historiography, was a product of the vibrant discursive rivalry and competitive dialectics between the schools of Isidore-Seville and Toledo-Agali. The second goal is to demonstrate, from this, that, since their inception, the historical representations of Isidore were part of this

---

1 An earlier version of this chapter is published as Michael J. Kelly, "The Politics of History Writing: Problematizing the Historiographical Origins of Isidore of Seville in Early Medieval Hispania," in *Isidore of Seville and His Reception in the Early Middle Ages: Transmitting and Transforming Knowledge*, ed. Andy Fear and Jamie Wood (Amsterdam: Amsterdam University Press, 2016), 93–110.

competitive moment. There never was in Visigothic Spain a singular representation of Isidore or the meaning or being of his works.

2   The Historiography of Isidore

There are four first-generation representations and historical accounts of Isidore. The first is the obituary praise known as the *Obitus Beati Isidori* written by Redemptus, a cleric at or near Seville. The text is from 636 and is preserved in a problematic eighth-century manuscript at El Escorial (R.II.14).[2] Second is Braulio of Zaragoza's *Renotatio Isidori a Braulione Caesaraugustano episcopo edita* (*Renotatio*) added to Isidore's *De Viris Illustribus* (*DVI*), and three of his letters (*Epistolae*), all of which are preserved in the ninth-century (c. 830–839), Toledo-Córdoban manuscript León Cathedral 22.[3] All that can be said of the dating of the *Renotatio* is that it was written before Braulio's death in 651. The forty-four letters in the collection were written over the course of two decades and include letters to and from Isidore. The third representation is Ildefonsus of Toledo's *De Viris Illustribus* continuation, written around the middle of the 660s. The oldest remaining copy is in the León Cathedral 22 manuscript.[4]

---

2   For the edited text, see *Scripta de Vita Isidori Hispalensis Episcopi*, Corpus Christianorum Series Latina 113B, ed. José Carlos Martín-Iglesias (Turnhout: Brepols, 2006), 379–88, or the older, *Obitus Beati Isidori*, Patrologia Latina 81, cols. 30–32.

3   For the most current edition and elaborate discussions, including full manuscript details, of the *Renotatio* see Martín-Iglesias, *Renotatio*, and Martín-Iglesias, *Scripta*. In general, these are the editions to refer to for the *Renotatio*, which Braulio may simply have titled, as a *DVI* chapter, *Isidoro episcopo* or *Isidorus episcopus* (Martín-Iglesias, *Renotatio*, 56). For editions of the letters and the *Renotatio* see also Patrologia Latina 80, cols. 649–700 and Patrologia Latina 81, cols. 15–17, as well as the edition of Lynch and Galindo containing a reproduction of the text of the León Cathedral 22 manuscript, *San Braulio, Obispo de Zaragoza (631–651), Su Vida y sus Obras*, ed. Charles H. Lynch and P. Galindo (Madrid: Instituto "Enrique Florez," 1950). The León Cathedral 22 manuscript is a composition of two manuscripts from 830 and 839. The first was made in Toledo and the latter in Córdoba. The first may have been a copy of an eighth-century exemplar. For a review of the bibliography of MS León Cathedral 22 see Martín-Iglesias, *Scripta*, 104–05. For translation and discussion of the letters see Claude W. Barlow, *Iberian Fathers 2, Braulio of Saragossa* (Washington, D.C.: The Catholic University of America, 1969), 15–112, and Miguel Franco, "Braulio de Zaragoza." For a recent translation of the *Renotatio* see *Etymologies*, trans. Barney, et al., 7–9, and for more information, Martín-Iglesias, *Renotatio*, 55–84 and 167–209, and José A. de Aldama, "Indicaciones sobre la cronología de las obras Isidorianas," in *Miscellanea Isidoriana* (Rome: Typis Pontificiae Universitatis Gregorianae, 1936), 57–89.

4   For the text and discussion see Ildef., *DVI*, 8 (Patrologia Latina, 96, cols. 201–2): Jacques Fontaine, "El *De Viris Illustribus* de San Ildefonso de Toledo: Tradición y originalidad," *Anales Toledanos III: Estudios sobre la España visigoda* (Toledo, 1971), 59–96; Carmen Codoñer

Finally, there is the second canon of the Eighth Council of Toledo, the oldest extant versions of which come from ninth-century manuscripts.[5] The council was held in December 653 and represents a production made chronologically somewhere between the respective works of Braulio and Ildefonsus; it is noted last of these four because it is in a mediating position – chronologically, formally and in terms of content – between the texts of Braulio and Ildefonsus and the wider debate of the schools. As such, first exposing the structural relationship between the texts of Braulio and Ildefonsus will make grasping the role of this passage in the debate easier.

3 The Representations

3.1 *Redemptus*

This short text of about seven hundred and fifty words is the obituary of Isidore composed by a cleric named Redemptus. The account is based on the first-hand experience of the clerics around Seville that knew Isidore the most intimately, and that were there for the last days of his life. This list includes, notably, John the bishop of Elepla (modern Niebla, due west of Seville) and Eparcius of Italica (a suburb of today's Seville). The *Obitus Beati Isidori* was the first postmortem account of Isidore. It is inherently important as the initial historical representation of Isidore. However, it does not reveal much about him, even if one tries to organize the collection of biblical and tropic references into a collected idea. The point of the short text is to announce Isidore's death, and to demonstrate that he spent his last days honorably, in peace, and in a proper Catholic manner.[6]

Merino, *El "De Viris Illustribus" de Ildefonso de Toledo* (Salamanca: Salamanca: Universidad de Salamanca, 1972); *Ildefonsus Toletani Episcopi: De virginitate Sanctae Mariae; De itinere deserti; De Viris Illustribus*, ed. Valeriano Yarza Urquiola and Carmen Codoñer Merino, Corpus Christianorum Series Latina 114A (Turnhout: Brepols, 2007); and, Carmen Codoñer Merino, "El libro de 'Viris Illustribus' de Ildefonso de Toledo," in *La Patrología Toledano-Visigoda*, ed. Joaquín Blázquez (Madrid: Consejo Superior de Investigaciones Científicas, 1970), 337–48.

5   For a full discussion of the manuscripts see *CCH* 6 (2002), 12–15.
6   See Pedro Castillo Maldonado, *La Época Visigótica en Jaén (siglos VI y VII)* (Universidad de Jaén, 2006), *Obitus B. Isidori a Redempto Clerico recensitus, Variae lectiones ex mss. Codicibus*, Patrologia Latina 81; Pedro Castillo Maldonado, "La Muerte de Isidoro de Sevilla: Apuntes de Crítica Histórico-hagiográfica," *Habis* 32 (2001): 577–96 (596); Gerd Kampers, "Exemplarisches Sterben. Der '*Obitus Beatissimi Hispalensis Isidori episcopi*', Klerikers Redemptus," in *Nomen et Fraternitas. Festschrift für Dieter Geuenich zum 65 Geburtstag*, ed. Uwe Ludwig and Thomas Schilp (Berlin: De Gruyter, 2008), 235–48.

3.2 *Braulio:* Epistolae, Renotatio, *and Isidore's* De Viris Illustribus

3.2.1 Epistolae

The three letters of Braulio that were written after Isidore's death do not give much description of Isidore, but they do demonstrate Braulio's fidelity to him. In the letter (14) written to Fronimian, a priest near the tomb of St. Aemelian, and perhaps the brother of Braulio, Isidore is cited in reference to liturgical protocol.[7] In another letter (22) to Eutropius, a bishop near Zaragoza, Isidore is noted because of his authority on the date of Easter. In letter 44, a response to Fructuosus, Braulio refers to Isidore as an unrivalled man of learning (*incomparabilis scientiae vir Isidorus*), using him to prove a point concerning the age of the biblical Mathusale. In addition to providing clear evidence of his support for Isidore, it has been argued convincingly that the letter collection was arranged by Braulio to advance a narrative of subtle antagonisms about the monarchy in Toledo. The form and function of the letter is consistent with the aims and methods of the school: subtle, sustained criticism of Toledo through carefully constructed representations of the past.[8]

3.2.2 Renotatio

The *Renotatio* of Braulio is a continuation chapter added to Isidore's *De Viris Illustribus*,[9] and is a much fuller account of Isidore's life and character than what is found in Braulio's letters or in the obituary by Redemptus. The *Renotatio* tells when Isidore lived, [supposedly all of] the councils he was at, and that he successfully fought heresy. Braulio also spends significant space telling his readers that Isidore was an eloquent, intelligent and talented orator, and a skilled and knowledgeable writer. Braulio even graces his readers with an *encomium* to Isidore, quoted from Cicero, *via* Augustine's *City of God* 6.2.[10]

The most important feature of the *Renotatio* is the list and short explanation of each of Isidore's works (*sans* a few small ones Braulio says). Braulio lists seventeen works by Isidore in an order that is generally accepted as chronological.[11] The list goes from *Differentiae*, *Proemia* (introductions to Holy Scripture),

---

7 That he was Braulio's brother is a weak argument based on Braulio's dedication of the *Vita S. Aemiliani* to his "brother" (*frater*), Fronimian. For an edited version of the text see Patrologia Latina 80, cols. 699–714, and for a translation see *Visigothic Fathers*, ed. and trans. Fear, 15–43.
8 See Miguel Franco, "Braulio de Zaragoza."
9 In lines 29–30 of the *Renotatio*, in the middle of the list and description of Isidore's works, Braulio adds "De viris inlustribus librum unum, cui nos ista subiunximus."
10 On the quote see Barlow, *Braulio*, 10.
11 Since Aldama's thesis, there have been challenges to the chronology of Braulio's list, from Jacques Fontaine to Pierre Cazier. The most recent is that of Martín-Iglesias, in his edition

De Ortu et Obitu Patrum, [*De*] *Origine*[*m*] *Officiorum* (known widely and incorrectly, since at least 1534, as the *De Ecclesiasticis Officiis*[12]) through his *Sententiae, Chronicon* (*Chronicles*), *De Origine Gothorum,* and his ultimate work, the *Origines* (*Etymologies*). Braulio uses the space not only for listing the works, but also for providing short descriptions about them and telling readers for whom they were made.

3.2.3   Braulio, Isidore, and the *De Viris Illustribus*

Isidore's *De Viris Illustribus* was written around the year 619.[13] It was a significant year for Isidore, in which he held the Second Council of Seville and finished up his first version of the *De Origine Gothorum*. It was also when Braulio may have left Seville to return to Zaragoza.[14] The year 619 is also when bishop Maximus of Zaragoza – a fellow attendee with Isidore of the contentious council of Gundemar – died, and his successor John, the brother of Braulio, took over the bishopric of Zaragoza.[15] It was at that point, the end of Maximus and the transfer of the bishopric to Braulio's family, and return of Braulio to Zaragoza, that Isidore ended his *DVI*.[16] In so doing, Isidore tied the city of Zaragoza to the illustrious list ranging from Hosius (256–359) the bishop of Córdoba, Nience and advisor to Constantine, to the bishopric of Zaragoza, and, more specifically, to the inception of the latter's spiritual orthodoxy and

---

and introduction to the *Renotatio*. Martín-Iglesias admits that there are potential problems with the order of the works, but that any alternative conclusions on the chronology should wait for reassessments of each work and their respective manuscript transmissions. For the theses and arguments see Martín-Iglesias, *Renotatio*, 74–84; Aldama, "Indicaciones sobre la cronología" in *Miscellanea Isidoriana*; and, Fontaine, *Isidore de Séville*, 217 and 436.

12   See the introduction to the *De Ecclesiasticis Officiis* by Christopher Lawson who proves the original name of *De Origine Officiorum*: *Sancti Isidori Episcopi Hispalensis, De Ecclesiasticis Officiis*, ed. Lawson, Corpus Christianorum Series Latina 113 (Turnhout: Brepols, 1989). Martín-Iglesias maintains this naming of the text in his edition of the *Renotatio* (*Renotatio*, ed. Martín-Iglesias, 260). For more, see Chapter 3, note 24 below.

13   For Isidore's *De Viris Illustribus* see Carmen Codoñer Merino, *El "De viris illustribus" de Isidoro de Sevilla: estudio y edición crítica* (Salamanca: Consejo Superior de Investigaciones Científicas, 1964), 132–53.

14   Barlow, *Braulio*, 4. On Braulio as Isidore's student see above Chapter 1, notes 64 and 71.

15   For records of the decretal and council of Gundemar see XII Toledo, *CCH* 6 (2002), 205–13.

16   In 619 there was also an inscription to *Saturninus prespiter* raised in Seville. The inscription, according to its inscribed dates, suggests that it refers to a local priest, but, given the relative lack of inscriptions from Seville and all that had been happening between Zaragoza and Seville in the year in which it was presented, one wonders if this did not also serve as a reference to that S. Saturninus of the Eighteen Martyrs of Zaragoza, the sepulchral site next to which John was abbot and to which Eugenius II would flee from Toledo. For the inscription see *Inscripciones Cristianas de la España Romana y Visogoda* (*ICERV*), ed. José Vives (Barcelona: Instituto Erique Flórez, 1969), no. 112, 38.

preservation or salvation by the family of Braulio. Furthermore, Isidore made this move, in the text, through Pope Gregory the Great and his (Isidore's) own brother Leander, thereby connecting Braulio's family and the cities of Seville and Zaragoza as the twin spiritual centers responsible for the conversion and continuing and future orthodoxy of the kingdom. This was not only a defense of their positions, and an affront to Toledo, but also a fine tribute by Isidore to his student Braulio. It was also a way to foster and sustain the close relationship with the important regional network in the Ebro valley, in between Toledo and its powerful connections in, and the families of, Narbonne. The overt allusion to the conversion of the kingdom to build legitimacy for the characters in the text and its narrative is a literary device common in the Isidore-moment, as will become evident throughout the following chapters.

In his editing of the *DVI*, Braulio appropriately repaid the favor to Isidore. Unlike his great teacher, Braulio did not write his own new *DVI*, only the addendum on Isidore. The *DVI*, as it stood, told the story of the peninsula's spiritual centers and illustrious figures properly in Braulio's eyes. Braulio's *Renotatio* was meant simply as an additional chapter to and continuation of Isidore's *DVI*, and it is with this text that the *Renotatio* is transmitted in the manuscripts, showing the perceived connection between the two.[17] The bishop of Zaragoza repaid the compliment from Seville with one for Seville, and the student also confirmed the legacy of his teacher within this traditional form of continuation…all in all, a pretty cozy affair of students, teachers and elite families maintaining supremacy over, and developing new channels between, centers and networks power.

Braulio did not write a new *DVI*. There was no need for him to do so since, so he felt, Isidore's trajectory of important ecclesiastic history was correct. Braulio was wholly faithful to his school, to such an extent that he adopted Isidore's ecclesiastical, historical lacunae. For example, in the *Renotatio*, Braulio states Isidore's role in the Second Council of Seville, yet he says nothing about the Third Council of Seville, which was also run by Isidore. Braulio definitely was aware of this council, yet he remained silent about it. In this, he was following the *damnatio memoriae* of the council established by Isidore-Seville with the *Hispana* in the early 630s and reinforced by the final proceedings of the Fourth Council of Toledo. In the *Renotatio*, Braulio afforded III Seville the same silence.[18] Braulio also remained quiet about Gundemar, not including him in

---

17 MS León Cathedral 22 may contain a copy of the original version of Isidore's *DVI*. See Barlow, *Braulio*, 9.

18 Braulio certainly knew of III Seville, since it was a significant topic of private as well as very public discourse. It was also a topic at IV Toledo, which Braulio attended and con-

the list of kings under which Isidore served, even though it is quite possible that Braulio was Isidore's student in Seville during Gundemar's reign, or near to it. This silence sustained another very important *damnatio memoriae* created and proliferated by Isidore.[19] In contrast, Ildefonsus would later re-introduce Gundemar to the list of kings associated with Isidore.[20]

3.3 Ildefonsus: Isidore and the De Viris Illustribus

Ildefonsus's text on Isidore is noticeably shorter than Braulio's *Renotatio*, leaving out much about Isidore's personality. The reader is not told about his charity, his fight against heresy, and his knowledge of antiquity. All that Ildefonsus repeated was that Isidore was a superb orator and a man with intelligence and propriety, and even in that he added a subtle critique, as noted below. The smaller quantity of general information about Isidore in Ildefonsus's account is complemented by an even more important feature, the cutting of the number of Isidore's texts down to ten. The ten texts on Ildefonsus's list of works attributed to Isidore are not in chronological order, contain almost no descriptions, and do not include all of the dedications of the books, for example, the [*De*] *Origine*[*m*] *Officiorum* to his brother Fulgentius, bishop of Astigi.

Ildefonsus cut the following works from Isidore's oeuvre:
- *De Numeris* (*Numbers and Scripture*)
- *De Nominibus Legis et Evangelorum*
- *De Haeresibus*
- *Chronicon*
- *De Viris Illustribus*
- *Monastica Regula*
- *De Origine Gothorum, et Regno Suevorum, et etiam Vandalorum Historia*

In other words, what Ildefonsus primarily excluded from Isidore's body of work were his historical writings and origins stories. Upon reading his account of Isidore's works one is provided with a different image of Isidore, one in which Isidore did not write on history or origins, not on spirituality and mysticism, and not on monasticism. He did not claim Swinthila was the king of *totius Spaniae* or declare Spain to be the "ornament of the world" (*ornamentum orbis*).[21] Ildefonsus's Isidore never wrote the texts that modern historiography is most attached to, nor is this Isidore the grand architect of consensus and

---

tributed to significantly. Finally, the epistolary exchanges suggest an awareness too of the council. There is no chance Braulio was unaware of III Seville. For more on III Seville and its *damnatio memoriae* see Chapter 4, § 4.

19 On the suppression of Gundemar from the record see Chapter 4, § 3.
20 Ildef., *DVI*, 9.
21 Isidore, *De Orig. Goth.*

unity through historical identity, discourse and representation. In this version of the story, Isidore also did not continue the *Chronicles* of Eusebius/Jerome and did not tie Swinthila or Sisebut to the victories of consensus-building happening in the Christian world in the 620s.[22]

Through Ildefonsus's representation of Isidore, three related conclusions are confirmed: first, that there were at least two distinct historical representations of Isidore concurrent in seventh-century Hispania. Second, that the significant points of contention between them were over Isidore's "historical" output. Third, that these differing representations came from the adherents of Isidore-Seville, on the one hand, and those of Toledo-Agali on the other, indicative of the competitive lines of the schools.

Ildefonsus's cutting of Isidore's *DVI* from the lists of his texts deserves special attention for its significance. Ildefonsus's representation of Isidore was meant as a chapter in his new version of the continuation of the *DVI*. Although he wrote a more elaborate continuation than Braulio had done, Ildefonsus also did not write a full *DVI*, which, given his starting point, is grounds alone for believing it was a response to Isidore's *DVI* and Braulio's addendum. As the recent editor of the *DVI* has pointed out, Ildefonsus's principal concern in writing the *DVI* was, in contrast to Isidore, to praise the *sedes regia*, Toledo, and insert Agali into the record.[23] Ildefonsus not only re-wrote the *DVI* in favor of Toledo-Agali, his praise for Isidore was always back-handed. In the preface to the work, he acknowledges that Isidore wrote a *DVI* but says that he did not do it well, hence the reason Ildefonsus needed to fix it.[24] This is fair evidence that Ildefonsus consciously excluded texts of Isidore's from the list of works in the entry on Isidore later in the text.

---

22   On the origins of the chronicle genre with Eusebius and Jerome see Pedro Juan Galán Sánchez, *El género historiográfico de la "Chronica." Las crónicas hispanas de época visigoda*. Anuario de Estudios Filológicos (Anejo 12) (Cáceres: Universidad de Extremadura, 1994), ch. 2.

23   Carmen Codoñer, "Los *De viris illustribus* de la Hispania visigótica. Entre la biografía y la hagiografía," in *Las biografías griega y Latina como género literario. De la Antigüedad al Renacimiento. Algunas calas*, ed. Vitalino Valcárcel Martínez (Vitoria: Universidad del País Vasco, 2009), 239–55.

24   *Ildefonsus Toletani Episcopi*, ed. Urquiola and Codoñer Merino, 110. The passive aggressive tone and false praise are reminiscent of the opening of Eudocia's Homeric cento, in which she honors the "clever" work of Patricius in compiling the cento while stating how, nevertheless, she really needed to fix it to make it work (see Arthur Ludwich, *Eudocia Augustae, Procli Lycii, Claudiani carminum graecorum reliquiae* [Leipzig: Teubner, 1897], 81–88). Generally speaking, the rewriting of texts for political purposes was a technique common not only to Iberian Christian writers, for example, see also Ambrose of Milan's revision of Cicero's *De officiis* (on which see Brown, *Through the Eye of a Needle*, 130).

Instead of writing from the second century forward, Ildefonsus provided his *DVI* with only thirteen entries, starting with the bishop of Toledo, Asturias. The next entry is on Montanus, the bishop of Toledo that oversaw II Toledo in 527. Ildefonsus rapidly moves forward, with the fourth entry, to Aurasius, the bishop of Toledo from 603 to 615. In between Montanus and Aurasius, Ildefonsus locates no bishops, not even Eufemius of Toledo, who led III Toledo, the council at which the Visigothic king and kingdom were converted to Catholicism. Instead, he includes Donatus, the North African monk that had come to Spain with dozens of monks and books.[25] In this entry, he says that Donatus was the first to bring a monastic rule to Spain, which likely was not true. Ildefonsus constructs this "fact," perhaps because it was Donatus's rule that Agali used, as has been implied by historians from evidence beyond Ildefonsus.[26] Ildefonsus's jump from Montanus to Aurasius allowed him to completely ignore III Toledo, and hence Leander of Seville. Ildefonsus changed the narrative from the moment when Seville entered the story in order to silence Seville's role in the conversion, but also of Toledo's: this was how important it was for Ildefonsus to exclude Seville.

In Isidore's *DVI*, the chapter on Gregory is followed by one about his brother, Leander, a key figure in converting the Visigothic monarchy. This literary construction placed Seville as the bishopric through which the peninsula and the kingdom became Catholic, legitimizing Seville as the spiritual primacy of the kingdom above Toledo, and, in fact, Isidore mentions none of the bishops of Toledo. Ildefonsus, on the other hand, glosses over the conversion and its figures, and charts an alternative story of ecclesiastical primacy in the kingdom. The gloss was so evident that later scribes felt the need to add their own entries about the figures of this period, especially Gregory.[27] Ildefonsus's version of the *DVI* leaves Leander out of the narrative and fills in the space with all of the bishops of Toledo since the beginning of the Isidore-moment, as well as a couple of distant bishops to provide the appearance of a continuation of Gennadius. Ildefonsus's *DVI* generated a Toledan-centered trajectory of historical Truth, with a capital "T."[28]

Ildefonsus's exclusion of Eufemius, the bishop of Toledo at III Toledo, may seem strange: if Ildefonsus was trying to build the legitimacy of Toledo as the

---

25 Ildef., *DVI*, 3.
26 Collins, *Visigothic Spain*, 153.
27 See Codoñer Merino, *De Viris Illustribus*.
28 On Ildefonsus's *DVI* empowering Toledo see Pedro Juan Galán Sánchez, "El *De viris illustribus* de Ildefonso de Toledo o la modificación del género," *Anuario de estudios filológicos* 15 (1992): 69–80; and, Jamie Wood, "Playing the Fame Game: Bibliography, Celebrity, and Primacy," *Journal of Early Christian Studies* 20 (2012): 613–40.

primary Catholic see of the kingdom, why would he not include Eufemius? One might reasonably believe that Toledo's bishop and signatory to the council at which the kingdom converted to Catholicism would be a necessary person to include in such a version of the narrative. However, since Gundemar's decretal had defamed Eufemius for his "mistakenly" having recognized Toledo as in Carpetania, not Carthaginensis, Ildefonsus had to be silent on Eufemius.[29]

Bishop Masona too is absent from Ildefonsus's *DVI*, and through this void one can get a glimpse of another major voice in the interpersonal and urban rivalries against Toledo, that of Mérida. Isidore is guilty too of ignoring Masona, but, to be fair, Isidore could claim his brother in this position in the *DVI*, whereas Ildefonsus does not suggest a suitable replacement, cutting both Leander and Toledo's own Eufemius. Also, the writer of the *Lives of the Fathers of Merida (Vitas Patrum Emeretensium* [*VPE*]), which praises and tells the life of Masona, was alive during the time of Isidore, and Isidore may have been in contact with Masona.[30] Isidore's brother Leander most certainly was a colleague of Masona, as seen in the records of III Toledo. The politics between them were vivid when Isidore left Mérida out of the *DVI*, and anyhow, his aim was to promote Seville. Also, Mérida and Seville, though competitive with one another vis-à-vis their texts, not to mention the real life history of the usurpers they hosted and fought against, both shared in the ongoing and increasingly difficult struggle to compete for spiritual supremacy against the growing aristocratic agency and internal patronage of Toledo, of the raising of its own local aristocracy to the bishopric.[31] Ruth Miguel Franco argues that in addition to their mutual personal affections, and the appreciation for each other's intellects, Braulio and Eugenius II were brought even closer together through their

---

29 See Chapter 4, § 3 on Gundemar's decretal, the problem of Eufemius's signature, the emergence of the region of Carpetania, and the metropolitan status of Toledo.

30 There is a single letter extant, from Isidore to Masona (Isid., *Ep.*, 4), though its origin is dubious. On the letters of Isidore see Patrologia Latina 83, vol. 6, ed. Arévalo, cols. 557–581; Roger E. Reynolds, "The "Isidorian" *Epistula ad Massonam* on lapsed clerics," in *Grundlagen des Rechts. Festschrift für Peter Landau zum 65 Geburtstag. Rechts-und Staatswissenschaftliche Veröffentlichungen der Görres-Gesselschaft* (Paderborn: F. Schöningh, 2000), 77–92; and, *The Letters of St. Isidore of Seville*, trans. Gordon B. Ford, Jr. (Amsterdam, 1970). For the authoritative edition of the *VPE* see *Vitas sanctorum patrum Emeritensium*, ed. Antonio Maya Sánchez, Corpus Christianorum Series Latina 116 (Turnhout: Brepols, 1992), and for discussion of it see below, Chapter 4, note 29.

31 The usurpers include Agila, Athanagild, Hermenegild, and Iudila. On the close affinity between the palace in Toledo and its local staff see VI Toledo 13: "Qui primatum dignitate atque reverentiae vel gratiae ob meritum in palatio honorabiles habentur, his a iunioribus modestus honor per omnia deferatur, qui etiam minores a senioribus et dilectionis amplectantur affectu et utilitatis imbuantur exemplo."

mutual struggles against Toledo, a situation that also seems true of Isidore-Seville and Masona-Mérida, despite Isidore's later rhetorical use of Mérida in the *De Origine Gothorum*.[32]

In addition to important exclusions, there are a few inclusions in Ildefonsus's *DVI* that could initially be considered problematic for the argument here presented, for instance, the chapters on Isidore, Braulio, and Braulio's brother John. Although not a Toledan or Agalian, John, bishop of Zaragoza from 619 to 631, was included probably because he was the head of the monastery of the Eighteen Martyrs to which Eugenius II fled from Toledo, before being forced into the bishopric of Toledo by Chindaswinth. Isidore and Braulio – the greatest symbols of local networks and alternative sites of power to Toledo – Ildefonsus simply could not ignore. Doing so would have created a very weakly legitimate *DVI*, the polemical intentions of which would have been too obvious and detrimental to the strength of the text. To avoid the danger of noting these figures, Ildefonsus created a literary structure of Toledan supremacy into which these men and their respective cities could fit neatly as anomalies. Isidore and Braulio, non-/anti-Toledan sources of authority, were presented so that the reader would be able to forget them: they exist in the text and are thus seemingly taken seriously, even if anomalies, and as such their presence creates a false impression to the reader of overall fidelity to historical truth.

In addition, for his chapter on Isidore, Ildefonsus appended the phrase "province of Baetica" (*provinciae Baeticae*) to the description of Isidore's bishopric. This, of course, was a true statement, but it was not a point Braulio felt compelled to note. Ildefonsus, the Toledan and metropolitan of Carthaginensis, did. Through this titular addition to the entry on Isidore, Ildefonsus may have been attempting to marginalize, in provincializing, Isidore's position and so Seville's and Baetica's wider claims to spiritual authority against Toledo and Carthaginensis.

Finally, Ildefonsus's erasure of Isidore's works from cultural memory – those works essential to the competitive dialectics of the period – effectively reshaped the legacy of Isidore and his school. Ildefonsus not only cut Isidore's texts from the record, he also re-wrote them in favor of Toledo-Agali. This section has discussed how Ildefonsus did this with his edition of Isidore's *DVI* and its reconstruction for Toledo-Agali, but Ildefonsus did this with other texts as well. For example, he cut Isidore's *Monastic Rules* from his list of Isidore's texts, and then wrote a new version representing authority from Toledo-Agali. This should be no surprise since Agali may never have adopted Isidore's rule,

---

32   Miguel Franco, "Braulio de Zaragoza," 172–73.

perhaps, as noted, using that of Donatus instead.[33] Ildefonsus's treatment of the monastic rules helps show the pattern of his reconstruction of the memory of Isidore-Seville, but it also demonstrates that he knew Isidore's texts and was not speaking out of ignorance when creating his list. Furthermore, this version of the *Monastic Rule* was followed by a common rule, or, *vulgata,* made around the turn of the eighth century. This is important to note because it represents a pattern of textual production first from Isidore-Seville, re-written in favor of Toledo-Agali, and then finally a vulgate version created anonymously in the northern regions of the peninsula, in the 690s and early 700s. This suggests that these texts were already being removed from the dialectics of power centering around Toledo's authority, perhaps from a sense of its doom, or at least its growingly farcical authority within, and marginality to, life in the north. Ildefonsus was the last bishop of Toledo to come to the bishopric through Agali and is the absolute end of the Isidorian event, the dialectics of which had been closed off by the *Liber Iudiciorum,* promulgated a few years before Ildefonsus's bishopric. Bishop Julian of Toledo continued Ildefonsus's *DVI* by adding a chapter about him, thereby proliferating the Toledan trajectory of this version of the *DVI,* but one that spoke within a post-Isidore-moment environment, even if it was concerned with the centrality of Toledan authority.[34]

3.4   VIII *Toledo 2*

"Nostri quoque seculi doctor egregius, ecclesiae catholicae novissimus decus."[35] These flattering words about Isidore presented nearly twenty years, and four plenary councils after his death represent the first recognition by Toledo of Isidore's authority. Followed by citations from two of his books – the *Sententiae* and the *Synonyma* – this marks the inception of the historical image and memory of Isidore by Toledo.

That this long overdue recognition of Isidore's spiritual authority was to happen at VIII Toledo should be no surprise. This council was a serious and

---

33   Ildef., *DVI,* 3. Donatus was a North African monk who brought the rule to Spain with him and who built the monastery of Servitanum. Ildefonsus claims that this was the first rule in Spain, a claim that Roger Collins says should be believed (Collins, *Early Medieval Spain: Unity from Diversity, 400–1000* [London: Macmillan, 1983], 81). In contrast, Andy Fear maintains that there were earlier rules in Spain (*Visigothic Fathers,* ed. and trans. Fear, 112). For discussion of the Visigothic monastic rules see Neil Allies, "Monastic Rules," 30–31.

34   See Jeremy du Quesnay Adams, "The Political Grammar of Julian of Toledo," in *Minorities and Barbarians in Medieval Life and Thought,* ed. Susan J. Ridyard and Robert G. Benson (Sewanee: University of the South Press, 1966), 179–95.

35   VIII Toledo 2.

impressive attempt by Recceswinth to soothe critical rifts caused by his father.³⁶ Recceswinth hoped to achieve this through an interrelated combination of concession and clemency, the association of this council to that of Reccared in 589, and, most importantly, the inclusion and sublimation of the school of Isidore-Seville into the authority of Toledo, completed with the *Liber Iudiciorum*.³⁷

In Chapter 5 it is shown how the *Liber Iudiciorum*, promulgated at VIII Toledo, was designed to associate Recceswinth's dynasty to the conversion of the kingdom, and, in a different way, to Liuvigild and Arian Visigothic kings. The proceedings and canons of VIII Toledo worked in complement to promote these aspects of the historical narrative of the *LI*.³⁸ Imaginary capital

---

36 For discussion of the events leading to VIII Toledo and Recceswinth's position in 653 see Chapter 5, § 3.

37 Although it may not have been the first attempt at incorporating the dynasty of Chindaswinth into the Isidorian historiography of the Goths in Hispania. The *Ortographia Isidori Iunioris* is an extension of Isidore's *De Origine Gothorum* that extends the text from Swinthila to Chindaswinth. Roger Collins argues that it is "feasible" that this "hybrid *Historia Gothorum*" was constructed during the reign of Chindaswinth, although such a conclusion is, as he notes, not one that can be proven. The continuation found in MS Madrid BNE 1346 (on which, see Chapter 3, note 39) folios 18ʳ–18ᵛ goes until the unction of Wittiza. For some discussion see Roger Collins, "Ambrosio de Morales, Bishop Pelayo of Oviedo and the Lost Manuscripts of Visigothic Spain," in *Wisigothica After M. C. Díaz y Díaz*, ed. Carmen Codoñer Merino and Paolo Farmhouse Alberto, MediEVI 3 (Florence: SISMEL – Edizioni del Galluzzo, 2014), 496, and Roger Collins, "Ambrosio de Morales and the *Codex Vetustissimus Ovetensis*," 29 (2018 draft of Collin's contribution to the festschrift for Tom Brown).

38 The use of the number twelve across VIII Toledo and the *LI* may have been a way to further associate them. For example, VIII Toledo has twelve canons, which is not a common number of canons for a council, and, in fact, only one other council in Spanish conciliar history has twelve canons (XIV Toledo, led by Julian of Toledo). In addition to having twelve canons, the *LI* has twelve books. Taken together, the number of canons and books in the council law-code seem to represent, complementarily, a symbolic connection to the Twelve Apostles and the Twelve Tables, a type of mysticism Isidore would have appreciated. For Isidore, mysticism is what elicited truth from "bodies and languages" (Isid., *Sent.*, 1.18.12). Isidore also lays out the theological and Christological importance of the number twelve in his book on numbers, "Sed per tres Trinitatis mysterium, per quattuor virtutum actio illustratur; ac per hoc in his partibus, ut per Trinitatis speciem actio virtutum perficitur, et per reparationem virtutum usque ad Trinitatis notitiam pervenitur. Rursum autem cum ad duodenarium surgit, et duodecim apostolos septiformis gratiae Spiritus perfectos ostendit, quorum praedicatio per quattuor virtutum genera Trinitatis fides in toto orbe crescit" (Isidore, *Liber numerorum*, in Patrologia Latina 83, vol. 5, ed. Arévalo, ch. 8, col. 229; Jean-Yves Guillaumin, ed. and trans. [Fr.], *Le livre des nombres = Liber numerorum, Isidore de Séville* [Paris: Belles Lettres, 2006], 45). Twelve was, otherwise, a significant number in the seventh century, as seen in the reference to the four passions, eight deadly sins, and six works of charity of Desiderius in Sisebut's *Vita Desiderii*, reflecting the Gospel of Matthew 25:35. Also, there are two anonymous poems, from the late seventh century, on the "twelve winds," from very early manuscripts (see *Index Scriptorum Latinorum Medii*

was ubiquitous at VIII Toledo, from superficial connections between the two names of the kings – Reccared and Recceswinth[39] – to their personal lineages to Liuvigild, to their votive crowns,[40] to their shared positions as the good, holy king in juxtaposition to their fathers. Also significant was Recceswinth's elevation of the bishops and bishoprics of Mérida and Seville to the top two spots as signatories of the Eighth Council of Toledo – although their bishops, Orontius and Antonius, were not the most senior at the council – as their predecessors had been at III Toledo. This dual promotion was meant to associate VIII Toledo with III Toledo, but it was also intended to satisfy Mérida, and the school of Isidore-Seville. VIII Toledo was one of only three plenary councils from the 630s to the end of the Visigothic kingdom in the 710s in which the signatory from Seville was higher than that of Toledo. One of these councils was Chindaswinth's VII Toledo, thereby illustrating Recceswinth's veneer of concessions covering the proliferation of his father's policies. The other example is XII Toledo, at which Julian and king Ervig reintroduced Gundemar's decretal to canonical records, a clear affront to the *damnatio memoriae* constructed by the Isidorian network.[41] Moreover, the lead signatory from Seville at XII Toledo, Julian, may in fact have been an appointee from Toledo.[42]

Making clear its theological position, the first canon of VIII Toledo proclaims Toledo's faith in the Holy Trinity, its consubstantiation, and in single

---

Aevi Hispanorum, ed. Manuel C. Díaz y Díaz [Madrid: Consejo Superior de Investigaciones Científicas, 1959], nos. 262 and 263). On the meaning of numbers in the period see Jean Leclercq, "Un tratado sobre los nombres divinos en un manuscrito de Córdoba," in *Hispania Sacra* 2 (1949), 327–38, and Fontaine, *Isidore de Séville*, II, 701, n. 5.

39   Though some historians argue that this is no coincidence, in that Recceswinth was related, by marriages, to Reccared's family (see García Moreno, "La sucesión al trono").

40   The votive crown was a practice imitating the Byzantines, and perhaps, specifically, the crowns in Hagia Sophia. It represented the symbolic connection between and opposition of the earthly diadem and Heavenly crown, and as such the duality of Christ, but also the cooperation between the Church and the monarchy. As Isidore says in *Sententiae*, 3.51.3, that royal power is only effective when subordinate to the higher authority. On the votive crowns see Moreno Martín, "Visigoths, Crowns, Crosses, and the Construction of Spain;" José Antonio Molina Gómez, "Las coronas de donación regia del tesoro de Guarrazar: la religiosidad en la monarquía visigoda y el uso de modelos bizantinos," *Antigüedad y Christianismo* 21 (2004): 459–72; *El Tesoro Visigodo de Guarrazar*, ed. Alicia Perea (Consejo Superior de Investigaciones Científicas, 2001), 295–386, in particular the chapters by Javier Arce, "El conjunto votivo de Guarrazar: función y significado," 347–54 and M. Cortés, "Influencias bizantinas," 367–76; Jacques Fontaine, *L'art préroman hispanique* I (La Pierre-qui-Vire [Yonne]: Zodiaque, 1973), 242–46; and, the *benedictio corone* in the *Liber Ordinum*, col. 165 (*Le "Liber Ordinum" en usage dans l'église wisigothique et mozarabe d'Espagne du cinquième au onzième siècle*, ed. Marius Férotin [Paris, 1904]).

41   On Gundemar's decretal and its significance to the Isidore-moment see Chapter 4, § 3.

42   See Introduction 1.3, entry on Julian of Toledo, and Appendix: Julian of Toledo Not an Agalian.

baptism. The second canon, in which Isidore arrives, is set out to deal with deserters and traitors (*refugis atque perfidis*), and the recent quagmire caused by the rebellion of Froia. Recceswinth had taken an oath to his father that demanded blinding and capital punishment for attempted usurpers and their associates, a rule that was confirmed by holy authority.[43] This commitment now put Recceswinth in a tough position. On the one hand, he needed to show clemency to the rebel Froia and his supporters (*fautoribus*), to show that faith and holy authority was above the law, while at the same time he had to maintain the integrity of oaths and the law, and deal with the real threat of rebellion. Recceswinth's solution was to cite Isidore – after promoting him to a doctor of the church – in a way that would satisfy Isidore-Seville's legalist position, and the calls for clemency from nobles and Toledan clerics. It is in this context that the historical Isidore finally became present in the records of Toledo. After citing the authority of ancient writers and doctors of the Church – Ambrose, Augustine, and Pope Gregory – and praising Isidore, the canon cites Isidore's *Sententiae* 2.31.9, which says that an oath promised incautiously should not be kept.[44] The canon goes on to cite Isidore again, this time from his *Synonyma*

---

43 On the oath, see VII Toledo 1, "omnes paene Spaniae sacerdotes omnesque seniores vel iudices ac ceteros homines officii palatini," a definition that Recceswinth essentially sums up in his VIII Toledo *tomus* when he says that "vos omnemque populum iurasse recolimus." On the rebellion of Froia, see the letter from Taio, bishop of Zaragoza, to the bishop of Barcelona, Quiricius: Taio, *Ep. ad Quiricium, Sententiarum* 5, Patrologia Latina 80, col. 727ff.; Julia Aguilar Miquel, "*Epistula ad Quiricum Barcinonensis antistitem y Epigramma operis subsequentis* de Tajón de Zaragoza. Estudio, edición crítica y tradicción," *Euphrosyne, Revista de Filología Clássica*, New Series 46 (2018): 181–204. For discussion of the council and rebellion, see Rachel Stocking, *Bishops, Councils and Consensus in the Visigothic kingdom* (Ann Arbor: University of Michigan Press, 2000), 1–4 (the title of this text will be referred to in the rest of the notes simply as BCC), and, Castellanos, "Political Nature of Taxation," 214. It is also possible that Eugenius II's *carm.* 20 and 36 refer to a rebellion of Froia: the former speaks of a current war in terms similar to Taio's description of Froia's attack on Zaragoza and the latter of the return of *refugi* after the war. For discussion of the possibility of their reference to Froia's rebellion, see Paulo Farmhouse Alberto, "Three historical notes on Eugenius of Toledo's *Carmina*," in *Poesía Latina Medieval (Siglos v–xv). Actas del IV Congreso del "Internationales Mittellateinerkomitee," Santiago de Compostela, 12–15 de septiembre de 2002*, ed. Manuel C. Díaz y Díaz and José Manuel Díaz de Bustamante (Florence: SISMEL-Ed. del Galluzzo, 2005), 109–22.

44 In the chapter *de iuramento*, it reads "Non conservandum sacramentum quod malum incaute promittitur, veluti si quispiam adulterare perpetuam cum ea permanendi fidem polliceatur: tolerabilius est enim non implere sacramentum, quam permanere in stupri flagitium." The citation from the *Sententiae* in the Vives edition of the canon is slightly different from other earlier and later editions. For instance, in Patrologia Latina 83 it reads *Non est conservandum*, and *quo* instead of *quod*, logically presents *adulterae* over *adulterare*, and reads *perpetuo* against *perpetuam* and *flagitio* over *flagitium*. Other than the differences with *perpetuam* and *flagitium*, the new critical edition of the *Sententiae* (Corpus Christianorum Series Latina 111) follows the Patrologia Latina version.

2.58.[45] As with the passage from the *Sententiae*, it explains that promises given in bad faith should be rescinded: that which was unwisely offered should not be maintained because an oath should not comply with an evil deed. Toledo's initial historical representation of Isidore was rooted in the context of a serious negotiation between Toledo-Agali and local networks of power, notably the school of Isidore-Seville.

Furthering this point, as the manuscript evidence makes clear, the *filioque* clause (*ex Patre Filioque procedit*) of the Latin version of the Nicene Creed was not part of the Creed pronounced in Spanish councils until 653, at VIII Toledo. It had not been in III Toledo or the Toledan councils since then, before VIII Toledo.[46] This is a significant point for the history of the Spanish Church, but also for the schools-competition, since it was likely Isidore that had introduced the clause. The *filioque* clause was added to the records of III Toledo by a tenth-century scribe, named Sisebut. This act effectively revised the conversion narrative and history of the Catholic Church in early medieval Hispania. The common assumption, over the centuries since then has been that the *filioque* was part of the Nicene Creed in Spain since the Visigothic kingdom's conversion in 589, but this seems to be incorrect. This mistake highlights the complicated problem of the historiography of Visigothic Hispania, particularly given that various scholars since the sixteenth century have suggested concern about the *filioque* being in III Toledo, yet the dominant narrative of the Latin clause since III Toledo has remained.[47] This small episode alone illustrates why a full, critical review of the manuscripts and historiographies of Visigothic Hispania is so important. The issue of the *filioque* clause is pertinent to the schools-competition as well. In the first canon of IV Toledo one reads "Spiritum vero Sanctum nec creatum nec genitum sed procedentem ex Patre et Filio profitemur," and it is possible Isidore drafted this, as seen in II Seville 13, which does not cite *filioque* but discusses at length the two natures, but single

---

45 "In malis promissis rescinde fidem, in turpe votum muta decretum quod incaute voviste non facias. Inpia est promissio quae sc[e]lere adimpletur."

46 See *CCH* 5 (1992), 67 and 386, and Peter Gemeinhardt, *Die Filioque-Kontroverse zwischen Ost- und Westkirche im Frühmittelatler* (Berlin: De Gruyter, 2002), 53–54.

47 For the historiography of the question and the defense of the later addition see Shawn Smith, "The Insertion of the *Filioque* into the Nicene Creed and a Letter of Isidore of Seville," *Journal of Early Christian Studies* 22 (2014): 265–69. For the conventional reading see Alberto Ferreiro, "*Sanctissimus idem princeps sic venerandum concilium adloquitor dicens*: King Reccared's Discourses at the Third Council of Toledo (589)," *Annuarium Historiae Conciliorum* 46 (2014): 43.

person, of Christ, and the equality of God and Son.⁴⁸ Shawn Smith argues that the Nicene Creed in Spain was changed to include *filioque* some time before Isidore's death, a conclusion based on his reading of Isidore's letter to duke Claudius as authentic.⁴⁹ The letter echoes the sentiments of Isidore found in II Seville about the Father and Son, but also in other ways, such as his warning not to engage theological disputes or use one's power over theological opponents without a full knowledge of the Scripture, a key aspect of Isidore's criticism of Sisebut. The appearance of *filioque* at VIII Toledo suggests the handiwork of Eugenius II and a concession to Isidore-Seville.

4 Other Contemporary Historical Representations of Isidore

Considering that he would become their most famous saint (and overall figure), it is a bit strange that there are no Visigothic hagiographies on Isidore.⁵⁰ However, in addition to the first-generation historical representations of Isidore already discussed, there are others claimed to be from, or close chronologically to, seventh-century Hispania. One of these is the *Vita Fructuosi* discussed in Chapter 1, plus the *Epitaphion beati Leandri, Isidori, et Florentinae* and the *Chronica Regum Visigothorum*.

4.1 *Epitaphion beati Leandri, Isidori, et Florentinae*
As preserved in writing, the short, metrical epitaph of twelve lines to the blessed Leander, Isidore, and Florentina – the *Epitaphion beati Leandri, Isidori, et Florentinae* – is from an inscription presented around the death of Isidore in

---

48 See Charles J. Hefele, *A History of the Councils of the Church from the Original Documents*, trans. Henry Nutcombe Oxenham (Edinburgh: T&T Clark, 1896), 450, n. 4, and for Isidore's authorship, see John N. D. Kelly, *The Athanasian Creed: The Paddock Lectures for 1962–63* (New York: Harper & Row, 1964), 38–39.
49 Smith, "*Filioque*," 270–86.
50 Although the first *vita* of Gregory the Great was not until a century after his death, written in the monastery of Whitby (Roger Collins, *Keepers of the Keys of Heaven* [Basic Books, 2009], 104). On the hagiographical tradition of Isidore see Ariel Guiance, "*Dormavit Beatus Isidorus*: Variaciones hagíográficas en torno e la muerte de Isidoro de Sevilla," *Edad Media* 6 (2003): 33–59; José Carlos Martín-Iglesias, "El corpus hagiográfico latino en torno a la figura de Isidoro de Sevilla en la Hispania tardoantigua y medieval (ss. vii–xiii)," *Veleia* 22 (2005): 187–228; and, José Carlos Martín-Iglesias, "El *Epitaphium Leandri, Isidori et Florentinae* (*ICERV* 272) o la compleja transmisión manuscrita de un texto epigráfico. Nuevo edición y estudio," *Euphrosyne: Revista de Filología Clássica, New Series* 38 (2010): 139–63. See also the eleventh-century *vita* in the MS Paris BN lat. 8093, which also contains the Isidore epitaph.

636. The possibility that this represents an authentic inscription from the 630s seems slim to fair based on the source evidence.[51]

A few puzzling questions come to mind when one reads the text. First, where is the rest of the family? Where is their brother Fulgentius who died several years before Isidore, and so should be listed? This absence implies that the person who wrote the epitaph was missing, or chose to ignore, basic information about the family. Second, the person who transcribed or copied the inscription either did not understand the Spanish dating system or did not know when Isidore had died. This is evident from the date of death assigned to Isidore as *era DCLXXXIII* (Spanish era year 683), the year 645. José Vives argues that this mistake was not the result of ignorance of the Spanish *era* system or of Isidore's date of death, but was, rather, a simple mistake by a later hand, that of the scribe of the eighth-century manuscript Paris BN lat. 8093 who "confundió la primera I con una X."[52] If Vives is correct, the transcription reflects an authentic inscription, despite there being no mention of it in the Visigothic sources, and the oldest preservation being an eighth- or ninth-century transcription.[53]

The epitaph to Isidore and family could be a later creation, from after the Visigothic kingdom's demise. However, there does appear to have been an earlier seventh-century tradition, in Seville, of inscribing or writing epitaphs to recently deceased bishops, as seen with the *Obitus Beati Isidori* and the epitaph to Isidore's immediate successor, the Sevillan bishop Honoratius, in the *Epitaphium Honorati episc. Hispalensis*, to which the *Epitaphion beati Leandri, Isidori, et Florentinae* could be further evidence.[54] However, for the moment, there appears to be more evidence that the *Epitaphion* was created after the collapse of the kingdom. Nonetheless, in light of the fact that the *Epitaphion* has been falsely attributed either to Braulio or to Ildefonsus, it stands as a good example of the confused historiographical legacy left behind by the initial historical representations of Isidore.[55]

---

51 For the most recent edition see Martín-Iglesias, *"Epitaphium Leandri."*

52 *ICERV*, ed. Vives, num. 272, 81.

53 On the manuscript tradition, see Giovanni Battista De Rossi, *Inscriptiones Christianae Urbis Romae, II* (Rome, 1861), 296–97, *ICERV*, ed. Vives, 80–81.

54 *Index Scriptorum Latinorum*, ed. Díaz y Díaz, no. 372, 98, and *ICERV*, ed. Vives, no. 273, 81–82, and 90, n. 287.

55 See Juan Pablo Ledesma, *El "De Itinere Deserti" de San Ildefonso de Toledo* (Toledo: Instituto Teológico San Ildefonso, 2005), 68, and *Index Scriptorum*, ed. Díaz y Díaz, no. 226, and no. 380. Finally, preserved only in the same manuscript that contains the *Epitaphium Leandri, Isidori et Florentinae*, MS Paris BN lat. 8093, there is an anonymous text, perhaps from the seventh century, titled *confessio beati Isidori dicta* (*Index Scriptorum*, ed. Díaz y Díaz, no. 307). In the ninth century, the anonymous *Ildemundus abbetis* and *versus de*

4.2 Chronica Regum Visigothorum

The *Chronica Regum Visigothorum* (CRV) is a non-descriptive list (*laterculum*) of the Visigothic kings from Athanaric in 362 to Ervig in 680.[56] It was originally composed in the late seventh century in the peninsula. Appended to the entry on Sisebut is a short note saying that he was king in the time of Isidore, "sisebudi temporibus fuit isidorus episcopus." Not much can be gleamed from this reference, since in it there is no detail about Isidore other than that he was bishop. Furthermore, the reference to Isidore is unlikely to be original to the CRV. The oldest extant manuscript of the CRV is the eighth-century Vat. Reg. lat. 1024, which also contains the most ancient copy of the *Liber Iudiciorum*.[57] Of the twelve extant manuscripts containing the CRV, only two include the reference to Isidore: the tenth-century Paris BN lat. 1557 (f. 20^v) and the eleventh-century MS Casinas n. 1. Since the latter manuscript was built from the former, there is only one manuscript family with this entry on Isidore, and it is a late one, from the tenth century.

In addition to being the only manuscript tradition of the CRV to mention Isidore, there are other anomalies of Paris 1557. First, there is no mention in any of the other copies of the CRV of any figures other than Visigothic kings. The scribe of this manuscript added Isidore to the reign of Sisebut, but also Pope Gregory and the Byzantine Emperor Maurice to the reign of Liugivild (*leuuigildus*).[58] The other anomaly that is worth mentioning is that in the Paris 1557 family, the CRV is not collected with the laws of the Visigoths, but rather, between a conciliar decree and letters of Gregory. These additions were simply meant to clarify, for the reader, the historical context of the life and times of Gregory, not to discuss Isidore.

S. Iohanne were added to the manuscript, and in the eleventh century a life of Isidore was also included in this dynamic manuscript (*Index Scriptorum*, ed. Díaz y Díaz, no. 370 and 377).

56   For the edition of the *Chronica Regum Visigothorum* (CRV) see the *Laterculus regum Visigothorum*, in *Chron. min.*, Monumenta Germaniae Historica, Auctorum Antiquissimorum 13, ed. Theodor Mommsen (Berlin: Weidmann, 1898), 461–68.

57   Three later manuscripts continue the list of kings: Soriensis (Wittiza, r. 694–702), Paris BN lat. 4667 (to Ardo, [supposed] r. 714–721), and Léon, c. 1057 (to Ordoño III of Léon, r. 931–951). For more on the manuscripts of the CRV see Mommsen, ed., 1898, pp. 461–63, and for its relation to the LI see Chapter 5, § 2.2–3.

58   This spelling reflects the general manuscript tradition, but also perhaps contemporary disregard for Liuvigild's attempt to Romanize (Byzantinize) his name into Leogivild. The evidence suggests that various mints in the kingdom purposely ignored royal instructions to write the king's name as "Leo-." On the coins and their relation to the names see Philip Grierson and Mark Blackburn, *Medieval European Coinage: The Early Middle Ages (5th–10th centuries)* (Cambridge: Cambridge University Press, 2006, orig. 1986), 49–54.

The entry on Isidore in the *CRV* appears to reveal little about the origins of the historical representation of Isidore in Spain. However, Braulio was the only early medieval author to associate Isidore and Maurice in the passage, and there is an early manuscript tradition of John of Biclar's *Chronicle* that continued it to 602 with supplementary discussions exclusively of Gregory and Maurice, hence the associations could reach back into the seventh century if Paris 1557 was built on these.[59] This is further supported by the claim of the author of the *Chronicle of 754* that their sources included a continuation of John of Biclar's *Chronicle* until the year 680, itself likely a continuation of the earlier one to 602 with its added emphasis on Gregory and Maurice.[60] It is possible that between these manuscripts and the Braulio reference a scribe of the tenth century read Isidore, Gregory and Maurice as integral to a chronicle. Yet, all that can be concluded confidently from the Isidore reference in the *CRV* is that there were divergent historiographical traditions about Isidore in the early middle ages.

4.3   *Continuatio Hispana*, or, *Chronicle of 754*

The *Chronicle of 754*, removed from the political world in which Isidore and the schools circulated and fought with each other, presents a rather neutral image of Isidore and his life.[61] The *Chronicle of 754* mentions Isidore together with, but only after praising, Helladius. All that it is said of Isidore is that he was an illustrious teacher and staunch defender against heresy.[62] Nonetheless, this is the first time that the two great, contemporary bishops, of Seville and Toledo respectively, were included in the same discussion. The anonymous chronicler synthesized the traditions of both schools, presenting what could be said to be a neutral discourse, or, a non-dialectical, or non-historical, one. However, this was not the case, as the chronicler was indeed speaking within a dialectics of power, but it was not the one colored by competition between schools of Christians, but rather promoting Christianity within an Islamic polity. The chronicler, writing in Toledo or in the southeast of the peninsula, was also concerned with the memory of Isidore, as the schools had been. However, his aim

---

59   See Manuel C. Díaz y Díaz, "La transmisión textual del Biclarense," *Analecta Sacra Tarraconnensia* 35 (1962): 57–76.

60   *Juan de Biclaro Obispo de Gerona, su Vida y su obra*, ed. Julio Campos (Madrid: Consejo Superior de Investigaciones Científicas, 1960), 100.

61   For an edition of the *Chronicle of 754*, see José Eduardo López Pereira, *Crónica mozárabe de 754: edición crítica y traducción* (Zaragoza: Anúbar, 1991), *Chronica Minora*, ed. Theodor Mommsen, Monumenta Germaniae Historica, Auctorum Antiquissimorum 11 (Berlin: Weidmann, 1894), 334–60. For discussion of the *Chronicle of 754*, see Ann Christys, *Christians in Al-Andalus, 711–1000*, 2nd edn. (New York: Routledge, 2010), 28–51 (esp. 33–35).

62   *Chron. 754*, 16.

was not to present a unique memory of Isidore *per se*, but rather to use him as historical evidence about the achievements of Christianity in seventh-century Hispania. Isidore was now part of a "unity" narrative which sought to see Christians in pre-Islamic Spain as one community united with its Catholic king (a key component of "Gothstalgie").

5   Conclusion

In summary, the following theses and points for further consideration can be drawn from the collective evidence of this chapter. First, the opening historical accounts of Isidore represent the schools active in the Isidore-moment. Second, the images of Isidore provided by these schools represent the entire first-generation of historical accounts in the peninsula. As such, any comprehensive historiography on Isidore must begin by engaging these texts as well as the dialectics in which they spoke, the discourse between the schools. Third, through this analysis of the initiation of the historical representations and historiography only of Isidore, it becomes possible to begin to see some common literary devices and tropes used in the schools-competition. We are also introduced to the real life institutional and geographical features endemic to this competition, and to authority in Visigothic Hispania. Fourth, and finally, the initial historical accounts of Isidore, followed by those of VIII Toledo and then Ildefonsus, demonstrate the vitality of the school of Isidore-Seville in the immediately post-Isidore generations. They also show its trajectory from hoped-for source of reconciliation and sublimation by Toledo to its waning influence and disappearance. Isidore's life and works were significant elements of an active and politically sensitive discourse that was symptomatic of the wider situations occurring in the kingdom. *How* the figures, events and ideas of the past were expressed, revealed, and interpreted – in whatever form this took, from a *DVI* edition to an origins-story to a canonical collection or law-code – mattered immensely, and these representations were fundamental products both for and of the virulent competition between networks of power. The form and content of the historical representations should not be separated from their wider political history, nor should pre-conceived notions about what constitutes a historical text limit the historian in the quest to understand the Visigothic kingdom, Isidore of Seville or the *Liber Iudiciorum*, especially insofar as what is meant by history is a method of discourse and dialectic. Various types of media – including letters, biblical texts, law-codes, lists of illustrious men, and origin-stories – with competing philosophies and methodologies of "history" were vibrant participants in the environment of life in the early middle ages.

CHAPTER 3

Origins and Histories: Creating New Chains of Signification

1   Introduction

In 1887, Thomas Hodgkin wrote that the Visigothic Church "does not need jealously to defend its privileges against the state when it is itself rapidly becoming conterminous with the state." Hodgkin was a member of a long-established Quaker family, the son of John Hodgkin, a Quaker minister. Thomas's father was the childhood friend of John Stuart Mill. While John Hodgkin received an education as a liberal Quaker, Mill was home-schooled by his father. Mill's father was a liberal philosopher and follower of Jeremy Bentham, author of *The Influence of Natural Religion on the Temporal Happiness of Mankind*, which was originally published under a pseudonym because of its negative conclusions on the utility of religion. Since they had been young, John Hodgkin and Mill had heard and had learned antagonistic views on state religion, which must have been a source of extensive thought and discussion. Mill became an atheist, in the manner of his academic supervisor, but Hodgkin maintained a strong liberal belief in religion. One may easily envisage the arguments witnessed regularly in the Hodgkin's household as Thomas was growing up. It would be unsurprising if Thomas, surrounded by debates on religion and state with family and friends, and a member of a minority religion in his own state, was to use the history of the Visigothic Church to espouse critical views of state religion. The Visigothic Church is imagined by him as a single unit that, since the conversion of Reccared, no longer needed to fight for its authority, to "guard jealously" its integrity and its privileges, which were secured within a mono-religious state. This was a critique of such a situation, given Hodgkin's views on religious plurality, but it was also the proliferation of a centuries-old historiography. After all, Hodgkin was writing primarily for "the general reader, who may not have his Gibbon before him," even if he re-shaped how it is possible to read Gibbon. The historiography of a unified Church and "state," real or desired, still tends to fuel scholarship about seventh-century Hispania. However, behind the imagined and constructed symbiosis was a serious contemporary, seventh-century struggle for autonomy from the central power and "state

Church" in Toledo.[1] Hodgkin may not have sensed this competitive situation, but he would have appreciated it.

A primary aim of this book is to reveal the subtle yet vicious competition between the schools of Isidore-Seville and Toledo-Agali lying subterraneous in the texts of the Isidore-moment. This chapter reveals how inventions and structures of historical narratives were used to create social and spiritual authority, in addition to political. The construction of historical representations, forms, and methods of narrating the past allowed authors to promote their positions, and schools, by offering multi-layered chains of signification suggesting the meaning of words, images, and events.[2] The historical texts of the period provided excellent platforms for the proliferation of the struggles between the two schools. Throughout them, one can detect an impressive collection of discreet criticisms lying beneath the veneer of literalness. The acts of nomination, labeling and description gloss over sublimated authorial exposition and critique, and offer multi-layered texts, modeled as brief for the sake of empowering its messages in the memories of audiences.[3] Evident is the

---

1 The first quote is from Thomas Hodgkin, "Visigothic Spain," *The English Historical Review* 2 (1887): 209–34 (223), and the second is from Hodgkin's Preface to the first volume of his *Italy and Her Invaders* (Oxford: Oxford University Press, 1880). On Hodgkin, see Wood, *Modern Origins*, esp. ch. 11; G. H. Martin, "Thomas Hodgkin," *Oxford Dictionary of National Biography*; and, Louise Creighton, *Life and Letter of Thomas Hodgkin* (London, 1917). Bentham's book was originally published in 1822 under the pseudonym Philip Beauchamp, out of fear of the Anglican authorities. The most recent edition is Jeremy Bentham, *The Influence of Natural Religion on the Temporal Happiness of Mankind* (New York: Prometheus Books, 2003).

2 For theoretical discussions of chains of signification and the deferral of meaning, and the symbolism of language, see Jacques Derrida, *Of Grammatology*, trans. Gayatri Chakravorty Spivak (Baltimore: The Johns Hopkins Press, 1997, orig. 1967); Andrea Mirabile, "Allegory, Pathos, and Irony: The Resistance to Benjamin in Paul de Man," *German Studies Review* 35 (2012), 319–33; and, Michel de Certeau, who maintains that "historical discourse acquires from its internal relation with 'chronicle' its status as being the knowledge of this chronicle, it is built upon a certain number of epistemological presuppositions: the need for a referential semanticization (creating the meaning of words, and chains of significations) [...] the possibility of fashioning a meta-language through the very language of the documents it uses." (Michel de Certeau, *The Writing of History*, trans. Tom Conley [New York: Columbia University Press, 1975], 94).

3 *Memoria* in the late antique world, in contrast to its English cognate "memory," had meaning beyond the political or social, and into the theological. One's memory on Earth could be related to their place in the afterlife. From the character of Trimalchio in the *Satyricon* to the discussion of memory by Varro (*Ling.* 6.49), to Isidore, memory in the classical and late antique world mattered tremendously, and it has been appropriately studied. For late antiquity, see Michael Koortbojian in *Art and Text in Roman Culture*, ed. Jas Elsner (1996), 210–34; Penelope J. E. Davies, "The Politics of Perpetuation: Trajan's Column and the Art of Commemoration," *American Journal of Archaeology* 101 (1997): 41–65; and, Janet Coleman, *Ancient and Medieval Memories: Studies in the Reconstruction of the Past* (Cambridge: University of

manipulation of memory through historical narrative, for the sake of present and future authority. This complements the use of absence and absent narrative space to provide a false sense of comprehensiveness and truth, and therefore legitimacy, as will be shown in the following chapters. This literary activity is evident throughout legal discussions and codifications, council records, and collections.[4]

The historical output of Isidore of Seville was the catalyst for the historiographical competition in this historical moment and was also, arguably, the most prominent collection of historical texts. This being the case, the primary focus of this chapter is the historical works of Isidore. These are often read as essentially royal propaganda, a collective defense of the Visigothic Crown in Toledo, in unison with Catholicism and the abstract referent "Hispania," "Iberia" or "Spain." This supposedly proves Isidore's unending loyalty (*loyalisme*) to the political authorities in Toledo.[5] Current scholarship generally proliferates this reading, which can be described historiographically as the "quest for unity" narrative, which reaches far back into the middle ages.[6]

Isidore was a master of language and wordplay, and exceptionally subtle, perhaps "overly subtle to the modern observer."[7] Beneath the layer of *loyalisme* evident in the texts, it is possible to discern a stream of criticisms and even, at times, vitriol. At the allegorical or mystical level of history-writing Isidore's

---

Cambridge Press, 1992). For the early middle ages, see Rosamond McKitterick, *History and Memory in the Carolingian World* (Cambridge: Cambridge University Press, 2004); Patrick Geary, *Phantoms of Remembrance: Memory and Oblivion at the End of the First Millennium* (Princeton: Princeton University Press, 1994); and, Chris Wickham and James Fentress, *Social Memory* (Oxford: Oxford University Press, 1992). For a theoretical exploration, see Ricoeur, *Memory, History and Forgetting*. The reader is also recommended to see the reading of Ricoeur's text by Alain Badiou in his article, "The Subject Supposed to be a Christian: On Paul Ricœur's *Memory, History, Forgetting*," trans. by Natalie Doyle and Alberto Toscano, *The Bible and Critical Theory* 2, no. 3 (2006).

4 The last point refers to Isidore's lesser *Chronicles*, which is re-dedicated in 654 to Recceswinth (see Marc Reydellet, "La diffusion des *Origines* d'Isidore de Séville au haut moyen âge," *Mélange d'Archéologie et d'Histoire de l'École Française de Rome* 78 (1966): 417–19. However, Julian of Toledo in the 680s may also have re-worked Isidore's *De Origine Gothorum* (see Chapter 3, note 87).

5 On Isidore's *loyalisme*, see Paul Séjourné, *Le dernier père de l'église, Saint Isidore de Seville* (Paris, 1936), and, John Henderson, *The Medieval World of Isidore of Seville* (Cambridge: Cambridge University Press, 2007).

6 For example, see Jamie Wood, *The Politics of Identity in Visigothic Spain: Religion and Power in the Histories of Isidore of Seville* (Boston and Leiden: Brill, 2012); Sam Ghosh, "The Barbarian Past in the Early Middle Ages" (Ph.D. diss., University of Toronto, 2009); and, Merrills, *History and Geography*.

7 See Merrills, *History and Geography*, 217, and Henderson, *World of Isidore*.

truths emerge: the Visigoths were not meant for salvation; their kingdom was on the path towards failure; and Toledo – its Crown and its Agalian-dominated Church – was in no way the true center of spiritual authority and legitimacy in the peninsula. The monks, bishops and school of Isidore-Seville were the guides and models for Christian life and death, for continuous conversion and, from it, the salvation of a re-born, baptized Hispania, or, Spania. For Isidore, conversion is a life-long endeavor that is never ultimately completed in life, but only in death, contrary to a political theology of forced conversions.[8] All being, alive or deceased, awaits the day of judgment; conversion is the continuous process of preparing for this day.[9] It is with this in mind that a text such as, for example, the *Obitus Beati Isidori*, should be read. Written, as noted, by a Sevillan cleric in the late 630s shortly after the death of Isidore, "post tot defectus Hispaniae novissimis temporibus suscitans," this text follows in the critical aesthetics established by Isidore in his historical writing and historiography.[10] This chapter reveals not only the centrality of historical writing and historiography to the schools-competition, but also the inherent antagonisms in Isidore's historical texts and the fragile *convivencia* that defines the Isidore-moment and its literary output.[11]

---

8   On Isidore's views of conversion, including as a gradual process of learning, see his *Sent.*, 2.8 and *DVI*, 28. In the secondary literature, see Henriette-Rika Benveniste, "On the Language of Conversion, Visigothic Spain Revisited," *Historein* 6 (2006): 72–87, and Wolfram Drews (*The Unknown Neighbour: The Jew in the Thought of Isidore of Seville* [Boston and Leiden: Brill, 2006], 224, n. 134), who argues that Isidore "regards the daily conversion of a Christian as a voluntary act. Every Christian is called upon to convert, which is understood as an active process [...]. The conversion is brought about and made by God's grace." Also, Jacques Fontaine calls the Isidorian Renaissance Isidore's "continuous conversion" of the Visigoths (Jacques Fontaine, "Conversion et culture chez les Wisigoths d'Espagne," *Settimane di Studio* 14 [1967]: 132). Isidore's theological position is mediated through Pope Gregory the Great who said, in a 591 letter to Virgilius and the bishops in Arles and Marseilles, "adhibendus ergo illis est sermo, qui et errorum in ipsis spinas urere debeat et praedicando quod in his tenebrascit inluminet." (*Gregorii I papae Registrum Epistolarum, Libri I–VII*, ed. Paul Ewald and Ludovic M. Hartmann, Monumenta Germaniae Historica [Berlin: Weidmann, 1891], I, 45, 71–72). There were multiple occasions on which Pope Gregory demanded kind treatment of Jews, about which see Solomon Grayzel, "The Papal Bull *Sicut Judeis*," in *Studies in Essays in Honor of Abraham A. Neuman*, ed. Meir Ben-Horin, Bernard D. Weinryb, and Solomon Zeitlin (Boston and Leiden: Brill, 1962), 243–80.
9   Revelations 20.
10 On the *Obitus Beati Isidori* see Chapter 2, § 3.1.
11 Jocelyn Hillgarth translates Américo Castro's famous dictum about medieval Spain, *convivencia*, as a "productive tension" between competing religious groups. This definition of *convivencia* also seems to characterize the schools-competition, despite the historical figures all being Catholic (Hillgarth, "Spanish Historiography and Iberian Reality," 33). For

2 Isidore's Literature of the Past

2.1 *Introduction*

Isidore's historical work, his writing about the past, or the "before now," is often considered a confusing enigma, a riddle that historians need to solve. This view suggests that the meaning of the texts was singular, not multi-layered. This is in contrast to texts by contemporaries in Toledo, such as king Sisebut's *Vita Desiderii* (*VD*) or those of other early medieval writers outside of the peninsula and kingdom.[12] However, this is hardly a fair assessment of Isidore's historical work. Isidore wrote many texts that could be considered "historical," depending on how one defines the meaning of the term. The argument throughout this book is that "historical" describes any narration that demonstrates a conscious consideration of the past, of the "before now," represented by a place in one or many imagined timelines. This is the meaning implied here when the term "historical" is used. Consequently, a fair variety of Isidore's texts should be considered historical, including his *De Viris Illustribus*, the *Hispana*, and some of the jurisprudence of the Second Council of Seville and Fourth Council of Toledo. These texts are considered elsewhere in this book, and so this chapter focuses on a number of other historical works of Isidore.

The texts considered in this chapter, as representations *of* pasts, offer alternative chains of meaning to promote the agenda of Isidore and his school.[13] The list of texts includes *Chronicles*, *De Origine Officiorum*, *Origines* (*Etymologies*), and *De Origine Gothorum* (*Historia Gothorum*). The "origins-story" holds a

---

Castro's use of the term see Américo Castro, *The Spaniards: An Introduction to Their History*, trans. Willard F. King & Selma Margaretten (Los Angeles: UCLA Press, 1971).

12 For example, Gregory of Tours and his *Decem Libri Historiarum*. For Sisebut's *Vita Desiderii* see *Vita Desiderii: Vita vel Passio Sancti Desiderii Episcopi Viennensis*, ed. Bruno Krusch, Monumenta Germaniae Historica, Scriptores rerum Merovingicarum 3 (Hanover and Leipzig: Hahn, 1896), 630–37; and, José Carlos Martín-Iglesias, "Une nouvelle édition critique de la *Vita Desiderii* de Sisebut, accompagnée de quelques réflexions concernant la date des *Sententiae* et du *De viris illustribus* d'Isidore de Séville," *Hagiographica* 7 (2000): 127–80. For discussion on the *Vita Desiderii* see Fontaine, "Sisebut's *Vita Desiderii*," in *Visigothic Spain*, ed. James, 93–129. About Gregory's text, see Martin Heinzelmann, *Gregory of Tours: History and Society in the Sixth Century*, trans. Christopher Carroll (Cambridge: Cambridge University Press, 2001), 192–201, and Helmut Reimitz, "Social Networks and Identities in Frankish Historiography. New Aspects of the Textual History of Gregory of Tours," in *The Construction of Communities in the Early Middle Ages: Texts, Resources, and Artefacts*, ed. Richard Corradini, Max Diesenberger and Helmut Reimitz (Boston and Leiden: Brill, 2003), 229–68.

13 On history-writing as a truth procedure, and on Christian forms of history-writing, see Björn Weiler, "Matthew of Paris on the writing of history," *Journal of Medieval History* 35 (2009): 254–78, and Rosamond McKitterick, "Christianity as History," in her *History and Memory*.

special significance in Isidore's spiritual-historical thinking. Each one was initially developed between the years 614 and 619 or 620. It is fair to call this period Isidore's "origins-moment." This "origins-moment" was, in part, related to Sisebut's interest in the meaning and origin of things, and perhaps his request for the *Origines*.[14] That is not to say that the books were "made-to-order" by Isidore for Sisebut, but that they were intended, though not exclusively, for audiences in Toledo and for its Agali circle.

The origins-stories provided Isidore and his school with an excellent opportunity to promote their interests. The creation of new chains of historical signification could be used, not only to subtly criticize the royal court, but also to tease out Isidore's theory of monarchy, and to generally promote, from the "inside," the metaphysical authority of Isidore-Seville over Toledo-Agali. The first version of the *Chronicles* was also produced during this time, around the year 615, and is certainly a representative part of Isidore's spiritual-historical thinking. The majority of the following discussion revolves, though, around the *De Origine Gothorum*. This is not because it necessarily contains quantitatively or even qualitatively more latent criticisms of the Visigoths and Toledo-Agali than the other texts mentioned, but it is an exemplary representative of the subtly vicious historical competition. None of Isidore's *origines* are strangers to the historiographical spotlight, medieval or modern. This is especially the case if one considers each manuscript as an individual historiographical act. However, with the exception of the *De Origine Gothorum*, only a short note will be made on the respective historiographies.

2.2 *Chronicles*

There were multiple continuators of the Eusebius-Jerome chronicles tradition.[15] Some of the authors in this body of literature were quite original in the continuities they drew: Count Marcellinus, Victor of Tunnuna, Marius of Avenches and John of Biclar can be counted among these. Isidore was unique in using

---

14 Isid., *Ep.*, 6: "Domino et Filio Sisebuto Isidorus: En tibi, sicut pollicitus sum, misi opus de origine quarundam rerum ex veteris lectionis recordatione collectum atque it in quibusdam locis adnotatum, sicut extat conscriptum stilo maiorum." For a discussion on the political significance of the first version of the *Origines* see Carmen Cardelle de Hartmann, "Wissenorganisation und Wissensvermittlung im ersten Teil von Isidors Etymologiae (Bücher I-X)," in *Exzerpieren – Kompilieren – Tradieren: Transformationen des Wissens zwischen Spätatike und Frühmittelalter. Millennium-Studien 64*, ed. Stephan Dusil, Gerald Schwedler, and Raphael Schwitter (Berlin and Boston: De Gruyter, 2017), 85–104.

15 Kim Bowes suggests a general "craze" for chronicles in late antiquity. See Kim Bowes, "Ivory Lists: Consular diptychs, Christian appropriation and polemics of time in Late Antiquity," *Art History* 24 (2001), 338–57, and, Arnaldo Momigliano, "The Origins of Universal History," in *On Pagans, Jews and Christians*, ed. Arnaldo Momigliano (Middletown: Wesleyan University Press, 1987), 31–57.

past chronicles as sites for the subtraction of information to construct an alternative historical narrative.[16] Isidore's closest associate in chronicles-writing was John of Biclar, who was a fellow Iberian and a colleague of Isidore's brother, Leander.[17] Isidore relied on John for a variety of information, yet the meaning of John's chronicle and Isidore's own are Other from one another. John and Isidore were different types of writers. John aimed to continue the existing chronicles, with the prevailing language of time and meaning, whereas Isidore represents a new aesthetic moment. Isidore sought to use the chronicle medium as a method to develop new sets of significations (part of the epistemological break of the Isidore-moment). It was not the chronicle tradition that Isidore was concerned with, but rather how he could use it. This is an example of the type (or aesthetic) of engaging with the past that was common during the period and the conceptual qualification of why John was not part of that moment.

Isidore developed his *Chronicles* with a complex set of interpretive layers, changing the narrative of past chronicles in the process. However, there is nothing elaborate in his conception of the chronicle model, Isidore's understanding of which was influenced by Cassiodorus, who imagined chronicles as narratives of the past that had an especially strong moral flavor. Chronicles were a category of histories for Cassiodorus, as they were for Isidore.[18] Isidore imbues the specific moral qualities of chronicles within a praxis of mystical and political significance into other modes of representing pasts, such as *origines* and, in a different way, *historia*.

Isidore produced two versions of his *Chronicles*, a long one and a short one. They are creatively referred to in scholarship as, respectively, the *maiora* and the *minora*, or the "greater" and "lesser." The lesser was made around 627 for inclusion into the *Origines*. The greater *Chronicles* was originally completed in 615 or 616, and then revised in 626.[19] Each version has its own peculiarities and

---

16 Goffart, *Narrators*, 9.
17 The term "Iberian" is used here as a geographical identifier. The peninsula was very likely referred to by John, Isidore and certainly others in real life at the time, amongst each other, as either "Hispania" or "Spania," as the extant texts and later manuscripts indicate. "Iberia" refers to an old Roman naming of the peninsula antiquated by this point (although other geographical identifiers once abandoned did return in this period, such as Carpetania). However, it is uncertain what identifying nominations, what identity labels, these individual figures attached to themselves in intimate conversations, in their minds, or whether others saw them the same way or, of course, whether such identities fluctuated throughout life and arose and disappeared according to the different contexts in which one found oneself.
18 Wood, *Politics and Identity*, 97.
19 It could also have been revised in the years 631 and 654. For the authoritative edition and discussion of the recensions of the *Chronicles*, see José Carlos Martín-Iglesias, *Isidori*

was produced for purposes most pertinent to the present situation.[20] Both versions of the *Chronicles* were impressively transmitted during the middle ages, and are well-preserved today in over eighty extant manuscripts, containing all or parts of the *Chronicles*. The oldest extant manuscript is Lucca 490, written about 796. There is also the "Fredegar" manuscript, Paris 10910, from the early eighth century, a complicated manuscript with various unresolved mysteries.[21]

2.3 De Origine Officiorum

The first of Isidore's origins-stories is the *De Origine Officiorum*. The precise date of provenance has not been determined, although it must fall between the years 598 and 615. The text is dedicated to Isidore's brother Fulgentius, the bishop of Astigi, and was written expressly for him. In the dedication, Isidore refers to himself simply by his name and not as bishop. This could indicate that he wrote the text before he was bishop, and so before 600, but it need not.

De Origine Officiorum is commonly referred to as *De Ecclesiasticis Officiis*, a title first attested in 1534. Its creation as such may have been influenced by its subsequently neat and holy-sounding abbreviation: DEO. The sixteenth century was an important period for early medieval history, when a host of new titles and "found" authors were invented and ascribed to early medieval texts. This is true for several of Isidore's texts, as it is famously with the creation of "Fredegar," a name first attested in 1579.[22] The most recent editor has shown

---

Hispalensis Chronica, Corpus Christianorum Series Latina 112 (Turnhout: Brepols, 2003), 119–23 (for dating); José Carlos Martín-Iglesias, "El capítulo 39 del libro V de la *Etimologías* y la *Crónica* de Isidoro de Sevilla a luz de la tradición manuscrita de esta última obra," in *Actas. III Congreso Hispánico de Latín Medieval*, 2 vols. (León, 26–29 de Septiembre de 2001), ed. M. Pérez González (León: Universidad de León, 2002); Marc Reydellet, "la diffusion des *Origines* d'Isidore de Séville," *Mélanges d'archéologie et d'histoire* 78 (1966): 383–437; and, Bernard Bischoff, "Die europäische Verbreitung der Werke Isidors von Sevilla," in *Isidoriana*, ed. Manuel C. Díaz y Díaz (León: Centro de Estudios "San Isidoro," 1960), 317–44.

20   Marc Reydellet, "Les intentions idéologiques dans la 'Chronique' d'Isidore de Séville," *Mélanges d'archéologie et d'histoire* 82 (1970): 363–400; Wood, *Politics and Identity*, 70–72; Bowes, "Ivory Lists," 338–57; and, Michael Allen, "Universal History 300–1000: Origins and Western Developments," in *Historiography in the Middle Ages*, ed. Deliyannis, 17–42.

21   The accepted provenance of MS Paris 10910 is Burgundy. See McKitterick, *History and Memory*, 51–52, and Roger Collins, *Fredegar: Authors of the Middle Ages* 13 (Brookfield: Variorum, 1996). On paleographical grounds, I have, in an unpublished conference talk, challenged this and offered a region of the north/north-west of Italy as an alternative site for where the manuscript was prepared.

22   Fredegar is the name of the author attributed to an anonymous chronicles text of the mid-seventh or early eighth century. For an edition of the *Chronicles* of Fredegar see *Fredegarii et aliorum chronica*, ed. Bruno Krusch, Monumenta Germaniae Historica, Scriptores rerum Merovingicarum 2 (Hanover: Hahn, 1888), 1–193. For a translation of book

convincingly that the Isidorian name of the text was *De Origine Officiorum*, and the modern edition provides a useful discussion of the evidence for this. One important example worth pointing out is how Braulio describes the text: "Ad germanum suum Fulgentium episcopum Officiorum libros duos, in quibus originem officiorum [...]."[23] Ildefonsus, perhaps slightly altering Isidore's intention, records the book as a *librum de genere officiorum*.[24]

2.4   Origines (*Etymologies*)

The historiography of the *Etymologiarum sive Originum Libri XX* is so extensive and laudatory that any introduction of it can put the author at risk of letting it take over the entire discussion. The significance of the *Origines*, it has been argued, cannot be overestimated and it could even be called the *Grundbuch des ganzen Mittelalters*.[25] The recent translators say that the *Origines* "was arguably the most influential book, after the Bible, in the learned world of the Latin West for nearly a thousand years."[26] General scholars of the Middle Ages tend to cite the *Origines* as the final word on Isidore, with little to no historicization, using Isidore and the text as blanket authorities for information, historical or otherwise. Ernst Brehaut went so far as to say that everything Isidore ever wrote is found in condensed form in the *Origines*.[27]

The boundaries of this chapter, and book, prevent elaborate exploration of the relationship between the *Origines* and the rest of Isidore's works. Suffice it to say, the *Origines* mediates and helps to expose the relationship between Isidore's historical, linguistic and etymological writings, and so his model of

---

four of the Chronicles see Michael Wallace-Hadrill, *The Fourth Book of the Chronicle of Fredegar* (Ann Arbor: University of Michigan Press, 1960). For a discussion of the authorship of the *Chronicles* see Collins, *Fredegar*, 1.

23   Braulio, *Renotatio*, ls. 14–15.

24   Ildef., *DVI*, 8. On the dating and naming, see *De Ecclesiasticis Officiis*, ed. Lawson, 13–14, and 119–21; Lawson confirms the dating of José Aldama (Aldama, "Indicaciones sobre la cronología" in *Miscellanea Isidoriana*, 87–88). For a recent challenge to Lawson's analysis see Thomas Deswarte, "Why a new edition of Isidore's *De Ecclesiasticis Officiis*: the 'De Acolythis' chapter and the three versions of the treatise," *Mittellateinisches Jahrbuch: international Zeitschrift für Mediävistik* 52, no. 3 (2017): 347–61.

25   The title reference is to *Isidori Hispalensis Episcopi Etymologiarum sive Originum Libri XX*, ed. Wallace M. Lindsay (Oxford: Oxford University Press, 1911). The quote is from Ernst R. Curtius, "Grundbuch des ganzen Mittelalters," in his *Europäische Literatur und lateinisches Mittelalter* (Bern: A. Francke, 1948), 496–97, trans. Willard R. Trask, *European Literature and the Latin Middle Ages* (Princeton: Princeton University Press, 1953), 24–29.

26   *Etymologies*, trans. Barney et al., 3.

27   See Jane Chance, *Medieval Mythography: From Roman North Africa to the School at Chartres, AD 433–1177*, Medieval Mythography 1 (Gainsville: University Press of Florida, 1994), 130, n. 17.

truth procedures. Henderson shows in brilliant, albeit at times be-wild-er[r]-ing fashion, how Isidore developed a deeply theological and ideological text by using the absolute extreme form of authorial absence: thesaurus, dictionary, or etymology.[28] Such techniques and truth procedures are evident throughout Isidore's historical writings. They also helped to influence and are on permanent display in the *Liber Iudiciorum*, which was begun several years after Isidore's death, around the time that Braulio was writing his *Renotatio*.

There are no single dates for the initial drafts and completion of the *Origines*. In his *Renotatio*, Braulio makes it clear that it was he who finished the text, at Isidore's request, in the late 630s or early 640s, but the precise beginnings of the *Origines* are uncertain. Isidore certainly worked on the *Origines* throughout his life: multiple drafts were made, updated and changed according to circumstances and information available.[29] Furthermore, around the year 627, the so-called lesser *Chronicles* was constructed for inclusion into the text. Since there is no reference to the *Origines* before the 610s, though, it is reasonable to conclude that that is when it was begun. The impetus for it seems to have been tied to the wider *origines* project that Isidore set to task in the 610s. This was influenced by a variety of factors, including potential requests for such a text from Braulio, and from Sisebut. Isidore developed the *Origines* as a text in dialogue with, at various times, both of them, as well as with other nobles and elite across the kingdom.[30] There are extant several letters between Isidore and Braulio that reference the text. There is also a short note to Sisebut, usually referred to as a dedication to him, in which Isidore sends him a copy of the *Origines*.[31]

What is the authentic name of the *Origines*? Several references to the *Origines* by both its author and editor – i.e. Isidore and Braulio – still survive. These are mainly found in the letter correspondence between the two, but there also exists the said note from Isidore to Sisebut. In correspondence with the king in Toledo, Isidore only ever refers to the text as the *Origines*, whereas with Braulio he refers to it as the *Etymologies*. Braulio mentions it at times as the *Origines* and at others as the *Etymologies*. The dating of the letters does not provide any solid clue to which title was first, since the dating of the earliest letters are no more dependable than the dedication to Sisebut. All that can be said is that some of these early letters were from the 610s. From the 610s to the 630s, the

---

28 Henderson, *World of Isidore*, Introduction.
29 See Braulio *Ep.*, 6 and 14. In *Ep.*, 3 and *Ep.*, 5, Braulio complains that the *Etymologies* has been completed and that others had been seeing finished drafts for some time. The letters are from the mid-620s and early 630s (see Martín-Iglesias, *Renotatio*, 57–58).
30 For a discussion on the dedicatees of the *Origines*, see Fontaine, *Isidore de Séville*, 876–77.
31 Isid., *Ep.*, 6.

title of the text fluctuated. After Isidore's death, Braulio edited the *Origines* into its final form and decided on the name *Etymologies*, as seen in the *Renotatio*.³²

The problem of which of the two names was the original could be resolved if we consider who was involved, rather than when the correspondences occurred. There may be a subtle nuance to the naming that could underscore an important ideological proponent to the name. The evidence of the dedication and letters implies that Isidore referred to the text as the *Origines* when in correspondence with the royal circle in Toledo, and as the *Etymologies* with Braulio. Isidore refers to the text as the *Origines* in communication with Sisebut, whereas in his letter to Braulio he calls it the *Etymologies*. Braulio usually refers to the text as the *Etymologies*, including in the final edition. However, Braulio's only reference to the *Etymologies* as the *Origines* is a late one, in a letter written between 632 and 633, and in Isidore's prompt response to this letter he refers to the text as the *Etymologies*. The use of the *Origines* title by Braulio c. 632–633 may be because he was sending it to Isidore in Toledo, where Isidore, who had arrived, it turned out, quite early for the Fourth Council of Toledo, was witness to Sisenand's securing his usurpation and attempt to "steal" the royal bishopric. Under such conditions, Braulio may have wanted to use the "royal" title of *Origines* in a letter sent to Toledo. Near the end of the same letter, Braulio refers to the *Origines* again as the *Etymologies*. It is a relatively long letter, and so it is possible that by the time Braulio was finishing it, the circumstances had changed in Toledo. Braulio himself was to head there for the council in 633. There would have been no point in going back to edit the title, since he and Isidore were well aware of both names. Regardless of the reasons for this confusion, one exception should not be enough to break the rule. It is evident that the *Origines* was referred to by both names, but that, from the evidence available, Isidore referred to it as the *Origines* with the king in Toledo and the *Etymologies* with his school. Given this and the fact that the earliest recorded reference by Isidore is to the *Origines*, that is the title adopted in this chapter and throughout this book.

From its completion in the late 630s and 640s, the *Origines* was apparently more popular outside the Visigothic kingdom than within it, and from after the kingdom's collapse than during its existence. This conclusion is based on the chance survival of evidence and the far better preservation of non-Visigothic manuscripts than Visigothic ones.³³ As such, it may not reflect the

---

32 "Etymologiarum codicem nimiae magnitudinis distinctum ab eo titulus, non libris, quem quia rogatu meo fecit, quamuis inperfectum ipse reliquerit, ego in viginti libros diuisi."

33 This is certainly not to say that later Visigothic writers did not at all read and consult the *Origines*. Julian of Toledo, for instance, cites it a few times in books 1 and 3, respectively, of his *Prognosticum futuri saeculi* (e.g. 1.4–5, 3.2, and 3.4). Moreover, although perhaps made to be sent to Ireland, the *Origines* was redacted in 655, somewhere in Hispania, in order to

actual situation. However, the relative lack of reference to Isidore's work in Hispania after the Isidore-moment, with the dominance of the school of Toledo-Agali from the 660s forward, does indicate that the manuscript situation reflects an historical reality. This pattern also matches that of other texts of Isidore and of the school of Isidore-Seville against those of Toledo-Agali.[34]

2.5 De Origine Gothorum

The *De Origine Gothorum* is shorthand for a set of texts meant by Isidore as a single work. It includes the *De Origine Gothorum* proper, a history of the Vandals and of the Sueves, and two texts referred as the *De Laude Spaniae* and *De Laude Gothorum* (or, *Recapitulatio*), which open and close the Gothic history. These play especially important roles in the narrative of the *De Origine Gothorum*, which is discussed below. The *De Origine Gothorum* is extant in two versions. The first was finished around the years 619 or 620, just after the unexpected death of Sisebut, evident from the hasty account of his demise, and does not contain the laudatory texts. The second version was finished around the year 625, after Swinthila's victory over the Byzantines in Spania and the elevation of his son Riccimir as co-ruler. It has been argued that there was a third version made by Isidore in

---

add to Book 6.17 the independent Visigothic continuation of Cyril of Alexandria's Easter table which advanced it from 532–626 (the first Visigothic continuation) to 627–721. This revised table was made in 632, but only added to Isidore's text in 655, shortly after the promulgation of the *Liber Iudiciorum*, Toledo's recognition of Isidore as a Doctor of the Church, and the closing of the Isidore-moment as described below in Chapter 5. This is evident from the (non-Visigothic) Longleat House flyleaf fragment, on which see the edition and discussion in James P. Carley and Ann Dooley, "An Early Irish Fragment of Isidore of Seville's *Etymologiae*," in *The Archaeology and History of Glastonbury Abbey: essays in honour of the ninetieth birthday of C. A. Ralegh Radford*, ed. Lesley Abrams and James Carey (Woodbridge: Boydell, 1991), 135-61. For more on the dating and Visigothic computistics see Immo Warntjes, "The Continuation of the Alexandrian Easter table in Seventh-Century Iberia and its Transmission to Ninth-Century Francia (Isidore, *Etymologies* 6.17)," *Revue d'Histoire des Textes* (2018): 185–94. Interestingly, it was between 655–664 also that the AD system was adopted in Hispania. The ongoing work of Evina Steinová should be consulted on all matters regarding the transmission of *Origines* manuscripts. One point that is particularly worth noting here from one of her forthcoming articles is that full manuscripts of the *Origines* are more common from late/former Visigothic territory than beyond it. This could indicate the growing fetishization of Isidore the figure, the icon, towards and in the eighth century. See Evina Steinová, "The Materiality of Innovation: Formats and Dimensions of the *Etymologiae* of Isidore of Seville in the Early Middle Ages," in *Entangled Manuscripts, c. 600–110*, ed. Anna Dorofeeva and Michael J. Kelly (Binghamton: Gracchi Books, forthcoming 2021), and Evina Steinová, "The Oldest Manuscript Tradition of the *Etymologiae* (Eighty Years after A. E. Anspach)," *Visigothic Symposia* 4 (2020): 100–143.

34   For a recent discussion on the *Origines* as a reflection of contemporary material culture see Scott de Brestian, "Material Culture in the *Etymologiae* of Isidore of Seville," *Journal of Late Antiquity* 11, no. 1 (2018): 216–31.

the early 630s, but its existence and moreover its association with Isidore and the Isidore-Seville school is doubtful.[35] This means that the writing of the two recensions coincided quite closely with the Second and Third Councils of Seville, as well as the revisions of the greater *Chronicles*, and may have been intended to function in different ways, according to the events of the time.

The proper naming of the *De Origine Gothorum* has been confused in the historiography, but should be dealt with in detail because it is important for grasping the significance of the text within this historical moment. Titles attributed to historical texts are critical clues in understanding their historical meaning: as seen with the *De Origine Officiorum*, the titles of texts are often changed throughout the centuries, and those ascribed in any given present do not necessarily reflect the original titles. There are multiple reasons why the intended names are lost. Sometimes it is due simply to scribal error. In the case of Visigothic texts, it is occasionally because seventh and eighth century manuscripts, or those that discuss the texts, do not provide names. For various reasons, later scribes or historians have provided titles, just as they have invented names of authors. In other instances, scribes and scholars have felt compelled to re-nominate texts in ways that appealed to, or would have been better understood by, their contemporary audiences.[36] Both of these activities were prevalent in the early modern period when titles and authorial ascription became important in the production of printed editions and translations.[37] However, inventing, altering and also translating titles into a different form happened in the early medieval world as well. The historiographies of the *Lex Visigothorum* and the *Hispana* are good examples. In contrast to later medieval and modern titles, each are referred to in the oldest extant manuscripts and references as, respectively, the *Liber Iudiciorum* and the *Liber Canonum*,

---

35 Theodor Mommsen believed that the *De Origine Gothorum* was from 625, that the original was lost, and that both existing recensions were built from this original version (*Historia Gothorum Vandalorum Sueborum*, ed. Mommsen, 254). The accepted dates in scholarship today are, respectively, c. 619/620 and c. 625. For a discussion of the dating and the problems of the recensions of the *De Origine Gothorum* see *Las Historias de los Godos*, ed. Rodríguez Alonso, 26–66, and Merrills, *History and Geography*, 179–85. There may also have been an extension of the *De Origine Gothorum* made in the 640s in Toledo, on which see Chapter 2, n. 37.

36 For instances of this specifically in the early middle ages, see Rosamond McKitterick, "The audience for Latin historiography in the early middle ages: texts transmission and manuscript dissemination," in *Historiographie im frühen Mittelalter* (Veröffentlichungen des Instituts fur Österreichische Geschichtsforschung 32), ed. Anton Scharer and Georg Scheibelreiter (Vienna: R. Oldenbourg Verlag, 1994), 96–114.

37 See *Documenting the Early Modern Book World: Inventories and Catalogues in Manuscript and Printing*, ed. Malcolm Walsby and Natasha Constantinidou (Boston and Leiden: Brill, 2013).

a significant relationship which is discussed below in Chapters 4 and 5. The invention of titles is meant to help audiences grasp the intention of the texts. The distance from the culture in which the text was produced, whether it be a century or a millennium, requires names that reflect current understandings of, for example, historical texts, to bridge the epistemological gap between the author and reader. Hence, later names tend to miss the meaning of early medieval texts in their historical contexts, substituting the original title with one subjected to, and translated for, understandings of the time.

Isidore's *De Origine Gothorum* is often referred to by modern scholars as the *Historia Gothorum* and, when translated, as the *History of the Goths*, the *Historias de los Godos*, the *Histoire des Goths*, etc.[38] That the original title was the *De Origine Gothorum* is evident from the historical and manuscript evidence. Starting with the former, Braulio's *Renotatio Isidori*, written shortly after Isidore's death, and the oldest and most reliable account of Isidore's writing, describes Isidore's work as the *De Origine Gothorum et Regno Suevorum et etiam Vandalorum Historia librum unum*. This is slightly different from that found in the nearly contemporary dedication of the text to Sisenand, which names it as *De Origine Gothorum Hispanorum Suevorum Vandalorum et Alanorum*.[39] There are lingering questions as to the historical authenticity of this dedication, which is transmitted by way of Jiménez de Rada and Lucas de Tuy in a lost thirteenth-century manuscript, recorded by a sixteenth-century scholar. However, the fact that the author of the manuscript refers to the *De Origine Gothorum* as the *Gotthorum historia*, the name that had become common by that time, while clearly having seen it as *De Origine Gothorum* [...] in the dedication to Sisenand, suggests that the description is late but the dedication with its title is authentic.[40] Assuming that the dedication is authentically seventh

---

38 For example, Rodríguez Alonso, *Las Historias de los Godos*, Fontaine, *Isidore de Seville*, and *Isidore of Seville's, History of the Kings of the Goths, Vandals, and Suevi*, ed. Guido Donini and Gordon B. Ford (Boston and Leiden: Brill, 1966).

39 See *Dedicatio ad Sisenandum, Chron. min. ii*, ed. Theodor Mommsen, Monumenta Germaniae Historica, Auctorum Antiquissimorum (Berlin: Weidman, 1894), 304. Given the title of the *De Origine Gothorum* in the *Dedicatio*, one wonders if it actually represents a text that was the source of the mysterious *Liber Itatii*, a list of Visigothic, Suevic, Vandal and Alan kings used by bishop Pelayo, and which exists now only in the late sixteenth-century manuscript by Ambrosio de Morales, Madrid BNE 1346 (the copy he commissioned of the *Codex Vetustissimus Ovetensis*). For discussion of the dedication and supposed 630s version of the *De Origine Gothorum*, see *Las Historias de los Godos*, ed. Rodríguez Alonso, 64–66. On the *Liber Itatii*, see Luis Vázquez de Parga, *La Division de Wamba* (Madrid, 1943), and John Wreglesworth, "The Chronicle of Alfonso III and its Significance for the Historiography of the Asturian kingdom 718–910 AD" (Ph.D. diss., University of Leeds, 1995), 27, 47, 380, n. 75.

40 For the text see *Roderici Ximenii de Rada Historia de rebus Hispaniae siue Historia Gothica*, Corpus Christianorum Continuatio Mediaevalis 72, ed. Juan Fernández Valverde (Turnout: Brepols, 1987), and *Lucae Tudensis Chronicon Mundi*. Corpus Christianorum

century, it could represent an important recension of Isidore's text, perhaps by the school of Isidore-Seville in response to the usurpation by a Frankish-backed rebel before the Fourth Council of Toledo. Such a revision, though, may have been anathema to the council's gestures.[41] That Braulio records the title slightly differently, but significantly, suggests either that he changed it to fit the post-Fourth Council situation, or that it was the original title before the revision including Sisenand.[42] It is likely that this revision, if it existed in more than name, was not by Isidore; the dedication is not from the school but rather from a pseudo-Isidore working in Toledo and writing at the beginning of the usurpation.[43] The dedication to Sisenand survives in several manuscripts, all of which derive from Toledan-family manuscripts, much like other royal, Toledan records with limited transmission. This pseudo-Isidore could have been the same as the anonymous editor of the *Chronicles* in 631, who seems to have been working in Toledo.[44] This is evident from the existence in one manuscript of an abbreviated form of the *Chronicles*, ending in 631 and edited by a user of the *Chronicles*, not by Isidore.[45] Perhaps this 631 version of the *Chronicles* and the *De Origine Gothorum* re-dedication to Sisenand were part of the same project.

Continuatio Mediaevalis 74, ed. Emma Falque (Turnout: Brepols, 2003). Luis Vázquez de Parga (de Parga, "Notas sobre la obra histórica de San Isidoro," in *Isidoriana*, ed. Díaz y Díaz, 99–114 [104]), and Cristobal Rodríguez Alonso (Rodríguez Alonso, *Las Historias de los Godos*, 64–66) believe that the dedication to Sisenand is entirely spurious.

41   On the relationship of Isidore's historical work with the agenda of the Fourth Council of Toledo see Helmut Reimitz, "The Historian as Cultural Broker in the Late and Post-Roman West," in *Western Perspectives on the Mediterranean: Cultural Transfer in Late Antiquity and the Early Middle Ages, 400–800 AD*, ed. Andres Fischer and Ian Wood (New York and London: Bloomsbury, 2014), 41–54.

42   This assumes that Braulio's list of Isidore's works is chronological, which editorial scholarship of Isidore's various texts generally confirms. Recently, however, it has been convincingly argued that Braulio's letter collection was arranged by him to advance a narrative of subtle antagonisms about the monarchy in Toledo. Such a conclusion is consistent with the overall argument of this book, but it does make one question the ordering of the *Renotatio*. For more, see Miguel Franco, "Braulio de Zaragoza."

43   Cazier argues that Isidore revised the text in the early 630s to cut Swinthila (Pierre Cazier, *Isidore de Séville et la Naissance de l'Espagne Catholique*, Collection Théologie historique 96 [Paris: Beauchesne, 1994], 62–68). This makes sense given the anathematizing of Swinthila and his family at IV Toledo, but is not entirely convincing given the altered title, the editing of the *Chronicles* at the time, and Braulio's recording of the text. The latter suggests that this supposed early 630s version was not Isidorian or was somehow antipathetic to IV Toledo.

44   See Roger Collins, "Isidore, Maximus, and the *Historia Gothorum*," in *Historiographie*, ed. Scharer and Scheibelreiter, 347–49.

45   It survives solely in MS Cologne Dombibliothek 8311, fs. 5–12, and was written by Archbishop Hildebold in Cologne circa 798.

Whether it was or not, the contemporary evidence indicates that the title of the text on the Goths was referred to during the Isidore-moment as the *De Origine Gothorum* and not the *Historia Gothorum*.

The manuscript evidence also supports the *origines* title, which is that found in the two oldest extant versions of the *De Origine Gothorum*. The oldest historical mention of the *De Origine Gothorum* is in Braulio's *Renotatio Isidori*, but it does not represent the oldest manuscript account. The oldest extant version of the *Renotatio Isidori* is preserved in the ninth-century Toledan-Córdoban MS León Cathedral 22. One of the oldest manuscripts containing the *De Origine Gothorum* is the MS Escurialensis R. II. 18. It is considered to be from the ninth century, but is a complicated manuscript with various problems of internal dating. In it, the *De Origine Gothorum* is the second text, introduced as *Incipit ex libro de origine Gothorum*. The histories of the Vandals and Sueves are absent. It should be noted that this manuscript also contains the dedication of the text to Sisenand. The fuller and more securely datable manuscript is Berlin Phillippsianus 1.885, written around the year 820 (before 846). This manuscript, without the dedication to Sisenand, records the texts true to the Isidorian dialectical reference for the titles, as the *de origine Gothorum et gestis*, the *storia Vandalorum*, and for the Sueves the story simply starts *Incipit Suevorum* (as does that of the Vandals, but its title is noted in its *explicit*). All ninth-century, and perhaps earlier, manuscripts refer to the text as the *De Origine Gothorum*. Whether dedicated to Sisenand or not, the integrity of the *De Origine Gothorum* title is secure.[46]

It is not absolutely certain when the *De Origine Gothorum* became a "*historia*" *Gothorum*. The general histories of Jiménez de Rada and Lucas de Tuy, and Alfonso X's *Estoria de Espanna,* are thirteenth-century examples, in Spain, of the various adaptations of the *De Origine Gothorum*'s name into a *historia*.[47] The archbishop of Toledo, Rodrigo Jiménez de Rada, as part of a project to "reinvent" Toledo – as a periphery-*cum*-center once again – wrote a series of historical texts such as the *Historia Romanorum, Historia Arabum, Historia Ostrogothorum*, and others, capped off by his *Historia Gothorum* (or, *Historia*

---

46 For a fuller discussion of the manuscripts and their transmission, see *Las Historias de los Godos,* ed. Rodríguez Alonso, 123–61 ([126–27 on MS Escurialensis R. II. 18, and 123–24 on MS Berlin Philipps. 1.885); Rodrigo Furtado, "Isidore's *Histories* in the Mozarabic scholarship of the eight and early ninth centuries," in *Ways of Approaching Knowledge in Late Antiquity and the Early Middle Ages: Schools and Scholarship,* ed. Paulo Farmhouse Alberto and David Paniagua (Nordhausen: Verlag Traugott Bautz, 2012), 264–83; Collins, "Isidore, Maximus," 348–49; and, Merrills, *History and Geography*, 180.

47 For the *Estoria de Espanna* edition with manuscript discussions and transcriptions, see the digital edition project led by Aengus Ward at www.estoria.bham.ac.uk/blog/.

de rebus Hispaniae).[48] Prior to these thirteenth-century texts, bishop Pelayo's early twelfth-century *Liber Chronicorum ab exordio mundi usque ad eram* MCLXX refers to the *De Origine Gothorum* as the *Historia de Regibus Gothorum, Wandalorum et Suevorum*.[49] In constructing his *Chronicles*, Pelayo had relied, in part, on the eleventh-century chronicle by Sampiro, which can be found in the *Historia Silense*, as a text contemporary to Pelayo's. However, neither it nor the chronicle by Sampiro mentions Isidore's historical work.[50] The oldest manuscript to refer to the Gothic section of the text specifically as the *Historia Gothorum* is the twelfth-century Paris BN lat. 4873, the only extant short recension, which labels the text as the *historia Gothorum, Wandalorum, Suevorum*. This is followed in an interpolation of the thirteenth-century MS Madrid univ. 134, and the fourteenth-century MS Paris bibl. de l'Arsénal n. 982, in which can be seen *Gothorum historia*.

This suggests that the *historia Gothorum* title developed around the eleventh or twelfth centuries as a result of new theories of history visible in Spain from the tenth century. It was at this time that the "quest for unity" narrative, which still dominates the historiography of Visigothic Spain, was earnestly developed. As noted previously, it was not in Visigothic Hispania that this idea persisted, or at least not during the Isidore-moment.[51] It was not until the end of the ninth or early tenth century that the Goths, as selected by God as rulers over the peninsula, were directly connected to the monarchy of contemporary Iberia.[52] This move towards divine authority for the Gothic and Spanish kings is evident in

---

48   For a short discussion and bibliography for these texts, see Lucy Pick, *Conflict and Coexistence: Archbishop Rodrigo and the Muslims and Jews of Medieval Spain* (Ann Arbor: University of Michigan Press, 2007), and, Norbert Kersken, "High and Late Medieval National Historiography," in *Historiography in the Middle Ages*, ed. Deliyannis, 193–210.

49   Wreglesworth, "Historiography of the Asturian kingdom," 29 and 107; Simon Barton and Richard Fletcher, *The World of El Cid: Chronicles of the Spanish Reconquest* (Manchester University Press, 2000); Linehan, *History and Historians*, 313–84; Francisco Javier Fernández Conde, "La obra del obispo ovetense D. Pelayo en la historiografia española," *Boletín del Instituto de Estudios Asturianos* 25 (1971), 249–91; and, *Crónica del Obispo Don Pelayo*, ed. Benito Sánchez Alonso (Madrid, 1924).

50   The *Historia Silense* preserved in the fifteenth-century manuscript Madrid BNE 1181. It gets its name from a note in the marginalia saying that the author of the *Historia* took his vows at the monastery of Santo Domingo de Silos. See Barton and Fletcher, *World of El Cid*, 71.

51   For important discussions on this, see Hillgarth, *Visigoths in History and Legend*, 1–21; *Las Historia de los Godos,* ed. Rodríguez Alonso, 11–20; and, Koon and Wood, "Unity from disunity," 793–808.

52   For elaboration of this point, see Chapter 5, § 3.1.

the famous tenth-century *Codex Vigilanus* and its chronicle of Alfonso III.[53] The *Historia Silense*, as the *Historia Roderici*, is an important text in the historiography of the meaning of "history." The author states his aims as objectively biographical. However, what the author does is develop a collection of historical vignettes, which serve as a framework to house a clear plot, a sustained, subtle critique of the ruling king, Alfonso VI.[54] There is also the beautiful, tenth-century *Codex Rotensis*, which strangely starts the reproduction of the *De Origine Gothorum* with the history of the Vandals (*Bandalorum Regnum*, fs. 156ʳ–157ᵛ), then the Sueves (simply as *Suevorum*, fs. 157ᵛ–159ʳ), and on to Isidore's *Chronicles* from f. 159ʳ to f. 167ʳ. The *De Origine Gothorum* begins only at f. 167ʳ without being named, as the other texts are. Instead, it is opened as "scitote, Gothorum antiquissimam esse gentem [...]." At the end of the text, on f. 176ʳ, it is, however, referred to as *Gotorum Regnum*, having imagined Isidore's text as a collection of royal biographies. This could have served as a model for the *Historia Silense*, but it draws no connections between Oviedo and Toledo, as it were. Yet, it serves as an important representative of the process of the gradual disappearance of *origines* as an historical model with unique meaning. Clearly discernible is a growing confusion and evolution in the tenth through thirteenth centuries of the aesthetic intentions for a *historia*, from promoting a *gens* to a more ambiguous method of royal biography, political satire, and universal history.

By the end of the thirteenth century, there was a solid conceptual shift in the way the past was conceived. History became closer to its modern form, the all-encompassing method and term for all history-writing and representations of the "before now." The first modern scholar of the *De Origine Gothorum* was Hugo Grotius, who wrote the title of the text as *Historia Gothorum*. This helped to cement the historiographical tradition of referring to the *De Origine Gothorum* sequence as such. This distorting of Isidore's title was not endemic to the copying and adapting of his historical work; it is reflective of a wider shift in medieval philosophy of history. Less than a century before Grotius, Johannus Magnus reworked Jordanes's *De Origine Actibus Getae* into *Historia de omnibus Gothorum Sueonumque*.[55] It was published in 1554, twenty years after Isidore's

---

53   For a full discussion of the *Codex Vigilanus* see Chapter 4, § 2.4. For the *Chronicle* of Alfonso III, and the Ovetense and Rotense editions see the long footnote with bibliography in Hillgarth, "Spanish Historiography and Iberian Reality," 27, n. 9, and Christys, *Christians in Al-Andalus*, 31.

54   See Barton and Fletcher, *The World of El Cid*, 9–23, and 90–98, and, Wreglesworth, "Historiography of the Asturian kingdom," 112.

55   For discussion see Kurt Johannesson, *The Renaissance of the Goths in Sixteenth-Century Sweden: Johannes and Olaus Magnus as Politicians and Historians* (Berkeley: University of California Press, 1991).

De Origine Officiorum appeared for the first time under the alternative title *De Ecclesiasticis Officiis*. The title *Historia Gothorum* has travelled well since Grotius and is still the most common way for scholars to refer to the text.[56]

The shift in titles through various manifestations from *De Origine Gothorum* to *Historia Gothorum* was not the result of uneducated, hapless re-nomination. Shifting titles were reflections of changing attitudes about history-writing.[57] In addition, the specific need to develop a non-original title may also have been influenced by the extant manuscripts. The lack of evident titles could have been a driving force of new names, or an unsolved problem, as in the case of the *Codex Rotensis*, for example. It may be that the oldest manuscript using *Historia Gothorum*, Paris BN lat. 4873, could reflect a twelfth-century dependence

56 See the use of *Historia Gothorum* in *Historia Gothorum Vandalorum Sueborum*, ed. Mommsen; Collins, "Isidore, Maximus and the *Historia Gothorum*;" Fontaine, *Isidore de Seville*; Luis A. García Moreno, "Prosopography and Onomastic: the Case of the Goths," in *Prosopography Approaches and Application: A Handbook*, ed. Katharine Keats-Rohan (Oxford: Unit for Prosopographical Research, University of Oxford, 2007), 347; Merrills, *History and Geography*, 170–228; and, Ghosh, "Barbarian Past," 17–76. Isabel Velázquez uses *Historia Gothorum*, suggesting that *De Origine Gothorum* was, interestingly, invented by Braulio (Isabel Velázquez, "*Pro patriae gentisque Gothorum statu* (4th Council of Toledo, Canon 75, A. 633)," in *Regna and Gentes. The Relationship between Late Antique and Early Medieval Peoples and kingdoms in the Transformation of the Roman World*, ed. Hans-Werner Goetz, Jörg Jarnut, and Walter Pohl (Boston and Leiden: Brill, 2003), 165. Merrills says that the *De Origine Gothorum*, often "referred to by modern scholars as the 'History of the Goths' [...] seems to have been imbued with a rather different significance in the seventh century," but does not elaborate the point (Merrills, *History and Geography*, 173).

57 For an example outside of Spanish texts, the so-called "*Historia Brittonum*," dated to about 829, is referred to in the oldest known manuscript as *origine et genelogia Britonum* (*Historia Brittonum, Chron. min.* iii, ed. Theodor Mommsen, Monumenta Germaniae Historica, Auctorum Antiquissimorum 13 [Berlin: Weidmann, 1898], 113). In the twelfth century, this text served as the major source of Geoffrey of Monmouth's adaptation, the *Historia Regum Britanniae*. In the fourteenth century, a translation of a German poem into Latin, the *De Origine Gigantum*, is attached as a complementing introduction to the *Historia* of the twelfth century. The history of this text is a good example elsewhere of *historiae* having become the primary mode of historical writing by the twelfth century. The late origins-story introduction suggests that *origines* had become a 'classicizing' narrative technique, meant to build authority based on an iconic or 'pre-*historia*' form of history-writing. The political events surrounding the production of the *De Origine Gigantum*, especially the Scottish declaration of origins, of Arbroath, confirm this. For discussion, critical edition and translation of the *De Origine Gigantum* see James P. Carley and Julia Crick, "Constructing Albion's Past: An Annotated Edition of *De Origine Gigantum*," in *Arthurian Literature* 13, ed. James P. Carley and Felicity Riddy (Cambridge: D. S. Brewer, 1995), 41–114; James P. Carley, "A Glastonbury Translator at Work: *Quedam Narracio de nobili rege Arthuro* and *De Origine Gigantum* in their Earliest Manuscript Contexts," *Nottingham French Studies* 30.2 (1991), 5–12; and, Ruth Evans, "Gigantic Origins: An Annotated Translation of *De Origine Gigantum*," in *Arthurian Literature* 16, ed. James P. Carley and Felicity Riddy (Cambridge: D. S. Brewer, 1998), 197–217.

on the shorter and earlier version of the *De Origine Gothorum*. The *De Origine Gothorum* was poorly transmitted outside of Spain in the middle ages, with only five manuscripts in circulation, despite its success within the peninsula.[58] This is not to say that Isidore conceived of the title as *Historia Gothorum* in his first draft of the text, but rather that, as an unfinished or rapidly terminated draft, Isidore had not yet set the title in the manuscript. The transmission of this version could have been without a title, allowing the title to develop along with the culture in which the text was reproduced. That the draft lay without a title and was imagined precisely as a draft of the *De Origine Gothorum* seems evident from Braulio's account of it in the *Renotatio*, in which he places the *De Origine Gothorum* late in the works of Isidore.

Overall, the evidence indicates that Isidore's imagined title for the text was the *De Origine Gothorum*. That he thought of it as such, and specifically not as a *Historia Gothorum*, is important, as is the point that the original title, for example, of the *Etymologies* was the *Origines*, and not, for example, *Historiae*. This reveals a lot about Isidore's intentions and attitudes about "*origines*" as an historical method. For the sake of convenience, *De Origine Gothorum* will be used as shorthand for the sequence of texts that includes it, the histories of the Vandals and Sueves, and the two laudatory texts, except when the latter are referred to directly.

What, though, is the extended historical significance of the title *De Origine Gothorum*? What are the structure and contents, and perhaps plot, of the *De Origine Gothorum*?[59] How are these entangled in a dialectics of meaning of the Isidore-moment? How do these affect the *De Origine Gothorum* as a multi-layered narrative, one which soothed Visigothic monarchs and select factions of nobles while also condemning them spiritually and politically?

The *De Origine Gothorum*, it has been argued, had no historiographical models when it was constructed.[60] To what extent this is true is arguable, but what is clear is Isidore's "ingenuity [...] in the way he transforms the meaning of his sources." This ingenuity is often interpreted as the ability to use antithetical texts to apparently praise the Goths, and Spain. Hillgarth suggests that Isidore changes a passage in Cyprian where he had questioned the security of even the richest of this world.[61] Isidore, in contrast, Hillgarth maintains, affirms that the "Gothorum florentissima gens" enjoys Spain and its great riches "(opes

---

58   For a list of manuscripts, see *Las Historias de los Godos*, ed. Rodríguez Alonso, 123–60.
59   It should be noted that some early medieval historians consider Bede to be the first writer of the period to develop plots. See, for example, Goffart, *Narrators*, 17.
60   Merrills, *Geography and Late Antiquity*, 173.
61   In a letter to Donatus, Cyprian (*Ep.*, 1.13) asks "An tu vel illos putas tutos, illos saltem inter honorum infulas et opes largas stabili firmitate securos, quos regalis aulae splendor fulgentes amorum excubantium tutela circumstat?" For the edited letters of Cyprian see

largas), imperii felicitate secura."[62] This can, however, be read in another way. In his *Sententiae*, Isidore warns that one should not indulge in self-confidence about one's salvation, no matter who the person or group may be.[63] In the *Synonyma*, Isidore warns: "nulla te securitas deceptum blandiatur."[64] Given the attitudes of Gundemar and Sisebut, and perhaps of Swinthila after his major military victories, this could be a warning or critique about the place of the Goths in salvation, compounded by their association with empire.[65] This, then, could read as a veiled critique made with flattering words about their security in the present, temporal world. Isidore's superficial praise for broader Hispania should not be taken for granted as such, since, for example, Isidore chose not to use Prudentius's patriotic images of the peninsula. Goffart contends that in "the guise of a Gothic history, the *Getica* celebrates Justinian's" conquests.[66] It may be fair to say that Isidore's *De Origine Gothorum* is a guise too: a veneer of support for the powers of Toledo over a subtle and consistently abusive narrative meant to promote, instead, Seville and its school. The use of the aera dating system confirms an official audience, while also providing a "legal" status to the text, potentially to comic effect for the Scripturally learned audience.[67]

As suggested by its full title of *De Origine Gothorum et Regno Suevorum et etiam Vandalorum Historia librum unum*, the *De Origine Gothorum* is part of a textual unit that includes an explicit *historia* of the Vandals and origins for the Goths, with the kingdom of the Sueves serving the mediating position, not an origins story or a history proper, yet a bit of both. The sequence of origins-stories and histories, with the mediating story of the Sueves is, as a nominative structure, meant to highlight the contrast between the stories, a

---

Cypriani episcopi Epistularium, Sancti Cypriani episcopi opera, ed. G. F. Diercks, Corpus Corpus Christianorum Series Latina 3b–c, 2 vols. (Turnhout: Brepols, 1994–1996).

62 For the ingenuity quote, see Hillgarth, *Visigoths in History and Legend*, 36, and n. 33 on that page for a short discussion and bibliography.

63 Isid., *Sent.*, 1.29.7.

64 Isid., *Synonyma*, 2.25. For the *Synonyma*, see the editions and important discussions, respectively, in Antonio Viñayo González, ed. and trans. (Sp.), *San Isidoro de Sevilla "Sinónimos"* (León: Universidad de León, 2001); *Isidori Hispalensis episcopi Synonyma*, ed. Jacques Elfassi, Corpus Christianorum Series Latina 111B (Turnhout: Brepols, 2009); and, di Sciacca, *Finding the Right Words*, 16–36. See also the English translation in Priscilla Throop, trans., *Isidore of Seville's "Synonyms" ("Lamentations of a Sinful Soul") and "Differences"* (Charlotte: Medieval MS, 2012), 9–85. For the quote above, *Isidori Hispalensis episcopi Synonyma*, ed. Elfassi, 81–82, ls. 244–247.

65 In the *De Origine Gothorum*, Isidore refers to the Visigothic kings as having an empire (see, for example, ch. 49).

66 Goffart, *Narrators*, 109.

67 On the ideological function of the aera dating system and its particular uses by Seville, see Handley, *Death, Society and Culture*, 135–39.

feature that is characteristic of Visigothic literature and rhetoric.[68] One might call the *De Origine Gothorum* a *historia tripartita*.[69] If this was Isidore's plan, he may have had one of several models in mind, such as Cassiodorus's/Jordanes's triple structure or Epiphanius's sixth-century *Historia Tripartita*. It may also be part of the spiritual-historical significance of Isidore's three-ages theory of universal history. It seems that Isidore did not know of Augustine's vision of the Six Ages when he first drafted the *De Origine Gothorum* in the 610s. In the sixth book of the *Origines*, written in the 610s, Isidore divides the history of the world into three ages, not six.[70] He also does so in his exposition on the Old Testament.[71] In the first recension of the *Chronicles*, written around 615, Isidore did not include any reference to the ages of the world. It was not until his later recension, around 627, that he would include Augustine's theory of the Six Ages.[72] This pattern of non-usage and usage of Augustine parallels that of versions of the *De Origine Gothorum* as well. In the first draft (the short recension), for instance, Isidore relies on a non-Augustinian source for his account of the sack of Rome by Alaric I. It is possible that in the 610s Isidore lacked access to important Augustinian texts, including sections of the *De Civitate Dei*. In fact, in a letter to Braulio, written in the 610s, Isidore asks Braulio

---

68 Pizarro, *The Story of Wamba*, 84–85.
69 See Goffart, *Narrators*, 20–111, on the tripartite structure of Jordanes's work, and on Epiphanius see McKitterick, *History and Memory*, 233–44.
70 Isid., *Orig.*, 6.17.16. It should be noted that in his *Differentiae*, written some time before 615, Isidore has a chapter (13) titled *De rerum gradibus*, in which he discusses the six categories of entities. His aim is to expose a six-part layering of the bodies and language of consciousness, being, and existence. For editions, discussion and translation of Isidore's *Differentiae* see *Isidoro de Sevilla Diferencias Libro I*, ed. Carmen Codoñer (Paris: Belles Lettres, 1992); *Liber differentiarum I*, ed. Faustino Arevalo, Patrologia Latina 83.9–70; and, *Isidorus Hispalensis Liber Differentiarum II*, ed. María Adelaida Andrés Sanz, Corpus Christianorum Series Latina 111A (Turnhout: Brepols, 2006), and translation: *Isidore of Seville's "Synonyms" (Lamentations of a Sinful Soul) and "Differences"*, trans. Priscilla Throop (Charlotte: Medieval MS, 2012).
71 Isid., *Expositio in Vetus Testamentum, Genesis* 18, ls. 1527–32: "Triduum autem illud in quo venerunt ad locum immolationis, tres mundi aetates significat: unam ante legem, aliam sub lege, tertiam sub gratia. Ante legem, ab Adam usque ad Moysen, sub lege, a Moyse usque ad Ioannem, inde iam a domino. Et quidquid restat, tertius dies est gratiae. In qua tertia aetate, quasi post triduum, sacramentum sacrificii Christi completum est." For the edited text and introduction see *Isidorus episcopus Hispalensis, Expositio in Vetus Testamentum: Genesis*, ed. and intro. Martine Dulaey and Michael M. Gorman (Freiburg: Herder, 2008), and page 58 for the lines quoted above.
72 For a discussion of the use of the adoption of Augustine's Six Ages see Wood, *Politics of Identity*, 123–24.

to send him Augustinian texts and acquaint him with Augustine.[73] If nothing else, this makes the relationship between Seville and Zaragoza much more reciprocal than it has been generally perceived to have been. It might be wondered, though, that if Isidore had had the three-age spiritual-historical model in mind with the first draft of *De Origine Gothorum*, would he not have altered the structure in the later version, as he incorporated the six-age model into the later *Chronicles*? In defense, it could be pointed out that the *Chronicles*'s purpose was not the same as that of the *De Origine Gothorum*, but also that the six-age model did not replace the three-age model in the revised *Chronicle*, or Isidore's wider works. It survived together as a complement to it, so there was no need for a change to the tripartite structure of *De Origine Gothorum* for it to maintain its spiritual-historical significance.[74] Although, "c'est parce qu'à l'exemple d'Augustin Isidore a voulu être la conscience chrétienne de l'Espagne de son temps, qu'il a conçu et exécuté la plupart de ses oeuvres," Isidore's doing so may have been, at times, more by Augustine's reputation in the peninsula than by way of an Augustinian hermeneutics.[75]

Ultimately, Isidore's use of origins-stories and history most closely resemble that used by Jordanes, or, as it may be, Cassiodorus. Isidore read some of Cassiodorus's works, although whether he ever read Cassiodorus's lost narrative of the Gothic past, or Jordanes's revision of it, is unknown. It has been argued widely that Isidore had no access to Jordanes's text, yet the similarities of the titles – *De Origine Gothorum* and *De Origine Actibusque Getarum* (referred to in shorthand as *Getica*) – is striking. It is commonly accepted that Isidore never, though, encountered the presumed Cassiodorian original or Jordanes's *Getica*.[76]

In conclusion, the form, content and names of the *De Origine Gothorum* sequence are intimately entangled with each other, and with Isidore's wider

---

73 *Ep.*, 1: "Dum pariter essemus, postulavi te, ut mihi decadem sextam sancti Augustini transmitteres; posco ut quoquomodo me cognitum ei facias." The "*ei*" could refer either to *Augustini* or to *decadem sextam*, although the latter seems the more correct choice given subject of the sentence. If so, Isidore would be asking only for assistance or acquaintance with that book.

74 See Wood, *Politics of Identity*, 123–28.

75 The quote is from Fontaine, *Isidore de Seville et la Culture Classique*, 876.

76 The relationship between Isidore's *De Origine Gothorum* and Jordanes's *Getica* is a complicated one. Walter Goffart is convinced that Isidore knew nothing of Jordanes's *De Origine Actibusque Getarum* when he wrote the *De Origine Gothorum* (Goffart, *Narrators*, 110). Hillgarth suggests that Isidore may have known Cassiodorus's historical work. Merrills too is less negative than Goffart in his response to this old question, saying instead that a "few echoes" can be found. In general, Merrills separates himself from Goffart's interpretations of Jordanes's *Getica*, for example, in emphasizing Jordanes's commitment to the prehistorical origins of the Goths, as an exercise in itself, as opposed to, according to Goffart, the importance of it later in the narrative, and the potential audience in Italy (Hillgarth, "Historiography in Visigothic Spain," 295, and Merrills, *History and Geography*, 174).

political concerns. They are also fundamentally part of Isidore's, and Braulio's, spiritual concerns and the project to advance the school of Isidore-Seville and preserve the autonomy of the Church from the Gothic monarchy. The entanglements of form, content and nomination allowed Isidore to develop a multi-layered text that could, as such, rival that being produced at the same time in Toledo by the king's circle, for example, the *Vita Desiderii*. Turning now to the details of Isidore's concepts of history, the use of history-writing and several examples of subtle criticisms hidden by an aesthetics of support help to show how the *origines* provide a veneer of cooperation covering a fierce struggle between competing networks of power and authority.

3   Isidore's [Use, Abuse and Philosophy of] History

3.1   *Introduction*

"Theory" and "philosophy" are not interchangeable words or concepts; each has its own conditions and contingencies, and is not the same in meaning, expression or form. What I call Isidore's philosophy of history has effectively been mentioned before, but is usually referred to as his concept, idea, theory or other categorizing noun. The most suitable phrasing, other than philosophy of history would be "theory" of history. I have chosen not to use this terminology because it suggests a one-dimensional, orthodox approach to Isidore's thinking about history and the past. Philosophy is, on the other hand, the general act of thinking. Isidore's thoughts and sentiments on the past are precisely of this complexity, *sententiae*, and it is in Isidore's text of that name that we first see his definitions of history. Thus, it is proper to refer to Isidore's philosophy of history, which includes his historical methodologies and theories of the past and historiography.[77]

The historian of today is often restrained by the "prison-house" of academic language when attempting to discuss history-writing in the early middle ages, lacking the terminology as well as the diversity of (historical) narrative or representational forms to do it justice.[78] In the early middle ages, the construction

---

[77]   The definition and interpretation of "philosophy" as the generic act of thinking is built from the work of various "non-philosophers," including Jean-Jacques Rousseau, Friedrich Nietzsche, Ludwig Wittgenstein, Alain Badiou, and François Laruelle. For a discussion see Alain Badiou, *Wittgenstein's Anti-Philosophy*, trans. Bruno Bosteels (New York: Verso, 2011), and François Laruelle, *Principles of Non-Philosophy*, trans. A. P. Smith (London: Bloomsbury, 2013).

[78]   For important discussions on issues of modern narrative performances of the "before now" see Fredric Jameson, *The Prison-House of Language: A Critical Account of Structuralism and Russian Formalism* (Princeton: Princeton University Press, 1972); Harry

of textual discourses about the past was a plural activity, in which the author had an array of accepted methods, some classical and others developed in late antiquity, to build their narratives. Late antiquity and the early middle ages were dynamic periods in the historiography of history: *the* past was not yet a concept as such.[79] What had happened "before now," was not a total experience of a single group, whether Roman, Christian, human, animal, nature, etc., but a diverse world of experiences and existences performing life to the tune of multiple possible imagined pasts. Today, historians tend to be in a less creative position, for a variety of reasons, not the least of which is the recent century of "exceptional" political and social events, the gradual collapse of Western democracy, and a decreasingly plural political world.[80] Whatever the reason, although we have multiple accepted methodologies and interpretative paradigms for researching and interpreting the past, "history" is ultimately the only generic concept used for thinking about the "before now." This requires the historian to refer to a variety of modes of representing the "before now," any imagined timelines or collections of times in which space-time are not yet permanently affixed, as historical writing, history, or historiography. This fails to capture the uniqueness of the modes for presenting what is "before now." This chapter passes through the various modes available to Isidore for representing the past – especially origins-stories and histories – in the course of teasing out the differences between them and the significance of their structural application. To prevent confusion, "history" in quotation marks is used to refer to early medieval methodology. When discussing the aesthetics of the past as a whole, or in general, the modern expression, history, is used, without any markings.

3.2 *History, Origins, and Chronicles*

In the sections below, it is shown how Isidore used history-writing to proliferate a struggle against the growing authority of the church and monarchy in Toledo, and its school. To make this evident, select content of the texts and manuscripts are discussed and partly deconstructed, and it is shown how important the naming and narrative forms of the text are in shaping both the superficial

---

Harootunian, "Uneven Temporalities/Untimely Pasts: Hayden White and the Question of Temporal Form," in *Philosophy of History After Hayden White*, ed. Robert Doran (London: Bloomsbury, 2013), 119–150; and, Elizabeth A. Clark, *History, Theory, Text: Historians and the Linguistic Turn* (Cambridge: Harvard University Press, 2004), esp. chs. 3 and 4.

79 On this, see the early chapters of Schiffmann, *The Birth of the Past*.

80 On the role of "exception" as an authoritative device in narratives of politics and history, see Carl Schmitt, *Political Theology: Four Chapters on the Concept of Sovereignty*, trans. George D. Schwab (Cambridge, MA: MIT Press, 1985), and, Giorgio Agamben, *State of Exception* (Chicago: University of Chicago Press, 2008).

and the sublimated, mystical intentions.[81] The aim of this section on Isidore's philosophy of history is to establish the meaning of historical-literary form for Isidore. In recent years, scholars have elaborated on the spiritual significance of language, of words, for the bishop of Seville, as evidenced in his *Synonyma*, *Differentia*, *Origines*, and elsewhere. The centrality of numbers, and law, has been less studied. However, when it has been, and when one examines Isidore's work in this field, it is evident that numbers and law are also part of the same "language of salvation": the plurality of form for history-writing served no less a purpose than this for Isidore.[82] In addition to providing entertaining media for political satire, beneath a veil of political expediency and cooperation, methods of history-writing and forms of expressing the past, in creating imagined pasts, gave Isidore a fierce pedagogical device that could shape memory and teach salvation. In using historical references and allusions about baptism and conversion, and in tying salvation to action – it is continuous effort that is spiritually beneficial, not the possession of ornament, whether *ornamenta verborum* or *ornamentum orbis* – but also historical determination, Isidore could effectively decide who was, and who was not, meant for salvation.[83] He did so through the content in the texts, but also by entangling that with the historical-literary form applied. It is especially the structural relationship between "history" and "origins-stories" with which Isidore had the most fun. It was the most effective antagonism of historical form used by him in promoting Seville against Toledo and in subtly, yet viciously, condemning the Gothic power structure, under a veneer of *loyalisme*.

---

81   As Merrills argues: "It is through the recognition of the demands of literary form that we can explain the huge generic variety that marked the historiography of the period (Merrills, *History and Geography*, 33)."

82   Karl-Ferdinand Werner, "Gott, Herrscher und Historiograph. Der Geschichtsschreiber als Interpret des Wirken Gottes in der Welt und Ratgeber der Könige," in *"Deus qui mutat tempora." Menschen und Institutionen im Wandel des Mittelalters. Festschrift für Alfons Becker*, ed. Ernst Dieter Hehl, Hubert Seibert, and Franz Staab (Sigmaringen: Thorbecke, 1987), 1–31.

83   Isid., *Diff.*, 2.39 (see also *Diff.*, 2.38): "Rerum enim studia prosunt, non ornamenta verborum;" and, *De Laude Spaniae*, ls. 5–7: "tu decus atque ornamentum orbis, inlustrior portio terrae, in qua gaudet multum ac largiter floret Geticae gentis gloriosa fecunditas." In *Diff.*, 2.40, Isidore divides ethics into four virtues: prudence, justice, fortitude, and temperance. Prudence, the first order of moral philosophy, is the recognition of the true faith and knowledge of Scriptures. It is through prudence that one must look at three modes of understanding: the first and foremost among these modes of knowledge of the Scriptures through moral philosophy is the knowledge of how things are accepted historically, without any obvious reference to a spiritual figure; the second is through belief in real events as such and as metaphors; third is by spirituality only.

3.2.1 Philosophy of History

Isidore's philosophy of history is an "evental" one, operating, as such, on two complementary levels. On the one hand, the "historical narrative gains its effect as an explanation by its revelation of the deeper meaning of the events it depicts through characterization in figurative (mystical) language."[84] On the other hand, the significant events in the narrative operate as nodes both for alternative historical or *origines* paths, and to signal the defining characteristic of an individual, place or group. As a category, Isidore says that history should preserve fidelity (faith), and so we must interpret it morally and comprehend it spiritually in order to preserve fidelity to the event, for example, of conversion.[85]

The evental as historical category, and history as a narration of fidelity, is not only a reminder of the direction of one's faith, whether proper or incorrect, or conscious or unconscious, but also a reminder that fidelity to this event should never reach completion in life. One should be nominated according to the event, e.g., as converted. Hence, Isidore's insistence that true conversion, fidelity to the event of true conversion, is a life-long process, one that is never completed and never reaches nomination. If and when conversion is forced, it is a false, nominated, truth, that is, once a truth becomes a name, a declared meaning, it retreats as a truth: Isidore was firmly against the act of forcing a truth. He felt that true belief was the product of a long process of thinking within a situation, and then the final announcement of the excess within one's knowledges. It is possible to say that Isidore's theory of monarchy and production of historical texts antagonistic to Toledo are a traumatic "acting-out" against actions by recent kings. They are, like his works on words, language and etymology, an "acting-out" against the forced [nominations of] conversions by Sisebut.[86]

3.2.2 Isidore and Popular Perceptions of History

What is "history" for Isidore, and what is the difference between "history" and other forms of representing the "before now"?[87] Historians have generally

---

84 Hayden White, "Historicism, History, and the Figurative Imagination," *History and Theory* 14 (1975): 63.

85 Isid., *Sent.*, 1.18.12: "[...] historiae oportet fidem tenere, ut eam et moraliter debeamus interpretare, et spiritaliter intelligere."

86 On the concept of historical writing as an "acting-out" of a single or collective trauma see Dominick LaCapra, *Writing History, Writing Trauma* (Baltimore: The Johns Hopkins University Press, 2001). On forcing, see Alain Badiou, *Conditions*, trans. Simon Corcoran (New York: Continuum, 2008, orig. 1992), 113–44, and, Katerina Kolozova, *Cut of the Real: Subjectivity in Poststructuralist Philosophy* (New York: Columbia University Press, 2014), 5. On Isidore's other texts as the "acting-out" of trauma see Chapters 4 and 5.

87 Julian of Toledo's history sequence, including "*historia*" and *insultatio*, operated in similar rhetorical fashion to Isidore's *De Laude Spania* and *De Origine Gothorum* sequence,

been dissatisfied with Isidore's historical method and philosophy of history: E. A. Thompson said about "the *History of the Goths* by St. Isidore of Seville," that, "as a history it is unworthy of the famous savant who wrote it." Luis Vázquez de Parga said that Isidore simply did not have the temperament of a historian. Ernst Brehaut declared that Isidore's "view of the past had no perspective."[88] Jacques Fontaine challenged existing views of Isidore's historical writings as worthless and unsophisticated. Appreciating the role of contemporary events, the meaning of history as a cultural product and the consistent epistemological function of Isidore's works, Fontaine re-evaluated Isidore's competency as a historian on grounds familiar to Isidore, within Isidore's own cultural milieu in which "les hommes du VIIe siècle (Isidore included) ont d'abord eu l'ambition d'écrire et de construire pour leur temps." The tradition that built up around Fontaine's re-interpretation is evident in the writings of Paul Merritt Basset, Marc Reydellet, Pierre Cazier, Andrew Merrills, Jamie Wood, and others.[89]

Since Fontaine and Reydellet, historians have begun considering Isidore's historical output as an oeuvre more related to his wider work, that his philosophy of history is not isolated from his ideology.[90] Goffart argued that historians should read the historical writings of early medieval authors within the contexts of their oeuvre, as well as within the contexts of their lives.[91] Jamie Wood has convincingly shown the integrity of Isidore's history-writing as a collection. However, we do not need to wait until Reydellet, Goffart and Wood for these important conclusions. Ildefonsus already in the 660s considered Isidore's history-writing as a single oeuvre, one with exceptional ideological significance, so much so that Ildefonsus decided to cut it, as a whole, from Isidore's list of publications. Isidore's history-writing can be viewed, fairly, as one expressive of his historical philosophy, but also of his abilities to weave that into popular

---

but perhaps with inverted intentions. For discussion on these connections, see Michael McCormick, *Eternal Victory: Triumphal Rulership in Late Antiquity, Byzantium and the Early Medieval West* (Cambridge: Cambridge University Press, 1990), 326, and Martínez Pizarro, *The Story of Wamba*, 154–59 and 222–30.

88   Thompson, *Goths in Spain*, 7; Vázquez de Parga, "Notas sobre," 100: Isidore "no tenía temperamento de historiador;" and Ernst Brehaut, *An Encyclopedist of the Dark Ages: Isidore of Seville*, Columbia University Studies in Economics, History and Public Law 48 (New York: Columbia University Press, 1912), 80.

89   Fontaine, *Isidore de Seville*, II, 737; Cazier, *Isidor de Séville*; Paul Merritt Basset, "The Use of History in the *Chronicon* of Isidorus of Seville," *History and Theory* 15 (1976): 278–92; Merrills, *History and Geography*; and, Wood, *Politics of Identity*.

90   See Reydellet, "Les intentions idéologiques," 363–400, and Marc Reydellet, *La Royauté dans la littérature latine de Sidoine Apollinaire à Isidore de Séville* (Rome: École Française de Rome, 1981), 505–97.

91   For some important clarifications on the general misreading of Goffart and literary theory in early medieval research see Martínez Pizarro, "Ethnic and National History," 47.

beliefs about history, to the benefit of his chains of meaning. The actualization of his philosophy of history in the form of a collection of diverse narrative structures allowed him an exceptionally wide option of literary language, tropes and types of figuration, or mysticism, by which to build multi-layered, falsely objective, authorially absent narratives.

For Isidore, "history" is narrative (*historia est narratio*).[92] This was a view common at the time, as seen in a letter between a monk, Mauricius, and the metropolitan bishop of Narbonne, in the early 610s, in which "history" is equated with narration.[93] However, "history" is not simply narrative for Isidore, it is *argumentum*, a term which implies narrative deception, and can be translated as "riddle," "trick," "sinister argument," or "plausible narration."[94] As "plausible narration," history as narrative always has at least two, and often three, layers of interpretation: the literal, the tropological, and the spiritual (mystical), or: body, language, and truth. The truth is hidden beneath bodies and languages, which are used to reveal the truth by those who are faithful to the Christ event, by the act of continuous life-long conversion. Without the mystical interpretation, the truth of the text is lost; it takes a true convert to read this level. We might even say that the body-language-truth triplet refers to Isidore's *De Origine Officiorum*, *Origines* and *De Origine Gothorum*: that is, to the origins of the church offices (the body of the church), of languages, and the historically-derived truth, "truth from pasts," except that each text produces its own truths by its own procedure.

For Isidore, literature, as a topos, (de)serves a place in universal history. Moreover, worldly history could, under the right conditions, be of the same essence as divine history, the Incarnation being the proof.[95] Such considerations allowed Isidore to create powerfully adaptive and effective political, social and spiritual texts from non-Christian ones, to re-construct Christian texts, and to treat the Bible as a collection of historical accounts. Isidore freely

---

[92] Or as Hayden White so aptly says in *Metahistory* (385), "Since the historian's main task is representation of the actual, his sifting of the documents is merely preparatory to the fulfillment of his principal aim: narration."

[93] *Ep. Wis.* 18: "Hos namque et alios quam plurimos Dei notatos electione multum sacra narrat historia, quos nec tempori nec loci coarctat necessitas per ordinem replicare." The see of the bishop referred to, Agapius, is uncertain, but it is most likely that he was the bishop of Narbonne. For a brief discussion see García Moreno, *Prosopografía*, no. 223.

[94] Isid., *Orig.*, 1.41.1 and 1.44.5. On the meaning of *argumentum* see Curtius, *European Literature*, 452–55, and *The Etymologies of Isidore of Seville*, ed. Barney et al., 67. In Roman law, *argumentum* is a general term for evidence (for reference see Alfred Berger, "Dictionary of Roman Law," *Transactions of the American Philosophical Society*, New Series 43 [1953]: 333–809).

[95] Isid., *Orig.*, 1.43.1, and 3.25.1–26.1; Isid., *De Fide Catholica*, 1.5.1–11 (Patrologia Latina 83, cols. 460–62); and, *De Fide Cath.*, 1.61.1–9 (Patrologia Latina 83, cols. 496–98).

interjects mythical and worldly figures with biblical ones. For example, in the greater *Chronicles*, Prometheus, Minerva, Athena, Atlas and Serapis appear together with the biblical Jacob and Joseph, and two chapters place Moses and the Oracle of Delphi on a familiar elevated plateau.[96] This conflux of characters presents the modern reader with a confusing hybrid story of a Christian-pagan past, like a novel built from the major events and characters of other ones. It is as if Stephen Dedalus could at any moment discuss theology with Alyosha Karamazov or philosophize with Pierre Bezukhov.

For his contemporary audiences, Isidore was able to play on shared notions of origins and universality to create contemporarily relevant historical narratives. He could also use this fusion as a multi-layering technique, to present an ideology of cooperation with Toledo over antagonistic criticisms of the monarchy and its church in the *sedes regia*.[97]

The relationship between "history" and the construction of multi-layered figurative historical narrative seems to be deeply embedded in Isidore's philosophy of history and popular conceptions of "history," and the differences between histories and origins-stories. Isidore uses the intriguing and rare term *historialiter* ("historically") on multiple occasions in his texts.[98] However, Isidore never once applies it in any of his "historical" writing, despite at least once suggesting its historiographical meaning.[99] It appears in the Gothic narrative of the *De Origine Gothorum*, but not in the histories of the Vandals or Sueves, or the *Origines*. Why? "History," or "historical" action, was not only fundamentally entangled with political intrigue and active propaganda, but also with "spiritual warfare." In contrast to origins-stories, historical action was intimately tied to heresy or some other form of non-salvific future, a didactic role consistent with Isidore's interpretation.[100]

---

96   Isid., *Chron.*, 38–53, 55, and 56.
97   On the culture of Christianizing the past in late antiquity see Bowes, "Ivory Lists: Consular diptychs," and, Arnaldo Momigliano, "Pagan and Christian Historiography in the Fourth Century AD," in *The Conflict between Paganism and Christianity in the Fourth Century*, ed. Arnaldo Momigliano (Oxford: Oxford University Press, 1963), 79–100.
98   Isid. *Diff.*, 2.29; *Proemia*, 63; *Quaestiones in Vetus Testamentum*, 1.1 and 14.14; *Contra Judaeos*, 9.13; *De Origine Officiorum*, 38.1; and, in *Allegoriae Quaedam Sacrae Scripturae* ch. 21 he uses the word *historialem*. It is also used, interestingly, in a mid-/later-seventh century text previous believed to be Isidore's, the *Liber de Ordine Creatararum* at 10.4 and 10.7. For more, see Marina Smyth, "The Seventh-Century Hiberno-Latin Treatise *Liber de ordine creaturarum*: a translation," *The Journal of Medieval Latin* 21 (2011): 137–222.
99   Isid., *Quaes. in Vet. Test.*, 1.1, ls. 73–75 (Gorman, ed., p. 4): "Creatura caeli et terrae quomodo historialiter ab exordio principii condita sit legimus; sed qualiter in ecclesia spiritaliter a doctoribus accipiatur, intellegamus."
100 Isid., *Orig.*, 1.43.

This meaning is consistent with literary and popular culture in the peninsula at the time, on both sides of the Visigothic-Byzantine "border."[101] In 615, Sisebut sent a letter, through his envoy Ansemund, to Caesarius, a patrician in Byzantine Spania. In it, he talks explicitly about the uses of history in the shared "spiritual warfare" (*spiritale bellum*) going on in Byzantine *Spania* and Visigothic *Hispania*: "Aliquae sane vestris tenentur affatibus, ubi pars figuraliter, pars historialiter intimatur, nonnulla tropicae narrationis obtinet locum."[102] In preserving this tripartite structure of classical narrativity – figuration, history, and tropic narration – Isidore maintains the latter two – history and tropic narration – while replacing the Roman "figuration," figurative or allegorical interpretation, with an explicitly spiritual (mystical) one, a *mystice intellegatur* that imbues allegory with spirituality. In *Sententiae* 1.18.12, Isidore claims that "Lex divina triplici sentienda est modo: primo ut historice, secundo ut tropologice, tertio ut mystice intellegatur. Historice namque iuxta litteram, tropologice iuxta moralem scientiam, mystice iuxta spiritalem intellegentiam." Moreover, for Isidore, wisdom is the power to understand the true meaning behind knowledge, to grasp the significance of (historical) contingency.[103] The evidence from the court in Toledo and the secular authorities in Byzantine Spania suggest their awareness of the "uses and abuses" of "history." The tone of the letter implies that each grasped popular episteme, the historical *a priori*, and imagined a wide audience for historical narration, that the texts of the Baetican "frontiersmen" in Seville, as Fontaine refers to them, were not simply a response to a sort of intellectual "challenge hurled at their own creativity."[104] Finally, in this episode is seen Isidore's awareness of the function of historicality, but also adapting its methodology to his philosophy of history, in which figurative allusion is imbued with absolute mystical significance. The spiritual meaning of the text is the deepest and "truest" layer, lying beneath the historical "facts."[105]

---

101 On the nature and existence of the border between the Byzantine province of Spania and the Visigothic kingdom see Gisela Ripoll López, "On the Supposed Frontier between the Regnum Visigothorum and Byzantine Hispania," in *The Transformation of Frontiers from Late Antiquity to the Carolingians*, ed. Walter Pohl, Ian Wood, and Helmut Reimitz (Boston and Leiden: Brill, 2000), 95–115, and, Wood, "Byzantine Spain," 292–319.

102 *Ep. Wis.*, 4.

103 Isid., *Diff.*, 2.36.

104 Fontaine, "Education and Learning," 741.

105 The "episteme" is what is for Foucault the historical *a priori*, the epistemological conditions through which an historical knowledge can develop and take form. Indebted to Foucault's concept of the episteme, but developing the idea further, Quentin Meillassoux argues that a [historical] "fact" is a representation that aspires to be a correct description of a reality. This represented reality must, however, also explain the conditions for the instance of reality in which the fact occurred. This explanation is what Meillassoux refers to as *facualité*, the "non-factual essence of fact," the necessity of the fact's coming into

3.2.3   History versus Origins-Stories

What is the difference between "history" and "origin-stories"? In the *Origines*, Isidore lays out the historiography of history, from the ancients to his own times, and elicits his matured definitions of "history." There are various types of "history," he says, including daily, monthly and annual, all of which are relatively ephemeral.[106] For Isidore, "history" represents times seen, and as such, events that end, like heresy, the kingdoms of the Vandals and Sueves, and sometimes (fidelity to) a conversion. Isidore defined chronicles, histories, and other types of representing the past, and lays out his philosophy of history in various texts, but he never explicitly addressed the meaning of "origins-stories."[107] Nevertheless, Isidore had a theory of origins-stories, and in using it as his historical narrative for the Visigothic past he was able to open up and play with, and play upon, the popularly perceived notions of "history" and literalness and the more deceptive narrative possibilities for "history" and origins-stories. To be part of "history" is to be left out of salvation. Those included in "history" are those whose pasts, whose identities, and so whose futures, are not connected to a salvific divine event, whether this be the Vandals' overwhelming Arianism, or the Romans' descent from pagan gods, or, in fact, the city of Rome, which lacked any known origin at all.[108] To be part of salvation, and to have authority in the present, one needed a known origin, an origins-story, but also a correct one. It is on the latter point that Isidore's multi-layering of superficial praise with deep theological critique pivots.

Origins-stories are not a type of "history" for Isidore, as, for example, chronicles are: they are categorically different, one might even say, Other.[109] Both forms employ imagined pasts to represent authority in the narrative present, but the ontologies are Other, "being" on the one hand temporal, material, and, on the other hand, universal and salvific. All "being" is from God: "Creator dictus pro totius mundi rebus ab ipso creatis; nihil enim est quod non origine a Deo traxerit."[110] However, not all is destined to return to God, for example, those

---

existence, its conditions. Isidore's *facualité* is a transcendental conditioning of the facts of the recent past and present made apparent by the necessity of Seville. See Michel Foucault, *Les Mots et les Choses* (Paris: Gallimard, 1966), and Quentin Meillassoux, *After Finitude: An Essay on the Necessity of Contingency*, trans. Ray Brassier (London: Bloomsbury, 2012).

106   Isid., *Orig.*, 1.41–44: *diurnus, kalendarius,* and *annales*. For a deconstruction see Henderson, *World of Isidore*, 72–98.
107   Isidore, however, read and cited Cato the Elder's *Origines*, which contained a definition of the genre.
108   Isid., *Orig.*, 15.1. The Romans were descended not from the lineages of Creation, but from Romulus, a direct descendant of Aeneas and so the pagan goddess Venus.
109   For a comparison of histories and chronicles see Wood, *Politics of Identity*, 67–70.
110   The quote is from Isidore, *Orig.*, 7.1.33, but see also *Orig.*, 5.1.1 and 7; 3.2, 9.2, 7.2.28, and 7.14.

in "history." For Isidore, origin implies something far more eternal and significant than "history"; it is what gives salvific meaning and direction, whether it is the origins of words providing them with meaning in the present, or the origins of ecclesiastical offices legitimizing and explaining them, or the use of the past as an "origin" to provide an apparent authority for the Goths.[111] Placing a "being-that-is-in-the-world" (person, group or entity), to adapt Heidegger's *sein und zeit* terminology, into an origins-story emplots them into the universal narrative, as the worldly, thanks to Christ, has this possibility.[112] That which has origins carries on into the final age of judgment, reconciliation and Shabbat. They are tied to the beginning and so simultaneously to the end-beginning, to the re-birth of that of humanity that will have no second death. Second death comes to those with incorrect, non-salvific origins.

3.2.4 Conclusion

To "make [it into] history," so vaunted as the ultimate act of mainstream confirmation in today's Western culture, was not a privileged place in Isidore's philosophy of history. In the historiography on Isidore's historical output, and most early medieval historical literature, it is widely asserted that a place in history could affirm a fortunate and advantaged position, in the world of the present, for those provided with the proper heritage. Weaving a person, empire, kingdom or gens deeply into an imagined past could provide cultural capital in the present.[113] This suggests a deep and shared cultural passion for historical authenticity, even in a society as widely diverse as seventh-century Hispania. The historians associating a group or person to an imagined past could also, however, severely deny them a place in the world. In the historical writing of Isidore, it does both. It affirms the contingent legitimacy in the present of the Visigothic position in broader Hispania, and yet denies a place in salvation. History in the Isidore-moment was used as cultural and spiritual capital.

This deeper layer of sustained theological critique is something that is lost in the post-Isidore-moment "quest for unity" narrative and the long, important

---

111   See *Orig.*, 6.2.51 on the lack of authority of those things that have origins unknown. See also the short note in Peter Brown, *The Rise of Western Christendom: Triumph and Diversity, AD 200–1000* (Oxford: Blackwell, 1996), 219–32.

112   Hayden White, *Metahistory: The Historical Imagination in Nineteenth-Century Europe* (Baltimore: The Johns Hopkins University Press, 1975), 7: "Providing the 'meaning' of a story by identifying the kind of story that has been told is called explanation by emplotment." On the theory of "emplotment," see White's *Metahistory*, and on the differences of "plot" and "story" see *Russian Formalist Criticism: Four Essays*, 2nd edn., ed. Lee T. Lemon and Marion J. Reis (Lincoln: University of Nebraska Press, 2012).

113   Goffart, *Narrators*, 3–19, and Wood, *Politics of Identity*, 1–22.

elaborations on how Isidore constructs the authority of the Visigoths in Spain, to which they are intimately tied. There is no denial of such a surface reading. However, this surface hides an entire world of mystical signification, tropological allusion and virulent, yet subtle political rhetoric and criticisms. To assist in grasping this reading we must keep in mind the events of the 610s with the founding and advancement of Agali, the events of Gundemar and Sisebut, the symptomatic "acting-out" by Isidore in his writing and the subsequent historiography and general competition of the period. Even without the conceptual framework of the Isidore-moment, however, the multivalent and consistent muted criticisms are evident. These would have been obvious to those readers and listeners who were supposed to catch them. Astute historians such as Jacques Fontaine, Roger Collins, Jocelyn Hillgarth, Peter Linehan, and others, have all made reference on occasion to subtly veiled criticisms in the writings from Seville and Toledo, but such references have remained fragmentary.[114] The following elaborates several examples as a way to begin tying together the history of this *convivencia*, the competitive but fruitful discourse that underlay the historical works of Isidore, as shown in the other chapters dealing with the historiography on Isidore and the historically-minded canonical, conciliar and legal codification projects.

4   Conversion and the Locating of Seville

This section illustrates, through several examples, the underlying and delicate critiques against the Visigothic Crown and its network in Toledo. It demonstrates the emplotment in the narrative of Seville as *the* mediator, model and constant source of proper conversion in Hispania, as Isidore's brother Leander had less assertively implied.[115] "Visigoth" will be synonymous here with "Goth," since it is the Visigothic polity or collective of Goths to which Isidore is referring.

---

114   Fontaine points to Isidore's ambivalent attitude towards the Goths (Jacques Fontaine, "Les relations culturelles entre l'Italie byzantine et l'Espagne visigothique: La présence d'Eugippius dans la bibliothèque de Séville," in *Tradition et actualité chez Isidore de Séville*, ed. Jacques Fontaine [London: Variorum, 1998], 9–26, at 10). Collins likewise suggests a "somewhat laissez-faire attitude in Isidore's thinking" about the monarchy in Toledo (as opposed to the rigid loyalism concluded by others). See Roger Collins, "Julian of Toledo and the Royal Succession in Late Seventh-Century Spain," in *Early Medieval Kingship*, ed. Peter H. Sawyer and Ian Wood (Leeds: University of Leeds, 1977), 47, and Collins, *Visigothic Spain* (Malden, MA: Blackwell, 2004), 75–77, n. 36. See also Hillgarth, "Coins and Chronicles," 483–508; Hillgarth, *Visigoths in History and Legend*, 31; and, Linehan, *History and Historians*, 44.

115   Subsequent referencing of the Bible will be from the Vatican's New Vulgate.

4.1 Seville as Model of Conversion

In Isidore's *De Origine Gothorum*, impious and other unfortunate events happen in Seville. That is the expressed historical reality, the world of early medieval Baetica, as the audience would understand it. Seville is not, however, a passive receiver of spiritual abuse. In each and every case in which something heretical occurs, Seville responds triumphantly by defeating the impiety, or with vengeance by divine grace. Faced with the reality of life and of Seville's position as a nexus for political and social activity in the peninsula, Seville, as the true convert, is able to respond appropriately to the events of the world. This model provides some agency in salvation, which is important in Isidore's theology and his warnings (as in the *Synonyma* or at the end of the *Chronicles*) not to speculate on or force the future, but to live and to act in one's own world. Conversion is a life-long and, at times, arduous endeavor, but it is also, as such, a truth contingent upon continuous actions of fidelity by bodies and languages: simply because a monarchy has "converted," for example, it is not destined for a salvific path, done with its task of conversion, or authorized to force speculations about the end or conversions. The embodiment of Seville as the model of conversion and the stories as examples of types of responses to spiritual abuses, combined with subtle criticism of Toledo's spiritual authority – both its monarch's and its Church's – in contrast to that of Seville's, is evident upon close examination of the role of Seville in Isidore's historical texts. Isidore's criticism of forced conversions is not only "opportune," but also endemic across his historical writing.[116]

4.2 Gunderic

The examples provided from the texts will run generally in chronological order. As such, the first is the story of the Vandal king Gunderic's (407–418) entry into Seville. In his *Chronicles* entry for the year 428, Hydatius says that Seville was protected by its Christian orthodoxy from destruction at the hands of the Vandals.[117] As a staunch defender of Seville as the site of orthodoxy in

---

116 For the reference to Isidore's opportunism see Yitzhak Hen, "A Visigothic king in search of an identity – *Sisebutus Gothorum gloriossisimus princeps*," in *Ego Trouble: Authors and Their Identities in the Early Middle Ages*, ed. Richard Corradini, Matthew Gillis, Rosamond McKitterick, and Irene van Renswoude (Vienna: Österreichische Akademie der Wissenschaften, 2010), 95–98.

117 Hydatius, *Chron.* 89: "Gundericus rex Vandalorum capta Hispali, cum impie elatus manus in ecclesiam civitatis ipsius extendisset, mox dei iudicio daemone correptus interiit." All citations of Hydatius's *Chronicles* are from those sections contained within Rodríguez Alonso's edition of the *De Origine Gothorum*, and otherwise to Theodor Mommsen's edition of Hydatius's *Chronicles*, *chron. min.* ii, Monumenta Germaniae Historica, Auctorum

the peninsula, it might be expected that Isidore would maintain this version of events. However, Isidore does not do so. Instead, he provides an alternative narration that defends Seville's spiritual and political authority in a way that was pertinent to the 620s and the plot of the narrative. In Isidore's account, the Vandals destroyed Seville and their king Gunderic attacked the martyrium of Vincentius, a site that is only ever mentioned by Isidore.[118] The impious Gunderic, whose religion is left ambiguous (allowing Isidore to use him as an allusion to any impious monarch), was successful in sacking the city and even taking violent actions against a Catholic religious site.[119] Hopefully, Gunderic enjoyed his spoils while he had them, for as the king was about to leave the city he was struck down and died at the gate of the shrine. As Isidore notes, "multos posse perire ex eis in die iudicii, qui nunc electi esse videntur et sancti, docente propheta."[120] The veiled critique of the royal presumption of power over the spiritual authority of Seville is, in this instance, perhaps not subtle enough: "qui (Gunderic) cum auctoritate regiae potestatis inreverentes manus in basilicam Vincentii martyris civitatis ipsius extendisset, mox dei iudicio in foribus templi daemonio correptus interiit."[121]

Isidore gives no indication that Seville was to blame for the violence that was done to it. Instead, Seville was a model for piety that taught patience for divine judgment – "Esto patiens, esto mansuetus, esto mitis, esto modestus. Serva patientiam, serva modestiam, serva mansuetudinem. Stude patientiae et

---

Antiquissimorum 11, 1–36). But see also Richard W. Burgess, ed., *The Chronicle of Hydatius and the Consularia Constantinopolitana: Two Contemporary Accounts of the Final Years of the Roman Empire*. (Oxford: Oxford University Press, 1993 [digitized 2017]).

118   The other reference is in chapter 30 of Isidore's *DVI*, produced at about the same time as the *De Origine Gothorum*. Given the rise in popularity of the Zaragozan martyr Vicentius in the earlier 600s, Isidore's creation of the story of Seville protecting him may have been an especially timely way to promote the spiritual authority of Seville and further tie Seville to Zaragoza.

119   Isid., *Historia Vandalorum* (*De Orig. Goth.* 73): "Qui (Gundericus) dum rupto foedere pacis 'Suevorum gentem' in Erbasis montibus obsideret relicta obsidione Suevorum Balearicas Terraconensis provinciae insulas depraedatur. Deinde Carthagine Spartaria eversa cum omnibus Wandalis ad Baeticam transiit Spalim *destruit* actaque caede in direptionem mittit. Qui cum auctoritate regiae potestatis inreverenter manus in basilicam Vincentii martyris civitatis ipsius extendisset, mox dei iudicio in foribus templi daemonio correptus interiit." Rodríguez Alonso prefers to use *diruit* instead of *destruit*, turning Mommsen's editorial choice around. Why Rodríguez Alonso has done so is unclear. *Destruit* is the term used in the oldest securely dated manuscript, Berlin Philipps. 1.885, while *diruit* is only used from the twelfth century. I have chosen to maintain Mommsen's editorial decision on this occasion. However, the meaning of the passage is the same whichever is used.

120   Isid., *Sent.*, 1.29.7.

121   Isid., *Hist. Vand.* (*De Orig. Goth.*, 73).

mansuetudini" – and that an impious monarch would meet their terrible fate soon enough.¹²² Every person should be more concerned with their own life than with wondering about the future: "Unus quisque ergo de suo cogitet transitu, sicut sacra scriptura ait: in omnibus operibus tuis memorare novissima tua, et in aeternum non peccabis."¹²³ The story has parallels to Agila's sacking of Córdoba, narrated later in the *De Origine Gothorum*, and discussed below. For the moment, suffice it to point out an important difference between the accounts: in the attack on Seville, Sevillans never use violence or force against heresy, unlike the Córdobans who take up arms against Agila. In both stories the king is killed by divine justice, but only in the account of Seville do the city and its people restrain from the performance of judgment (thought). This story should be read as a criticism both of the royal power of Toledo against the spiritual authority of Seville and a proliferation of the position against Sisebut's, and any royal, attempt to force conversions or interfere in the Church's spiritual authority. When the version from the shorter and longer recensions of the *De Origine Gothorum* are compared, it is evident that this was a specifically royal critique made during the reign of Swinthila against Sisebut specifically, but perhaps also Swinthila. In the longer version, from around 625, Isidore has Gunderic attack religious authority in Seville on grounds of the *auctoritate regiae potestastis*, thereby associating such [ab]use of power with the subsequent divine vengeance. In the shorter version, Isidore only says: "cum omnibus Vandalis ad Baeticam transiuit captaque Spali cum inreverentes in ecclesias ipsius civitatis manus extendisset, mox dei iudicio daemone correptus interiit." The divine vengeance is enacted because of attacking Seville and the holy site within it, without any reference to the power of royal authority. The subtle critique that Isidore was reluctant to advance in his first draft, he did so in the later. Moreover, we see in the story, as Isidore re-narrates it, not only divine vengeance, but also the model of conversion, re-baptism of the religious site and its city. This alternative narrative serves to emphasize the especial spiritual power and piety of Seville.

In Isidore's narration of events – about twelve years after the Gunderic affair (c. 440) – the Suevic king Recchila conquered Seville. Recchila is not said to have destroyed the city or to have attacked any religious sites. Moreover,

---

122   Isid., *Synonyma*, 2.31.
123   The full quote from Isidore's greater *Chron.* 418 is: "Residuum saeculi tempus humanae investigationis incertum est. Omnem enim de hac re quaestionem dominum Iesus Christus abstulit: non est vestrum nosse tempora vel momenta, quae pater posuit in sua potestate, et alibi, de die autem, inquit, et hora nemo scit neque angeli caelorum nisi solus pater. Unus quisque ergo de suo cogitet transitu, sicut sacra scriptura ait: in omnibus operibus tuis memorare novissima tua, et in aeternum non peccabis."

his son Recchila converts to Catholicism around the same time, or not many years later, certainly before he became king in 448. He married the daughter of the Visigothic king Theoderic, bringing Seville, nuptially, under a Catholic monarch already in 440, long before the Franks or Goths had converted. Even though this marital situation would fail, it adds further depth to the story of Seville's conversion, and serves as a foreshadowing of the conversion of the Goths by Seville.[124]

4.3 Theudisculus

In the forty-fourth chapter of the *De Origine Gothorum*, Isidore provides another example of Seville as the great defender of orthodoxy in Hispania and against impious kings. The example he uses is the short reign and personal life of the Visigothic king Theudisculus (r. 548–549), or Theudegisel, who reigned for the year or two before Agila, the civil war, and the intervention of the Byzantines. As with the story of Gunderic, Isidore subtracts information from his source(s) then uses it to re-write a narrative supporting his agenda. As the royal critique is in the Gunderic story, Isidore adds new information not found in his source for the passage, or in his first draft of the *De Origine Gothorum*.[125] Particularly significant is the reference to the death of Theudisculus in Seville. In this episode, Seville serves as the "vanishing mediator," the character that enters the story to highlight the underlying truth, then disappears or fades away into latency.

According to Isidore, Theudisculus was a vicious, impious king who created a mass of antipathy, with many desiring his death. His major crime, it seems, was turning the wives of elite men into public prostitutes (*prostitutione publica*). A condemnation even harsher than those made by Suetonius against Domitian, who also defiled and abducted the wives of the elite.[126] Isidore

---

124 Isid., *Historia Suevorum* (*De Orig. Goth.*, 85–86).
125 The reference to Seville is only in the longer version of the *De Origine Gothorum* and also not in Isidore's source, which simply reads: *Thiudi mortuo Thiudisculus Gotthos regit an. I m. VII* (Anon., *Consularia Caesaraugusta*, entry for 544). Often referred to as the *Chronicle of Zaragoza*, the newest edition of the text re-nominates it as a *Consularia*. It is suggested that the *Consularia* is a set of annotations on the *Chronicles* of Victor of Tunnuna and John of Biclar, and never transmitted separately from them as a chronicle. For edition and commentary, see *Victoris Tunnunensis Chronicon cum reliquiis ex Consularibus Caesaraugustanis et Iohannis Biclarensis Chronicon*, ed. Cardelle de Hartmann and Collins, and Collins, "Isidore, Maximus and the *Historia Gothorum*," 356.
126 Suet., *De Vitis Caesarum, Domitian*, ch. 1: "Ne exsequar singula, contrectatis multorum uxoribus, Domitiam Longinam Aelio Lamiae nuptam etiam in matrimonium abduxit." For Suetonius, the Loeb Classics volumes are used, but see also Robert Kaster, ed., *C. Suetoni Tranquilli: De Vita Caesarum Libros VIII et De Grammaticis et Rhetoribus Librum*,

condemned prostitution in the strictest of terms. That a king was engaged in the crime of prostitution, in addition to forced adultery and, we may fairly conclude, rape, not only de-legitimizes his right to rule, but it also associates him with heresy. For Isidore, prostitution was intimately tied to paganism.[127] For these crimes, Theudisculus is killed at a banquet in Seville, run-through with a sword by conspirators.

Did the author of the *Vitas Patrum Emeritensium* several years later have Isidore's account in mind when he or she narrated the story of the failed plot to kill Masona in a similar fashion?[128] Whether or not they did, the point of Isidore's story is certainly not that Arian leaders meet horrible fates, since Catholic kings do as well. Witteric (603–610) suffers a similar death: stabbed with a sword by conspirators during a dinner.[129] Reccared's son Liuva (601–603) was also murdered, in even more horrific fashion. Sisebut met an unexpected end, killed by poison. After Reccared, Gundemar is the only Catholic king in the *De Origine Gothorum* to die naturally, without any mysterious circumstances.

The significance of Gundemar's reign to Isidore is discussed in the next chapter, but for now the point is that Isidore's intention in the Theudisculus story is to promote, once again, Seville as the bulwark against royal impropriety and heresy. In contrast to the case of Gunderic's death, which sets up the model response of a conversion community, Theudisculus is killed by human agents. This establishes another option, one with less agency, and more unpredictable, therefore not the primary model for a baptized life: divine grace working through the human body. It is by divine grace that, with minds cleared, the murderers' actions are spiritually acceptable and successful in defending the piety and fidelity of their wives.[130] Divine grace is instilled before man is able to make any judgment or have any corrupting thoughts. The killing was not a forcing of human judgment, since it was pre-thought.[131] Moreover, the stress laid upon the sanctity of marriage is an integral aspect of the wider narrative and should be kept in mind. Finally, if Sisebut did in fact have kinship ties

---

Oxford Classical Texts (Oxford: Oxford University Press, 2016 [digitized, 2018]). Isidore read several texts of Suetonius, as is evident in the *Origines*, but it is not clear if he specifically read the *De Vitis Caesarum*.

127 Isid., *Orig.* 18.42.
128 For further information about the *VPE*, including the edition, authorship and dating, see Chapter 2, note 30 and Chapter 4, note 29.
129 Isid., *De Orig. Goth.*, 58, 57, 61.
130 Isid., *Diff.*, 2.32: "Nullus autem liber arbitrii quidquam potest praevalere virtute, nisi spernae gratiae sustentetur juvamine."
131 Isid., *Diff.*, 2.32, and, Isid., *Synonyma*, 2.7: "Culpam ibi emenda, ubi nascitur; in ipso initio cogitationi resiste, et evades caetera. Adversus initium cogitationis decerta, et vinces; caput cogitationis exclude, et caetera superantur."

with the Ostrogothic Amals, and hence Theudisculus, the criticism of the latter could also have served the purpose of a careful critique of Sisebut's reign. The criticism of Sisebut otherwise is included in the long version of the *De Origine Gothorum*, as is the critique of Theudisculus.

4.4 Agila – Athanagild

The third example is the account in the *De Origine Gothorum* of kings Agila (r. 549–555) and Athanagild (r. 555–567). In this story, Seville plays an active and passive role, as both a scene of the action and as a site from which actors derive for activities elsewhere (e.g. Mérida). Isidore's pattern of constructing the narrative is similar to the examples of Gunderic and Theudisculus above. The role of Seville in the struggle between Agila and the usurper Athanagild is invented by Isidore as part of the maturing of his text in the 620s. Seville is not mentioned in Isidore's source or in the first draft of the *De Origine Gothorum*.[132]

The story goes that Agila led a violent, military campaign against the city of Córdoba. Like Gunderic, he attempted to harm, in some way, a martyrial site. Unlike Gunderic, Agila was successful in having "profanely defiled" (*profanator polluerit*) the holy church of the blessed martyr Acisclus. Isidore is somewhat vague about Agila's reasons for profaning the site. Agila is said to have done so out of contempt for Catholicism ("in contemptu catholicae religionis"), however, there is no mention of Arianism. In fact, like with the associations of paganism above, it seems that Agila's crime was also some sort of pagan ritual involving the bringing of enemies and livestock ("inferret hostiumque ac iumentorum horror") to a holy sepulcher. For these acts, Agila received divine punishment in the form of the death of his son, the confiscation of his treasure, and the loss of extensive forces (presumably those under his son's command). Agila survived, but he lost much of his power, and he also lost his heir to the throne. This may be why he fled directly to Mérida and not to Seville, which refused to accept Agila after his acts in Córdoba and defeated him when he did try to re-enter the city. When Agila returned to Mérida, he was murdered by his own troops. Seville once again had defended the spiritual orthodoxy in Spain against royal interference and aggression.

After Agila's defeat, the Visigoths (the entire Visigothic army), fearing destruction by rival Visigothic kings, and Byzantines, capitulated to the new king in Seville. The messages from Isidore are a bit mixed in this regard. Seville serves as the site where the Visigothic army was subdued and ended,

---

132   The source is *Cons. Caesaraug.* a. 545 & 552: "Thiudisclo mortuo Agila Gotthos regit annos v m. vi & Agilane mortuo Athanagildus, qui dudum tyrannidem absumpserat, Gotthorum rex efficitur. Regnat an. xv."

effectively, the immediate war with the Byzantines. In this way Seville prevented further bloodshed. Seville's role in such a merciful conclusion to war would be a message well encouraged by Isidore. So too would the idea that a Visigothic king's power rests entirely on his connections with Seville. The problem is that Isidore has tough words to say about the usurper Athanagild, calling him a tyrant. This may simply be the result of Isidore's need to sustain the integrity of his monarchy theory – that usurpation is wrong – representing yet another layer of the text. This is supported by the fact that the *way* Athanagild came to power is the only sure criticism Isidore expressed about the king. The only other perceived criticism of Athanagild by Isidore is his relationship with the Byzantines. Isidore says that Athanagild invited the Byzantines, but it is never fully clear from Isidore's texts whether he saw this as a positive or negative factor.

This episode is important as it supports Isidore's running narrative of Seville's defense of orthodoxy and site of religious authority in Hispania. Isidore is diligent in his associating, or not, the Visigothic monarchy with Seville, a reason why he fails to mention the location of Hermenegild, or especially that he had made Seville his capital.[133] The inclusion of Córdoba in the story of Agila is significant because it was not mentioned in Isidore's sources or in his earlier draft. Isidore's sources associate Athanagild and Liuvigild with actions in Córdoba, but not Agila. Isidore excludes those references to Córdoba and replaces them with the story of Agila in Córdoba.[134] The actions of Agila against Córdoba were developed for the narrative flow and plot of the longer *De Origine Gothorum*. This must be related to the troubles and confusions in the 620s, which included the collapse of the Byzantine province, the crisis of III Seville, and the various legal cases, especially from Córdoba, against Isidore's brother Fulgentius. The invention of the Agila-Córdoba story would have served as a reminder to Córdoba that Seville had an established history of protecting the religious wrongs done to Córdoba, despite anything happening in the present.

---

133 That Seville was Hermenegild's capital see the Seville inscription by Hermenegild and the numismatic evidence in Handley, *Inscriptions and Epitaphs*, 60 and McCormick, *Eternal Victory*, 317. See also recent numismatic works, such as: Ruth Pliego, "La Moneda Visigoda, Anexo I," SPAL: *Revista de prehistoria y archaeología de la Universidad de Sevilla* 21 (2012), 209–232 (215), and 231; Ruth Pliego, *La Moneda Visigoda: Historia Monetaria del Reino Visigodo de Toledo* (c. 569–711), 2 vols. (Seville: Universidad de Sevilla, 2009); and, *Corpus Nummorum Vis.* For forgery of Visigothic coins, especially of Sisenand's, see Ruth Pliego Vázquez, "La falsificación de la moneda visigoda," in *Falsificació i manipulació de la moneda: XIV Curs d'Història monetaria d'Hispania* (Barcelona: Museu Nacional d'Art de Catalunya, Gabinet Numismàtic de Catalunya, 2010), 81–102.

134 *Cons. Caes.*, a. 568, and John of Biclar, *Chron.* a. 572.

There was, Isidore implies, an uninterrupted symbiotic, orthodox friendship between the two cities.

4.5 *Conclusion*

In conclusion, consistent with his historical literature, this model of Sevillan conversion functions on at least two levels. On the one hand, Seville is projected as *the* bulwark of Catholicism, repeatedly avenging the acts of heretical activities and Visigothic kings. It is also a site that exists in the realities of the present. Seville is the mediating site for the conversion of all of Hispania; it is the master-signifier as quilting point performing the (chain of) signification that baptizes the peninsula and so allows salvation since, as Isidore says, to be born only once is to remain forever in sin.[135] Seville's history reveals its consistent and central role in that conversion, and at times foreshadows Zaragoza's coming centrality to it. The audience of the text is witness to various moments along an invented chain of allegorical episodes in which Seville appears as the vanishing mediator and master-signifier that both "sets everything right" and elicits the truth (true meaning of the events).[136] Seville's role in the gradual conversion represents a "mystical level" of the *De Origine Gothorum*, a "true" story of the conversion of Spain with the assistance of Seville, and also Seville's role against royal interference and other rival sites, such as Mérida. Seville is the model of conversion: gradual, realistic, full of real-world challenges, acting with wisdom, divine grace, never speculating about the future, never forcing the process of conversion. The *De Origine Gothorum* is a promotion of Seville's spiritual authority, but it is also laced with a subterfuge of criticism against the Visigothic kings for their actions, their [ab]use of Christianity and the fate-less path upon which they were setting themselves, about which the next section will elaborate.

5 The Goths in Isidore-Seville's Historical Representations

5.1 *Introduction*

The aims of the *De Origine Gothorum* were theo-political, praising proper Catholic conversion and Seville's role in converting the peninsula and kingdom. Seville, it is intended, is to be an icon of Spanish orthodoxy: frozen, sacred,

---

135   Isid., *Orig.*, 8.10.2.
136   On the vanishing-mediator as literary and narrative device see Alain Badiou, *Theory of the Subject*, trans. Bruno Bosteels (London: Continuum, 2009, orig. 1982), and Slavoj Žižek, *For They Know Not What They Do* (New York: Verso, 2002).

and compulsively repeating itself. The Visigoths are a rather stock figure, or even foil, inserted to promote, and to draw out, the character of the true protagonists, Seville and Catholicism, and the struggles against monarchy, impiety, and improper theology. In a master-servant dialectic between Isidore and the Visigoths, the Goths play the role of the fearful servant whose conscious existence depends on the master, rewarded and felicitous when they serve.[137] The Vandals and Sueves are not part of this privileged dialectic.[138] They are examples of the failure to convert and dangers of apostasy, barbarians who do not manage to become part of universal time, for "melius est enim non promittere quam fidem promissi non exsolvere; melius est enim non vovere quam post votum promissa non reddere."[139] The Visigothic kings, once baptized as Catholics, remain so. However, their growing authoritarianism over the Iberian Church and their attempts at totalizing (as part of centralizing) power, coupled with their increasingly zealous theological interpretations and religious actions, anathema to the school of Isidore-Seville's theology from Augustine and Gregory the Great, mean that the Visigoths serve as a model of the "good" barbarian, but they maintain this status only if the master proliferates the fallacy of the dialectical positioning.

5.2 *Gog and Magog*

In the eleventh chapter of the *De Origine Gothorum*, Isidore says that the Goths were brought into the Empire under their king Athanaric, who was invited by the Spaniard and emperor Theodosius in 381 into Constantinople, and soon thereafter died. The Goths, having seen the benevolence of Theodosius, submitted themselves to him. This is the beginning of the Gothic connection to Hispania, which is inaugurated by an allusion to their self-subjugation to it. It is also a reference to their subjugation to the Romans. This situation did not last long. In the very next chapter, the Goths revolt against this submission and famously sack Rome. The latter had not been, it turned out, *imperii felicitate securas*.[140] Like the apocrypha, Isidore says, the city of Rome has no authority because it has no known origins.[141] "I know of no precedent for Isidore's

---

137   On the master-servant dialectic see Chapter 1, note 59.
138   For a new perspective on the Vandal situation and Isidore's employment of the Vandals as a "useful illustration for a complex argument in a carefully crafted history of the Goths" see Andrew Merrills and Richard Miles, *The Vandals* (New York: Wiley-Blackwell, 2010), 6. See also their updated 2014 volume.
139   Isid., *Synonyma*, 2.58. The clause contains a quote by Isidore from *Ecclesiastes* 5.4.
140   Isid., *De Laude Spaniae*.
141   Isid., *Orig.*, 15.1. For secondary discussion see Luis A. García Moreno, "Expectatives milenaristas y escatológicas en la España tardoantigua (ss. v–viii)," *Spania. Estudis d'Antiguitat*

intimate association of Hispania with the Goths," Jocelyn Hillgarth has argued.¹⁴² True as that may be, the Goths, for Isidore, also have a known origins-story, and it begins before their direct association with Spain. In fact, it goes back to the very beginning of Creation: a direct lineage from Adam and Eve.

In the long recension of the *De Origine Gothorum* the Goths are descended from "Gog and Magog." The development of the couplet "Gog and Magog" is a distortion of biblical texts, which develops throughout the course of late antiquity and the early middle ages. In Genesis 10, Magog (מגוג) is the grandson of Noah and son of Japhet. In 1 Chronicles 5, Gog (גוג) is a direct descendant of Shem, Japhet's brother.¹⁴³ Thus, Gog and Magog are related to each other through Noah.¹⁴⁴ The relation is stretched, though, over many centuries. At some point in biblical exegesis, Gog becomes attached to Magog, and together they refer variously to places, to peoples, and as allusions to particular ideas. The confusion is due both to the ambiguity of the Hebrew passages in *Ezechiel*, and to a misreading of the Hebrew.

Isidore makes the Goths direct descendants specifically of Magog and, in so doing, Marc Reydellet rightly argues, is the first author to tie a barbarian group directly with the lineage of Magog.¹⁴⁵ Isidore does not suggest a singular Gothic descent from Gog, but rather, from Magog, saying only that in the

---

Tardana oferts en homenatge al professor Pere de Palol i Salellas (Barcelona: Publicacions de l'Abadia de Montserrat, 1996), 103–09.

142 Hillgarth, *Visigoths in History and Legend*, 35.

143 In the Babylonian Talmud, Og is simply a huge man (Erubin 30a).

144 Interestingly, in the Babylonian Talmud (B Megillah 9b) Japheth equates to Hellenism and Shem is rabbinic Judaism. Moreover, according to the Noahide laws of rabbinic Judaism found in the Talmud (T Avodah Zarah 8.4; b. Sanhedrin 56a–b, and perhaps also referred to in Acts 15), the descendants of Noah are the Gentiles and these gentiles deserve a place in the world to come, even though they are not Jews. So, as a grandson of Noah and son of Japhet, Magog would be a Hellenic (and pagan) gentile. In contrast, Gog as a descendant of Shem, would be a Jew. According to rabbinical thinking, then, Judaism and "Noahide" gentiles are brothers. It is tempting to speculate on Isidore's knowledge of this reading and through it further condemning of the Goths. It is almost certain that Isidore was unaware of the Talmudic traditions, although it is not inconceivable that this thread, at least, circulated in Christian intellectual circles.

145 Isid., *Orig.*, 9.2.27 and *De Orig. Goth.*, 1: "Magog a quo arbitrantur Scitas et Gotos traxisse originem, and, Gothorum antiquissimam esse gentem, quorum originem quidem de Magog Jafeth filio"; see *Etymologies IX*, ed. Marc Reydellet (Paris: Les Belles Lettres, 1984), 55, n. 54 and 91; 93. Arne Søby Christiansen says that already in the fourth century, the Goths were tied to Gog, by Ambrose of Milan. Isidore could have read Ambrose, but he definitely did not copy him, since he tied the Goths specifically, and crucially, to Magog. Gog and Magog should not be conflated in this instance. See Arne Søby Christiansen, *Cassiodorus, Jordanes and the History of the Goths. Studies in Migration Myth* (Copenhagen: Museum Tusculanum Press, 2002), 44, and Ian Wood, Review of Søby Christiansen,

past the Goths have been associated with both Gog and Magog, ancestors of the Scythians (*De Origine Gothorum* short recension) and Goths (*De Origine Gothorum* long recension). Isidore begins the long recension by saying that "Gothorum antiquissimam esse gentem, quorum originem quidem de Magog Jafeth filio suspicantur a similitudine ultimae syllabae." He goes on to say that "Retro autem eruditi eos magis Getas quam Gog et Magog appellare consueuerunt."[146] Isidore not only connects the Goths to Magog, but also, in drawing the distinction between Magog and Gog, he opens important narrativic possibilities.

Josephus (and Jerome) connects the Scythians to Magog.[147] In the short recension of the *De Origine Gothorum*, Isidore ties the Goths to the Scythians, but he cuts the association of either group with Magog (or Gog). When Isidore returned to his text to produce the longer recension, he decided to reintroduce the lineage with Magog. To do so, he replaced the Scythians with the Getae, suggesting that Gog and Magog were synonymous with the Getae. Having already considered the Goths to be the same as the Scythians, a relation which will re-appear in the *De Laude Gothorum*, Isidore makes the seemingly simple move of tying the Goths directly from Magog. There is a very subtle, but important difference between a lineage from Gog or Magog. Descent from either one implies an ancestry tied directly with the origins of Creation. However, only Magog is mentioned in *Genesis*, with Gog in *Ezechiel*, a story with which Isidore had some fun.[148] Isidore, in his expositions on the Old Testament,

---

Cassiodorus, Jordanes and the History of the Goths. Studies in Migration Myth (Copenhagen: Museum Tusculanum Press, 2002), *Historisk Tidsskrift* 103 (2003): 465–84.

146   The line is taken almost exactly from Jerome (see the following note), albeit the meaning is different, since Isidore before draws the evident connection between Goths and Magog.

147   Josephus, *Antiquitates Judaicae*, 1.6, where Josephus says that "Scythian" is an adaptation of Magog by Greeks, cited by Jerome, *Liber Hebraicarum Questionum in Genesim*, 10.2: "Filii Iafeth Gomer et Magog et Madai, et Iauan, et Thubal, et Mosoch, et Thiras [...]. In Europa uero usque ad Gadira, nomina locis et gentibus relinquentes: e quibus postea inmutata sunt plurima. Cetera permanent ut fuerunt. Sunt autem Gomer Galatae, Magog, Scythae [...]. Et certe Gothos omnes retro eruditi, magis Getas quam Gog et Magog appellare consueuerant. Hae itaque septem gentes, quas de Iafeth uenire stirpe memoraui, ad aquilonis partem inhabitant." It should be noted too that for Jerome, the Iberians, Hispali and Celtiberians were descendants not of Magog, but his brother Tubal. Isidore could have used these to tie the Goths to Spain, since this would have made the Goths cousins of these "native" groups. All reference to Josephus is from the Loeb Classical Library edition by H. St. John Thackeray (Cambridge: Harvard University Press, 1965), and for the citation here of Jerome, see Jerome, *Hebraicae quaestiones in libro Geneseos; Liber interpretationis hebraicorum nominum*, ed. Paul de Lagarde, Germain Morin, and Marc Adriaen, Corpus Christianorum Series Latina 72 (Turnhout: Brepols, 1959), 11, ls. 5–24.

148   Ezechiel 38:17 and 39:16.

never mentions Gog or Magog.[149] Isidore wrote these expositions in 624, after he had in various ways analyzed and engaged the New Testament in his writings.[150] This means that the Old Testament texts, which include the referenced discussions of Gog and Magog, were not only known by Isidore at the time of writing the long recension of the *De Origine Gothorum*, but also that questions about it were fresh in his mind. There can only be a very deliberate reason for the unique associations drawn.

Furthermore, this imbued Isidore's text with a poignant power to influence his lay readership in Hispania, royal or otherwise. This is because the Goths were associated in contemporary, popular culture with the Getae, and the Goths themselves seem to have taken some pride in this lineage. This suggests not only that the association was well known, but also that it held cultural capital in Hispania in the early seventh century. This is evidenced by an extant marriage contract from the year 615 from Córdoba, found in the *Formulae Visigothicae*. In it, the Goths are equated with Getae: "Insigni merito et Geticae de stirpe senatus. Illius sponsae nimis dilectae ille. Praemia nubentum ratio praescribere cartis [...]."[151] This was a popular belief with some legacy in early medieval Spain. It can be found at least up to the ninth century, with the heirs of the Gothic nobility proudly referring to themselves as *Getae*.[152] This episode helps to connect Isidore to the mundane world around him. Indeed, it is not the first time in this chapter that we are witness to Isidore's familiarity with popular language, ideas and belief. This shows Isidore's ability to converse with diverse crowds, and his famed "eloquence for every occasion," despite Ildefonsus's subtle but illuminating, and perhaps comical, criticism that listeners of Isidore needed his texts repeated several times before they made any sense.[153]

---

149 Isid., *Expositiones Sacramentorum Seu Quaestiones in Vetus Testamentum*, Patrologia Latina 83, cols. 207–424.
150 As, for example, in his *De ortu et obitu patrum, De nominibus legis et evangeliorum liber*, and the *Sententiae*.
151 *Form. Wis.* 20, in *Formulae Wisigothicae*, ed. Olaitz, 105–12. The *Formulae Wisigothicae* is a Córdoban collection that made its way to Oviedo and was copied, along with other Andalusian manuscripts, into the now lost *Liber Ithatium*. The *Form. Wis.* survived in early modern manuscripts. See *Miscellanea Wisigothicae*, ed. Gil, 10–15; Luis A. García Moreno, "Building an Ethnic Identity for a New Gothic and Roman nobility: Córdoba, 615 AD," in *Romans, Barbarians, and the Transformation of the Roman World*, ed. Ralph W. Mathisen and Danuta Shanzer (Burlington: Ashgate, 2011), 271–82 (273); and, Manuel C. Díaz y Díaz, *De Isidoro al siglo XI* (Barcelona: Ediciones El Albir, 1976), 70ff.
152 See Luis A. García Moreno, "Spanish Gothic Consciousness among the Mozarabs in al-Andalus," in *The Visigoths*, ed. Ferreiro, 303–24.
153 Braulio, *Renotatio* ls. 4–6: "Vir in omni loquutionis genere formatus, ut inperito doctoque secundum qualitatem sermonis existeret aptus, congrua vero opportunitate loci

The elevation of the Getae in the long recension of the *De Origine Gothorum* is more than a sign of Isidore's abilities to satisfy a diverse readership, and to play smartly to it on religious and socio-political sentiments. To elicit the significance, we can return to the king that first introduced the Goths to Hispania: Athanaric. After the death of Athanaric in Constantinople, the Goths selected Alaric as king (in 382). However, in 399, the Goths decided to split, with some following Alaric and others an alternative king, Radagaisus (r. 399–405/409). Several years later they reconciled over the issue of a common enemy: Rome. The story parallels that of the one told about the reigns of Agila and Athanagild, who lead different factions of Goths that came together to fight the Romans. This is not coincidental in Isidore's narrative, for it is the loss of Agila that ends the royal line from Alaric I. Noble factionalism in Gothic society was prevalent all the way through the end of the Visigothic kingdoms. Radagaisus was killed by the Romans some time between 405 and 409. Isidore relates that Radagaisus was a pagan who had made it his mission in Italy to pour out libations of blood to his pagan gods, and for that divine vengeance, or grace, stepped in to settle the matter. Especially important here is that Isidore also claims that Radagaisus was a Scythian.

Thus, to claim that the Goths were descended from the Scythians implies that they were descendants not of Alaric's line, but of Radagaisus's. This somewhat less-than-subtle criticism of the Goths was left out of the *De Origine Gothorum* with the replacement of the Scythians by the Getae. However, the association with the Scythians returns in the *De Laude Gothorum*, which is full of satire, and deep theological critiques. It will be referred to again shortly. Here it should be noted that according to Isidore, Alaric announces, during the sack of Rome, that his fight is not against the Apostles, but against Rome. The story is an invention of Isidore's, and it serves to show the contrast between the two lines of the Goths. It is the (holy) line of Gothic kings from Athanaric and Alaric I that founded the Visigothic kingdoms in Toulouse and Toledo, but which has been extinguished by this point, the potentially salvific line of Gothic leadership is dead. The significance of that is open-ended, but it should be noted that despite the warming Apostles story, Alaric dies after sacking the holy city, as Gunderic, Theudisculus and Agila each died after their impieties. Isidore needed to invent the point about the Apostles in order to prevent his audiences from assuming Alaric's death was from divine justice.

Isidore spent considerable energy to construct an origins-story for the Goths that would superficially tie them to salvation history, provide transparent

---

incomparabili eloquentia clarus;" Ildef., *DVI*, 8, and on Ildefonsus's critique in this passage, Linehan, *History and Historians*, 44.

origins that would promote the Visigothic authority in the present, and flatter common audiences. The significance of the text, the real truth, however, is in the mystical reading. Isidore invented a multitude of new and alternative chains of historical signification, and beneath each are serious criticisms, two of which will be further elaborated.

5.2.1   Gog, Magog, and the Enemies of God
First, in alluding to a Gothic descent from both Gog and Magog, while only specifically referencing Magog in the present, Isidore is able to safely make a damning allusion about the Goths. In the Scriptural passage Isidore refers to, *Ezechiel* 38–39, Gog as a person and people are the ultimate evil.[154] They ride down from the north, vicious, strong and mounted on horses, destroyers of the metaphorical Israel, who will cover the holy land and be wiped out by God to make room for His people. The allusions of Gog to the Goths are extensive. In the *De Laude Gothorum*, which could easily be read as a dark satirical comedy, Isidore "celebrates" how the Goths came down from distant northern lands, caused chaos, and were feared by all of the people of Europe.[155] Moreover, Isidore associates the Goths three times as talented equestrians. This may also be a subtle joke, built from Petronius's *Satyricon*, about the *nouveaux riches* of Toledo.[156] It is hard not to chuckle along sardonically when Isidore asks "Sed quis poterit tantam Geticae gentis edicere virum magnitudinem?"

In *Ezechiel*, Gog is the ultimate metaphor of evil. Moreover, in *Ezechiel* Gog is only ever referred to as Gog (גוג), never as Magog (מגוג). Yet Isidore makes a

---

154 Following the Talmudic tradition (see Chapter 3, note 144), the people of Gog are the Jews.
155 Sons of Japhet that inhabited the area around Crimea and the northern Black Sea, according to Josephus, *Antiquities of the Jews*, 1.6.
156 In hilarious fashion, Petronius, in his *Satyricon*, references the equestrian order and its relationship to the "newly rich," freedmen. Isidore read the *Satyricon*, citing it multiple times in the *Origines*, where he makes it evident too that he was well aware of the place of the equestrian order in Roman society. Other elites at the time probably knew it perfectly well too, as the (late) Roman titular system was still functioning to some degree. The bishop in Toledo at the time the *De Origine Gothorum* was written was Helladius, an Agalian who had been, before entering the monastery, *rector rerum publicarum* (Ildefonsus, *DVI*, 6). For the edited *Satyricon*, see *Satyricon. Apocolocyntosis*, ed. and trans. Michael Heseltine and W. H. D. Rouse, and rev. Eric Herbet Warmington, Loeb Classical Library 15 (Cambridge: Harvard University Press, 1913); and, *Petronius Satyricon Reliquiae*, ed. Konrad Müller (Leipzig and Stuttgart: Tuebner, 1995). For discussions on Isidore's knowledge of the *Satyricon*, or lack thereof, see Jesús Rodríguez Morales, "¿Petronio en la Biblioteca de Isidoro de Seville?," *Helmantica: Revista de filología clásica y hebrea* 43 (1992): 69–77; and, Patrick Breternitz, "Was stand in Isidors Bibliothek? Zur Petronrezeption in den Etymologien Isidors von Sevilla," *Rheinisches Museum für Philologie* 159 (2016): 99–112.

point of saying that the book of *Ezechiel* refers to Magog.[157] This may be a matter of confusion in translation from Hebrew into Greek and then into the Latin that Isidore was using. However, the Vulgate version of *Ezechiel* refers almost exclusively to Gog.[158] In the fourth century, Ambrose of Milan wrote a letter to Emperor Gratian (r. 375–383) to assure him of victory against the Goths, within which he ties the Goths only to Gog. To do so, he cites the same chapters of *Ezechiel* that Isidore later would.[159] Isidore carefully chose to tie the Goths to Magog. Tying the Goths specifically to Magog, while referring to their relationship to Gog through the Getae and a manipulation of the wording in *Ezechiel* allowed Isidore to provide biblical lineage to the Goths. Thus, what appeared to be praise was also a subtle representation of the Goths, to those who knew Scripture, as the enemies of God. Magog is also, in *Ezechiel*, the land, and so it may be a latent criticism of the Visigothic kingdom as well. Unsurprisingly with Isidore, we see the very smart use of language, by a master of wordplay.

Isidore uses the Magog lineage to draw an allusion of the Goths as the enemies of God, but also the enemies of Hispania. In the passage in the *Origines* (9.2.89) in which Isidore notes the origin of the Goths from Magog, his source is not *Ezechiel*, but rather, a single line from Lucan. In it, the Goths and the Dacians (an offshoot of the Goths) are attacking Iberians. This history of the Goths begins with them attacking the peoples of Iberia, since "Hispani ab Ibero (Ebro river through Zaragoza) amne primum Iberi, postea ab Hispalo (Seville) Hispani cognominati sunt."[160] Since the Iberians were connected

---

157 Isid., *De Orig. Goth.*, 1: "Gothorum antiquissimam esse gentem, quorum originem quidem de Magog Jafeth filio suspicantur a similitudine ultimae syllabae; et magis de Ezechiele propheta id colligentes."

158 In twelve instances Gog is used, and in only two Magog. Gog and Magog are also referred to in Revelations 20:8 as the enemies of God, but Isidore only references Ezechiel, so it is to that which reference is made.

159 Ambrose, *De Fide as Gratianum Augustum Libri Quinque*, 2.16: "Namque et futuram nostri depopulationem, et bella Gothorum Ezechiel illo jam tempore prophetavit; sic enim habes: Propterea prophetiza, fili hominis, et dic: O Gog, haec dicit Dominus: Nonne in die illa cum constituetur habitare populus meus Israel in pace, surges et venies de loco tuo, ab extremo Aquilone: et gentes tecum multae, sessores equorum omnes, congregatio multa et magna, et virtus copiosa; et ascende ad populum meum Israel ut nubes operire terram in novissimis diebus, etc. *Gog iste Gothus est*, quem jam videmus exisse, de quo promittitur nobis futura victoria, dicente Domino: Et depraedabuntur eos, qui depraedati eos fuerant, et despoliabunt eos, qui sibi spolia detraxerant, dicit Dominus. Eritque in die illa, dabo Gog, hoc est, Gothis, locum nominatum, monumentum Israel multorum virorum congestum, qui supervenerunt ad mare: et per circuitum struet os vallis, et obruet illic Gog et totam multitudinem ejus, et vocabitur Ge Polyandrium Gog; et obruet eos domus Israel, ut purgetur terra."

160 Isid., *Orig.*, 9.2.109.

singularly to Zaragoza and Seville, the Goths were a particular affront to the school of Isidore-Seville. Isidore knew the *Ezechiel* passage and of other ways to connect the Goths to Magog and Gog, but for the *Origines* he (or Braulio) chose a passage clearly painting the Goths as an affront to Seville-Zaragoza, the school of Isidore-Seville. This would have been especially pertinent at the times of the *Origines*'s drafts, of the ten books around 619 when Sisebut received a copy, and in the early 630s when the school was passed on to Braulio, who edited the *Origines* into final version. Around the year 619 was also when Isidore produced his *De Viris Illustribus*, which ties Seville and Zaragoza together in especial union.[161]

Certainly, there were many layers of references in the historical texts that must be impossible to see through modern eyes, and what the text indicates about social relations also leads to intriguing questions. The key one here is whether Isidore was condemning a whole *gens*, and so all of the Gothic community, or only the monarchy. It is not possible to discern for sure, but what is certain is that any audience that was reasonably educated and knew the Scriptural material would have been well aware of the terrible associations of, and critiques against, the Goths, and so the monarchy in Toledo. Perhaps this is why the *De Laude Gothorum* is extant in only three manuscripts, none of which contain the royal dedication of the text.[162] The association of the Goths with Gog and Magog implicates them in biblical disasters and subtly removes them from Salvation History.

5.2.2   Marriage, and Love?

In Jordanes's *Getica*, the Romans (Byzantines) marry the Goths, and all live happily ever after in shared origin and future. Isidore's *De Origine Gothorum* narrative was constructed in much different contexts. Instead of a period of Byzantine conquest in the West, it was a moment of Byzantine defeat and Gothic conquest in Hispania. The way Isidore deals with the marriage theme is appropriate to the moment when he was writing: writing-out the Romans and introducing the Goths. In Isidore's narrative, the nuptial relations between the Goths and Romans are grimmer than in Jordanes's account.

In the *De Laude Spania*, Isidore claims that the Romans were once married to Iberia (Hispania). The Romans, noted in the present tense as the "head of nations," were no longer betrothed to Hispania: the Romans and Hispania were

---

161   See Chapter 2, § 3.2.3.
162   MSS Bern 83, Leningrad (Leninopolitanus) Bibl. Imp. QI 20, and, St. Gall 133.

now divorced, a narrative that Julian of Toledo later reverses.[163] The reasons for the failed marriage seems to be that the Romans no longer made the appropriate effort for Hispania, which deserved more than what the Romans could offer; it deserved a relationship with one that would continuously make efforts towards betterment, conversion.[164] The Goths, on the other hand, had become wealthy and powerful, and had gained possession of Hispania. The late classical and late antique images of the *nouveaux riches* and their grotesque abuse of power and displays and uses of wealth seem as evident here as in the *De Laude Gothorum*. The newly found positions of wealth and authority of the Visigoths, allusive to both the Crown in Toledo and Toledo's Agali monastery, gave them a heightened sense of power, a feeling that they could be "secure in the felicity of empire," in the possession of things, a security Isidore elsewhere notes as anything but secure. There are more disturbing aspects, though, of the narrative of the replacement of the Romans by the Goths.

The Gothic conquest of their new bride is, at its core, a violent one. Moreover, the associations made between Gothic actions and emotions are no less disturbing to a modern audience than they were to Isidore's. The Goths, perhaps because of their "freedman" status, were anything but gentle, tender and caring in the process of Hispania's re-marriage to them. This is emphasized fiercely by Isidore who says that the Goths "raped" (*rap[u]it*) Hispania.[165]

---

163   From a canon preserved only in the *Juliana* version of the *Hispana*, Drews argues that Julian of Toledo was attempting to (re-)connect the Goths to the Romans, as a way to denigrate "primitive" Jews. If this interpretation is correct, then we can see Julian, as part of his project to re-build the authority of Toledo, working hard to reverse Isidore's narrative in the *De Origine Gothorum* that dissociates Romans from Goths, demonstrating the political expediency of the Goth-Roman narrative also late into the seventh-century. It is another example of Isidore-Seville's text being either forgotten or re-interpreted after the Isidorian period. For Drews's interpretation see Drews, "Jews as Pagans?," 189–207. For a recent and important re-thinking of identity and the use of Goth and Roman in Visigothic Spain see Manuel Koch, *Ethnische Identität im Entstehungsprozess des spanischen Westgotenreiches* (Berlin and Boston: De Gruyter, 2011).

164   It appears that the Goths are meant as the only "man" between the Romans, Goths and Spain, but issues, meanings and intentions of gender are unclear here. The implied relationship of gender could be an allusion to popular beliefs about Roman and Gothic differences of perspective, or related to the harsh treatment by the Goths of Spain. For some discussion on contradictory views of spousal abuse and masculinity in late antiquity, see Leslie Dossey, "Wife Beating and Masculinity in Late Antiquity," *Past and Present* 199 (2008): 3–40.

165   In his edition, Mommsen uses "*rapuit*," whereas in his, Rodríguez Alonso prefers "*rapit*." *Rapuit* and *rapit* are of the same root word, so the argument concerning its significance should be similar whichever version is chosen. However, they are in different tenses between the editions, implying slightly different meanings. *Rapuit* reflects the past tense, and *rapit* is in the present. The implications of the latter are that the Goths are still

Perhaps this is too harsh a translation for *rapit*, but the evidence suggests that this intensity conveys Isidore's meaning. Before turning to Isidore's uses of the word, let us look at how some of his primary sources use it.

In the New Testament, the use of the verb *rapere* infers violent capture or seizure. The Gospel of Matthew says that the violent take the earth by force (*rapiunt*). It also associates raping (*rapit*) with the devil taking what was in one's heart. In the Gospel of John too, and Acts, *rapere* is a seizure or capture by force. Elsewhere in Acts and in Paul's letter to the Corinthians, a noun version, *raptum*, refers to a violent abduction.[166] Outside of Scripture, Orosius uses *rapere* in similar ways.[167]

The *De Laude Spania* is the only time Isidore uses the verb *rapio* in the *De Origine Gothorum*. Elsewhere in the *De Origine Gothorum* sequence he uses the noun *rapinis* to mean "robbery" and "plunder."[168] Isidore's use of this is consistent in other texts as well.[169] These uses all imply various levels of force in the conquest of Hispania by the Goths. Force is anathema to the school of Isidore-Seville, and there was no Christian concept yet of "just war" or force, despite the later association of it with Augustine.[170] Rome too was a conqueror (*victrix*) in its marriage with Hispania, Hispania's first marriage. There is, though, something more sinister in the Gothic actions, that becomes evident when Isidore's explicit definition of *rapio* is consulted.

In the *Origines*, Isidore is quite clear what the verb *rapio* means. In its past participle form, Isidore defines it as an expression of sexual rape: "Stuprum.

---

violently handing Hispania. *Amavit* is in the past tense in both Mommsen and Rodríguez Alonso, and it was probably for the sake of consistency that Mommsen changed *rapit* to *rapuit*. There seems to be no other explanation, since there is no discrepancy in the manuscripts. Thus, in forcing the consistency of the edition, Mommsen may have missed a very important distinction in the wording of the text, chosen carefully by its author. This highlights the need for new and extensive manuscript research and awareness by current scholars.

166   Matthew 11:12 and 13:19, John 6:15, 10:12 and 28, Acts 6:12 and 23:10, Paul, 2. Corinthians 12:2 and 4, and Acts 8:39 and 19:29.
167   Orosius, *Hist. adv. pag.*, 7.8 and 7.9.
168   Isid., *De Orig. Goth.*, 51 and 84.
169   Isid., *Sent.*, 1.12.6b: "Quae uarietas malae motionis tunc menti inhaesit, quando ab aeternorum contemplatione primus homo recedens in illo stare noluit, a quo male recessit, et iusta damnatione inconstans per rerum raptus uarietatem defluxit […];" Isidore, *Sent.*, 2.12.7: "Quo mens hominis iusti ex uera conpunctione rapiatur, et qualiter infirmata reuertatur degustatae lucis magnitudine, illum nosse posse qui iam aliquid exinde gustauit;" and, Isid., *Sent.*, 3.60.4: "Pro diuersitate usus alii de rebus mundanis pereunt, quas cupidius rapiunt."
170   See Phillip Wynn, *Augustine on War and Military Service* (Minneapolis: Fortress Press, 2013).

Raptus proprie est inlicitus coitus, a conrumpendo dictus; unde et qui rapto potitur, stupro fuitur."[171] In referring to *raptus* as the act of illegal intercourse, Isidore who also has it follow the word *stuprum*, illicit sex, furthermore suggests that *raptum* is committed by a figure that delights in the sexual pleasure derived from taking a victim by force.[172] Not a pleasant picture of the Goths, especially in light of the fact that Isidore considered fornication the parent of all sins.[173] Striking too is the coupling of *rapit* and *amavit*: through rape was produced love. For the Goths, rape and love were intimately entangled. As a Goth could truly express love by using physical force to connect the two "partners," to build a union, so could the Gothic kings expect to create true Christian love by force. Thus, the Gothic marriage to Hispania was a forced one, a conquest. For Isidore, there was no union of Goths with Hispania, but rather violent suppression. This fits perfectly well with the array of critiques, alternative narratives and *damationes memoriae* throughout the school of Isidore-Seville's collection of texts.

The marriage theme runs throughout the *De Origine Gothorum* sequence, fundamental to the re-birth and conversion narrative. It is introduced at various points to function in ways similar to one another: tying together different peoples and places to each other and to the various timelines; separating them from one another and the timelines, whether universal salvific or otherwise; and, in general, offering a consistent trope for historical and mystical allusions and truths.[174] As noted, the Goths first become entangled with Hispania (not with the pre-Spanish Iberians) when Athanaric was invited into Constantinople by the Spaniard emperor Theodosius. The successor to Athanaric was Alaric I, whose lines went on to found the early Visigothic kingdoms. Alaric's

---

171 Isid., *Orig.*, 5.26.14.

172 Also, as Jinty Nelson and Alice Rio point out, in almost all early medieval law codes the word *raptus* has a fluid meaning, ranging from rape to assault to simple unapproved eloping. Exceptionally, the *Liber Iudiciorum* is the only early medieval law code to use raptus exclusively as forced rape. For their discussion, see Janet Nelson and Alice Rio, "Women and Laws in Early Medieval Europe," in *The Oxford Handbook of Women and Gender in Medieval Europe*, ed. Judith Bennett and Ruth Karras (Oxford: Oxford University Press, 2013), 7.

173 Isid., *Synonyma*, 2.8: "fornicatione contaminari deterius omni peccato puta, omnibus peccatis fornicatio major est."

174 Despite Cazier's 1994 chapter "Le mariage de Gots avec l'Espagne," Fontaine first notes the importance of the nuptial theme in the *De Laude Spaniae*, but without elaborating the discussion into the *De Origine Gothorum* proper. For the Cazier chapter see Cazier, *Isidore de Séville*, and for the Fontaine reference, Jacques Fontaine, "Un manifeste politique et culturel: Le *De Laude Spaniae* d'Isidore de Séville," in *Le discours d'éloge entre Antiquité et Moyen Age*, ed. Lionel Mary and Michel Sot (Paris: Éditions Picard, 2001), 64.

immediate successor was Athaulf, who married Gallia Placidia, the daughter of Theodosius. The marriage was the result of force. Gallia Placidia had been captured by the Goths (*Gothi ceperant...adsumpsit*) in Rome. It should be noted that, on this occasion, Isidore uses the verb *capio* and not *rapio*; the Goths "rape" Spain but not the Romans, consistent with the *De Laude Spaniae* narrative. Two kings later, Wallia returns Gallia Placidia to Rome. The marriage fails, but the Goths are re-united with Rome and Hispania after they subject themselves to the Romans. Wallia pledges Gothic loyalty to Rome, and in return the Goths are invited into Hispania to work on Rome's behalf, and, in honor of that good service, are given land (freedom).[175] The story of Gallia Placidia highlights the continuous dialectic between Romans and Goths in the *De Origine Gothorum*, but it is also a foreshadowing of Hispania as a passive mediator between Roman and Gothic marriage, and portends the violence that the Goths would commit against the peninsula.

6 Conclusion

In conclusion, scholars have extensively written about Isidore's adapting methods and narratives of Roman and Christian historiography – on concepts of geography, political others, barbarians, heresy, and orthodoxy – to legitimize Visigothic control of Hispania, and the importance of the Church to this.[176] On the surface, that neat narrative of the Visigoths' proper place in Christian, Spanish history is evident. However, when deconstructed, it becomes clear that Isidore's historical writings are smartly crafted, multi-layered literary constructions that are also full of latent criticisms for and a general disdain of the Visigothic power-structure in Toledo, not a genuine praise of it. These texts represent a traumatic "acting-out" against the actions of the monarchy and its allies in Toledo, and are central components of the competitive dialectics between the schools.

This "acting-out" is a symptom of the growing authoritarianism of the Church and monarchy in Toledo since the founding of the monastery of Agali in the early 600s, the promotion of it as the "prep-school" for the bishops of Toledo, and then in Gundemar's actions, discussed in the next chapter, which shocked Isidore and his network. Sisebut was no exception to the trend,

---

175   Isid., *De Orig. Goth.*, 19–22.
176   Isidore emulates Sidonius Appolinarus's geographical exposition of Clermont: see Sid. Ap., *Letter* 4.2.5 (Sidonius Apollinaris, *Sidonius: Poems and Letters*, 2 vols., Loeb Classics, ed. and trans. William B. Anderson [Cambridge: Harvard University Press, 1965], 2:142).

initiating his reign by solidifying Gundemar's authoritarian actions, confirming Toledo's position over the Church, and its church over the provincial sees. Shortly into Sisebut's reign, in response to the events, Isidore began constructing a theory for proper monarchy, and developed a series of origins-stories that confirmed to his audiences that the Church, independent of the monarchy, defended by Seville, had both historical and spiritual claims for autonomous authority unmatched by the new power of Toledo. In the origins-stories, we can see the promotion of this Sevillan agenda, the defense of the provincial churches, and law, and of historical authority, but also outright antagonism and spiritually damning critiques of the Visigothic power-base in Toledo. Sisebut was no exception to this rule.

Isidore had a particular connection with Sisebut, as opposed to other kings, but this should not necessarily be equated with affection. With no other Visigothic king did Isidore exchange so much written material, but also, no other king during Isidore's bishopric had attempted to force conversions and to promote his political agenda via a distorted, and perhaps populist, version of orthodoxy. Sisebut never once sought ecclesiastical approval for his actions, ones that included forced conversions, the building of churches (St. Leocadia in 619 [a fact that Isidore silences]) and the appointment of bishops around the kingdom.[177] Nor did Sisebut ever allow a council in the metropolitan of Carthaginensis. The first council to be held in the metropolitan see of the province was twenty-three years after Gundemar moved the metropolitanate from Cartagena to Toledo. During Sisebut's reign, Isidore, however, held a significant council in Seville in 619, confirming Seville as the bulwark against heresy in Spain, or so the historiography of Isidore-Seville claims, in contrast to that of Toledo-Agali.[178] The exchange of letters and texts from the school were from a real fear – a reversal of the master-servant dialectic propagated in Isidore's historical narrative – not evidence of inherent loyalism by Isidore or of him and Sisebut as "twin pillars" of a renaissance, except in the sense of a *convivencia*, an antagonistic relationship that produced interesting and impressive results.

Isidore's historical writing is a complex, multi-layered network of associations and significations that reveals deep antagonisms between the two schools. A view beyond the texts themselves to the acts of constructing their historical narratives, their delivery to audiences and their use of popular beliefs helps not only to disentangle the serious religious and political crises of the Isidore-moment, but also allows scholars to paint a fuller picture of life in early seventh-century Hispania.

---

177 See Drews, *The Unknown Neighbour*, 219.
178 The only contemporary Spanish source to discuss II Seville and praise Isidore's role in combating heresy is Braulio in his *Renotatio*, ls. 50–3.

CHAPTER 4

The Historical *Lacunae* and *Damnatio[nes] Memoriae* of the *Hispana*

1   Introduction

"Isidore and our other [contemporary] feeble sources" suppressed the complexities of the historical dynamics of the early seventh century. It is precisely in this "feebleness" that important clues as to the mysteries of the Isidore-moment lay.¹ The historical *lacunae* and *damnationes memoriae* of specific people, places and events reveal the deep entanglement between the authors, texts and competing discourses for power otherwise suppressed in the historical records. When critically exposed, they reveal the extent to which the texts of the period, across genres, were in direct and argumentative dialogue with one another.²

---

1   Thompson, *Goths*, 157.
2   The concept of *damnatio memoriae* is a Roman one, found across material and written culture and especially popular in late-Roman and post-Roman ("vulgar") legal codification. The use of *damnatio memoriae*, in which the condemned person is written-out of textual records or the texts containing their name and signature are destroyed, can be found, for example, throughout Justinian's *Corpus Iuris Civilis*, in laws that deal with political, social and religious infamy: in *Codex* 1.3.23 Eutyches is condemned by a Catholic council for impiety, while *Dig.* 28.3.6.11 demands the condemnation of a person's memory because of treason or other similar offence. The most interesting case is perhaps *Inst.* 3.1.5, which explains the damnation of memory as a way of blocking the heirs of the condemned. In a sense, this is what Isidore-Seville was attempting with the *damnatio memoriae* of Gundemar: erasing him from memory to prevent heirs to the throne acting in the same manner. The Roman phrase for such erasure from the records was, to be precise, *memoria damnata* (but see also *Codex* 1.5.4.4, 7.2.2 and 9.8.6, *Dig.* 28.3.6.11 and 31.76.9, *Inst.* 3.1.5 and 4.18.3). However, the term *damnatio memoriae* is used in this book because it is the common term employed to discuss this legal evidence of *memoria damnata. Damnatio memoriae* is, to be precise, an early modern term, first appearing in scholarship in 1689 as the title of a Ph.D. dissertation by Christopher Schreiter, *Iuridicam de Damnatione Memoriae, Praescitu Superiorum*. For a short discussion see Peter Stewart, "The Destruction of Statues in Late Antiquity," in *Constructing Identity in Late Antiquity*, ed. Richard Miles (London: Routledge, 1999), 184, n. 3, and for a view of the general subject from a non-literary point of view, see Eric R. Varner, *Mutilation and Transformation: "Damnatio Memoriae" and Roman Imperial Portraiture* (Boston and Leiden: Brill, 2004). The use of *damnatio memoriae* continued on well past late-imperial Rome, for example, by Jordanes in his politically expedient constructions of the past concerning the Goths and Romans in broader Byzantium. For Jordanes's *damnatio memoriae* see Goffart, *Narrators*, 97–111, and for its employment by Carolingian writers see Yitzhak Hen, *Roman Barbar-*

In the two previous chapters, the emphasis was on eliciting and explaining the construction of alternative chains of signification in historical narrations, the "ideologizing of memory."[3] This competition extended through the historical and into the meta-historical-, theological- and legal-literature. In this chapter, the emphasis is on *historical lacunae* and *damnationes memoriae* that also considerably altered the history and memory of seventh-century Hispania. Evidence for their purposed construction is demonstrated by a case-study of the history and historiography of the Iberian Church and its conciliar, canonical and legislative actions and activities, as laid out in the early seventh-century canonical collection known as the *Hispana*. Of particular concern here are the absences from the *Hispana* of the reign and council of Gundemar and the Third Council of Seville. Through a detailed interrogation of select *lacunae* and *damnationes memoriae* of the *Hispana*, and a historicization of its textual tradition, with appropriate reference to its transmitted legacy, it is possible to continue demonstrating how representations of the past, and the manipulation of memory, were central to building authority. The attempts at negating the past evident in the *Hispana* and the subterfuge of *lacunae* that they overlay, when dynamically exposed and explained, can provide crucial flesh to the reconstruction of complex realities and depth to our understanding of the schools and the discursive competition that later framed the *Liber Iudiciorum*.

2   The *Hispana*

This chapter revolves around the historical *lacunae* and *damnationes memoriae* of one textual tradition, that of the *Hispana*, and its historicization. As such, it is imperative to begin by explaining the text, its history, and the historiography of the peninsula's early church councils. The *Hispana* is a chronological recording of the Catholic conciliar activities of Hispania from late antiquity through the late seventh century. The contents of the *Hispana* are, other than the late addition of a sixth-century council of Narbonne, exclusively from the Iberian Peninsula. There are three distinct seventh-century versions of the *Hispana*, all of which were made either in Seville or Toledo. The respective authors and editors of each of these versions were either part of the school of Isidore-Seville

---

ians: *The Royal Court and Culture in the Early Medieval West* (New York: Palgrave MacMillan, 2007), and by the Anglo-Saxon writers, Tom Shippey, "The Merov(ich)ingian again: *damnatio memoriae* and the *usus scholarum*," in *Latin Learning and English Lore: Studies in Anglo-Saxon Literature for Michael Lapidge*, vol. 1, ed. Katherine O'Brien O'Keffe, and Andy Orchard (Toronto: University of Toronto Press, 2005), 389–406.

3   Ricoeur, *Memory, History, Forgetting*, 448.

or of Toledo-Agali. They included the records and history of conciliar activities and pronouncements that suited their own expedient political and pedagogical needs. Although the *Hispana* may have been meant as a pedagogical text in the sense of being a body of canons to be referred to and updated by bishops going forward, a *Ius* or *Liber Canonum* or *Lex Canonica*, as in Merovingian Francia, it could only have been so to some extent.[4] The history and structure of the *Hispana* – its exclusions and inclusions, redactions and recensions, and manuscript transmission – show that it was a rhetorical product of the ongoing struggle for present and future authority played out through constructions of the past.[5]

As a multifaceted text, the *Hispana* represents not only the inception of the history and historiography of the Catholic conciliar activities in Spain – and further indicates the "uses and abuses" of historical writing by Visigothic writers and the connection of it to legal codification – but is also almost their exclusive representative throughout Visigothic history and the history of the middle ages.

There are select Spanish councils recorded in other manuscripts, but such non-*Hispana* transmission is rare. Two significant cases of such an exception are the so-called St. Maur collection and Novara collection.[6] The collection of St. Maur was compiled at the end of the sixth century, in Gaul. It is likely that the collection was put together in Arles or Narbonne.[7] It contains the Third Council of Toledo and the only usable manuscript of it is The Hague, Rijksmuseum Meermanno-Westreenianum, M 10 B 4. This manuscript allowed

---

4 See Hubert Mordek, *Kirchenrecht und Reform in Frankenreich. Die Collectio Vetus Gallica, die älteste systematische Kanonessammlung des fränkischen Gallien. Studien und Edition* (Berlin: De Gruyter, 1975), and Gregory I. Halfond, *The Archaeology of Frankish Church Councils*, AD 511–768 (Boston and Leiden: Brill, 2010), 137–38 and 175.
5 On canonical collections as historical texts, see McKitterick, *History and Memory*, 255.
6 For an extended discussion see Gonzalo Martínez Díez, "Dos nuevos firmantes del Concilio III de Toledo," *Anuario de Historia del Derecho español* 42 (1972): 637–42; Gonzalo Martínez Díez, "La colección del ms. de Novara," *Anuario de Historia del Derecho español* 33 (1963): 391–538; Félix Rodríguez, "Los antiguos concilios españoles y la edición crítica de la colección canónica Hispana," in *Monumenta Iuris Canonici, Vol. 6, Proceedings of the Fifth International Congress of Medieval Canon Law*, ed. Stephen Kuttner and Kenneth Pennington (Biblioteca Apostolica Vaticana, 1980), 3–13 (8–9, n. 9); Ettore Cau, *Scrittura e cultura a Novara (secoli VIII–X)* (Pavia: Università degli studi di Pavia, 1971–1974); and, Lotte Kéry, *Canonical Collections of the Early Middle Ages (ca. 400–1140). A bibliographical guide to the manuscripts and literature, History of Medieval Canon Law* (Washington, D.C.: The Catholic University of America Press, 1999), 32 and 45–46. For a critique of Kéry see McKitterick, *History and Memory*, 250 ff.
7 The collection of St. Maur may be a direct descendant of the late fifth-/early sixth-century *Collectio Quesnelliana* from Arles. On the latter see Kéry, *Collections*, 27–28.

Philippe Labbe in the seventeenth century to add two new signatories to III Toledo: bishop Commundas of Egitania and a representative of the bishop of Tarragona.

The second of these non-*Hispana* traditions is the Novara collection, named after a family of manuscripts in Novara dating from the eighth century. As a document in its original form, the Novara collection was first constructed in Tarragona around the year 550, far earlier than the date of birth of the *Hispana*. The Novara collection was revised only once. This revision occurred in Tarragona, in 638, the year both of VI Toledo and when the transgressions of III Seville were revealed by inquisition. This may well indicate that the revision was Tarragona's response to the Sixth Council's inquisition and to the construction of the *Hispana*.[8] The Novara collection contains the record of six councils: Tarragona, Gerona, Lérida and II, IV and VI Toledo.[9] It is important not only for preserving these councils, but also for providing an example of raw signatures. *Es bien conocida*, Félix Rodríguez argues, that copyists of the councils tended to condense the signatures of the councils to their bare essentials. The collection of Novara, unlike the carefully edited *Hispana*, provides rare explications of the signatures, showing their actual and apparently unedited diversity of form.[10]

These two non-*Hispana* collections provide additional data about the councils of seventh-century Hispania, in terms of locations, dates, attendees and forms of signatures. Furthermore, they reveal the silencing of various aspects of the participation of Tarragona in the councils and in the recording of them. Their absence from the *Hispana* reinforces our interpretation that the *Hispana*

---

8   Such a conclusion is possible not only by its *terminus post quem* of 638, but also by the situation of the signatures which indicate that it was paid little attention beyond this date. The Novara collection could have been a response to the collections of Gallic conciliar activities happening at the time. Finally, given that this line of canonical recording turned out to be a cul-de-sac in Spain, it is reasonable to see this 638 revision as a response to Tarragona's decreasing significance in the central power structure of the kingdom. On the Novara collections see Sanchez-Arcilla Bernal, "Historial del Derecho Español," *Boletín Mexicano de Derecho Comparado* 105 (2005): 1111–17, and Léopold Delisle, "Manuscrits bénéventins et wisigothiques. Observationes paléograpiques sur les traits caractéristiques qui sont communs aux anciennes écritures de l'Italie méridionale et à celle de l'Espagne," *Bibliothèque de l'École des Chartes* 21 (1910): 233–35. On the decline of Tarragona see Francesc Rodríguez Martorell and Josep M. Macias Solé, "Buscando el siglo VIII en el Puerto de Tarracona: entre la residualidad y el desconocimiento," in *Cerámicas Altomedievales en Hispania y su entorno (siglos V–VIII d.C.)*, ed. Iñaki Martín Viso, Patricia Fuentes Melgar, José Carlos Sastre Blanco, and Raúl Catalán Ramos (Valladolid: Glyphos, 2018), 573–89.

9   See Enrique Flórez, España sagrada 6 (Madrid, 1751), 144 and 149, and Martínez Díaz, "Dos nuevos firmantes del Concilio III de Toledo," 637–41.

10 Félix Rodríguez, "Los antiguos concilios españoles," 9.

represents a particular struggle for authority between the schools, one that left little space for other centers.[11] The absence of a suffragan of the bishop of Tarragona, a council of Tarragona and the very tradition of conciliar recording, of writing the history of the councils, in Tarragona, seems to indicate not a fading away of conciliar activities in this city, but a purposed silencing of it from the records.[12] Who did this and why cannot be shown for certain, but it is reasonable to conclude that it was a representative of either of the schools.[13]

2.1 The Conditions of the Hispana's Birth

In the words of its authoritative editors, the *Hispana* was constructed as a text in its *forma más primitiva* in Seville between the years 633 and 636. This places its provenance to the seminal years of the early 630s, between IV Toledo and the death of Isidore before V Toledo.[14] This dating makes sense in a variety of ways and, as will be shown, the *Hispana* is certainly a product of the historical milieu of these years, closely associated with the canonical project of IV Toledo and its relationship to, amongst other participants, the school of Isidore-Seville.

The timing and structure of the *Hispana* demonstrate that it was more than a capstone to Isidore's career. It was a politically expedient text, an important function of which was to promote the Sevillan School in the present and near future. This included the passing on of leadership of the school from Isidore to Braulio, from Seville to Zaragoza,[15] in a rhetorical-mnemonic form like that used to promote these two sites of authority in Isidore's *DVI*.[16] The *Hispana*

---

11 A Catalonian/Pyrennean collection purportedly of the *Hispana* has caused some confusion, having been dated to the 590s, mid-seventh century, or later. Whatever the case, the most ancient manuscript representing this Catalonian/Pyrennean collection is no older than the ninth-century *codex Gerundensis* in the Archivo de la Santa Iglesia Catedral Basílica in Barcelona (see *CCH* 1 [1966], 141–42 and *CCH* 2 [1976], 501–83).

12 It is curious too that there is a total absence from the conciliar records of Tarragonian bishops and church officials for nearly forty years, from 646 (VII Toledo) to 683 (XIII Toledo).

13 If the collection of St. Maur was from Narbonne, it too is an example of such a phenomenon. However, it seems more likely that it was a collection from Arles.

14 On the dates of the construction of the *Hispana* see *CCH* 1 (1966), 306–54; *CCH* 6 (2002), 9ff.; *Concilios Visigoticos*, ed. Vives, xiv; Séjourné, *Saint Isidore*, 92–94; and, Stocking, BCC, 14–18, n. 51, 108 and 114.

15 It is the site, in the 630s, of the elevation of a king and the transfer of spiritual authority from Isidore and Seville, but it is also the site of the only plenary council to occur outside of Toledo, in 691 (II Zaragoza).

16 By rhetorical-mnemonic device is meant a learning technique by which one is able not only to remember a list of information (mnemonics), but also its meaning (the aim of rhetoric). In the *DVI* of Isidore and the Sevillan version of the *Hispana*, information is translated into a particular form meant to produce a particular memory to help the reader

inaugurates the story of the inception and growth of Catholicism in Hispania. It begins with a Catholic council held in Seville's province, Baetica. From that point, the *Hispana* takes the reader rapidly to the conversion of the peninsula through Leander. This is followed by the exclusive defense of Catholicism in Hispania by Seville for forty-four years: all provincial councils between III and IV Toledo (589–633) are excluded except for the First (590) and Second (619) Councils of Seville. The story ends with the transfer of this defense of orthodoxy safely into the hands of Braulio. The *Hispana* is a text whose coming into existence depended on the desire to promote the school of Isidore-Seville, not only in the present but also beyond, past the life of the school's grand-master Isidore, and his family, and into the able hands of the person (Braulio), and ecclesiastical see (Zaragoza) of his chosen successor.[17]

The political act of creating a literary text to support and encourage the lasting power and authority of Isidore-Seville is an important one. It provides further evidence of the vigorous and essentially discursive struggle of the schools, and how that differed in nature to the reaction by other regional centers, like Mérida. Considered in the context of the broader situation happening within the kingdom at the time, and of the specific Isidore-Seville censorship evidenced in the text, the *Hispana*'s construction also adds depth to the historical picture of the early 630s, a period of turbulent politics, significant changes of authority, and the production of an array of related texts. As mentioned, the *Hispana* came to fruition around the time of IV and V Toledo. This coincided not only with the closing years of Isidore's life,[18] but it was also in 633 that Isidore lost his beloved sister, the nun Florentina, for whom he had written the *Contra Judaeos* in the 610s.[19] However, the promotion of Braulio, and Isidore's own

---

remember information in a certain way. These texts present patterns of information that assist the reader with remembering the primary ecclesiastical significance of Seville and its ecclesiastical representatives, which is then passed on to Zaragoza and its ecclesiastical representatives. In this way they are mnemonically affiliated.

17 Such connections between Seville and Zaragoza may suggest that it was the school of Isidore-Seville that encouraged the silencing of the tradition of conciliar activity, and of writing its history, in Tarragona. This is because Zaragoza was in the province of Tarraconensis, the metropolitan see of which was Tarragona. It would have been more sensible to pass ecclesiastical and spiritual authority from Isidore-Seville to Tarragona, if the aim was to preserve a site of authority away from the church and monarchy in Toledo. However, what was present was the proliferation of a specific network of authority, not a united struggle against Toledo's growing authority.

18 It was perhaps because of the stress of travel in his old age that he ignored Sisenand's call to return home in 632.

19 For Isidore's travels to Toledo at this time, see his letter to Braulio, letter six in the manuscript collection of Braulio's letters. For a fuller discussion, see Miguel Franco, "Braulio de Zaragoza," 155–76.

personal and family circumstances, were not the only nor even the most pressing items on Isidore's and others' minds in the early 630s. The two years leading up to IV Toledo in December 633 was a period of considerable political activity.

In 631, Sisenand, as previously noted, a Frankish-aided rebel for the Visigothic Crown, and potentially a noble from Narbonensis (as Gundemar had been[20]), successfully deposed the Visigothic king Swinthila, the great victor over the Byzantines, and king of *totius Spaniae*, as Isidore referred to him around 625. Sisenand was proclaimed king in Zaragoza, perhaps by way of royal unction.[21] Given the turn of events, it is reasonable that there arose significant trepidation and confusion concerning the positions of various networks of power.[22] Even though it was nobility in Hispania who had initiated this change, this was not an ordinary usurpation and struggle for the throne played out amidst the characters of the inner circles of court and church in the normal style of Visigothic regime change. Although a king's overthrow, even in the typical way, was a good opportunity for rebellion, in this instance a particular vacuum or gap in the established power structure seems to have opened up. Perhaps there was some sort of actual or hoped-for return of local autonomy for the cities of former Byzantine Spania, foreshadowed, it could be said, at Gundemar's council in 610 and at II Seville in 619.[23] Regardless of the reasons, it seems that a general breakdown of "order" had been growing in the south throughout the years leading into the power-grab of Sisenand with the help of Dagobert I and the Franks. This situation of confusion in the cities and bishoprics of the crumbling and collapsed Byzantine enclave, and local economy, may explain why at least some parts of the south at this time supported another rebel to the

---

20 Gundemar was governor of the province of Narbonensis, as seen by the letter to him from Count Bulgar (*Ep. Wis.*, 14).
21 On Sisenand's elevation at Zaragoza, see Fred., *Chron.*, 4.73. For a discussion of the possibility of the use of royal unction by Sisenand, see King, *Law and Society*, 48, n. 5.
22 On the challenges to Swinthila leading up to the moment of Sisenand's usurpation, see Luis A. García Moreno, "La oposición a Suinthila: Iglesia, Monarquía y Nobleza en el Reino Visigodo," *Polis* 9 (1991): 13-24.
23 See II Seville 2, 3 and 6 in their discussions on problems in Cartagena and in Córdoba, a city that had a tradition of autonomy, and the bishoprics of Écija, Illiberis and Cabra, which had taken control of areas formally held by the see of Málaga. II Seville 1 provided restitution of property to rightful owners in Málaga. These areas were for sure in Visigothic hands, with the area at least to Illiberi (Elivira)/Granada, if not even closer to the coast, having been taken by Witteric, as is seen by the consecration of a church of St. Stephan there in Witteric's name (*domini nostri gloriosi Witerici regis*) in 607 (*ICERV*, no. 303). A coin inscribed *Gundemarus re[x ---pius Eliberri* (*ICERV*, no. 455; Pliego Vázquez, *La Moneda Visigoda* II, no. 226), puts the length of Visigothic control to about thirty miles from the sea. Thus, under Gundemar, the Byzantines were pinned pretty tightly along the coast.

throne, Iudila, in competition to the northern/Gallic-backed Sisenand. This Lusitanian and Baetican-sponsored rebellion was not a short and weak one. It lasted for some time, perhaps two years, ending only in 633 when its leader Iudila became a victim[24] of a formal *damnatio memoriae* in direct response to the political events on the ground.[25] Iudila's rebellion was a major event that not only precipitated multiple *damnationes memoriae* in the period, some of which were related to the rebellion and others which were not, but it was also responsible for the lengthy postponement, by Sisenand, of the Fourth Council of Toledo.[26]

Not long after the suppression of Iudila's Mérida-centered rebellion, an anonymous author from Mérida wrote the hagiographical text, the *Vitas Patrum Emeritensium*. As with all hagiography, the VPE should be read within the precise context of its composition.[27] The VPE was meant as a gesture to promote the ecclesiastical authority of Mérida, and thus its wider theo-political significance. It is a good case-study too in the importance of "the book," in its content, but also as a material object in a shared, but not unified, religio-political struggle against the growing centrality of Toledo. This is why the story, in the VPE, of Liuvigild trying to steal the robe from Masona is so central to the text, even if out of date as an historical event. Toledo, in the form of Liuvigild, tried every means it could to create for itself the same spiritual status as, in this

---

24 If Swinthila was edited out of the *De Origine Gothorum* in the early 630s, then it may be that he was the first victim of *damnatio memoriae* in these years.

25 Iudila's rebellion is known from two coins, one from Mérida and the other from Eliberri. Mérida must have been a serious site of rebellion in Sisenand's reign, not only because of Iudila's revolt, but also that more than twice as many gold coins were produced in that city than any other during Sisenand's reign. This indicates a real need to pay extensively for support and perhaps for local militias. For a discussion of this revolt and for the Iudila coins, see Collins, *Visigothic Spain*, 72 and 80; *Corpus Nummorum Vis.*, 409–12; Pliego Vázquez, *La Moneda Visigoda*, II, 303; and, George C. Miles, *The Coinage of the Visigoths in Spain: Leovigild to Achila II* (New York: American Numismatic Society, 1952), 30 and 321, plate 34.

26 On the councils as places for nobles to try to gain leverage over the monarchy, especially starting with IV Toledo, see Miguel Pino Abada, "El Papel de los concilios visigodos en la defense de los intereses nobiliarios frente al rey," *Hispania Sacra* 68 (2016): 119–26.

27 As Ian Wood argues, in discussing the writings of Jonas of Bobbio (Ian N. Wood, "The Use and Abuse of Latin Hagiography," in *East and West: Modes of Communication*, ed. Evangelos K. Chrysos and Ian N. Wood [Boston and Leiden: Brill, 1999], 93–110 [100]), all hagiographical texts need "to be read in the precise context of their composition." There is, however, some debate about the historical uses of hagiographical texts and their value for historical reconstruction. For another view, see Isabel Velázquez, *La Literatura Hagiográfica: Presupuestos Básicos y Aproximación a sus Manifestaciones en La Hispania Visigoda*, Libros Singulares 17 (Burgos: Fundación Instituto Castellano y Leonés de la Lengua, 2007). For a discussion of the debate, see Santiago Castellanos, *La Hagiografía Visigoda: Dominio Social y Proyección Cultural* (Logroño: Fundación San Millán de la Cogolla, 2004).

instance, Mérida. Liuvigild tried to subtract spiritual authority from Mérida and add it to Toledo by seizing Eulalia's robe for the royal city. This fight for "the robe was a fight for supremacy between the two cities. And this is clearly evidenced by the *Vitas*. Every reader could understand it."[28]

This example of the use of force to build religious conformity and spiritual power for Toledo is symptomatic of the seventh-century responses by Toledo to non-conformity. It is symptomatic too of the confrontations between Toledo and the authority and sometimes even theology of the ecclesiastical authorities and their sites of power. This includes, and in the *VPE* is an allusion to, Mérida in the 630s. In this sense, the meta-narrative of the *VPE* is comparable to that of the *Hispana*, even if its internal, literary logic may not be. It is significant not only that this text was first produced during the early 630s, as part of this flourishing of competitive and reactive discourses of authority, but also that its second recension was made between 670 and 680, around the time that Julian revised the *Hispana* and added Gundemar's conciliar activities to it. There is an important parallel with the *VPE* and the *Hispana*, therefore, in the history of their production and revision.[29]

In addition to the *Hispana* from Isidore-Seville and the *VPE* from Mérida, and connected to both literary-political events, the Isidorian network at this time also composed or edited into final versions other dynamic and rhetorical texts such as the *Origines*, and perhaps also recensions of the *De Origine Gothorum* and the *Sententiae*.[30] In response to hagiographical-historical output, used to defend respective spiritual and religio-political authority, an anonymous

---

28   Javier Arce, "The city of Mérida [Emerita] in the *Vitas Patrum Emeritensium* [VIth c. A. D.]," in *Modes of Communication*, ed. Chrysos and Wood, 1–14 (5).

29   Previous confusions concerning the dating and authorship have been resolved by the suggestion that the *VPE* was produced in two recensions, the first written between 630 and 638, and the second between 670 and 680. Antonio Maya Sánchez suggests that it was the second recension that was written by a deacon of Mérida named Paul. The first recension was also written by a deacon of Mérida, perhaps working in the basilica of St. Eulalia, but whose name eludes historians (see *Vitas*, ed. Maya Sánchez, and Arce, "The city of Mérida," 3). This conclusion seems to clarify the apparent problem of authorship as expressed by Fontaine who dated the text to 633 and 638, with the sole authorship of the *VPE* to Paul of Mérida (Fontaine, "Conversion et Culture chez les Wisigoths," 108, and see Joseph Garvin, The *"Vitas Sanctorum Emeritensium"* [Washington, D.C.: The Catholic University of America Press, 1946]). Also, it should not be assumed that the anonymous author was male. Women also wrote historical and historiographical works in the early middle ages, see Janet Nelson, "Gender and Genre in Women Historians of the Early Middle Ages," in *L'Historiographie médiévale en Europe*, Jean-Philippe Genet (Paris: Éditions du CNRS, 1991), 149–63.

30   The authenticity of a dedicated version of the *De Origine Gothorum* to Sisenand from a later medieval manuscript and edited by Mommsen is debated. For more on this see Chapter 3, note 39.

writer in Toledo put together the *Passio S. Leucadiae*. Leocadia was the saint for whom the recently deceased bishop of Toledo, Helladius, had consecrated a church, consecrated by Sisebut on October 26, 618.[31] Braulio also finished his *Vita S. Aemeliani* some time during the year 636.[32]

Therefore, in addition to the potential editing and redacting at this time of Isidore's *Chronicon, Sententiae* and *De Origine Gothorum*, at least five major texts were produced and re-published: the *Hispana* and canons of IV Toledo, the *VPE, Passio St. Leocadia, Vita S. Aemeliani*, and the *Origines*, which were re-credited at this time and passed on for editing to Braulio, who, it is reasonable to believe, was also a general editor of the *Hispana*.

Seville (and its nexus with Zaragoza) and Mérida were not the only significant sites of local and regional power in terms of production, administration, economy and taxes into the fisc.[33] However, they were prominent spiritual centers, locations of wealth, and historic cultural capitals capable of being perpetual sites of political opposition to Crown and Church in Toledo. The constant pressure that the school of Isidore-Seville put on Toledo to match its rhetorical vigor, if it wanted to advance its central authority, manifested itself in Toledo's competitive redactions, recensions and, on occasion, texts

---

31 The oldest manuscript of the *passio S. Leucadiae* is from the tenth century, but the original text was likely written slightly before 633. See *ICERV*, no. 93, and Ángel Fábrega Grau, *Pasionario Hispánico (Siglos vii–xii)* (Madrid-Barcelona: Consejo Superior de Investigaciones Científicas, 1953), 65–67 for the text, and 262 for the dating. The church of St. Leocadia in Toledo was consecrated by Helladius on October 26, 618, a point later mentioned in the mid-ninth century by Eulogius of Córdoba, in his *Liber apologeticus martyrum*, xvi 5 (*Corpus Scriptorum Muzarabicorum*, ed. Juan Gil [Madrid: Instituto Antonio de Nebrija, 1973], ii. 483).

32 In this year, someone in the kingdom also updated the 95-year Alexandrian Easter table to 627–721 (from 531–626). For more on that see above, Chapter 3, n. 33. For an edition of Braulio's *Vita Aemiliani* see *Vita Emiliani Sancti Braulionis Caesaraugustani Episcopi. Edición crítica*, ed. Luis Vázquez de Parga (Madrid: Consejo Superior de Investigaciones Científicas, 1943), and for discussion see Santiago Castellanos and Santiago Fernández Ardanaz, *Hagiografía y sociedad en la Hispania visigoda. La "Vita Aemiliani" y el actual territorio riojano (siglo VI)*, Biblioteca de temas riojanos 103 (Logroño: Instituto de Estudios Riojanos, 1999); Santiago Castellanos, *Poder social, aristócracias y "hombre santo" en la Hispania visigoda. La "Vita Aemiliani" de Braulio de Zaragoza*, Biblioteca de investigación 20 (Logroño: Universidad de La Rioja, 1998); Salmonte, "Análisis y funcionalidad de la '*Vita Aemiliani*,'" 247–66; and, the short introduction in Barlow, *Braulio of Saragossa*.

33 Tarragona and Córdoba, for example, seem to have been far more vibrant centers of life in the peninsula during the seventh century. See Pérez Martínez, *Tarraco*, and, Martínez, "Aqueducts and Water Supply." For a recent discussion on the Visigothic collecting of taxes, see Damián Fernández, "Statehood, Taxation, and State Infrastructural Power in Visigothic Iberia," in *Ancient States and Infrastructural Power: Europe, Asia, and America*, ed. Clifford Ando and Seth Richardson (Philadelphia: University of Pennsylvania Press, 2017), 243–71.

of compromise. This discursive competition is at the very heart of the history of the *Hispana* and the ways in which its versions and manuscripts deal with Gundemar's council and the Third Council of Seville.

2.2 *The Three Versions of the* Hispana

It was this complicated historical situation out of and into which the *Hispana* was conceptualized and actualized, but it is not only this historical moment that defines the history of the *Hispana*. Three versions of the *Hispana* were produced in the seventh century, between the years 633 and 694/702. Although each served its historically associated purposes, no Visigothic version of the *Hispana* was ever compiled outside of Seville or Toledo. This makes Isidore-Seville and Toledo-Agali *the* voices of the canonical past in pre-Islamic Spain and of the Spanish historiography into the centuries following. Collectively titled *Hispana*, these three versions are known individually as the *Isidoriana*, the *Juliana*, and the *Vulgata*.

2.2.1 *Isidoriana*

The *Isidoriana* is the earliest form of the *Hispana*, written, as its name implies, by Isidore-Seville, between 633 and 636. The *Isidoriana* is a redaction of the conciliar past, presented in chronological order. It did not make its way safely through the rough and tumble of Mediterranean time, but it is known to have existed from eighth-century textual and manuscript references,[34] and has been reconstructed by the authoritative editors of the *Hispana*.[35]

2.2.2 *Juliana*

Subsequent to the so-called *Isidoriana*, two revisions of the *Hispana* were made, both in Toledo. The first full revision was made around 681, and XII Toledo, the council that reintroduced to the *Hispana* the conciliar activities of Gundemar.[36] At some point between Wamba's Eleventh Council of Toledo

---

34 *Chron. 754*, 18, and MS Vienna 411, a *Vulgata* recension transmitted to Francia (perhaps from Galicia), and the *Codex Rachionis*, compiled by bishop Rachio of Strasbourg circa 787–788, but burned with the town library of Strasbourg in 1870. There is a description of the manuscript by Dom Pitra in Séjourné, *Saint Isidore*, 514–23, but for discussion and bibliography see Bernard Franck, "Recherches sur le manuscrit de l'Hispana de l'évêque Rachio," *Archives de l'église d'Alsace*, new series 7 (1956): 67–82.

35 CCH 1 (1966), 11–15, 103–205, 384–86; Gonzalo Martínez Díez, "Concilios españoles anteriores a Trento," in *Repertorio de Historia de las Ciencias Eclesiasticas en España, vol. 5, Siglos i-xvi* (Salamanca: Universidad Pontificia, 1976), 306–07; Rodríguez, "Los antiguos concilios españoles," 3–13; and, *Stocking, BCC*, 15–16 and 108–114. For an argument antithetical to Martínez Díez's conclusions, see Charles Munier, "Nouvelles recherches sur l'Hispana chronologique," *Revue des Sciences Religieuses* 40 (1966): 400–10.

36 On the second revision, see CCH 1 (1966), 324, and CCH 2 (1976), 350.

in 675 and Ervig's opening council of 681, Julian repaired, re-ordered and had the *Hispana*'s material re-adjusted.[37] This editorial action created the version of the *Hispana* that would become the revision attributed to Julian, and that would become the primary version of the *Hispana* transmitted. The *Juliana* has its own peculiar inclusions and exclusions, the most important of which, in terms of the present discussion, are the reintroduction of Gundemar's decretal with its related constitution, and the continued silence on III Seville. The reintroduction of the Gundemar material was meant to adjust the *Hispana* to an alternative political context and, in making it a defense of the authority of the church and monarchy in Toledo, seriously alter its original significance.[38]

2.2.3 Vulgata

The second revision of the *Hispana*, and the only other extant version, is an anonymous recension of the *Juliana* made in Toledo, and known as the *Vulgata*. It was made at some point shortly after XVII Toledo in 694, after the bishopric of Julian and not long before the collapse of the kingdom in 710–712.[39] The *Vulgata* is important here specifically for some of the councils it uniquely brings to light and which indicate further attempts at *damnationes memoriae* by Isidore-Seville and Toledo-Agali.

2.3 The Contents of the Recensions

The contents of the *Hispana* differ in each version. The *Isidoriana* ends with the transference of the school to Braulio, the *Juliana* with Julian's conciliar activities, and the *Vulgata* at XVII Toledo. Overall, dozens of Iberian councils are included in the *Hispana*, ranging chronologically from the period of the pagan Western Roman emperor Constantius Chlorus, with the Council of Elvira c. 306, to king Egica's XVII Toledo in 694. The council of Elvira's eighty-one short

---

37 This may have been part of the wider reforms and efforts at uniform practice going on, including the production and formalization of church ritual in the *ordo de celebrando concilio*. The basis of the *ordo*, like the *Hispana*, lay in the efforts of IV Toledo, in this instance, its fourth canon. On the creation of the *ordo de celebrando concilio* in the 670s and wider portrayal of early medieval conciliar ceremony see Charles Munier, "L'*ordo de celebrando* concilio wisigothique," *Revue des Sciences Religieuses* 37 (1963): 250–71.

38 Interestingly, Julian leaves XI Toledo out of his redaction, although he was there. Julian may have excluded the record of his presence at this council as a way to disassociate from Wamba after the affair of Ervig's apparent usurpation and Julian's potential role in it. Doing so would have been quite difficult, though, one may imagine, given the *Historia Wambae*, so it is unclear why Julian did this. For further discussion, see Appendix: Julian of Toledo Not an Agalian.

39 See Félix Rodríguez, *Observaciones y sugerencias sobre algunos manuscritos de la Colección Canónica Hispana* (Burgos: Facultad Teológica del Norte de España, 1975), 139–42.

canons, opening list of signatures, reference to a non-present Roman emperor, and total lack of any representation from Toledo, stand in stark contrast to XVII Toledo's long opening royal pronouncement from a Visigothic king centered in Toledo, eight detailed canons, closing list of signatures and concluding *lex in confirmatione concilii*. Indeed, a simple comparison of the *Hispana*'s opening council and the last Visigothic one recorded in it presents a fine microcosm of the internal history of the Iberian councils from late antiquity to the end of the Visigothic kingdom: from independent ecclesiastical activities pursued within a part of the Roman Empire to official voices of, often expressed directly to, a barbarian king located at the heart of the peninsula.[40]

What this chapter is especially interested in is the deceptive appearance of totality put forth by the *Isidoriana* and the extensive censorship that it hides. The *Hispana* was conceived by Isidore-Seville as a text to provide the reader, through the structural relationship of its contents, with a sense of comprehensiveness to the story. This was meant to build trust and confidence in this school by making the reader and audience feel that the author was comprehensive in their compilation of historical pasts. Therefore, the reader and audience felt comfortable believing that recorded faithfully were the proceedings of conciliar councils of Hispania, provincial and plenary, either from the early fourth century or at least from the early sixth century to 633. This was a lie, a false totality and "image of continuity, coherence and meaning" that presented the "true" story of the unique centrality of Seville to orthodoxy in Spain and as the only true rival to Toledo (or vice versa).[41] As, borrowing a concern from Marrou, Danuta Shanza warns, "Many students of canons and canonical lists fall victim to the fallacy of demanding a higher degree of precision or exhaustiveness from their sources than those very sources required or were intended to have."[42]

It is not only Gundemar's conciliar activities and III Seville that were excluded from the *Hispana* by Isidore-Seville, although these are the focus of this chapter, but also, for example, multiple councils from the end of the sixth century and early seventh century: Narbonne (589), II Zaragoza (592), Huesca

---

40   For a recent critical examination of the historical council of Elvira, see Josep Vilella Masana, "Los obispos y presbíteros del supuesto concilio de Elvira," in *El obispo en la Antigüedad tardía. Homenaje a Ramón Teja*, ed. Silvia Acerbi, Mar Marcos, and Juana Torres (Madrid: Editorial Trotta, 2016), 335–54.

41   Hayden White, "The Value of Narrativity in the Representation of Reality," in Hayden White, *The Content of Form* (Baltimore: The Johns Hopkins University Press, 1987), 11.

42   Danuta Shanzer, "Augustine's Disciplines: *Silent diutius Musae Varronis*?," in *Augustine and the Disciplines: from the Cassiciacum to Confession*, ed. Karla Pollman and Mark Vessey (Oxford: Oxford University Press, 2005), 99.

(598), Toledo (of 597), II Barcelona (599), and Egara (614).[43] Comparable to the situation of the limited transmission of Gundemar's council, but even more pronounced, these councils remain extant in only one medieval manuscript, the *codex Aemelianensis* (Escorial d.I.1, fs. 222^v–226^r). It may be that they represent the transmission of another independent collection of councils from Tarragona, referred to as the *Epitome Hispana*. This collection was compiled in Tarragona in the early 600s around the time of Gundemar's council.[44] The dates of the councils recorded in the *Epitome Hispana* range from the years 589 to 614. All of the councils in the *Epitome Hispana* were left out of the *Hispana* by Isidore-Seville. This means that the only councils in between the conversion of the kingdom at III Toledo in 589 and IV Toledo in 633 were two councils of Seville, in 590 and 619. The image the *Isidoriana* provides to its readership and audience is a clear line of orthodox spiritual authority in Hispania, running from Leander of Seville at III Toledo through the councils of Seville to the early 630s' conciliar activities in Toledo led by Isidore, and Braulio, who then takes over authority from the aged Isidore.

2.4   The Transmission of the Hispana, and the Case of Gundemar

The *Hispana* was transmitted reasonably well throughout the middle ages, with multiple adaptations of its *Juliana* and *Vulgata* versions used for Gallic collections. Yet, the transmission of the conciliar activities of Gundemar is limited to one family of Spanish codices.[45] Gonzalo Martínez Díez and Felix Rodríguez have studied all twenty-four extant medieval manuscripts of the *Hispana*, plus two whose records of Iberian councils derive wholly or partly from the *Hispana*: Paris BN lat. 3846 and Paris BN lat. 1460.[46] The extant

---

43   In the edited version of the *Hispana* there are two councils listed as the Second Council of Zaragoza. This is because the council in Zaragoza in 592 was not recorded in the *Hispana* and so that of 691 was listed as the Second Council of Zaragoza. The council of 592 is listed only in this compilation in the *codex Aemelianensis*. It should be noted too that the Council of Egara was only recorded in writing at the Council of Huesca, ten years later, showing that council decisions were not always recorded in formal writing. This means that more councils than are known may have occurred, and also that recording them was a significant event. On the exclusions from the *Hispana* tradition, see Stocking, *BCC*, 16, n. 57.

44   On the independent transmission of the *Epitome Hispana*, see *El epítome hispánico, una colección canónica española del siglo VII*, ed. Gonzalo Martínez Díez (Comillas: Universidad Pontificia, 1961), and Kéry, *Collections*, 57–60.

45   For a helpful list of these manuscripts, collections and related bibliography see Kéry, *Collections*, 57–86.

46   For the comprehensive list and authoritative discussion of the manuscript tradition of the *Hispana*, including a detailed list of the extant, destroyed, missing and extraneous manuscripts, see the Introduction and Chapter 2, respectively, of *CCH* 1 (1966) and *CCH*

manuscripts range in date and place of provenance from the eighth century to the thirteenth century and from across Europe; most often, they are written in Visigothic script. Surprisingly perhaps, and in any case disappointing, not a single remaining manuscript of the *Hispana* is from Toledo.[47]

The oldest extant manuscript of the *Hispana* is the eighth-century Frankish *codex Vindobonensis*, or Vienna 411, housed at the Oesterreichische Nationalbibliothek in Vienna.[48] The manuscript is of Gallic origin, written in pre-Carolingian (non-Visigothic) minuscule, representing a Gallic adaptation of the *Vulgata* version of the *Hispana*. The manuscript does not contain the records of Gundemar's council, which are found only in the Spanish manuscripts.[49]

The oldest extant Spanish manuscript of the *Hispana*, and the second oldest extant *Hispana* overall, is the Escorial e.I.12, or *Codex Oxomense*. The lost Ur-model for the *Codex Oxomense* is an eighth-century Spanish manuscript made in Córdoba around the year 775.[50] The *Codex Oxomense* is a *Juliana* redaction from the ninth century, written in Visigothic round minuscule script.[51] It is shown by Martínez Díez and Rodríguez to be the archetype, in turn, of MS Escorial d.I.2, or, *Codex Vigilanus* (or *Codex Albedense*) and MS Escorial d.I.1, or *Codex Aemelianensis*, also written in Visigothic minuscule. The *Codex Vigilanus* was produced some time between 974 and 976 at the now ruined monastery of St. Martin de Alveda (Logroño) by the monks Vigila, Sarracino, and Garcia. The *Codex Aemelianensis* was put together between 992 and 994 by a bishop named Sisebut, at San Millán de la Cogolla, the old stomping grounds of Fronimian, Braulio's colleague and potentially biological brother.[52] Taken

---

6 (2002). For other excerpts of the *Hispana* and transmission of individual councils see *Index Scriptorum Latinorum Medii Aevi Hispanorum*, ed. Manuel C. Díaz y Díaz.

47 *CCH* 6 (2002), 41.

48 For a complete facsimile and notes see Otto Mazal, ed., *Wiener Hispana-Handschrift: Vollständige Faksimile-Ausgabe im Originalformat des Codex Vindobonensis 411*, Codices selecti phototypice impressi 41 (Graz: Akademische Druck-und Verlagsanstalt, 1974).

49 MS Vienna 411 represents the anonymous, severely limited and still unedited late seventh-century *Collectio Hispana Gallica*. For a discussion, see *CCH* 6 (2002), 103–09. For another list of the manuscripts related to the *Collectio Hispana Gallica*, see Kéry, *Collections*, 67–68.

50 On the relations to a lost 775 manuscript and the Córdoban origins of it in MS Escorial e.I.12, see Manuel C. Díaz y Díaz, "Pequeñas aportaciones para el estudio de la 'Hispana'," in *Revista Española de Derecho Canónica* 17 (1962): 373–90 (382–83).

51 *CCH* 6 (2002), 109ff.

52 See *CCH* 1 (1966), 109–32, and *CCH* 1 (1966), 30–33 and 111–19. The manuscripts contain more material than the *Hispana* collection, including the *Liber Iudiciorum* and the first record of Arabic numerals in Europe (García López, *Lex Wisigothorum*, 121–25). Although it is not a member of the oldest extant family, the *Oxomense* MSS, it is worth pointing out the existence of a fragmentary eleventh-century *Vulgata* from Córdoba, MS Escorial e.I.13, or, *Codex Soriensis*.

together, the Codices *Oxomense, Vigilanus* and *Aemelianesis*, and their Ur-text, represent a single manuscript tradition surviving from 775 to the 990s.

This independent Spanish tradition is a Toledan-centered one, and a cul-de-sac of its kind, being the only *Hispana* tradition to contain the *Appendix Toletana*, a list of seven Toledan documents, mostly from the first two decades of the seventh century.[53] These few manuscripts represent the only tradition to preserve the Gundemar texts. Of this family of Spanish manuscripts, the *Codex Vigilanus* is remarkably faithful to the preservation and promotion of Toledan documents and interpretation. So much so that its compilers actually went back through Isidore's *Chronicles* and added a whole new chapter praising the ecclesiastical activities of Toledo, namely, the building in that city of the church of St. Leocadia by Sisebut in 619.[54] This is the only manuscript to contain this chapter in Isidore's *Chronicles*, and so it could be reasonable to read it as a minor addition to Isidore's text. However, it may be that, as with the more significant material, for example, Gundemar's council and the other contents of the "Toledo Appendix," the *Codex Vigilanus* provides a unique glimpse into a Toledan response to Isidore's history-writing. Sisebut, the scribe of the *Codex Aemelianensis*, was no less fidelitous to Toledo and was ready to edit texts in a way that manipulated historical memory. For example, Sisebut was the first to add the *filioque* clause to III Toledo of 589. This changed the conversion narrative of Toledo to one in which Toledo had, from Reccared's conversion, embraced the Latin editing of the Nicene Creed. In actuality, the *filioque* addition was a development of Isidore-Seville from the 620s forward, and it did not appear in Hispanian councils until 653, at VIII Toledo, at which the *Liber Iudiciorum*, the first Visigothic law-code by a Catholic king, was promulgated.[55]

In the centuries in between the creation of the *Codex Aemelianensis* of 994 (the latest member of the *Oxomense* family) and the so-called *Proceso* of the mid-thirteenth-century edition of this *Hispana* tradition, another version of Gundemar's acts existed. These are now lost, but must have been used in the thirteenth century. This alternative text is evident in the almost complete

---

53 In Escorial e.I.12 & d.I.2, the *codices Oxomense* and *Vigilianus*, the records of I and II Seville are at the end, after the *Appendix Toletana*, which could indicate that Julian cut all of the Seville councils out of the record.

54 The chapter is listed by Mommsen as 416ª (*Chron. Min.* ii, 480). That Isidore left this important moment out of the *Chronicles* is significant evidence of the dating of the editions and Isidore's intended meanings for the text. Furthermore, this addition to the *Chronicles* reveals its lack in the contemporary period of its life, and enhances the interpretation concerning the significance of the early 630s production of the *Passio St. Leocadia*, and perhaps revision of the *Chronicles*.

55 On this, see Chapter 5, note 133.

re-arrangement of the order of signatories to Gundemar's decretal.[56] Moreover, the presence of another version of Gundemar's decretal used in the middle of that century is not surprising, given the fascinating story of the re-emergence of Gundemar's decretal and constitution in the thirteenth century, highlighted by a desire for accuracy, legitimacy, and legal clarity. This was manifested in a calculated drive from 1238 to the middle of 1240, led by royal, ecclesiastical actors in Spain, in dialogue with the Pope, to bring together all the records of the *Hispana*.[57] Interestingly, the thirteenth-century bishops of Toledo were unaware of the *Oxomense* tradition, and its only traceable owners – the abbot of Oña, the bishop of Oviedo, and the abbots of Sahagún, Silos, Cardeña, and Carrión – were all located relatively close to one another in the northern Duero plateau in various nearby valleys nourished from the melting snow of the Cantabrian mountains.[58]

2.5 Modern Edition: the Hispana vs. Edited Councils

Since the editorial work of Ambrosio de Morales in the sixteenth century, the *Hispana* has undergone significant modern editing. The first authoritative version of the twentieth century was that published by José Vives in 1963. This edition is very helpful since it also contains the translation of the *Hispana* into a modern language. Nevertheless, this useful edition and translation is problematic because it is based on only eight manuscripts.[59] The authoritative edition of the *Hispana* is now within the multi-volume series *La Colección Canónica Hispana*, by Gonzalo Martínez Díez and Félix Rodríguez. The first two volumes were produced only by Martínez Díez, with Rodríguez joining him for the third volume, published in 1982. The most recent volume was published in 2002. The entire, centuries-long story of the editing of the *Hispana* is not paramount here.[60] What should be pointed out, however, is that any editorial attempt at a comprehensive *Hispana*, one that includes all the texts from the various *Hispana* traditions, would be an attempt to invent a very different text, in that it would confuse an edition of the *Hispana* with an edition of the councils.[61] This is important to keep in mind, since it is the peculiarities of each of

---

56 CCH 6 (2002), 44–48.
57 CCH 6 (2002), 33–50.
58 See Vicente Castell Maiques, *Proceso sobre la ordenación de la Iglesia Valentina (1238–1246)*, 2 vols. (Valencia: Corts Valencianes, 1996), I, 194–203.
59 *Concilios Visigóticos*, ed. Vives, VIII.
60 On the history of the modern editing of the *Hispana* from 1597 to the present, see Rodríguez, "Los antiguos concilios españoles," 3–13.
61 Rodríguez, "Los antiguos concilios españoles," 9–10.

the three versions of the *Hispana* – their unique inclusions, exclusions and editing – that make the *Hispana* a valuable piece of contextual evidence.

3   The Example of Gundemar and his Council (610)

In writing his *Chronicles*, Isidore completely ignored the Visigothic king Gundemar, and in his *De Origine Gothorum* Isidore presented him as nothing more than a footnote to the history of the Visigothic kingdom, let alone the history of Hispania. Fast forward about a millennium and a half to the premier scholar of Isidore, Jacques Fontaine, who remains true to Isidore's historiography on Gundemar. In his massive, two-volume, thousand-page classic *Isidore de Seville et la Culture Classique*, Fontaine only mentions Gundemar once, on a single page, briefly, as a small part of a footnote. Gundemar is mentioned only in passing to connect the Visigothic hostility towards Brunhild, seen in Sisebut's *Vita Desiderii*, back to Gundemar, as evidence that Sisebut was maintaining a tradition of antipathy towards Brunhild.[62] For Fontaine, Gundemar is demoted to a marginalized footnote in history. The sole purpose for his presence in the historical text is as a supplement to the actions of his successor. The maintenance of such a near *damnatio memoriae* of Gundemar over fourteen centuries is remarkable.

The focus of the following discussion is not on reconstructing the history of Gundemar or the manuscript legacies *per se*, although this is part of the effort, but rather the origins and story of the construction and proliferation of the historiography of Gundemar as first begun by Isidore-Seville. In particular, the emphasis is on the decision of the school not to include in the *Hispana* the records of the 610 conciliar activities of Gundemar. These council records are constituted by a very important royal decretal, signed by Isidore, and an associated constitution expressing episcopal discontent with (but not formal disapproval of) that decretal. Such an antagonistic constitutional tone is the only of its kind from the Visigothic kingdom of Toledo and stands in stark contrast to the constitutional expressions of its later *Liber Iudiciorum*.

The council of Gundemar is fundamental for the history of Gundemar, and of the relations between the monarch in Toledo and church figures in the kingdom, inside and outside of Toledo. Gundemar's council is also essential to the history of Isidore and the direction of his writings, and to explicating the development of the competitive discourse between – to varying degrees mutually

---

[62]   Fontaine, *Isidore*, 841, and Fontaine, "Sisebut's *Vita Desiderii*," in *Visigothic Spain*, ed. James, 123 and 127.

marginalized – sites of authority and power in Hispania. Despite the *damnatio memoriae* of him, Gundemar was a fitting king to place in the pantheon of more-than-"note"-worthy Visigothic kings, yet he was not.[63] Gundemar's activities had a profound effect on Isidore and neither they nor Gundemar himself were marginal notes in Isidore's mind, nor should they be to historians. The decretal and constitution constellation re-defined the direction of Isidore's writing in the 610s, leading him into a flourish of historical writing and formalizations of the theory of proper kingship and affecting the way he dealt with Toledo and Toledo-Agali (king and bishops).

There are a variety of reasons why, in the early 630s, the school of Isidore-Seville would have wanted to formally suppress the memory of the council of Gundemar, with its decretal and constitution. These are explained more fully below, but for now it is worth pointing out that the decretal with Isidore's signature, shows his presence at the council in Toledo, at the council that marks not only his entry into the historical record but also his explicit approval of Gundemar's problematic activities and the potential disregard for junior and other bishops. For these and other reasons, the school felt compelled to suppress the memory of Gundemar's decretal and constitution by leaving them out of the *Hispana*, as Isidore had done already in his historical *origines* texts.

3.1 The Conciliar Activities of Gundemar: What's All the Fuss?

On October 22, 610 Gundemar, not long in office, held a council in Toledo.[64] By some interpretation this was a plenary council and could have been listed

---

63   For more on Gundemar's reign, see Michael J. Kelly, "Gundemar the Ghost, Isidore the Historian: Rethinking Visigothic History from the Whispers of its Literature," in *Creative Selection: Emending and Forming Medieval Memory*, ed. Sebastian Scholz and Gerald Schwedler (Berlin: De Gruyter, in press [2021]).

64   In the past, scholars have had doubts concerning the historical authenticity of Gundemar's council, but it is today accepted that it was a real event and the records authentic. In support of the authenticity of Gundemar's council and decretal see Kelly, "Gundemar the Ghost, Isidore the Historian"; *Concilios Visigoticos*, ed. Vives, 403–10; CCH 1 (1966), 209–20; Séjourné, *Saint Isidore*, 86–88; Thompson, *Goths*, 159–60; José Orlandis and Domingo Ramos-Lissón, *Historia de los concilios de España romana y visigoda* (Pamplona: Universidad de Navarra, 1986), 248–52; Isabel Velázquez Soriano and Gisela Ripoll López, "*Toletum*, la construcción de una *urbs regia*," in *Sedes Regiae (ann. 400–800)*, ed. Gisela Ripoll, Josep María Gurt, and Alexandra Chavarría Arnau (Barcelona: Reial Acadèmia de Bones Lletres, 2000), 521–71; Pérez Martínez, *Tarraco*, 403; and, Stocking, BCC, 121, and n. 13. For arguments questioning the authenticity of the texts, see Giovanni Domenico Mansi, *Conciliorum omnium maxima collectio*, 10.511; Felix Dahn, *Die Könige der Germanen* 5 (Leipzig, 1885), 175; Antonio González Blanco, "El decreto de Gundemaro y la historia del siglo VII," in *Los Visigodos. Historia y civilización* 3, 159–69; and, Antonio González Blanco,

in the *Hispana* as the Fourth Council of Toledo.[65] It was attended by bishops from every province and dealt in its content with ecclesiastical matters that directly addressed multiple provinces and which affected them all.[66] As either plenary or provincial, Gundemar's council was not included in the *Isidoriana*. The main function of the council was to pronounce a decretal, the *decretum Gundemari regis*, concerning the bishoprics of Cartagena and Toledo.[67] The decretal contains the signature of Gundemar, written in his own hand, plus the signatures of twenty-six bishops from every region and province of the kingdom, including Narbonensis, although authority over the latter is vague.[68] Only two bishops attested to being there for the decretal, Isidore and Innocentius, bishop of Mérida,[69] although all of the signatories were likely present.

In addition to the decretal, there was a supplementary *constitutio Carthaginensium*, pronounced by Gundemar the day after the council, containing signatures from fifteen bishops from around Carthaginensis/Carpetania. This Carthaginian constitution was meant, from Gundemar's point of view, to buttress the council's actions as expressed in the decretal, which it did. However, the *constitutio* also provides a rare glimpse into the serious conflicts and politicking, subtle incriminations, and the heated discourse of the early 610s, otherwise veiled in the historical record.

"La historia del S. E. peninsula entre los siglos iii–viii d.C. (Fuentes literarias, problemas y sugerencias)," *Antigüedad y Christianismo* 23 (2006): 53–79 (71).

65   It could also be considered the Fifth Council of Toledo if the 598 Toledo was plenary (bishops from every province were in attendance, including Masona, but not, interestingly, Leander or as a lower clerical representative, Isidore).

66   IV Toledo 3 defines a plenary council as one that dealt with matters relevant to the whole church ("fidei causa...aut quaelibet alia ecclesiae conmunis"), which the restructuring of the metropolitan statuses of two provinces and the seat of the king seems to fit. The compilers of the *Juliana* attached it to the proceedings of XII Toledo, perhaps because they did not know how to introduce it without otherwise disturbing the numbering of the Toledan councils. For the councils in Toledo in 655 and 675, both of which, by canonical definition, were provincial councils, the *Juliana* numbered them as plenary councils. The *Vulgata* recension introduces to the record the council of Toledo of 598, which also could have been a plenary council, by conciliar definition, at that point, but was not included as such, perhaps to maintain the integrity of the numbering as well.

67   *CCH* 6 (2002), 201.

68   "ob hoc, quia una eademque provincia est, decernimus ut sicut Betica, Lusitania vel Tarraconensis provincia, vel reliquae ad regni nostri regimina pertinentes."

69   To some extent, this mimics the signatory structure of Reccared's III Toledo, in which other than the bishop of Toledo, the top two signatories were from Mérida and Seville, Masona and Leander. Also, only a small sampling of the signatories actually attest to being there in Toledo in person, in particular, the five metropolitan bishops: Masona, Eufemius, Leander, Micecio of Narbonne, and Pantardo of Braga.

Following the *constitutio* and its signatures are three short *suggessiones* on behalf of Emilanem, bishop of Mentesas in Carthaginensis.[70] Such an ordering in the texts and use of the *suggessiones* in this way implies that those at the council and those working in Gundemar's court, although there are no records of any strictly secular laws by Gundemar, knew their way around the Romano-Visigothic legal tradition. The *suggestio* was traditionally, in late Roman imperial law, a question or advice submitted by a lower official to the emperor or other higher office holder, directly associated with imperial constitutions. This particular adherence to Roman legal tradition as it came down to Hispania, both in Visigothic and Byzantine circles, is a symptom of the broader dedication to legality in the records of the council. Not only do the *suggessiones* used in the constitution represent classical and late Roman imperial legal codification, but the decretal and constitution do as well. In classical Roman law and late imperial codification, as well as the Breviary of Alaric II (*Breviarium Alaraci*), or, *Lex Romana Visigothorum* (*LRV*), the decretal was essentially an imperial decision written down to be disseminated and universalized as law across the Empire or unified political unit, such as a kingdom, although its specific function varied according to the situation. It is reasonable to think that Gundemar's court saw the decretal as just such a final decision: a royal writ that became universal law across a unified political entity, and thus a smart legal move and definite affront to the Byzantines.[71]

The conciliar activities of Gundemar demonstrate the presence of keen jurists and other legal officials in Gundemar's court and their appropriate education in, awareness of, and versatility for adapting Imperial and Visigothic law. Evident in the council too are legalist conciliar innovations that are normally attributed to Isidore's II Seville in 619, as well as explicit imitation of Byzantine practice for the purpose of affiliating Gundemar with the Byzantine emperor.[72]

---

70   *CCH* 6 (2002), 212–14.
71   There is some inconsistency in terms of the title of the document by Gundemar. The decretal is opened as such, but in the signatures Gundemar, in his *propria manu*, refers to the text as *edicti*, hence the reference to the decretal as the *Edictum Gundemari*. If Gundemar saw the decretal as an edict, this further suggests its intention as a royal proclamation, a *lex in confirmatione*. On the history and function of the *decretum* and *constitutio* in Roman and late Roman law, see Ernst Levy, *West Roman Vulgar Law* (W.S. Hein, 1951); *Pauli Sententiae* (Ithaca: Cornell University Press, 1945); Jill Harries, *Law and Empire in Late Antiquity* (Cambridge: Cambridge University Press, 2004); Kaius Tuori, "Legal Pluralism and the Roman Empire," in *Beyond Dogmatics: Law and Society in the Roman World*, ed. John W. Cairns and Paul J. du Plessis (Edinburgh: Edinburgh University Press, 2007), 39–52; and, the introduction to David Johnston, *Roman Law in Context* (Cambridge: University of Cambridge Press, 2004).
72   Stocking, *BCC*, 129–30, and Orlandis and Ramos-Lissón, *Historia de los Concilios*, 252–90.

Gundemar approaches this task from multiple angles, for example, signing the decretal as *Flavius Gundemarus rex*. This action indicates that the council was an "ornate event," and reveals the intention to imitate Byzantine-style authority in the presence of the collected Spanish bishops. It was the tradition for the Visigothic king to sign a text as *Flavius* only when it served rhetorical, Byzantinizing purposes, in front of Spanish audiences. For example, Reccared signs III Toledo and a formal *decretum* as *Flavius*, but signs personal letters to Pope Gregory simply as *Rex*.[73] Much can be learned about Gundemar's reign from his conciliar activities, which, at the very least, indicate the legal adeptness of his court. It is perhaps not surprising to learn that a Visigothic king and his royal court displayed such characteristics, however, considering the general historiography of Gundemar and his reign, initiated by Isidore and his school, this is a notable discovery.

3.2 Rationale of Gundemar's Decretal

The decretal's explicit purpose was twofold: first, it involved the demotion of the bishopric of Cartagena from its status as metropolitan see of the province of Carthaginensis. This demotion would be so absolute that no bishop of Cartagena would ever sign a Spanish (Visigothic) council, from 610 until the end of kingdom in the 710s. In the one instance in which a representative of Cartagena's bishop signed the records, at XI Toledo in 675, the signature was excluded, by Julian, from the *Hispana*, and would only re-appear in tenth-century manuscripts.[74] This shows Toledo's lingering anxiety about former Roman provincial capitals, whether Cartagena or Seville, and could help explain Isidore's lamentations over Cartagena in the 630s.[75] The second function of the *decretum* was to elevate the bishopric of Toledo to the vacated post of metropolitan see of Carthaginensis. In so doing, decades after Liuvigild declared Toledo the *sedes regia*, Gundemar became the first Visigothic king to formally elevate the city of Toledo to metropolitan status of Carthaginensis.[76]

---

73 For the letter, see *Gregorii I papae Registrum Epistolarum, Libri viii–xiv*, ed. Ludovic M. Hartmann, Monumenta Germaniae Historica (Berlin: Weidmann, 1899), IX, 227, pp. 220–21.
74 On Julian's exclusion of XI Toledo see *CCH* 6 (2002), 15–18.
75 See Chapter 1, § 3 on Leander and Isidore, and Isid., *Orig.*, 15.1.67.
76 At the turn of the seventh century, Toledo had outside its city walls the monastery of Agali, as well as four abbeys, two cathedrals and a basilica. On the history of the development of Toledo as ecclesiastical metropolitan see and royal city, see José Orlandis, *La Iglesia en la España visigótica y medieval* (Pamplona: Ediciones de la Universidad Navarra, 1976), 93; Pérez Martínez, *Tarraco*, 283–92; and, Velázquez and Ripoll López, "*Toletum*;" Lauro Olmo Enciso, "El Reino visigoda de Toledo y los territorios bizantinos. Datos sobre la heterogeneidad de la peninsula ibérica en época visigoda," in *Coloquio Hispano-Italiano de Arqueología Medieval*, Publicaciones del Patronato de la Alhambra (Granada: Patronato de la Alhambra y Generalife, 1992), 185–98; and, Claudio Sánchez-Albornoz, *El aula*

The promotion of Toledo over Cartagena was meant to deface and challenge the Byzantine position in Cartagena and the wider peninsula, perhaps in anticipation of conquering the city.[77] The message of victory expressed by the conciliar activity was surely an act of propaganda that was part of the ongoing discursive competition and war of rhetoric between Visigothic and Byzantine officials in Hispania/Spania.[78] Gundemar opens the decretal with a practical, or popular, appeal to the bishops of Carthaginensis in a manner somewhere in between the legalist approach and the pathos of Sisebut's *VD* only a few years later.[79] Gundemar quickly acknowledges that much wrongdoing had been done recently in Toledo, explaining how it was manipulated during his predecessor Witteric's time, when it was subject to corruption and conspiracies and, in general, not well respected.[80] Gundemar would restore glory, order, piety and prestige to Toledo and its Church.[81] In addition, Gundemar points out that the Byzantines had also done a poor job defending the integrity of Cartagena, and the metropolitan Church of Carthaginensis,[82] which had recently been

---

regia y las asambleas políticas de los godos, Cuadernos de historia de España 5 (Buenos Aires: Facultad de filosofía y letras, 1946), 5–110.

77 Gundemar's armies may have reached Cartagena or near to it, and he may have taken Barbi, only four miles west of Antequera, which was re-taken in 612 by the Byzantines. On Barbi, see Maragarita Vallejo Girvés, "El sistema viario peninsular en los límites de la provincia bizantina de Spania," in *Camineria hispánica: actas del II Congreso Internacional de Caminería Hispánica,* ed. Manuel Criado de Val (Madrid: AACHE Ediciones, 1987), 95–108 (100), and Peter Bartlett and Gonzalo Cores, "The Coinage of the Visigothic king Sisebut [612–621] from the Mint Barbi," *Gaceta numismática* 158 (2005): 13–17. On Cartagena, see Paul Goubert, "Administration de l'Espagne Byzantine: Les Provinces," *Revue des Études Byzantines* 6 (1946): 71–133. For a discussion and criticism of Goubert, see Ripoll López, "On the Supposed Frontiers," n. 20.

78 This is seen clearly in the Comentiolus inscription of 589 or 590, on which see Wood, "Byzantine Spania," 292.

79 *CCH* 6 (2002), 205.

80 "[...] sed etiam aeternorum adipisci gloriam meritorum Nonnullam enim in disciplinis ecclesiasticis contra canonum auctoritatem per moras precedentium temporum licentiam sibi de usurpatione praeteriti principes fecerunt, ita ut quidam episcoporum Carthaginensium provinciae non revereantur contra canonicae auctoritatis sententiam passim ac libere contra metropolitane ecclesiae potestatem per quasdam fratrias et conspirationes inexploratae vitae omnes episcopali officia provehi atque hanc ipsam praefatae ecclesiae dignitatem imperii nostri solio sublimatam contemnere, perturbantes ecclesiastici ordinis veritatem euisque sedis auctoritatem quam prisca canonum declarat sententia abutentes."

81 In the Oxomensis, Vigilianus and Aemeliensis manuscripts (*CCH* 6 [2002], 20).

82 "Quod nos ultra modo usque in perpetuum fieri nequaquam permittimus, sed honorem primatus iuxta antiquam synodalis concilii auctoritatem per omnes Carthaginensis provinciae ecclesias Toletanae ecclesiae sedis episcopum habere ostendimus, eumque inter suos coepiscopos tam honors praecellere dignitate quam nominis iuxta quod de metropolitanis per singulas provincias antigua canonum traditio sanxit et auctoritas vetus permisit."

subject to the assassination of its bishop Licinianus, the deposition of its governor Comentiolus, and the intrigues of one bishop Stephanus.[83] Gundemar was doing the province of Carthaginensis a favor by demoting Cartagena and promoting Toledo in its place as metropolitan see. Gundemar would defend the interests of the true faith and (im)movable property of the see, and restore Cartagena's dignity and standing, despite stripping it of its metropolitan authority.

3.3 Gundemar's Legitimization of the Decretal

Gundemar built legitimacy for the ancient authority of Toledo as primatial see of Carthaginensis by tying this power back to the formal Catholic foundations of the kingdom at III Toledo, signed by the Catholic bishops, senior Goths (*omnes Gothorum seniors*), and several Arian bishops.[84] At this council, Gundemar claims, Toledo was elevated to metropolitanate of Carthaginensis. Gundemar's council was ratifying this move, and it was also correcting an existing ecclesiastical error from III Toledo. At that council, the bishop of Toledo, Eufemius, signed as "Eufemius in Christi nomini ecclesiae catholicae Toletanae metropolitanus episcopus provinciae Carpetaniae," suggesting that Toledo was not even in Carthaginensis, let alone the center of its spiritual life. However, Gundemar says that neither bishop Eufemius nor by implication any of the other signatories, including Reccared, Leander, Masona and the senior Goths, accurately understood the location of Toledo. Rest assured though, as Gundemar tells his audience through an appeal to commonsense, Carpetania and Toledo were "undoubtedly" (*procul dubio*) part of Carthaginensis, and so the matter was settled.[85]

---

83   See Wood, "Byzantine Spania," 315, and *Greg., Reg. Libri. viii–xiv*, ed. Hartmann, XIII, 47–50, pp. 410–18. That Cartagena was fully stocked with Justinian's *Corpus Iuris* is evident from the 603 *Exemplum Legis* from Cartagena/somewhere in Byzantine Spain, which cites the *Novella* and *Digesta*, and lays out the case against bishop Stephanus (*Diplomática*, ed. Canellas López, 176).

84   At the end of the *acta* of III Toledo are *subscriptiones virorum illustrium* rejecting the Arian heresy in favor of Catholicism ("post subscriptiones episcoporum, presbyterorum, diacorum confessi catholicae et damnationi haeresis Arianae subiectas sequuntur"). The list of signatories ends with "similiter et omnes seniores Gothorum subscripserunt." The small number of signatures of Arians and the number of revolts surrounding III Toledo imply that this list represented only a handful of Arian bishops.

85   "Illud autem quod iam pridem in generalis synodo concilii Toletani a venerabili Eufemio episcopo manus subscriptione notatum est, Carpetaniae provinciae Toletanam esse sedem metropolis, nos eiusdem ignorantiae sententiam corrigimus, scientes procul dubio Carpetaniae regionem non esse provinciam sed partem Cartagensis provinciae, iuxta quod et antiqua rerum gestarum monumenta declarant." On Gundemar's argument that Toledo had always been the metropolitan see of Carthaginensis, see Orlandis and

Gundemar's explanation for the move of the metropolitanate of Carthaginensis to Toledo, which was effectively a Carpetanian city at this point, could provide a peek into what may have been a significant debate, or even a wider social tension and contemporary discourse on identity and authority, about which next to no historical evidence remains. If Carpetania and Carpetanian identity had re-emerged in a profound way, it is interesting that Gundemar gave little thought to suppressing it.[86] Formally speaking, his decretal starts with an implied demotion, or rather negation, of Carpetania, which, at least since the conversion of the kingdom, had been the province or provincial region of the *sedes regia*. Gundemar bolsters the force of this move with an allusion to the twelfth canon of the Council of Chalcedon (451), which says that a province should not be split in two: "secundum antiqua Patrum decreta singulos noscuntur habere metropolitanos [...]."[87] This was meant as a way to "encourage" the bishops of Carthaginensis and Carpetania to sign the decretal and constitution, since the rest of Chalcedon 12 warns that any bishop participating in the splitting of a province shall lose their episcopal positions.[88] In accepting the suppression of Carpetania, the bishops may have been ignoring

---

Ramon-Lissón, *Historia de los concilios*, 246–60. On the use of "common sense" as a rhetorical device in late antiquity, see Brown, *Needle*, 57.

86 Carpetania lay within the northern plateau, stretching from Pallencia and Uxama in the north, to Toledo and Segobriga at its southern boundaries. Recent research illustrates that the emergent identity and uniqueness of this central region, and the re-emergence of Carpetania and Carpetanian identity with it, was a real phenomenon. See Martínez, *Tarraco*; Luis A. García Moreno, "Los orígenes de la Carpetania visigoda," in *Toledo y Carpetania en la Edad antiqua: simposio celebrado en el Colegio Universitario de Toledo 6 al 8 noviembre 1986*), ed. Jaime Alvar and Carmen Blánquez (Toledo: Colegio Universitario, 1990), 240ff.; Juan Antonio Quirós Castillo, "Early medieval landscapes in northwest Spain: local powers and communities, fifth-tenth centuries," *Early Medieval Europe* 19 (2011): 293; Castellanos, *Los godos*, 168–76; Alexandra Chavarría Arnau, "Churches and aristocracies in seventh-century Spain: some thoughts on the debate on Visigothic churches," *Early Medieval Europe* 18 (2010). 160–74; and, Tamara Lewit, "Pigs, presses and pastoralism: farming in the fifth to sixth centuries AD," *Early Medieval Europe* 17 (2009): 89ff. On the re-emergence and/or persistence of identities and localized rivalries see the chapters on Spain in *Urban Interactions*, ed. Burrows and Kelly.

87 For the Latin version of the Council of Chalcedon, see *Acta Conciliorum Oecumenicorum* II, ed. Eduard Schwartz (Berlin: De Gruyter, 1914). For discussion and translation of the Council, see Michel Jan van Parys, "The Historical Evidence on the Council of Chalcedon: the Council of Chalcedon as Historical Event," *Ecumenical Review* 22 (1970): 305–20, and *The Acts of the Councils of Chalcedon*, ed. and trans. Richard Price and Michael Gaddis, 3 vols. (Liverpool: University of Liverpool Press, 2005).

88 The decretal also has a bishop from Carthaginensis, and the constitution has bishops from what was Carpetania or Tarraconensis.

or dismissing the local identities and sentiments of those outside their small circles, a discontent evident in the constitution.

The constitution approves the demotion and promotion, respectively, of Cartagena and Toledo, and provides glimpses into otherwise unseen tensions. As such, it challenges the argument that Gundemar's actions represent an institutionalization of a *de facto* position, one that was already accepted by "la asamblea episcopal penisular."[89] In the constitution, one sees, if not an outright condemnation of Gundemar's authority, then dissenting opinions by bishops in Carthaginensis.[90] In the constitution, the bishops, almost all junior or in some way marginal, state that they in no way condone Gundemar's actions, or rather, the precedent of royal authority over ecclesiastical appointments and administration.[91] They confirm that Toledo is a metropolitan see only on the basis of canon law, by canonical precedent reaching back to bishop Montanus of II Toledo in 527. They never state explicitly that Toledo is the metropolitan see of Carthaginensis, only that it is a metropolitan see: "fatentes huius sacrosanctae Toledo ecclesiae sedem metropolitani nominis habere auctoritatem."[92] Moreover, at the start of the constitution's signatory list, Gundemar is referred to only as *Gundimari regis*, not *Flavius Gundemarus rex*, as Gundemar refers to himself in the decretal, and how Visigothic kings are mentioned in such texts. This was a potential challenge to Gundemar's elevated authority.

Regardless of the potential dissension at the council, which also divided local bishops in a least one city in Carthaginensis,[93] the transfigurative feature of Gundemar's conciliar activities appears evident.[94] By transferring the metropolitanate from Cartagena to Toledo, Gundemar, in anticipating the eventual Visigothic victory, pre-established a way to maintain the ecclesiastical unity of Carthaginensis a decade or so before Toledo's actual conquest. After Gundemar's council there was no need for any subsequent Visigothic king or council to expressly make this move, and no bishop of Toledo ever again signed Toledo

---

89 Pérez Martínez, *Tarraco*, 364.

90 Such expressed dissension is almost unprecedented in conciliar legislation. The only other place it appears is in III Seville, the other council presided over by Isidore and suppressed by Isidore-Seville from the *Hispana*.

91 Previous kings had exercised power over ecclesiastical appointments, for instance when Liuvigild replaced Masona with Nepopis, according to the author of the VPE, 5.6. However, Gundemar was institutionalizing the practice, with the authority of the church.

92 On the letters of Montanus of Toledo, see Céline Martin, "Las Cartas de Montano y la autonomia episcopal de la Hispania septentrional en el siglo VI," *Hispania Antiqua* 22 (1998): 403–26.

93 Venerius and Teudorus both sign as bishops of the Carthaginian bishopric of Castolonensis. The former signed the decretal, while the latter signed the constitution.

94 See Pérez Martínez, *Tarraco*, 363.

as in Carpetania or elsewhere other than Carthaginensis. Moreover, with the council, Gundemar also moved the Toledan monarchy closer to Roman tradition, giving it the cultural capital it needed against the Byzantines.[95] The ancient boundaries of Carthaginensis were revived at the expense of Carpetania, which held no cultural capital over the Byzantines, or anyone else that Gundemar cared to impress. Cementing Gundemar's move, the next bishop of Toledo, appointed by Sisebut around 614, the *vir illustris* and *dux* Helladius was, prior to his giving up public life for monastic life at Agali, the governor of Carthaginensis.

3.4 Effect of Gundemar's Actions

Isidore had much to regret about his role in Gundemar's council. The subsequent actions of Sisebut would not have been legally defensible in canon law or acceptable without the complicity of Isidore in prescribing the decretal of Gundemar in a way that paid tangential attention to proper conciliar precedent and which authorized, with his leading signature, if not the absolute authority of the Toledan monarchy over the Hispanian Church at least a step in that direction. This was a power that Sisebut immediately put to use, inaugurating his reign by appointing bishops.[96] In addition to his inaugural appointments, in 614 Sisebut reprimanded the bishop of Tarragona, Eusebius, and in a letter to him demanded the elevation of the bearer of the letter to the bishopric of Barcelona.[97] Sisebut made it clear that he was head of the kingdom and the Church, and was not afraid to ignore any cleric's advice – including that from Isidore – to act unilaterally.[98] It was at this time that Isidore began constructing his argument against this new power. He did so in a way that would characterize he and his school's relations with Toledo: subtle yet sustained discursive aggression, manipulation and the use of education and texts to promote the view of Isidore and the School, and the proliferation of an image of Isidore-Seville as the source of spiritual authority and defender of church rights against Toledo. It was the traumatic moment of Gundemar's council, followed rapidly by Sisebut's institutionalizing royal prerogative, that caused

---

95 Pérez Martínez, *Tarraco*, 363.
96 There is no example of a Catholic king before Gundemar doing this, unless we count Reccared's actions against the Arian church and its clergy or his edict at III Toledo. See *Leges Visigothorum antiquiores*, ed. Karl Zeumer, Monumenta Germaniae Historica, Legum Nationum Germanicarum 1 (Hanover and Leipzig, 1902), 418–20, and *Diplomática*, ed. Canellas López, 97.
97 *Ep. Wis.*, 7.
98 For brief discussion of this point, see Fontaine, "Sisebut's *Vita Desiderii*," in *Visigothic Spain*, ed. James, 126, n. 1.

the fatal rift between Isidore and his school with Toledo-Agali, the monarchy and its bishops.

A close examination of Gundemar's council reveals the exceptional employment of legalism and historicism in the period. It also suggests to what degree these activities represent a true peripeteia in terms of the relationship between the Visigothic monarchy and the Church. During this moment, the traumatic gap between the reality of this peripeteia and the desire of Isidore-Seville occurred. This soon became manifest in Isidore's *Sententiae* and *De Origine Gothorum*, texts that foreshadowed the cuts and *damnationes memoriae* of the *Hispana*.[99] What were the specific ramifications of all of this on the *Hispana* and the memory of Gundemar and his actions? Why exactly did the school cut Gundemar? The cuts are a product of the events of Isidore, the council, and then Sisebut and those subsequently of the 610s, but they are, as well, part of a sustained effort by Isidore and the multilayered response to the complicated situation in the early 630s.

3.5 *Why the* Damnatio Memoriae *by the School of Isidore-Seville*

In the late sixth century, two rival Constantinopolitan patriarchs, John Scholasticus and Eutychius, "drew up competing lists of conciliar decisions to support their opposing positions."[100] One need not, then, wait until the Byzantine iconoclast controversy from the eighth century forward to see the use of canonical lists not only as pedagogy, or as a way to Christianize the past and the present identity supposedly arisen from it, but also as a primary source in a fierce competitive discourse between rivals for authority *vis-à-vis* an early medieval capital city. To discover this in the seventh century, in the early medieval west, a region generally "characterized by diversity, not uniformity" one can look to the precedent of the *Hispana*.[101] As discussed in the previous chapters, Isidore-Seville promoted the historical and theological supremacy and tradition of authority for Seville over the rest of the peninsula, and certainly against Toledo. The event of Gundemar's council and reign were particularly poignant, representing a turn of focus in his writing, a new direction in his thoughts, and a traumatic moment symptomized by the emerged gap between thoughts and actions, not to mention his introduction into history.

Four reasons are proposed in this section for why Isidore-Seville cut Gundemar's council from conciliar records: first, including it would have meant

---

99   On the dating of Isidore's *Sententiae* to between 612 and 615, see Chapter 5, note 75.
100 Cameron, "Remaking the Past," 5.
101 See Cameron, "Remaking the Past," 16, and, for wider discussion, Brown, *Rise of Western Christendom*, "Divergent Legacies 500–750," part II.

presenting this school, and Isidore in particular, as defenders of the prerogative of the monarch over internal Church affairs;[102] second, it would have presented them as bullies over other provinces and episcopal brethren, and, third, implied the elevation of Roman law over canonical law; and, fourth, it could potentially have strained the important relationship between Isidore's family and that of his successor as head of the school, Braulio. For these reasons, Gundemar's council was excluded from the *Hispana*.

Before elaborating on these reasons for why Isidore-Seville cut Gundemar's conciliar activities from the record, it should briefly be reiterated that they did in fact cut the records. No seventh-century manuscripts of the *Hispana* remain, but it has been firmly established that Gundemar's conciliar activities were authentic and were reintroduced by Julian of Toledo and placed at the end of XII Toledo.[103] The non-chronological position of Gundemar's council, out of place from the rest of the councils, indicates that it was an addition by the *Juliana* redactors. Furthermore, one can be confident that Gundemar's council was purposely left out of the *Hispana* on two grounds. First, the denunciation and manipulation specifically of the memory of Gundemar is a persistent and wider situation in the writing of Isidore, which goes on to create a nasty and almost unbelievable historiographical legacy. Second, as indicated already, cutting conciliar activities that ran counter to the pedagogical intentions and political aspirations of Isidore as an individual and as the network was not a problem. They created historical *lacunae* to direct knowledge and memory in a way that promoted their authority over Toledo's, with competitive discourse, smart applications of language, education and keen networking being their main forces against the *sedes regiae*, who repeatedly responded confrontationally, for example in the *Juliana*. In addition to cutting Gundemar's council, which Isidore was at, along with his brother Fulgentius, the *Isidoriana* authors cut from the *Hispana* at least one other council, if not two councils, led by Isidore personally. The most certain of these councils censored from the *Hispana* is the Third Council of Seville. The other is a council (*synodi*) held in Toledo but led by Isidore sometime between 610 and the early 620s, in which one Sintharius was "cooked but not purified" ("igni etsi non purificatus") by inquisition.[104] The manuscripts, editions, political history of the seventh

---

102   Contrary to Isidore in his *Sent.*, 3.2 and *De Orig. Offic.*, and IV Toledo 75.
103   There they remained in the Spanish tradition throughout the middle ages and into modern editions, in the middle of the manuscript, suggesting that it was there in that place originally in the *Juliana*. In Escorial d.I.1, the *Codex Aemilianensis*, Gundemar's decretal and council are in fs. 185^r–186^v, and in Escorial d.I.2, the *Codex Vigilianus* fs. 193^v–202^r.
104   Braulio, *Ep.*, 3. This could refer to Sinthasius, the grandfathered-in Arian bishop that signed the Council of Egara in 614.

century, and precedents for such particular *lacunae* about Gundemar present strong evidence that Isidore-Seville excluded the Gundemar material from the *Hispana*. There were logical reasons for doing so, longstanding ones related directly to Gundemar's reign and the issues it raised.

3.5.1   Defending the Royal Prerogative: A Problem of the 630s and Before
Of the four explanations laid out in this section for why Isidore-Seville left Gundemar's council out of the *Hispana*, the most prominent issue, and the one most contemporaneous to the construction of the *Hispana*, during the reign of Sisenand, is that of royal prerogative in Church affairs, and the legacy of this prerogative since Gundemar. What is apparent in an exchange of letters between Isidore and Braulio is that each one of them, by the early 630s, expected the king to exercise, without any reservation, full and final authority over ecclesiastical appointments.[105]

The anonymous chronicler of 754, the first Christian to write a history in and of Spain after the Islamic conquest of Toledo, relates that Sisebut was a wise and learned king, Swinthila worthily received the kingship and was successful in his reign, Chintila held an enlightening council, and Tulga was of good character and ancestry. Despite the praise for each of his near predecessors and successors, all that the chronicler says of Sisenand is that he was placed on the royal throne after seizing power.[106] Despite being a relative of Sclua, the bishop of Narbonne at IV and VI Toledo, and of Fructuosus, the reputation of Sisenand was not a stellar one in the peninsula.[107] His relatively short reign saw significant revolts, including the two-year struggle against the usurper, Iudila, who had the support of the impressive metropolitan city of Mérida, and some regions of Baetica.[108] There were revolts against Sisenand from other directions

---

105   Braulio, *Ep.*, 5 and 6. These letters refer to Sisenand's decision to appoint the new metropolitan of Tarraconensis. Audax was consecrated, but it is unknown whether or not he was the person Braulio had wanted.
106   *Chronicle of 754*, chapters 13, 16, 18, 19, and 17: "Huius Eraclii temporibus Sisebutus in era DCL (612AD) [...] ut vir sapiens, nimium literature deditus retentat annos per octo [...], Huius Eraclii temporibus Suintila in era DCLVIII...digne gubernacula in regno Gothorum suscepit sceptra x annis regnans. Hic ceptum bellum cum Romanis peregit celerique victoria tocius Ispanie monarchiam obtinuit, Cintila...Hic concilium Toletanum XVIIII episcoporum habitum agitat, ubi non solum de rerum mundanis, verum etiam de divinas multa ignaris mentibus infundendo illuminat, and Tulgas bone indolis et radix." About Sisenand, the chronicler says, "Sisenandus [...] per tirannidem regno Gothorum invaso, quinquennio regali locatus est solio."
107   In contrast to what is said about him by Franks, e.g. Fredegar.
108   The chronicler of 754 says five years, 631–636, while the *CRV* pinpoints it as four years, eleven months and sixteen days (*CRV*, ed. Mommsen, 1898, p. 467).

as well. The Basques had invaded down the Ebro, perhaps taking advantage of the usurpation(s) going on in Toledo, and the revolt of Iudila elsewhere.[109] On the whole, the revolts and incursions were so serious that Sisenand, having called for a plenary council already in 632, likely to affirm his position and condemn Swinthila, had to cancel it, telling bishops to go home, which Isidore kindly refused to do.[110] As such, Isidore may have been in Toledo to witness Sisenand's possible support for the attempted "usurpation" of the bishopric of the metropolitan Church by Gerontius, from Justus, the rightful Agalian heir to the bishopric of Helladius.[111] Usurpation, then, was the mediating point for the early Spanish historiography of Sisenand.[112] It was the lens through which Sisenand was seen and seems a fair way to imagine how Isidore, Braulio and others in the peninsula witnessing the events saw him.

After Sisenand's usurpation of the throne was secure, with Iudila defeated, and entirely erased from history, and the curious situation between Gerontius and Justus resolved, IV Toledo was finally convened in 633. Once the council opened, Sisenand spared no time in condemning specific rebels, either or both Swinthila and Iudila, and passing a canon (45) against rebellion generally. This was reinforced, it was hoped, by the elaboration of the role of the king and Church in canon 75. The Fourth Council of Toledo was, like Gundemar's council and the *Hispana*, above all else a hotly political affair. Indeed, this is solely how it is constructed in the initial Spanish historiography, with the astute chronicler of 754, the first writer to mention and admit to using as a source the *Hispana*, saying that the council's whole purpose was simply "to consider various issues." In contrast, the anonymous chronicler says that v Toledo, otherwise considered unimpressive by historians, "enlightened the minds of the ignorant on many things, both sacred and profane."[113] IV Toledo was impressive, the chronicler relates, for only two reasons: Braulio's performance, and the large number of bishops in attendance, from Hispania and Narbonensis. This demonstrates the political character of IV Toledo, at which Isidore also passed on guidance of the school to Braulio.[114] It may be that historians have over-inflated the contemporary significance of IV Toledo. It could also be

---

109 Braulio, *Ep.*, 5.
110 Braulio, *Ep.*, 6.
111 Gerontius was roundly admonished for the affair later. See Ildefonsus, *DVI* preface and ch. 7, and the potential reference to the affair in Braulio in *Ep.*, 35.
112 The Franks/Burgundians spun the story in the opposite direction, diminishing Swinthila and elevating/praising Sisenand (see Fred., *Chron.*, 4.73).
113 *Chronicle of 754*, chs. 18–19.
114 On Isidore's role at IV Toledo see Orlandis and Ramon Lissón, *Historia de los concilios*, ch. 4.

that the chronicler's copy of the *Hispana* was an *Isidoriana* that ended with V Toledo, led by Braulio, thereby painting *it* as the ultimate fruition, to that point, of the Catholic vision in Spain, through Isidore-Seville.[115]

The overarching point here is that Sisenand's power and authority, both as *a* king and as *the* king in Toledo, was the main agenda in the first half of the 630s, in which the *Hispana* was born absent of Gundemar's council. Sisenand's reign was especially disconcerting not only because he was a foreign-backed usurper, but also that his usurpation caused revolts and may have created a local schism within the metropolitan of Carthaginensis. Moreover, IV Toledo was called largely to promote the king's authority, which extended, Isidore and Braulio knew, to ecclesiastical appointments. This was not a sign of consensus between equal partners. However, the most unnerving aspect of all of this, for Isidore and Braulio, was that Sisenand never felt the need to defend his position over the Church. This royal prerogative was well enough entrenched in Toledo without the need for him to refer to any legal precedent for employing it. Such power had been formalized in 610 by royal and canonical legislation in Gundemar's council. This certainly was known by Isidore, and likely on the minds of he and Braulio – whose father signed the records of Gundemar's council, as did Maximus, predecessor as bishop of Zaragoza – during this affair. With the coming to the throne of a Frankish-backed usurper, the last thing Isidore and Braulio wanted was the further entrenching of this prerogative, or its extension. This is why the *Hispana* could not include Gundemar's council, which provided conciliar authority to royal appointments and, moreover, demonstrated Isidore's explicit endorsement of another Narbonnian/Gallic-supported king, Gundemar, to the Toledan Crown's institutionalization of the power of the king over the wider Church outside of Toledo.

Isidore and his school were in a difficult position with Sisenand. On the one hand, they needed to be pragmatic, knowing that, since Gundemar, the king had had the legal authority to unilaterally decide on major ecclesiastical decisions. On the other, they also needed, especially at this moment, a vital point in the school's leadership and continuity, to express somehow the image that they were protecting the autonomy of the Church, its authority and spiritual independence, in the face of Toledan aggression, usurpers, and Gallic intrigues. Pragmatic politics is one thing, while the preservation and propagation, within a pedagogical text like the *Hispana*, of the structure that led to and

---

115 In fact, this makes even more sense if we consider the exceptional diligence of the bishops of VI Toledo held two years later in 638, and so two years after Isidore's death, in exposing the injustices and crimes committed at and supported by Isidore and his network at III Seville.

symptomized royal, Toledan domination over the church, was another. Politicking was no surprise, what was, was the pragmatic activity and the contrast between it and the story told in the texts from both Seville and Toledo, a real gap between what could be done and what could be said, between actual life, authority and power, and the utopian desires for the future.[116] If Isidore and Braulio had no real power in the present against the political pragmatics of the situation, they could use their learning, wisdom and abilities to present and sustain discourses that stood against this situation. This is precisely what they did by cutting Gundemar's council, thereby leaving out of the historical record the legal and formal authority of the king, Sisenand or otherwise, to make such appointments in the future.

This general struggle to maintain provincial, regional church autonomy and episcopal authority, while at the same time respecting the king (and his army), was not uncommon throughout the kingdom. It was just that Isidore-Seville had particularly well-connected and smart writers at its disposal, thanks in large measure to Isidore's own resources, education, school, and diligent networking able to challenge Toledo's (meta-)authority, or at least present an image and memory that they had done so. As such, it was they who were the main source of antagonism for Toledo.

3.5.2   Collegiality?

The decretal and the constitution, as events of lasting significance to the kingdom and to the Spanish Church, may have caused or sustained divided loyalties and personal opinions to a much greater extent than the evidence allows one to conclude. Isidore cut the records of the Third Council of Seville from the *Hispana* in part because it made him look overbearing towards junior colleagues. He could also have been seen this way from the Gundemar affair, a reason for him not to include the council in the rhetorical, and pedagogical, *Hispana*.

The decretal and constitution records seem to show that at least some junior colleagues may have been pushed to the side, for example, in the confusing case of Venerius and Teudorus,[117] but also in the variations in the signatures of

---

116   Although such a gap is present in varying ways in cultures, this particular *caesura* between actions and words, evident throughout the history of Isidore, his school, and writing more widely in the period, is wrapped up with paradoxes of late antique and early medieval Christian culture, especially when the Roman legal(ist) tradition confronted new ideals. One example from Isidore is his demanding prayers for the poor, charity, forgiveness, etc. (*Sent.*, 3.60) and yet, in *Sent.*, 3.53, saying that the poor should not be shown mercy in court, out of respect for legal fairness, of course.

117   On Venerius and Teudorus, see Chapter 4, note 93.

Isidore and Innocentius: "dum in urbem Toletanam pro occursu regio euenissem (Isidore)/aduenissem (Innocentius), agnitis his constitutionibus assensum praebui atque subscripsi."[118] This need not suggest that they were the only two there, but it does show the special relationship of Seville and Mérida with Toledo. More importantly, the slight differences in the language between the signatures indicate a close cooperation between Gundemar and Isidore, with Innocentius brought in to approve the actions upon which they had decided. However, this may have been an established situation, of Isidore's dominance over the passive Innocentius, a man the *VPE* calls "innocuus semper et pius."[119]

Nevertheless, whether in the curious case of Venerius and Teudorus, of the dominance of Isidore over Innocentius, or the fact that these two bishops are the only in the decretal to explicitly state being there in Toledo for the council, there appears a general lack of collegiality in the council, which runs counter to Isidore's expressed vision. Indeed, it is the "special duty" (*speciale officium*) of a bishop, Isidore says, not only to read the Scripture and the canons (hence the pedagogical and political function of the *Hispana*) and to guide the priests ("'Scopos' [...] ergo 'episcopin' latine superintendere possumus dicere"), but also not to admonish or look down upon any of them ("nec quemquam ex membris suis dispicere, nullum [...]"). The bishop is to be at complete peace with his brothers ("cum fratribus habere pacem"), a situation the decretal and constitution does not represent.[120]

3.5.3 Family, Friends, and Cartagena

It is a spirit of collegiality, in a sense, that suggests another reason why Isidore-Seville excluded the decretal and constitution from the *Hispana* (and *De Origine Gothorum*). Namely, it was a way to respect the position and memory of family and friends, some of whom may still have been in Cartagena.

For his sister Florentina, who died around the time of the construction of the *Hispana*, Isidore had written and dedicated his book on the Jews (*Contra Judaeos*), a pedagogical text meant for the assistance of her nunnery.[121] Isidore

---

118 *CCH* 6 (2002), 208.
119 *VPE*, 5.14.1–2.
120 Isid., *De Orig. Offic.*, 2.5, ls. 70–72 and ls. 173–75. Concern for brethren is otherwise evident in *Sententiae*, 3.32.2: "Qui veraciter fraternam vult corripere ac sanare infirmitatem, talem se praestare fraternae utilitati studeat, ut uem quem corripere cupit humili corde admoneat, et hoc faciens ex conpassione quasi communis periculi, ne forte et ipse subiciatur temptationi." Isidore may have been adapting Augustine's monastic egalitarianism, on which see Peter Brown, *Religion and Society in the Age of Saint Augustine* (New York: Harper & Row, 1972), 266.
121 On the death of Florentina, see the inscription noted in Chapter 2, § 4.1.

dedicated another pedagogical book, the *De Origine Officiorum*, to his problematic younger brother and episcopal colleague, the bishop of Astigi (Ecija), Fulgentius, who stood with Isidore at Gundemar's council, signing the decretal as the signatory from Astigi. Fulgentius also signed II Seville, at which a jurisdictional dispute concerning his episcopal jurisdiction was at the top of the agenda (canon 2). Isidore may have needed to protect Fulgentius by later "bending" the secular and canon laws at III Seville, which involved the bishop of Astigi, Martianus, the successor of Fulgentius, who was unlawfully, and by brutal means, including the torturing of women, deposed from his seat in favor of a certain Aventius.[122] III Seville was also excluded from the *Isidoriana* for multiple reasons, one of which may have been the role of Fulgentius; it was important for Isidore-Seville to limit exposure to Fulgentius in the historical record.

Isidore never wrote a book during Leander's lifetime, and never dedicated one to him. He nonetheless admired his older brother and spent much of his episcopal and literary career defending the great legacy of Leander. Whether in preserving Seville as the new Constantinople and site of spiritual authority of Hispania, praise in his *DVI*, or the defense and promotion of Leander's grand achievement, the conversion of the peninsula and kingdom, Isidore was a consistent proponent of his immediate family and a diligent sibling able and willing to use his authority, training and connections to preserve his family's name and legacy. He did so even if it meant having to break the law, bend canonical rules or manipulate the living and historical records and memory of the past.

Despite the lack of overt attention paid to his family in his extensive writings, which some historians have seen as a lack of concern for them, Isidore was deeply committed to his "circle" – his family, friends, and students. This was regardless of the borders of the Visigothic kingdom and Byzantine Spania, namely its capital, Cartagena.[123] As such, it is possible that Isidore would have wanted to cut Gundemar's council from the records, especially after the Byzantine collapse and Visigothic conquest of Cartagena. This is because in this scenario the city lost its privileged status, while Toledo gained ecclesiastical and spiritual authority. This was a double blow to Isidore-Seville. It was a move authorized, embarrassingly and regretfully, by Isidore, who in the 630s lamented the Gothic destruction of the city. As recent archaeological work suggests, this claim by Isidore may have been an exaggerated rhetorical one,

---

122 See *Exemplum* B.2, C.1, and Stocking, "Martianus, Aventius and Isidore: Provincial Councils," 168–92.
123 On the "border" between Visigothic and Byzantine Spain, see Chapter 1, note 4.

made to denigrate the Gothic kings. Found only later in the *Origines*, it could also have been a metaphorical statement, alluding to Cartagena's loss of status since Gundemar, a lamentation.[124] Such a conclusion of ultimate regret would be consistent with and further clarify the reasons for why Gundemar's council is never included by Isidore in any of his historical writing, from the *De Origine Gothorum* through the *Hispana*, despite his presence at the council and its definite significance for the kingdom and churches around the peninsula.

Isidore's association to Cartagena was not merely nostalgic, though it is not impossible that nostalgia for his family's apparent hometown and the place of his birth played some role in not wanting to preserve a record of his demoting its bishopric.[125] Beyond this sentimentality lay firm connections with the city, including Leander's movements through it in his trips to and from Constantinople. Throughout the Byzantine occupation, even after the conversion of Toledo, Leander remained in close contact with Cartagena, including with its bishop Licinianus.[126] Isidore must have been associated with and potentially in contact with people like Licinianus as well, whether or not he had travelled himself back to Cartagena, as his brother Fulgentius had done in the late 570s.[127] This is definitely the case with Leander's old colleague, John of Biclar, who travelled through Cartagena back and forth between Constantinople and was exiled to Barcelona by Liuvigild until the end of that king's lifetime. John was not only close to Leander, but also certainly in touch with and influential upon Isidore, who set out to continue John's *Chronicle* shortly after John's death, although he would do so in a very different vein. John was also one of the signatories of Gundemar's decretal, led by Isidore. Pope Gregory's letters through Cartagena to Leander, and possibly other materials as well, also reached Isidore in Seville. The numismatic evidence shows, in Isidore's time, the continued circulation of gold and even copper coins between the cities, as

---

124 Isid., *Orig.*, 15.1.67. On the archaeology of Cartagena revealing that it was not destroyed, see Sebastián Ramallo Asensio, "Aproximación al urbanismo de Carthago Nova entre los siglos IV–VII D.C.," in *Spania: Estudis d'antiguitat tardana oferts en homenatge al profesor Pere de Palol i Salellas*, 201–08, and Sebastián Ramallo Asensio and Elena Ruiz Vaderas, "Cartagena en la arqueología bizantina en Hispania: estado de la cuestión," in *V Reunió*, ed. Gurt and Tena, 316–21.

125 On the love of one's hometown in late antiquity, see Brown, *Through the Eye of a Needle*, 64.

126 Isidore, *DVI*, ch. 29; Licinius, *Epistula* 1 (*Liciniano de Cartagena y sus cartas. Edición crítica y estudio historicó*, ed. José Madoz [Madrid, 1948], 84 and 92–93); *Epistulae Liciniani episcopi Carthaginensis*, ed. Ángel Custodio Vega (El Escorial: Typis, 1935); and, Wood, "Defending Byzantine Spania," 315.

127 Leander, *Regula*, ch. 23.

does the archaeology show the circulation of goods, such as African Red Slip (which disappears with the collapse of Byzantine Spain).[128]

Finally, although slightly askew from a family or Cartagena context, but very much in line with the fidelity to the school of Isidore-Seville, there is the issue of the signature in the constitution of Gregory of Oxomensis, the father of bishop John of Zaragoza and his brother Braulio. This is, ironically or fittingly, the site from which Gundemar's council was ultimately preserved (through the MS Oxomensis). Back at the time of the council, it was a young bishopric, born around the time of III Toledo, and one that was, in fact, in the see of Carpetania suppressed at Gundemar's council.[129] Even if the rift evident in the decretal and constitution was not remarkably divisive, it stands to reason that with Braulio, the son of Gregory, member of a prominent Ebro valley family, in Seville at the time or having been there recently for his education and training, or even simply working closely with Isidore, it would have been a nice gesture not to mention Gundemar's council in the 610s. That this was on Isidore's mind is a reasonable conclusion since only a few years later, when he wrote his *DVI*, he structured it in such a way as to complement and promote the family of

---

128 The extent of the connections has led historians to argue that Seville was part of Byzantine Spania for some time. This traditional view was expressed by Karl F. Stroheker in "Das spanische Westgotenreich und Byzanz," *Bonner Jahrbuch* 163 (1963): 252–74. Several years later, Thompson (*Goths*, 368) authoritatively argued that Seville was never controlled by the Byzantines. For two very interesting copper coins from Seville from the period see numbers 11 (07GV11) and 12 (07VG12) in the Gale Collection of the Australian Centre for Ancient Numismatic Study. The obverse sides of each coin contain the letters "S" and "P" for [I]Spali. On the no. 12 coin, the "S" and "P" flank the stem of a cross, demonstrating a clear local association of the city with its church. For a comparative look at the Byzantine tremiss of Spania (minted in Cartagena and Malaga), see Peter Barlett, Andrew Oddy, and Cécile Morrisson, "The Byzantine gold coinage of Spania (Justinian I to Heraclius)," *Revue Numismatique* 167 (2011): 351–402. For more on the copper coins, see Ruth Pliego, "The Circulation of Copper Coins in the Iberian Peninsula during the Visigothic Period: New Approaches," *Journal of Archaeological Numismatics* 5, no. 6 (2016): 125–60, and for a bronze coin from Seville see Ruth Pliego Vázquez, "Kings' Names on Visigothic Bronze Coins: A New Minimus from Ispali in the Name of Leovigild," *American Journal of Numismatics* 30 (2018): 219–32. On silver coinage, see Miquel Crusafont, Jaume Benages, and Jaume Noguera, "Silver Visigothic Coinage," *Numismatic Chronicle* 176 (2016): 241–60. On the local production of base-metal coins and their circulation within Baetica and Spania, including Seville and Cartagena, see Kurt, *Minting, State and Economy*, 114–15, 277–79.

129 Gundemar's council dealt with and represented multiple re-emergent and new sees and bishoprics, not only Carpetania and Oxomensis, but also Celtiberia, Oretum, and that of Laberricensis whose see is never heard of again after its bishop Vitulacius signed the decretal of Gundemar in 610. For discussion of the bishopric of Oxomensis, see Pablo C. Díaz, "La diócesis de Osma en la Antigüedad," in *Arte e historia de la diócesis de Osma* (El Burgo de Osma, 1998), 215–25.

Braulio and their taking over of the bishopric, in the form of his brother John. This move was made over and against the previous bishop of Zaragoza, Maximus, who was also at Gundemar's council, having signed the decretal, and was the author of a *"historiola"* that was subsequently lost.[130] The role of Maximus in all of this is unclear, but regardless, the final act in this play between Isidore and Braulio's family would have been the maintaining of this silencing of the council of Gundemar when Isidore-Seville produced the *Hispana*, at the same time that the leadership of the school was passed on to Braulio, who, it is not unreasonable to believe, was involved in some way with the text's construction. It is possible, then, that the school cut Gundemar's council for reasons related to Braulio's family, out of friendship and for the future position of the school.

For Isidore, family and friends were significant influences that determined the actions of his life and his writing, in the form of text production on a whole, but also, very significantly, the way texts, including council records memorialized in the *Hispana*, were written. This is true also in regards to his tight relations with his specific network and school, some of which involved the family of Braulio, his connections to the Ebro valley, and, of course, to Cartagena. This city represented for Isidore not only a nostalgic hometown, but also a site of important personal and political connections, a complex, multi-faceted symbol of his past, of the Byzantine past, and of their and its place and meaning of his kinship and networking ties in the Hispania of the 630s, and forward towards the full conversion. There is no simple explanation possible for how the demotion of Cartagena and the potential propagation and further dissemination of this information and formalization would have affected Isidore and his school, how they would have perceived the potential repercussions, and how that determined their reason not to include Gundemar's council in the *Hispana*. Nevertheless, it is reasonable to conclude that the fact that it was Cartagena in particular that was being demoted, let alone in favor of Toledo, complicated matters and must somehow have been a factor when Isidore, Braulio, and others of the Isidore-School decided to maintain this historical *lacunae* and the wider *damnatio memoriae* of Gundemar's reign.

3.5.4 Roman Jurisprudence

Excluding Gundemar's decretal and constitution from the record presents, in the *Hispana*, the image of the development, or rather the preservation, of the Roman-Visigothic legal tradition through the provincial councils *via* Seville, as opposed to through Gundemar and Toledo. This narrative structure invented a clear chain of signification that associated Isidore-Seville with the legal

---

130   On this text see Collins, "Isidore, Maximus," 345–58.

tradition for the better – since they also left out III Seville – that found fruition in Braulio, Eugenius II, the *Liber Iudiciorum* and VIII Toledo. Furthermore, the inclusion of Gundemar's council in the *Hispana* would have meant that any subsequent attempt to ignore or challenge the Visigothic king's prerogative over church appointments would be breaking canon law, a situation one might assume Isidore and others were not keen to lay out so openly. Also, although it may not be expected to have been the type of present-day specifics included in the *Origines*, it nevertheless should be pointed out that Isidore's book on laws and times (*Orig.*, 5, *de legibus et temporibus*), effectively an origins-story of law, ignores Gundemar's decretal as well.

3.5.5 Conclusion

If Gundemar's council was so antithetical to Isidore's vision of monarchy and the authority of the church relative to it, one may ask: why did Isidore lead the council and sign off on royal prerogative? This would, however, be a misleading question. Although a variety of potential reasons for Isidore's actions could be pondered, it is important to keep in mind that it was only after Isidore's participation in the council and soon after the use of it by Sisebut for royal prerogative that Isidore began formulating, in already his tenth book (*Sententiae*), his theories of monarchy and consensus. It was his participation in the council and its aftermath that retrospectively created the problems relative to Isidore's and his school's visions of the role of the monarchy and the Church in the kingdom. Isidore participated in and signed the decretal for several local and immediate reasons. These had to do with the breakdown of the Byzantine province of Spania, and the protection during this crisis of the bishoprics, bishops and other clergy of Baetica, and his family and friends in Cartagena and around Baetica. His concern was for the autonomy and authority of the regional bishoprics, and here for Cartagena, evident in his II Seville and letters to Cartagena, and the implied relationships from that and Leander's movements through the city. This episode represents well the persistent contrast between pragmatic politics and competing visions of religious autonomy and spiritual utopianism, and its awkward relationship with realism.

The reasons for Isidore-Seville's exclusion of the council of Gundemar from the *Hispana* are related to the event of Gundemar's council itself, to Isidore's regret about his involvement in it, and especially to the immediate political circumstances of the early 630s. The *Hispana* was an immediate political agent, but also one that promoted the long-term spiritual authority of the school, now led by Braulio. It is with all of this in mind that the *Hispana* and its silence on Gundemar's council should be considered a savvy theo-political move by Isidore-Seville. Cutting from the story of Spanish conciliar history the council of Gundemar, which formalized Toledo's authority over the Church with Seville's approval, makes perfect sense under the historical conditions of the early 630s and furthermore indicates the complicated relationship in the Isidore-moment between Isidore-Seville and Toledo-Agali, periphery and center, the actions and voices of consent versus the competition put to pen.

In deleting Gundemar's actions from the *De Origine Gothorum* and the *Hispana*, Isidore denied historical agency to Toledo's spiritual primacy even of its own province, to eliminate the origin story, it could be said, of Toledo's becoming metropolitanate. Without an origin how could there be a legitimate future? As Walter Benjamin argued, and as is reverberated in literature by George Orwell, and Orwellian in character Isidore sometimes feels, "Who controls the past controls the future. Who controls the present controls the past."[131] Gundemar had to die twice for the full vigor of his significance to be felt. The Hegelian theory of repetition in history is that every *body* must die twice. First, there is the biological death, part of the natural cycle of generation, corruption and transformation, and of chance and contingency. Second, there is the absolute death, the destruction of the historical cycle itself. This frees history, as nature, from its own laws, allowing radical, alternative existence to emerge.[132] When Isidore announced Gundemar's absolute death in the *Hispana*, he broke the historical cycle of Gundemar. In its place he substituted an alternative chain of signification, a new "real and ratified existence."[133] The *Hispana* represents the body that is beyond the biological, beyond the cycle of the present, of reality. The *Hispana* is a "sublime object of ideology," an alternative ideology (or body) to the one pervasive in the existing world of the early 630s where kings had the legal right to make ecclesiastical appointments.[134]

This reinforces the idea that one should not readily associate Isidore's actions and words, for often these are not the same and are, rather, adapted to the immediate present. One aspect of Isidore that is notably consistent is not his writing as a reflection of his and his school's real actions, but rather the use

---

131 See George Orwell, *Nineteen Eighty-Four* (London, 1949).

132 On Hegel's (dialectical idealist) argument for historical discontinuities, and so break with Romanticism's views of the "natural course" of history and defense of continuity over disruption, see Georg Lukács, *The Young Hegel: Studies in the Relations between Dialectics and Economics*, trans. Rodney Livingston (Cambridge: MIT Press, 1975), 301–05.

133 Georg W. F. Hegel, *The Philosophy of History*, trans. John Sibree, Dover Classics (Mineola: Dover Publications, 2004, orig., 1837), part 3, "The Roman World;" Slavoj Žižek, *The Sublime Object of Ideology* (New York: Verso, 1989), ch. 4; and, Jacques Lacan, *Écrits*, Parts 1 and 4 especially.

134 See Miran Božovic, "Immer Ärger mit dem Körper," *Wo es war 5–6* (1988), and Žižek, *Sublime Object of Ideology*, ch. 4.

of writing for self-promotion, of him, his family, and school. Moreover, he has a tendency to change his mind in texts, adapting them to current circumstances and using them as clear tools of propaganda and overt manipulation that, if need be, were redacted later to erase or reconstruct the memory of this action. When a text he was involved in no longer suited this purpose, whether it was Gundemar's council or III Seville, it was cut from the written records, from "history," and so from the future memory of Spaniards.

4 The Example of the Third Council of Seville (624)

The second case-study of this chapter exploring omissions from the *Hispana* by Isidore-Seville, examines the Third Council of Seville. As with Gundemar's council, this council was formally led by Isidore, and subsequently left out of the *Hispana* in the early 630s. Unlike Gundemar's council, however, it never found its way into later versions of the *Hispana* or any manuscripts whatsoever. Nevertheless, there are important historical parallels between these two councils. Both councils make evident the existing discontent between local and regional bishops, the importance of local networks of power to achieve one's aims, the defense of such local networks above any wider unity, and the problems of conciliar justice more widely. In being erased from the *Hispana*, these two councils also share parallels in their representations of Isidore's, and the school's, attempts to present an image and narrative of it as the correct spiritual guide and holy authority for the kingdom. The case of III Seville also presents other Isidorian interests: the promotion of regular provincial councils, the application of Roman legal principles in conciliar justice, and the defense of patronage, family and local networks of authority as a social structure. Furthermore, the case of III Seville enhances the argument for the absolute interconnectivity of and dialogue between texts in the Visigothic kingdom and the (often historical) discourses in and about them. In particular, we see the close, and antagonistic, relationship between records of III Seville, the *Hispana*, and IV and VI Toledo. When read as a continuous and often competitive discourse, leading to the *Liber Iudiciorum* and VIII Toledo in 653, we see the deep political entanglements that drove Visigothic literature of all types in the period.

4.1 *Records of the Third Council of Seville*

The historiography of the Third Council of Seville is far less complicated than that of Gundemar's council. However, it is still imperative to begin the inquiry with the state of the records and the historical authenticity of III Seville. Following this, the council's contents will be explained, hypotheses introduced as to why Isidore-Seville left III Seville out of the *Hispana*, and finally the conclusion presented as to the significance of this exclusion to the Isidore-moment and its wider historical narrative.

The actual records and canons of III Seville are lost. It has been argued that one of the council's canons found its way into IV Toledo 57, but this is doubtful.[135] Unlike the council of Gundemar, which was not included in the

---

135   IV Toledo 57, found in the *Juliana* manuscripts of the *Hispana*, promises not to force Jews to convert, but prescribes force for maintaining fidelity to Christianity upon those who were forced to convert by Sisebut (Séjourné, *Saint Isidore*, 29 and 253; Drews, *The Unknown Neighbour*, 220, n. 112; and, Drews, "Jews as Pagans?," 206). From the latter point, Drews argues that Isidore, at III Seville, supported Sisebut's general policy of forced conversion, despite Isidore criticizing Sisebut's anti-Jewish policy in the second draft of the *De Origine Gothorum*, made about the time that III Seville was held. From the juxtaposition, Drews claims that Isidore personally supported Sisebut's policies of forced conversion (for Drews, this is also evidence that it is impossible to trace any clear and consistent line of thinking by Isidore on the position of Jewish conversion [Drews, *The Unknown Neighbour*, 219ff.]). Drews's conclusion could be challenged on a few grounds. First, the canons of IV Toledo represent a collective effort, even if led by Isidore personally. Second, the canon in question states that nobody should ever be forced to convert: "Ergo non vi sed liberi arbitrii facultate ut convertantur suadendi sunt non potius inpellendi." True conversion is a matter of internal decisions, not external pressure: "[…] sicut enim homo proprii arbitrii voluntate serpenti obediens periit, sic vocante gratia Dei propriae mentis conversione homo quisque credendo salvatur." It supports the use of force, though never of forced conversion, under one condition: to maintain the fidelity of those who were *already* Christian. This is all consistent with the theology of Isidore-Seville – from Isidore's position in *de fide Catholica contra Judaeos*, written in 614–615, just after Sisebut's laws on forced conversion, to Braulio's defense of the Patristic tradition in his letter to Pope Honorius – and it does not suggest support for forced conversion or require the canon to be from III Seville. Such a prescription evident in canon fifty-seven would have been a perfectly sensible independent result of the discussions of IV Toledo, given the spirit of the council and the situation at the time. The bishops were trying to defend the integrity of the churches around the kingdom and to promote ecclesiastical authority, both of which would have been damaged if baptism and the receiving of the body and blood of Christ were not sufficient to formally convert a person. Once the obligations to Christ and the Christian sacraments were made, they needed to be safeguarded (see Drews, *The Unknown Neighbour*, 224 and Chernin, "Visigothic Jewish Converts: A Life in Between"). For Isidore, anyone who departed from the unity of the faith was not just a heretic, but also an antichrist: "Sed et ille Antichristus est qui negat esse Deum Christum. Contrarius enim Christo est. Omnes enim, qui exeunt de Ecclesia et ab unitate fidei praeciduntur, et ipsi Antichristi sunt (*Orig.*, 8.11.22)." Furthermore, IV Toledo 57 makes it clear that past wrongs, for example forced conversions, were not to be reconciled. Rather, those present at the council, in accepting past errors, mistakes and other problems, instead of trying to revive and resolve them, were doing what was best for the present and the future, to prevent wrongs from happening again. This matches the two points of canon fifty-seven which say that nobody should be henceforth forced to convert, but that the situation that existed from past errors was to be maintained, in cases where people had been forced

Isidoriana, but was later introduced into the *Hispana* tradition by Julian of Toledo, III Seville was erased from the conciliar records permanently. Its canons and its text never emerge from the shadows of the past. They were never found sitting in an archive in the middle ages and introduced into medieval manuscripts. There were not even medieval discourses about the canons of III Seville, or about the council at all. There were no later medieval attempts in Spain, as there were for the council of Gundemar, to use the Visigothic document for religious, legal or political purposes. The records of III Seville never appear in the *Hispana* or any of the manuscript traditions recording the Spanish councils. They were not in the *Codex Oxomense*, nor are they in the *Codices Vigilianus* or *Aemelianensis*.

It seems that the records of III Seville have been missing for quite some time, almost 1400 years. In fact, they may have gone all-but-missing not long after the council was held in 624. This interpretation depends on how we read one of Braulio's letters, in which he asks for the records of the council from Isidore and, perhaps, from king Swinthila. Certainly, the records of the council were hard to find fourteen years after the council, in 638, when a case from the council was reinvestigated at VI Toledo. Such a situation is corroborated by the record of this inquisition, which states that none of the bishops of Baetica, who were at III Seville, knew then where the records were. Nevertheless, it appears that some interested party brought forth the records, at least those concerning the specific case-at-hand, the appeal of Martianus, to the investigators at VI Toledo.[136] These records were not, however, added to the recently constructed *Hispana*. The suppression of the limited case records and those of the whole III Seville was certainly a purposed affair, a very serious one, and one that was calculated originally by Isidore himself in the 620s and institutionalized in the 630s by their absence from the *Hispana*.

Despite the *damnatio memoriae* of III Seville, that it did occur, when, and where, are evident from several sources, which also shed light on some of its content. The most important source for III Seville is the *Exemplar iudicii inter Martianum et Auentium episcopos* found in the ninth-century Toledan-Córdoban MS León Cathedral 22, at folios 44^r–48^v.[137] The *Exemplar* is a record

---

    to convert or bishops who had unfairly gained bishoprics, as in the case of Aventius. Therefore, it seems likely that canon fifty-seven was, even if the direct product of Isidore-Seville's stance against forced conversions, a product of the dialogue at IV Toledo. The canon is unlikely to be from III Seville, and, in fact, could stand as a microcosm of the entire essence of IV Toledo.

136 See *CCH* 1 (1966), 318–21, and the *Exemplar iudicii*.
137 The *Exemplar* is printed in three primary editions, the most recently edited of which comes from 1885. It has never been translated into English, but in one edition there is a

of the second appellate defense of Martianus in the case brought against him by Aventius at III Seville. The bishops at that council, led by Isidore, voted to strip Martianus of his title of bishop and of his see of Astigi, and to give both title and bishopric to Aventius instead. In the *Exemplar*, Aventius is stripped of his ill-gotten bishopric, but allowed to keep the rank of bishop on condition of penance. The *Exemplar* provides numerous examples, it claims, of injustices committed at III Seville, which broke both canonical and secular laws (of the *Breviarium Alarici*).[138] From the *Exemplar*, important details come to light about the original case of Aventius vs. Martianus, and therefore about III Seville. The *Exemplar* does not, however, cite any canons from the council, leaving one to wonder about the extent of III Seville's activity. Although the case of Aventius vs. Martianus could not have been the entire purpose of the council, it appears to have caused significant discontent amongst the clergy and local populaces, particularly in Baetica. This discontent was part of that which led to multiple canons against conciliar corruption at IV Toledo, and to the council hearing the first appeal of the case by Martianus. The unsatisfied discontent and the way the appeal was handled at IV Toledo also led to a permanent *damnatio memoriae* of III Seville in the *Hispana*, to the second appeal of Martianus, and an inquisition of III Seville at Chintila's VI Toledo. The problems of the case also resulted in at least one public inscription in support of Martianus. These socio-political effects represent only those that are known of confidently. The effects of the case, III Seville, and subsequent appeals, were perhaps more widespread than is evident from the sources. Although this case was especially significant, this was not the only publicly witnessed fight between bishops going on in the 630s, as seen, for example, with the struggle between Gerontius and Justus in Toledo.

In addition to the evidence of the *Exemplar*, which relates information about the case of Aventius vs. Martianus, but not the council as a whole, as proof of III Seville is a reference to it by Braulio (*Ep.* 3) and several allusions to it in IV Toledo.[139] There remains some circumstantial evidence as well,

---

Spanish translation. For the text, see Enrique Flórez, España Sagrada 15 (Madrid, 1787), with Spanish translation, Fidel Fita y Colome, *Suplementos al Concilio Nacional Toledano* VI (Madrid, 1881), or *Die Könige der Germanen*, 6, ed. Felix Dahn (Leipzig, 1885), 615–20, with commentary from pages 623 to 641. Martínez Díez and Rodríguez do not include the *Exemplar* in their edition of the *Hispana*, since neither it nor the Third Council of Seville were ever part of the *Hispana* (see CCH 6 [2002], 9–11). For a review of the bibliography of the MS León Cathedral 22, see *Scripta de vita*, ed. Martín-Iglesias, 104–05.

138 II Seville 1, 3 and 8 allude to the Breviary of Alaric, as does IV Toledo 46. The *Exemplar* cites *Breviarium, Pauli Sententiae*, 1.1.2(4) directly.

139 IV Toledo 21, 24, 28, 29 and potentially 57.

particularly as reference to III Seville's case of Aventius vs. Martianus in a fragment of an inscription from Astigi. The inscription refers to the protection of Martianus, the bishop who was wrongly accused and stripped of his bishopric. The inscription, if referring to this same Martianus, should be from between 623/624 or the years 638 and 640, the dates of Martianus's bishopric. However, if this inscription is read as a public demonstration of support for Martianus or a call for him to be returned to his bishopric after being stripped of it in 624, then it is possible that the inscription could be from between the years 623 and 638.[140] Either way, it is an important display of public support for the beleaguered Martianus.[141]

Of the evidence other than that of the *Exemplar*, the letter of Braulio is the most useful. It helps date the council and adds to our knowledge of some otherwise unknown content of the council, namely about the case of one Sintharius. Since this case was not discussed in the *Exemplar*, one can be confident that the *Exemplar* does not in any way represent the whole activities of III Seville.

Braulio's letters survive in only one manuscript, the aforementioned León Cathedral 22. The *Exemplar* also survives in only one manuscript, León Cathedral 22. This manuscript also contains a stand-alone letter to Pope Honorius (fs. 65^r–67^v) and a profession of faith by Jews in Toledo (fs. 48^v–51^v). Both of these can be dated to around the time of VI Toledo, when the *Exemplar* was written, and at which a letter from the Pope was received, according to Braulio.[142] The *Exemplar*, and the letter in which Braulio discusses it, were part of a collection

---

140 José Vives suggests that this inscription refers to the bishop Martianus of III Seville (*ICERV*, no. 409). This is reasonable given that it is an inscription from this same bishop's district. García Moreno questions this conclusion on archaeological grounds, saying that it must be an inscription from centuries earlier (García Moreno, *Prosopografía*, no. 193, n. 1).

141 There is also a letter that may refer to III Seville. The letter was written by a monk Leo around the year 629, and is known as the *epistola ad Sisuldum arcidiaconum de conpoti ratione* (*Index Scriptorum*, ed. Díaz y Díaz, no. 96). The oldest version of it is in the ninth-century MS Köln BC 83.

142 It is likely that all of these were related to one another. The letter from the Pope, now lost, which condemned the Spanish Church for the lack of force it applied to converting Jews arrived around the time of VI Toledo. In that council a canon was passed urging stronger actions against Jews. Chintila sent the Pope a gift inscribed with a personal dedication, perhaps written by the king himself (see the *Anthologia Latina*, ed. A. Riese, 1.2 [Leipzig, 1906], no. 494, and short discussion in Collins, "Literacy and the laity," in *Uses of Literacy*, ed. McKitterick, 115). Indicative of the different attitudes of the schools, in contrast to sending a gift, Braulio wrote a harsh response to the Pope, in which he firmly suggested the Pope stay out of the Spanish Church's affairs. For further discussion of this matter see note 135 above and 161 below. For more on the letters between the Hispanian Church and the Papacy see Alberto Ferreiro, "The Bishops of Hispania and Pope Innocent I (401–47)," *Visigothic Symposia* 3 (2018): 19–35 and Alberto Ferreiro, *"Epistolae Plenae": The*

of records from the 620s and 630s held probably together in the same archive at some point, presumably originally in Toledo. Since Braulio signed the *Exemplar*, it could also be that this material was brought together as part of the Braulio collection, which contains not only the letters, but also his *Renotatio*.

It is from the third letter in Braulio's epistolary collection in this manuscript that a bit more can be learned about the activities of III Seville, and one can begin constructing an argument for when it actually took place. From Isidore's response to the letter, five or six years later, we may also have written testimony of Isidore's supposedly accidental misplacement and losing of the records of III Seville. In this letter, Braulio, who was still only an archdeacon at the time, asks Isidore to use his influence with Swinthila to have him (Braulio) sent a copy of the council that condemned Sintharius. At this council, one Sintharius "was wholly cooked even if he was not completely purified" by the inquisition of Isidore. Braulio was seeking the records in order to find out the truth about this, apparently infamous, council.[143] Sintharius appears to have been a heretical bishop "cooked" (*decoctus*) at III Seville, in the year 624. This conclusion is drawn from the following points. First, Braulio went to Isidore for the records of this council, implying that the council had been led by Isidore, in Seville, and Braulio says directly that Isidore was the inquisitor. Second, the action against Sintharius seems to fit the tone of III Seville, from what is known of it from the *Exemplar*. Third, Sintharius is not mentioned in the record of any of the extant councils of the period, meaning that the case against him must have been at this council, or some other unknown council. Fourth, the timing of Braulio's letter confirms that he was referring to III Seville. Claude Barlow dated Braulio's *Ep.* 3 to the year 625. More recently, José Carlos Martín-Iglesias dated it to between the years 626 and 627. The latter is the currently accepted date for the letter's composition.[144] Whether Braulio wrote the letter as early as 625 or as late as 627, he wrote it while he was still only an archdeacon, which means it must have been before March 631, when he became bishop of Zaragoza.[145] It also means that III Seville must have taken place before the year 627. The consensus today is that III Seville was held in 624. This is based on the dating of Braulio's letter, but it also depends on the year of death of Fulgentius,

---

Correspondence of the Bishops of Hispania with the Bishops of Rome: Third through Seventh Centuries, The Medieval and Early Modern Iberian World (Boston and Leiden: Brill, 2020).

143 "Gesta etiam synodi in qua Sintharius examinis vestri igni [etsi non purificatus, invenitur tamen decoctus] quaeso, ut vestro instinctu a filio vestro Domino rege nobis dirigantur cito. Nam et nostra eius sic flagitavit gloriam suggestio, quia multum in concilio pro investiganda opus est veritate."

144 See Martín-Iglesias, *Renotatio*, 28–30, and Stocking, BCC, 139–42.

145 See García Moreno, *Prosopografía*, no. 207.

Isidore's brother. Fulgentius was the bishop of Astigi, having been appointed some time before the year 610, when he signed the council of Gundemar (the decretal) as bishop. This is important because the next two bishops of Astigi were the Martianus and Aventius whose case was heard originally at III Seville. Fulgentius must have been dead when the council took place because Martianus was already the bishop of Astigi.[146] Two possible dates have been proposed for the death of Fulgentius: 623/624 or 628/629.[147] Since the *terminus ante quem* of Braulio's *Ep.* 3 is 627, it is reasonable to suggest that III Seville was held in 623 or 624, after Fulgentius was dead and Martianus had been raised to the bishopric.[148] It is most likely that the council was in 624 because Martianus would have needed the time to commit all of the offenses that he was accused of in the council. Aventius would also have needed the time to interrogate and torture witnesses and collect the testimony he needed for the case against Martianus.[149]

Finally, Isidore's strange and symptomatic response to Braulio's *Ep.* 3 should be briefly pointed out. The most immediate oddity is that Isidore does not return the message for at least five years: he responds to Braulio only once Braulio had reached the bishopric of Zaragoza. The timing of the response may have less to do with Braulio's title, *per se*, than with the raising of the rebel Sisenand to the throne in Braulio's city in the same month that Braulio became bishop there (March 631). Isidore's response to Braulio was written in the Sisenand-held Toledo.[150] Regardless of whether there was some connection between the timing of Isidore's response, the raising of Braulio to the bishopric and elevation of Sisenand to the throne, the content of Isidore's letter (*Ep.* 4), and then Braulio's response in turn (*Ep.* 5), reveal that Isidore was certainly up to something discreet concerning records and, moreover, that Braulio became

---

146 There is also no record of Fulgentius's deposition, or evidence of him being alive later.
147 On it see Aldama, "Indicaciones sobre la cronología," in *Miscellanea Isidoriana*, 61, who sees the date as 624, Enrique Flórez (*España Sagrado* 10, 107), who sees it as 629, and Séjourné (*Saint Isidore*, 55) who believes this all refers to II Seville since, he argued, Fulgentius died in 619.
148 For further discussion on the dating of III Seville and the defense of 624, see Drews, *The Unknown Neighbour*, 220, n. 109; Ramón Hernández Mártin, "La España visigoda frente al problema de los judíos," *La Ciencia Tomista* 94 (1967): 627–71 (677); Séjourné, *Saint Isidore*, 31; and, Stocking, "Martianus, Aventius and Isidore: Provincial Councils," 171. José Orlandis suggests a date between 622 and 624 (José Orlandis, *Die Synoden auf der Iberischen Halbinsel bis zum Einbruch des Islam* [Paderborn: Ferdinand Schöningh, 1981], 143).
149 Such confessions by torture as expressed supposedly at III Seville, although anathema to Christian prescriptions, were acceptable in the legal culture of the time. On the use of torture and pain in the period, see Harries, *Law and Empire*, esp. 118–52.
150 On the dating of Sisenand's elevation at Zaragoza, see Fred., *Chron.*, 4.73 and *CRV*, 35.

aware of this from him. Isidore tells Braulio that he had lost his letter. Not only this, it seems that all of his papers had gone missing: "[...] reversus e palatio regis, non solum scripta tua non inveni, sed etiam quidquid aliud in chartis fuit, periit." Isidore, so he said, had no idea what Braulio had requested of him. Moreover, whatever it was, Isidore no longer had it, since everything had been lost, and furthermore Swinthila was now dead. Isidore's eventual reply to Braulio not only gave Isidore more time, if needed, to find the Toledan copies of the council and fully suppress these records, but also a very good excuse for not sending them, or any other records. In a lengthy response, Braulio was critical of Isidore, starting off the letter by saying that a man is usually happy to receive a letter from a friend, but not, he implies, on this occasion: "Solet repleri laetitia homo interior ac spiritualis, cum inquisitione fungitur amantis [...]." Braulio felt that Isidore's misplacing of the letter was an excuse for not sending the requested material, yet, in his response, Braulio only refers to the *Etymologies* request from *Ep.* 3, not the records of the council in which Sintharius was "cooked." This likely indicates two very important points. First, instead of Isidore needing more time to suppress or destroy the records of III Seville, an act already accomplished, what he was doing was stalling in finishing the *Origines*. Second, even if Isidore was, in his response in *Ep.* 4, stalling about the records of III Seville, it is evident that between *Ep.* 4 and *Ep.* 5 he got word to Braulio that this affair needed to be hushed up, or he got him the records, since after *Ep.* 3 Braulio never mentions the council again, or the case of Sintharius.

4.2 The Successful Plaintiff Aventius and the Appeals of Martianus

Little is known positively about III Seville, but one aspect that is certain is that Aventius won his case against bishop Martianus.[151] This is evident from the appeals, which will be discussed in a moment. At III Seville, the bishops decided to strip Martianus of his rank and see and to transfer both to Aventius. They did so, supposedly, after rigorous inquiry and application of canonical and Roman legal principles, as set out in Visigothic law and in II Seville. They tried the case according to the letter of law and the result was a fair and total victory for Aventius. This was the message that was meant to be conveyed, however, wider doubts about the legality and justice of the council's bishops and their decisions appear to have emerged shortly after the council. When, and to what extent, the uncertainties about the case, and the belief in a miscarriage of justice, or an injustice, against Martianus surfaced is not clear. However, it is evident that injustices were well-rumored to have occurred by the time of the

---

151 Martianus was convicted of sex with a slave, doubting the faith and speaking against the king, all quite serious charges.

first appeal of Martianus in 633 at IV Toledo. Five years later the inquisitors at VI Toledo elicited the details of the injustices. The appeals make evident that the bishops at III Seville, led by Isidore, violated secular and canon law on multiple occasions. The council paraded a veneer of Roman and canonical legality as a way to make the promotion of Aventius seem legitimate, when in fact it was a matter of a more powerful and well-networked noble, Aventius, usurping the bishopric illegally from Martianus.[152]

What do the appeals reveal about the case and the miscarriages of justice or injustices of III Seville? Martianus's appeal was first heard at IV Toledo, or, as the *Exemplar* refers to it, the previous universal council. It is important to remember that the records of this appeal were also excluded from the *Hispana* by Isidore-Seville, and so the details of it primarily come from the *Exemplar*. The *Exemplar* reveals a couple of important points about Martianus's appeal at IV Toledo. First, that the bishops there restored Martianus to his rank, but not to his see. Second, that although the appeal was heard it was not investigated fully because the council ran out of time: "Iam enim in praecedenti universali concilio (IV Toledo), ex parte fuerat auditus, et gradui tantum, et non loco restitutus, quoniam angustia temporis ne ad plenum negotium suum ventilaretur fuerat interceptum."[153]

There are several reasons which help to explain why the appeal was not investigated completely at IV Toledo, and why Martianus was only restored to his rank, but Aventius not stripped of his ill-gotten see. First, the tone of IV Toledo was one of reconciliation, in which the bishops tried to deal fairly and equitably with all of the many wrongs that had been happening in the kingdom: from usurpations to conciliar injustice, to lack of provincial conciliar activity. To do so, and for the sake of moving forward, consensually, they

---

152 One could say that their apparent adherence to the letter of the law was "a public display of the fact that things were being done properly; indeed, were being done 'by the book'." This is Roger Collins's assessment of the use of the *Liber Iudiciorum* by judges in ninth and tenth-century Galicia and Castile (the *LI* being called then either *Forum Iudicum* or *Librum Gothicum*), which seems an appropriate interpretation of the use of Roman and Visigothic law in III Seville as well (Collins, "Literacy and the Laity," in *Uses of Literacy*, ed. McKitterick, 130).

153 The *Exemplar* here implies that V Toledo (636) was not in fact a plenary council, which may have been the real reason why the appeal was not heard until VI Toledo in 638. Felix Dahn (*Die Könige der Germanen* 6, 624) argues that the universal council referred to in the *Exemplar* was V Toledo. However, Séjourné and Thompson convincingly show that the universal council mentioned is a reference to IV Toledo, the "universal council par excellence," Thompson exclaims (Thompson, *Goths*, 287, n. 6). See also, Séjourné, *Saint Isidore*, 196 and 328.

announced a blanket amnesty for all of those involved in unsavory intrigues: nobody present would be condemned for actions done in the past.[154]

This should be kept in mind when considering the case of Martianus's appeal. If the investigators at IV Toledo decided to bring to light the full events of III Seville and all of its miscarriages of justice, they would have had a hard time not implicating those present, including especially, but not only, Isidore. Certainly, this would have run against the spirit of reconciliation at the council. Also, and even more of a threat to the fragile agreement and veneer of consensus, if the case was completely re-investigated the proper legal solution would have been to do as those in the *Exemplar* later did, depose Aventius and restore Martianus. This was precisely the type of disturbance to the balance of interests that the bishops of IV Toledo tried desperately to avoid.

The bishops, then, were in an awkward position when it came time to hear the appeal of Martianus. On the one hand, they needed to handle the matter quickly, so as not to raise much of what happened at III Seville, and so potentially condemn anyone present. On the other hand, the bishops at IV Toledo had just passed a canon saying that all ecclesiastical business at councils was to be handled in full, and that no bishop was to leave before all matters were settled.[155] It seems that they were so desperate to avoid episcopal commotion, and to avoid upsetting the balance of agreements, that they were willing to violate at least one canon of IV Toledo. It is evident from the *Exemplar* that the answer to this problem for the bishops was a compromise between the options. They did not hear the case in full, because of a lack of time, but, in a backhanded reprieve, they restored Martianus to his rank, but not his seat as bishop.[156] Aventius maintained his rank and position as bishop of Astigi.

There were some problematic results of IV Toledo's rushing the appeal. One was that it led to the violation of the council's canons, for the sake, it was hoped, of maintaining the fragile consensus between parties in the council. This established a fatal precedent for ignoring conciliar legislation if there was a perceived need to do so, a precedent which the bishops at VI Toledo would take advantage of in overturning the results of III Seville. Moreover, the partial restitution of Martianus, to his title but not his see, left the door open for further discontent and, of course, the second appeal of Martianus five years

---

154 IV Toledo 75: "nullum ex nobis praesenti atque aeterno iudicio."
155 IV Toledo 4.
156 They also seem to have put the blame for Martianus's situation on Martianus himself, since he was unable to present witnesses to testify on his behalf, because he could not defend himself.

later, in 638, at VI Toledo, held in the church of St. Leocadia, led by the Toledo-Agalian bishop of Toledo, Eugenius I.

At the second appeal, the evidence of the case was exhaustively evaluated, with at least seventeen witnesses interviewed, including Gothic nobles. From the opening lines of the *Exemplar* it is clear that the inquisitors were especially hostile to III Seville and its bishops.[157] Throughout the *Exemplar*, the various legal errors of the bishops at III Seville are raised, with the reasons for their illegality explained.[158] For example, Aventius accused Martianus of consulting a female diviner, a woman named Simplicita, about the life of Swinthila. As evidence, Aventius used only two witnesses. This was not an overwhelming condemnation; however, it was strong enough in Visigothic law to hold up as evidence, so long as the witnesses were liable to give testimony. One of these witnesses was a young boy named Recceswinth, who was at the time under the age of fourteen. This meant that he was legally a minor and could not, as such, provide legal testimony. Therefore, there was only one legal witness, Dormitio. According to the *Breviarium*, the testimony of a single witness was not admissible as proof in court. The charge against Martianus for consulting a diviner should have been thrown out, but it was not.[159] Examples like this, when compiled together in the *Exemplar*, make it clear that Aventius's case never should have been sustained in court.

---

157   "Saepe improbitatibus malorum quatitur vita innocentium, et interserit se sub colore justitiae iniquitas fallaciae quum diabolicis insidiis infligitur macula in ecclesiis, quoniam semper aemula virtutibus invidia illum vulnerat mendacio criminis, quem nequit perimere opere actionis. Hinc est enim quod dudum in concilio Spalensi Martianus Astigitanae ecclesiae episcopus falsis criminibus exauctoratus, ad universalis praesentis concilii confugit remedium purgandus, indignoque questu, ut judicium damnationus suae retractaretur est deprecatus."

158   For a concise discussion of all of the legal errors and injustices laid out in the *Exemplar*, see Thompson, *Goths*, 287–89.

159   The *Exemplar* says that at III Seville, Sciuila and Gundulfus confirmed Recceswinth's ability to give testimony: "Insuper adstiterunt testes Sciuila et Gundulfus, qui sub iuramento testificati sunt ipsum Ricesuindum non suisse aetatis legitimae ad testificandum, eo quod non habebat quartum decimum annum et e duobus testibus Dormitio cum remansisset solus, inlicitum suit soli credere." Was this Sciuila the Sclua who was bishop of Narbonne at VI Toledo, and relative of Fructuosus and the previous, usurper-king Sisenand? It is possible that Sclua was in such a position of authority in 624 at III Seville, given also his relation to the bishop of Béziers, Peter, and the fact that he was a bishop himself some time before IV Toledo. If Sclua was the one to give such false testimony certainly another level of intrigue is added to the affair of Martianus vs. Aventius and III Seville. If this false testifier was the same Sclua, could we then be witnessing in VI Toledo a serious condemnation against Sisenand, attempts at reconciliation between various parties, and could this explain Fructuous's (a relative of Sclua and Sisenand) problems with the monarchy and his demand to free captives held since Chintila?

The final outcome of the case between Martianus and Aventius was that, on the one hand, Martianus was fully restored to his rank and see. On the other hand, Aventius, thanks to the moderation of VI Toledo, according to the *Exemplar*, was deposed from his see but allowed to keep his rank as bishop, so long as he performed proper penance.[160] It is important to stress, again, that the case of Aventius vs. Martianus was not necessarily the primary purpose, or even the main task, of III Seville. Nor was the second appellate case of Martianus vs. Aventius the primary task of VI Toledo. This council had a lot of important and significant work to do. For example, it passed a harsh canon against Jews, multiple canons condemning various active practices, from the selling of clerical offices and clerical sexual misconduct to the fleeing of people "to the enemy" (*ad hostes*).[161] Other canons were issued dealing with the litany, with confirming that members of the palace were to be young, modest and ordinary citizens, and at least one lays out the idea that it was "inhuman" (*immanum*) not to reward the faithful. Also included are canons that defended the king, that continued to prescribe rights of select groups to succession, and that made it illegal for anyone to suggest a successor while the current king was alive (a canon which Braulio and other bishops would later break).[162] That the

---

160 "[...] exquisivimus: ipsius autem unius subreptionem, et alterius innocentiam comprobantes, judicii sui decreto elegerunt removere de Sede Astigitanae ecclesiae Aventium episcopum, atque, ac si sera, restituere pontificem Martianum: quorum sententiae, tam divina pietas, quam nostrae Congregationis unanimitas, favorem exhibentes, quoniam (ut quidam Patrum ait) nunquam puduit in melius retorsisse sententiam, meliori eorum judicio consona voce praebentes assensum, robur conferimus Deo confirmante perpetuis temporibus valiturum. Porro de Aventius episcopo haec nostrae moderationis sententia humanitate Concilii promulgatur, ut pro praemissis excessibus suis sub satisfactione poenitentiae apud fratrem nostrum honore retento subdatur, quatenus et crebra compunctione purgetur, et a tanti facinoris vitio corrigatur."

161 The reasons for the passing of the anti-Jewish canon appear to have been complex, though there is a general "Heraclian" context. Its promulgation may have been deeply influenced by Pope Honorius's recent letter to the Spanish church, condemning it for not treating Jews harsh enough. The letter appears to have arrived around the time, if not during VI Toledo. This timing seems evident from the Papal letter associated with this council in the MS Cathedral León 22 (fs. 65^r–67^v). What the effect of this was on the canon, and council, is unclear. What is evident is that the canon ran contrary to Braulio's, and the School of Isidore-Seville's, ethos for the treatment of Jews and the role of conversion. In his letter to him (*Ep.* 21), Braulio actually goes so far in defending the Spanish Church's Isidorian position that he corrects the Pope's knowledge of Scripture in favor of the Isidorian reading. He also cites Timothy to show that the Spanish church was in fact working according to Scripture, by converting people through love and preaching, not by violence. This ran contrary to Pope Honorius's desires and the canon in the VI Toledo.

162 See Braulio *Ep.*, 37 in which he, after consultation with other bishops, urges Chindaswinth to raise Recceswinth to the throne as co-king.

council found the time to so thoroughly "cook" Isidore and his School's actions in Seville, is a testament to the significance of the continuing competition for spiritual and legal authority between the schools.

The sense one gets from the *Exemplar* is that there was a deeply political, extra-legal and extra-religious motivation for the inquisition.[163] Although the *Exemplar* appears to have heard the case properly, in contrast to earlier councils, many of the bishops and other clergy in attendance apparently left the council before the hearing was complete. This is evident by the fact that forty-eight bishops, two deacons and three presbyters sign the records of the council, but only forty bishops, one deacon and one presbyter sign the *Exemplar*. As such, VI Toledo also violated the fourth canon of IV Toledo in its hearing of the appeal of Martianus. If the concern was on promoting and correcting conciliar justice, in maintaining the integrity of the secular and especially canonical law, as opposed to making a political statement, then its bishops would not have violated canon four of IV Toledo. In implicating bishops and Gothic nobles in illegalities and crimes committed before 633, they were also violating the spirit of IV Toledo 75.[164]

The overall narrative that emerges from the *Exemplar* is not one of absolute conciliar justice and the advancement of canonical precedent. Rather, it is that Toledo-Agali, both its monarchy and its Church, in the forms of Chintila and Eugenius I, knew the secular and canonical laws and law-codes better, and were more judicious in their application of them, than Isidore-Seville and the bishops of Baetica. It is clear that the competition between networks of authority continued to supersede the desire for unity around a single site of power. The antagonism between wanting to do what was best for the Church and what was best for one's patronage or other network is evident.

---

163 This is a reasonable conclusion based on the evidence, since, why would the bishops at VI Toledo have bothered to hear the second appeal of Martianus at all, and, moreover, to run such a full inquisition into the case of III Seville? The case was almost fifteen years old, the bishops involved were advanced in years (Martianus died a year later), and leading figures of the original trial were dead. Furthermore, and one may presume, most importantly, a full interrogation was a threat to the established status-quo and the fragile, if still existing, consensus. Thus, there seems to have been no obvious reason to hear the appeal other than overt political reasons. The only other possibility is that they were legally required to do so. This would have been true if VI Toledo was the first plenary council since IV Toledo in 633. Even if this were the case, though, it would not explain the apparent passion put into the inquisition, which is to a degree not otherwise seen in the council records.

164 NB, Chintila was elected king according to the prescriptions of IV Toledo 75.

4.3 Why the Damnatione Memoriae *by the School of Isidore-Seville?*

Several reasons have already been presented which allude to why Isidore-Seville would have wanted to suppress III Seville from the records, and why it was left out of the *Hispana*. The *Exemplar* shows that III Seville would have reflected poorly on the legal, religious and spiritual authority of the school, giving the school ample reason to erase it from memory and public discourse. However, there were also further considerations for excluding it from the *Hispana*.

First, Isidore may have wanted to deny III Seville its place in the memory of the Spanish church to protect his family legacy. The case of Aventius vs. Martianus was a dispute over the bishopric of Astigi, which had been, prior to Martianus's bishopric, in the hands of Isidore's family for nearly two decades. As such, it was important for Isidore to defend the integrity of the bishopric of Astigi. The need to defend this bishopric was even greater, because, not long before the case of Aventius vs. Martianus, the bishopric had been the focus of intrigue. During the bishopric of Isidore's brother Fulgentius (early 600s to early 620s), Astigi was accused of usurping surrounding jurisdictions and the authority of bishops. This is evident in the case of Theodulfus of Málaga against Fulgentius, heard at II Seville in 619, and in the case also brought against Fulgentius by bishop Honorius of Córdoba. The bishopric of Astigi was a thorny issue for Isidore and for the Sevillan church more widely. The cases involving Fulgentius suggest nepotism, abuse of conciliar justice, and, at the very least, a lack of consensus amongst bishops in Baetica, let alone the entire kingdom. If Isidore-Seville could not secure fair agreement between bishops in its own province, and including close relatives, what claim did it have to any larger authority and role in kingdom-wide spiritual power?

Second and third, there are the issues of the violation of Roman and Visigothic law and legal principles that occurred in III Seville, and what this would mean for unity and authority of the church. The records of II Seville "reflect a remarkable confidence in the efficacy of conciliar judicial procedure in ordering the local churches of Baetica."[165] The violations, errors and miscarriages of justice that occurred at the very next council in Seville, the very next provincial council in the kingdom, would have been a particular embarrassment to the school. The failure of II Seville's pronouncements to lead to justice at III Seville would not have been a conclusion Isidore-Seville would have wanted commemorated in the *Hispana*. Moreover, the records of III Seville would have shown just how manipulable the law and judicial procedure were, especially in the face of intimidation by powerful local and provincial networks of power.

---

165   Stocking, *BCC*, 131.

This would have been a dangerous precedent to approve of, and preserve, in the *Hispana*. Serious problems with ecclesiastical consensus, and so the right to broader social authority, were already quite evident, sometimes to the public-at-large, as shown in the cases of Venerius vs. Teudorus, Fulgentius vs. Theodulfus, Fulgentius vs. Honoratus, Gerontius vs. Justus, Aventius vs. Martianus, and also perhaps with Isidore vs. Helladius. Isidore-Seville would have had no desire to propel this image of discontent and the failure of provincial conciliar justice by including III Seville. The Third Council of Seville would have presented local bishops with a fine case in point as to why they should not hold or attend provincial councils. This would have run contrary to the visions of Isidore-Seville, expressed at IV Toledo and then later in the *Liber Iudiciorum* and VIII Toledo. It did not, however, bother the bishops or the king at VI Toledo, who were more concerned with asserting their particularist agendas over a universalist one.

4.4 Conclusion

In conclusion, the *damnatio memoriae* of III Seville is a good case-study in the struggle between the schools, for several reasons. First, it is another example of Isidore-Seville manipulating the history of the Spanish Church and its canonical activities in order to fit a story and teach a past that promoted and supported it as *a* or *the* proper ecclesiastical authority in the peninsula. Second, the history of III Seville reveals the important relationships of the Fourth, Sixth and Eighth Councils of Toledo, and the *Liber Iudiciorum*, and shows, in turn, the deeper levels of connection between them, the *Hispana* and the schools. The push, in IV Toledo, to institutionalize and universalize provincial councils was, in significant part, a response to the abuses of III Seville, which, for the sake of consensus, the bishops at IV Toledo went a long way not to mention directly. The promotion of cooperation, the protection against abuses of power, and the defense of provincial rights and conciliar justice, in IV Toledo and in the *Hispana*, as it was constructed, were the legacy of Isidore-Seville. Moreover, it is evident that VI Toledo, perhaps the first plenary council after Isidore's death – or after sufficient time for a new bishop of Seville to be established and for Isidore to have been mourned – was, in its attack on III Seville, a reaction against the school.[166] It may also have been a reaction against the *Hispana* – which would help to make sense of the so-called Novara collection made in Tarragona in that same year, 638 – although no formal edits are made

---

166 This is not to say that he was mourned formally, since mourning was, as Braulio points out in a letter to the nun Basilla, apostolically forbidden (Braulio, *Ep.*, 15, citing Jerome, *Ep.*, 3.3, and 1 Thess. 4:13).

to the *Hispana* by Toledo until the 670s, after the Isidore-moment. Third, the case of Aventius vs. Martianus further reveals the firm commitment of Isidore to his family, even to the extent of severe nepotism, and the promotion of his family over the law. The cutting of III Seville from the *Hispana* also reveals the gap between the reality of Isidore's commitment to family (over the concern for Astigi) and the story that he, and his school, told in their texts. Fourth, III Seville is another example, like Gundemar's council, of the existence of serious antagonisms and possibly dissenting opinions expressed at a council. Yet, there are only two clear instances from seventh-century Hispania of such discontent: that of the conciliar activities of Gundemar and that of III Seville.[167] Both of these were excluded from the *Hispana*. Given these exclusions, and that both councils were led by Isidore, they serve not only as further evidence of how carefully crafted an image of Sevillan authority Isidore-Seville erected, but also just how much medieval and modern consensus narratives, and *loyalisme* interpretations notably, rely on the sleight-of-hand constructed by that school or network.

---

167   For more on the dissenting opinions recorded in the *Exemplar*, see Stocking, "Martianus, Aventius and Isidore: Provincial Councils."

CHAPTER 5

Pinnacle and Twilight: The *Liber Iudiciorum* and the "Historical" Fulfillment of the Isidore-Moment

1   Introduction

This chapter provides the final case-study of the Isidore-moment: the *Liber Iudiciorum* (*LI*) issued by king Recceswinth in 654.[1] The *LI* is a prime example of the ongoing competitive dialectics between Isidore-Seville and Toledo-Agali, and is a manifestation of its literary and historical modes. More significantly, the *LI* appropriates and sublimates the Isidorian school, and in so doing draws to a close the competitive dialectics between the schools. The *LI* is the embodiment of the pinnacle and twilight of our historical moment. The Toledo-Agali school disappeared following the episcopate of Toledo's next bishop, Ildefonsus, the last Toledan bishop to be raised from Agali.

The aim of this chapter is to provide closure to the historical moment that is the core focus of this book: the Isidore-moment effectively ended with the *Liber Iudiciorum*. After this, the construction of texts – biographical, historical, conciliar, and legal – and their meaning and significances, the networks and competitions in which they spoke, and of which they were products, were categorically different from those previously. The *LI*, promulgated at the end of the Eighth Council of Toledo in December 653, sublimates the school of Isidore-Seville permanently into a Toledan framework. The promulgation of the *LI* coincided with Toledo's first and formal recognition of Isidore, and that he was dead, as was, recently, Braulio.[2]

---

1   A new critical edition of the *Liber Iudiciorum* is currently in preparation. This international project, co-directed by Michael J. Kelly and Isabel Velázquez, will be published open-access in series over a number of years on behalf of Networks and Neighbours (www.networksandneighbours.org). For now, unless otherwise noted, all reference is made to the editions of Zeumer: *Lex Visigothorum* in *Leges Visigothorum antiquiores*, ed. Karl Zeumer, Monumenta Germaniae Historica, Legum (Hanover and Leipzig: Hahn, 1894 and 1902), 21–313 and 33–456. A new English translation of the *Liber Iudiciorum* is currently being prepared by Damian Fernández and Noel Lenski to be published in Liverpool's translation series. For a Spanish translation, see the *Liber Iudiciorum* in *El Libro de los Juicios* (*Liber Iudiciorum*), ed. Rafael Ramis Barceló, trans. Pedro Ramis Serra and Rafael Ramis Barceló (Madrid: Agencia Estatal Boletín Oficial del Estado, 2015): 41–877.
2   Isidore was acknowledged as a doctor of the Church at VIII Toledo 2.

The secondary aim of this chapter, complementing the first, is to show that the *Liber Iudiciorum* is symptomatic of the literary and historical methods of the Isidore-moment, and how its historical structure represents the fulfillment of this situation. This is done by showing how its structure and content, and its use of the past and the "before now," imbue it with particular meaning, or significance, and function. The purpose of the *LI* is explicable when considered within the literary and dialectical competition endemic to the moment. The *LI* is not singularly a law-code or piece of legal history, it is also a pointed engagement with the past and a literary figuration with significance in its context. For this reason, this chapter is primarily concerned with the *LI* as a text, referring in detail to only a few layers of content – monarchy theory, territoriality and regionality, and Jewish legislation – as a way of buttressing the structural conclusion. Consistent with the methodology of the other chapters, this is not, *per se*, a hermeneutic, philological or deconstructive reading of the *LI*, yet it is also not strictly structural. It is a reading of the text in its cultural environment, in which historical fulfillment mattered.[3] Frederic Maitland, echoing Friedrich Carl von Savigny, called for a methodology for studying the history of law determined equally by content analysis and philosophical approaches, and Patrick Wormald maintained that post-Roman law in Europe was never disentangled from literature. It is, to some degree, these spirits of inquiry that guide this one.[4]

---

3   For an overview of Visigothic legal history, see José Manuel Pérez-Prendes y Muñoz-Arraco, "Historia de la legislación visigótica," in *San Isidoro Doctor Hispaniae* (Seville: Centro Cultural El Monte, 2002), 51–67, and the classic study by Rafael de Ureña y Smenjaud, *Legislación Gótico-Hispana* (Madrid, 1905). It is also worth the time to review Charles-Louis Montesquieu's *De l'Esprit des Lois* (Paris, 1758), in which he advanced several conclusions that influenced the development of the historiography, especially the idea that the law was a key component for the drive of the Visigothic kings to consolidate power. Montesquieu's interpretations were largely taken from Pithou's edition of the *LI*, which also includes Isidore's *Chronicles*. In the twenty-eighth chapter of *De l'Esprit des Lois*, for example, Montesquieu cites Pithou's preface to his edition of the *LI*. For a new interpretation of Merovingian *leges* that may also shed comparative light on Visigothic legislation see Thomas Faulkner, "Carolingian kings and the *leges barbarorum*," *Historical Research* 86 (2013): 433–64.
4   "Why the History of English Law is Not Written," in *Collected Papers: The Collected Papers of Frederic William Maitland*, ed. Herbert Albert Laurens Fisher, 3 vols. (Cambridge: Cambridge University Press, 1911), I, 480–97, and Patrick Wormald, *The Making of English Law* (Oxford: Oxford University Press, 1999), esp. ch. 6.

2 What Is the *Liber Iudiciorum*?

2.1 Dates and Provenance

The *Liber Iudiciorum* is a law book issued by Recceswinth in 654, promulgated at the Eighth Council of Toledo in the Praetorian Church of Sts. Peter and Paul.[5] After Recceswinth, the *LI* was edited or added to in various ways by subsequent kings leaving three distinct versions of it: that of, respectively, Recceswinth, Ervig, and Egica.[6] The dates of the three versions are 654, 681, and 692, with each having their own contemporary political significance.[7] Each king added laws and adapted the meaning and sentiment of the code according to their own wishes and the situations at the time. This chapter, and this book, interrogates the version of Recceswinth because of its relationship to the Isidore-moment.[8]

2.2 Manuscripts

The *Liber Iudiciorum* was remarkably well preserved in the middle ages. This was, in part, because it continued to be used in various ways in the peninsula until at least the thirteenth century and was copied through the fourteenth. In the middle ages, the *LI* was used, cited, and picked apart to construct Alfonso x's *Las Siete Partidas*, although it preserved its own separate, and often more preferred, legal existence, and generally maintained its validity in Christian Spain. Don Fernando III, also in the thirteenth century, confirmed the legality

---

5   See *Chron. 754*, 35, and the opening of the council: "Anno quinto orthodoxi atque gloriosi et vera clementiae dignitate praespicui Recesuinthi regis, cum nos omnes divinae ordinatio voluntatis euisdem principis serenissimo iussu in basilicam sanctorum apostolorum ad sacrum synodi coegisset aggregari conventum [...]." This church would become the site where kings were anointed and blessed before going off to war, and was raised by Wamba to the status of being its own see. Thus, just outside the walls of Toledo there was a competing bishop and site of royal, ecclesiastical authority. The progress towards total royal authority in the king seems to have reached new heights, to the extent that the king created a parallel church authority. This may have been the reason for Julian of Toledo apparently leading a coup to overthrow Wamba. For the primary evidence of this see XII Toledo 9, and for discussion see Collins, *Visigothic Spain*, 100. XII Toledo is also the council in which Gundemar's actions over the church were reintroduced into the record.
6   The Egica version has been known as the *Vulgata* since Zeumer's edition.
7   Roger Collins agrees with Karl Zeumer that the final recension is a vulgate one, not an official recension issued by Egica, based on the diversity in the manuscript and because it contains only three laws of Egica. See Collins, *Visigothic Spain*, 233–36, and García López, *Lex Wisigothorum*, 36–37.
8   See Céline Martin, "Le *Liber Iudiciorum* et ses différentes versions," *Mélanges de la Casa de Velázquez, Nouvelle series* 41 (2011): 17–34.

of the *LI*, and even decreed that it be translated into Castilian and used for the *fuero* of Córdoba. The examples from the Spanish middle ages could be elaborated.[9] Suffice it to say that, even in 1788, Charles III explicitly declared that the *LI*'s constitutions had never been repealed and could still be used.[10]

The story of the code's post-Visigothic life is a long and dynamic one, and because of this later success, historians are in a good position concerning *LI* manuscripts. More than forty manuscripts remain, some of which contain a whole version. The *LI* also features in the manuscripts of the *Hispana* discussed in Chapter 4, MSS Escorial d.1.2 and d.1.1, but the oldest extant manuscripts, both Recceswinth versions, are Vatican Reg. lat. 1024 and Paris BN lat. 4668. MS Reg. lat. 1024 was produced either in the late seventh century or first half of the eighth century and was made somewhere in the region around the Pyrenees, probably near Urgel or Cerdaña.[11] It is the only manuscript of the *LI* to contain nothing of the later versions of the text. As such, it allows a fair opportunity to see what Recceswinth and those at the Eighth Council were doing with the text. Furthermore, MS Reg. lat. 1024 has almost no markings, and appears to have been used very little in its time, suggesting that the later versions had replaced it. At the end of Reg. lat. 1024 is the list of Visigothic kings known as the *Chronica Regum Visigothorum* (*CRV*).[12]

2.3 Naming and Authorship

In the margins on folio 1^r of Reg. lat. 1024 the text is referred to as the *Liber Iudiciorum*, suggesting that this was how it was known at the time, but not necessarily in its original context. Other eighth-century sources and manuscripts refer to the *Hispana* as the *Liber Canonum*. This presents a visible pattern of nomination in the eighth century that reflects contemporary terminology, but reaching back into the seventh century.[13] However, this cannot be confirmed, no thanks to Fredegar who, writing in the 650s, did not mention these texts. García López suggests that reference to the code as either *Lex Gothorum* or *Lex*

---

9 For discussion on the transmission and influence of the *Liber Iudiciorum* before the twelfth century, see García López, *Lex Wisigothorum*, 41–151, and for after the twelfth century, Marie R. Madden, 2nd edn., *Political Theory and Law in Medieval Spain* (Clark: Lawbook Exchange, 2007), 43–98.

10 *Los Codigos Españoles concordados y anotados* (Madrid, 1847), I, xlvii.

11 See García López, *Lex Wisigothorum*, 41.

12 The oldest manuscripts of the Ervig version are Paris BN lat. 4418 and Paris BN lat. 4667, from the ninth and tenth centuries, respectively. On the manuscripts, see García López, *Lex Wisigothorum*, 35–69. On the *CRV*, see also Chapter 2, § 4.2.

13 The *Liber Canonum* is mentioned in *Chron. 754*, 22. The oldest extant manuscript, which reads *Liber Canonum*, is the eighth-century MS Matritensis Londoniniensis (formerly *codex Alcobaciensis*).

Visigothorum was a later ninth-century creation, given the re-imagination then of the Gothic past. This is a sensible conclusion, yet it should also be noted that the eighth-century manuscript's CRV may reflect the scribe's reading of the law-code's title, *Lex Visigothorum*. The term *Visigothorum* was certainly used in the seventh century, for example in the *Inventio Zoili*, a text relating the finding of the relics of the Córdoban martyr Zoylus.[14] Ultimately, it is not possible to securely state what the original title was, or even if there was one, but the earliest extant evidence of the name is *Liber Iudiciorum*.[15]

In the ninth and tenth centuries the name was adjusted to reflect desired associations with the Goths, and in the twelfth century it was referred to as the *Forum Iudicum*. It was re-promulgated in translated form by Fernando III as the *Fuero Juzgo*.[16] As with the titles of other texts discussed throughout this book, it was the activity of sixteenth-century scholars that led to the modern naming of early medieval texts. The influence of these scholars on modern interpretations of the early middle ages should not be underestimated.[17] There have been more than a dozen editions of the *Liber Iudiciorum* produced since the first edition in 1579 by Pierre Pithou, who gave the LI the title *Codex legum Wisigothorum*. From that, *Lex Visigothorum* became popular, and then authoritative with Karl Zeumer's 1894 edition *Leges Visigothorum*.[18]

---

14   See Fábrega Grau, *Pasionario Hispánico*, 379–81.
15   On the naming of the text, see García López, *Lex Wisigothorum*, 41; *Leges Visigothorum*, ed. Zeumer, I (1894), xix; Collins, *Visigothic Spain*, 224; and, Roger Collins, "Sicut lex gothorum continet: Law and Charters in Ninth and Tenth-century León and Castile," *English Historical Review* 100 (1985): 489–512.
16   See *Fuero Juzgo en latín y castellano* (Madrid: Real Academia Española, 1815).
17   See Chapter 3, § 2.3 for a discussion on the sixteenth-century editing and nominations of the *De Origine Officiorum*, and of an anonymous chronicle to "Fredegar."
18   Pierre Pithou, *Codicis legum Wisigothorum libri XII, Isidori Hispalensis Episcopi de Gothis Wandalis et Sueuis, Historia siue Chronicon* (Paris: Sébastien Nivelle, 1579). On the political significance of the history of the early *Liber Iudiciorum* editions, see Michael J. Kelly, "From Rhetoric to Dialectic: the Becoming 'Germanic' of Visigothic (Legal-)Literature, and (Postulating) the End of a 'Truth'," in *Interrogating the 'Germanic': A Category and its Use in Late Antiquity and the Early Middle Ages*, Ergänzungsbände zum Reallexikon der Germanischen Altertumskunde 123, ed. Matthias Friedrich and James M. Harland (Berlin: De Gruyter, 2020), 127–143. On the editing of the LI, see Ruth Miguel Franco, "Braulio de Zaragoza y la corrección del Fuero Juzgo," *Helmantica* 57 (2006): 67–89, and Madden, *Political Theory*, p. 29, n. 2. For examples of the continued use of *Lex Visigothorum* and *Leges Visigothorum*, see Guilio Vismara, "*Leges Visigothorum*," in *Lexikon des Mittelalters* 5 (Munich and Zurich: Artemis Verlag, 1991), 1804–05; Hermann Nehlsen, "*Lex Visigothorum*," in *Handwörterbuch zur deutschen Rechtsgeschichte*, vol. 2 (Berlin: E. Schmidt, 1978), 1966–79; Drews, *The Unknown Neighbour*, 220; James N. Adams, *The Regional Diversification of Latin 200BC–AD600* (Cambridge: Cambridge University Press, 2007), 428; and, Castellanos, "Political Nature of Taxation in Visigothic Spain," 225.

The inclusion of the CRV in the oldest manuscript of the *Liber Iudiciorum* is relevant not only to the naming: it suggests a fundamental relationship between legal codification as history and historical memory, particularly on behalf of Recceswinth, but also more broadly in the early middle ages. Recceswinth's *LI* may be the first genuine instance of this, but it is not the only.[19] The inclusion of historical texts and historical lists with legal codes happened on multiple occasions in the early middle ages. Several manuscripts of Lombard laws include the king's list of Rothari, as well as an origins story of the Lombards. This expressed association, in Lombard texts, between history and law goes back at least to Paul the Deacon.[20] There are examples too amongst Frankish laws and histories, and the earliest manuscript of Alfred's law book has been connected closely with the *Anglo-Saxon Chronicle*, and then later with Bede's *Ecclesiastical History*. The Scandinavian law book of Gotland was also complemented by a historical narrative, the *Historia Gotlandiae*. All of this, Patrick Wormald argued, suggests an extra-practical reason for the law-codes. They often made, first and foremost, literary sense, and served ideological, or literary, purposes.[21]

---

19   As noted elsewhere (see, for instance, Chapter 2, notes 56–57), the CRV is a comprehensive list of the legitimate Visigothic leaders and kings from Athanaric to Ervig and, as such, is a historical complement to the *LI*. Attached to one manuscript of the *Codex Theodosianus* is a short laterculum of emperors. However, the list contains only those emperors who are mentioned in that code, with the exclusion of a couple (Constantine II and Jovian). As such, it serves more as an index of sorts than as a historical complement in the way of the CRV. That said, it is interesting that the oldest manuscript containing the CRV (Vatican Reg. lat. 1024) and what was the only manuscript of the *Codex Theodosianus* laterculum (Turin, Biblioteca Nazionale Universitaria, A.II.2 – destroyed in 1904]) have a *terminus ante quem* of the eighth century for their origin. Are they both eighth-century additions to their respective law codes? For the *Codex Theodosianus* laterculum, see *Laterculi Imperatorum Romanorum Codici Theodosiano Adiuncti*, in *Chron. min.*, ed. Theodor Mommsen, Monumenta Germaniae Historica, Auctorum Antiquissimorum 13 (Berlin: Weidmann, 1898), 411–13. For more on its manuscript, see Tino Licht, *Schriftkultur im Zeitalter der ersten lateinischen Minuskel (III.–IX. Jahrhundert)* (*Quellen und Untersuchungen zur lateinischen Philologie des Mittelalters* 20) (Stuttgart: Anton Hiersemann, 2018).

20   For the manuscripts with the Lombard edict and the *Origo Gentis Langobardorum* see *Leg. Lang.*, xxvii–xxviii, xxxvii–xliii, and, *The Beneventan Script*, ed. E. A. Lowe, 2nd edn. (Rome, 1980), 11. For Paul the Deacon, see *Pauli Historia Langobardorum*, ed. Ludwig Bethmann and Georg Waitz, Monumenta Germaniae Historica, Scriptores Rerum Langobardicarum et Italicarum, saec. VI–IX (Hanover: Hahn, 1878), 12–187.

21   Patrick Wormald, "*Lex Scripta* and *Verbum Regis*: Legislation and Germanic Kingship from Euric to Cnut," in his *Legal Culture in the Early Medieval West: Text, Image and Experience*, by Patrick Wormald (London: The Hambledon Press, 1999), 37, and Fontaine were part of the 1960s–1980s anti-functionalist group of scholars who developed a firm reaction against historians of the previous generations who had interpreted early medieval texts

The step Wormald did not take was in suggesting the fundamental relationship between legal collections and historical discourse. This significance is evident in the *LI*, in which the historical narrative, constructed as it was, spoke specifically to those used to similar literature and literary methods in the first half of the seventh century in Iberia.[22] Moreover, the capstone of Isidore's book on law in the *Origines* (*Etymologies*), *de legibus et temporibus*, is his lesser *Chronicles*. In 654, when the *LI* was promulgated, this Isidorian integration of law and history was re-dedicated to Recceswinth.[23] Law served a spiritual function for Isidore, entangling historical and spiritual knowledge.[24] The advent of Jesus brought understanding of the mystical sense of the law, and so humanity's ability to know, love and follow it correctly.[25] Embracing this discourse, history, law and spirituality were also intertwined in the form, presentation, meaning and intention of the *LI*, despite the emphasis on supposed secular matters in many of its constitutions.

The authorship, or editorship, of the *Liber Iudiciorum* has often been attributed to Braulio, based on a letter exchange he had with Recceswinth. In one letter, Braulio complains about the horrific state of a manuscript that he was asked to edit by the king.[26] Historians cannot be sure if this *codex* was the *LI*, but there is a good chance that it was.[27] What the letter shows is that, assuming Braulio was editing the *LI*, the state of the *codex* was in a deplorable condition at the end of the 640s, and that Braulio essentially re-constructed the laws into a new, clear *codex*. Moreover, it was Recceswinth who commissioned Braulio and sent him the material. However, Braulio died roughly three

---

as "functional." In response, Fontaine and others claimed that these texts were aesthetic, hence the construction of the theory of the Isidorian Renaissance. But, perceptions of law and history in relation to aesthetics have now been made more dynamic, less reactionary, since the Deleuzian-turn in aesthetics.

22 See Wormald, "*Lex Scripta*," 19–21.
23 See Reydellet, "La diffusion des *Origines* d'Isidore de Séville," 417–19.
24 Isid., *Sent.*, 1.19.6: "Vel quod lex non tantum historice, sed etiam spiritualiter sentienda sit." For a theoretical discussion of history as an epistemological and eschatological project, see Paul Ricoeur, *History and Truth*, trans. Charles A. Kelby (Evanston: Northwestern University Press, 1965).
25 Isid., *Diff.*, 33: "Ante adventum enim Redemptoris nostri, gentilis populus ideo non obtemperavit legi, quia nondum intelligebatur sensu spirituali. Lex enim gravia atque dura secundum litteram jubebat, ideo contemnebatur. Venit autem gratia Evangelii, temperavit legis austeritatem, applicavitque sibi gentilem populum."
26 Braulio, *Ep.*, 38.
27 For discussion of the evidence and defense of Braulio's editorship, see Ruth Miguel Franco, "*Sub Titulis Misi, in Libros Diuisi*: Braulio of Zaragoza and His Arrangement of Materials," *Visigothic Symposia* 1 (2017): 131–49; Miguel Franco, "Braulio de Zaragoza y la corrección del Fuero Juzgo;" and, Lynch, *Saint Braulio*, 135–40.

years before the code was promulgated, so he could not have been the person who produced the final draft. This task may have been accomplished by Taio, Braulio's successor as bishop of Zaragoza and perhaps also his former student. The evidence of Taio's editing comes from letters between him and bishop Quiricius of Barcelona, in which they discuss the *codex* that Taio's predecessor had been editing.[28] The other potential (co-)editor was Eugenius II, the "intellectual grandchild of Isidore," a non-Agalian, and, as discussed in Chapter 1, a voice in Toledo sympathetic to, if not in some ways a proxy of, Isidore-Seville.[29]

Recceswinth had, then, entrusted the editing of the *LI* in large measure to the school of the Isidorian network. The king's choices for editorship suggest a desire for integrating the schools of Toledo-Agali and Isidore-Seville, by allowing the latter a complementary voice in the economy of power in Toledo and thereby subduing opposition in the form of the competitive dialectics of the moment. For the sake of simplicity, but more importantly because he ordered and oversaw its construction, and promulgated and issued it in his name, the author of the *LI* will be referred to as Recceswinth.

2.4 *Contents*

The *Liber Iudiciorum* is a collection of laws organized into twelve books, each of varying length. The books of the *LI*, and the laws within them, are ordered by topic, as opposed to by dates of promulgation. In this sense, the *LI* is consistent with other law-codes and historical constructions from Toledo, such as the *Vulgata* version of the *Hispana*. The *LI* is not a blanket collection of existing laws, although its contents are quite diverse. In the *LI*, there are laws taken from, or influenced by, a range of codifications and texts, some Visigothic and others not. The Visigothic sources include the *Codex Euricianus, Breviarium Alarici*, Visigothic Formularies, Isidore and II Seville, the councils of Toledo, and unreferenced laws of Swinthila.[30] There are also remnants of Gothic traditions and language,[31] and foreign sources, including Justinian's *Corpus Iuris*

---

28   For the Taio and Quiricius exchange, see Taio, *Sententiae*, Patrologia Latina 80, col. 727.
29   See de Jong, "Adding Insult to Injury," 376.
30   CE: *LI*, 2.1.14, 5.4.13; LRV: *LI*, 2.1.10, 2.1.18, 2.1.24, 2.2.7, 2.3.7, 5.2.6, 6.4.2, 7.6.1–2, 10.1.5; Visigothic Formularies: *LI*, 2.1.23, 3.1.5, 5.7.1, 10.1.18; Isidore: *LI*, 1.1.4–5 (unnamed), 2.1.3 (attributed to Recceswinth); II Seville: *LI*, 10.3.4, ascribed to Recceswinth, and 10.3.5 titled *antiqua*; IV Toledo: *LI*, 5.7.9, referred to as *antiqua*; V Toledo: *LI*, 2.1.7; VII Toledo: *LI*, 2.1.6; VIII Toledo: *LI*, 2.1.5: Swinthila: *LI*, 2.1.5, attributed to Chindaswinth.
31   *LI*, 2.1.14.

Civilis, as well as Burgundian laws.³² The notable absence of the Ostrogoths could shed further light on the authorship of the *Edictum Theoderici* (ET).³³

The first book of the LI is the so-called "Visigothic constitution" because it elicits the instruments of law (*de instrumentis legalibus*).³⁴ The opening book lays out the purposes, reasons and roles of and for the law, and prescribes the regulations for *princeps* and *legislatores* (the king and the jurists in his court).³⁵ The second book expands these prescriptions, picking up where the last one left off, discussing at some length the importance of being a fair king (*princeps*), and further binding him to the laws.³⁶ The prescriptions in the LI laying out the role and proper activities of the king are mirrored in the canons of VIII Toledo. Judges, courts, contracts, property, mercantilist activities, criminal laws, degrees of relationship, fugitives, and land boundaries otherwise constitute the bulk of code. The laws of Recceswinth's LI attend largely to civil matters, except for book 12 and its legislation against Jews and Jewish life in the kingdom. This book was significantly supplemented by Ervig with a major new section (LI, 12.3) containing twenty-seven laws against Jews, a revision of the conclusion, and an entire reconstruction of the book's narrative.³⁷

In total, there are more than three hundred "ancient laws" (*antiqua*), and about one hundred laws, and ninety laws, respectively, from Chindaswinth and Recceswinth. There are only five laws from other named kings: three from Reccared, and two from Sisebut. This means that about forty percent of all law by the 650s was, according to the LI, very recent legislation. The code calls

---

32   Justinian's *Corpus*: LI, 3.1.5, 6.1.7, 8.4.2, 9.1.10, and 10.1.17 (attributed to Chindaswinth); Burg.: LI, 2.1.11, 3.2.8, 3.4.4, 5.6.6, 8.3.10, 8.4.1, 9.1.3, 9.1.5–6, and 9.1.13.

33   The lack of overtly Ostrogothic material in the LI suggests possible Visigothic provenance of the ET. On the ET see Chapter 5, note 135.

34   See Madden, *Political Theory*, 30, who saw LI 1 as a constitution. Dietrich Claude defended and expanded this position, arguing that the constitutional elements apparent in the LI are comparable to modern constitutional frameworks (Claude, "The Oath of the Allegiance and the Oath of the King in the Visigothic kingdom," *Classical Folia* 30, no. 1 [1976]: 6). For a comparative look at another potential legal guide from the period, for the *Lex Salica*, see Karl Ubl, "Eine Verdichtung der *Lex Salica*. Die *Septinas septem* der Handschrift Paris, BN lat. 4411," in *Exzerpieren – Kompilieren – Tradieren: Transformationen des Wissens zwischen Spätatike und Frühmittelalter. Millennium-Studien 64*, ed. Stephan Dusil, Gerald Schwedler, and Raphael Schwitter (Berlin & Boston: De Gruyter, 2017), 223–44.

35   Associating the Visigothic king with the authority of the Roman emperor, the king is referred to in the LI as *princeps*.

36   See LI, 2.1.2 and 5.

37   On Ervig's changes, see Michael J. Kelly, "The *Liber Iudiciorum*: A Visigothic Literary Guide to Institutional Authority and Self-Interest," in *The Visigothic Kingdom of Toledo: Concepts and Forms of Power*, ed. Paulo Pachá and Sabine Panzram (Amsterdam: Amsterdam University Press, 2020): 257–72.

all laws *antiqua* that it suggests were promulgated before the Visigothic kings converted to Catholicism; it provides the names only of select, Catholic kings.[38] The significance of these figures and this use of nomination in the historical narrative will be explained below. Finally, the *Liber Iudiciorum* was meant for diverse audiences, demonstrating its important rhetorical function, and a law in the *LI* specifically dictates rules for translated versions.[39]

3   Interlude: Short Historical Background

Before eliciting the fuller meaning of the text and its contents, a short history of the immediate years leading up to the promulgation of the *Liber Iudiciorum* can assist with grasping its framing. As discussed in this book's introduction, seventh-century Hispania was an exceptionally literate society in which laws were known, used, written, referred to and potentially even taught. The 640s and 650s were vibrant in the production of legal texts: there are extant mandates of judges, judiciary securities, charters, testaments of bishops, constitutions, legal signatures, and subscriptions. The history of Visigothic law was already a long one, reaching back into the fifth century. The aim here, though, is not to place the *LI* into a chain of legal history, but properly into its own historical context. It is the dialectics of power between secular and ecclesiastical – as initiated by the founding of Agali, Gundemar's reversals of Reccared's positions, and Isidore's responses – that is central to this historical moment, and which helped forge the fissures and literary culture endemic to it.

3.1   *The Tremors of Chindaswinth, and Recceswinth's Reaction: Securing a Dynasty*

The *Liber Iudiciorum* was originally conceived, some historians believe, by Chindaswinth, the father of Recceswinth.[40] Chindaswinth certainly was an

---

38   For example, a ruling from Isidore's II Seville is labeled as ancient (*LI*, 10.3.5), as is a canon from IV Toledo (*LI*, 5.7.9).

39   *LI*, 2.1.9. Alberto Ferreiro suggests that Recceswinth spoke Gothic, as was related by the *Chronicon* of Pseudo-Isidore. Does this law suggest that Recceswinth was not the only person who could speak Gothic in mid-seventh-century Hispania? On Recceswinth's Gothic, see Ferreiro, "Saint Martin of Braga and the Germanic Languages," 298–306. In the 610s, Gothic custom was present in functioning law in the peninsula, but it is uncertain whether or not this was the situation in the 650s or whether it implies any knowledge of Gothic language by the parties involved (see the *Libellus Dotalis Morgingeba*, in *Misc. Wis.*, no. 20, and *Diplomática*, ed. Canellas López, no. 100, 181–82).

40   For example, King, *Law and Society*, 18, and ibid., "King Chindasvind."

active lawmaker, but the *LI* was developed and promulgated by Recceswinth, as evidenced from the letters between him and Braulio, followed by VIII Toledo. The reign of Chindaswinth was a firm and consistent one, albeit one that must have been traumatic for the elite of the kingdom, both secular and ecclesiastical. It began with Chindaswinth, with the support of various nobles, usurping power from the supposedly weak king Tulga, a violation of the canons of the Fourth and Sixth Councils of Toledo.[41] The aged Chindaswinth, in his late 70s, was raised to the kingship, with the support of these nobles, in the far north of the peninsula, either Pamplona or Pampliega (Burgos).[42] One of Chindaswinth's first orders of business was to prevent any rebellions, in turn, against him. Sisenand had done this by making rebellion anathema in the Fourth Council of Toledo. Chindaswinth, although the structure of his usurpation had similar features to Sisenand's, was a different sort of king. Instead of working through conciliar legislation, he killed those whom he perceived to be potential threats to his authority, two hundred Gothic nobles (*primatis Gotorum*) and five hundred members of the "middle class" (*mediogrebus*).[43] One could, at first glance, say that Chindaswinth was an ideal Machiavellian prince: Machiavelli argued that the best situation for a prince is to be both loved and feared. To do so, he should kill all of his detractors immediately at the beginning of his reign, since, over time, people would forget individual events and deaths, and from fear would come virtue and love. However, if a prince killed people only individually, but consistently, he would be feared and hated, and not loved. This seems to have been Chindaswinth's course of action, and the sentiment that he fostered, over the eleven years of his reign, from 642 to 653.[44] Fredegar relates that Chindaswinth killed seven hundred nobles of

---

41   IV Toledo 3. The Sixth Council of Toledo, canon seventeen, declared that nobody should prepare a new king while the current one was alive, let alone usurp the living monarch. In the next canon, it is said that the murder of a usurped king should be avenged, a prescription Chindaswinth avoided, whether he cared to or not, by tonsuring Tulga. This depends, in part on how we read, and believe, the sources. According to Fredegar (*Chron.* 4.82), Chindaswinth took power with the approval of certain Visigothic nobles and others, in northern Spain, and subsequently had Tulga tonsured. According to the *Chronicle of 754*, Chindaswinth's usurpation was done by means of an outright revolt.

42   See the discussion in García Moreno, *Prosopografía*, no. 33, n. 1.

43   Fred., *Chron.*, 4.82.

44   Though he only effectively reigned until 649 when he raised Recceswinth to the throne as co-king. From this point on, Chindaswinth spent his time in penance, while Recceswinth seems to have taken control of the functioning of the kingdom, issuing laws, as seen in the *LI*, and consecrating churches, such as the new church of St. John the Baptist in Toledo (Baños de Cerrato). On the latter, see *Diplomática*, ed. Canellas López, no. 129. On Machiavelli's ideas see his *Il Principe*, chapters eight and seventeen.

various classes, individually (*sigillatem*), and continued to kill people at will throughout his reign.⁴⁵ He was more of a paranoid Stalin, in this sense, than the confident ideal prince described by Machiavelli. The secular and ecclesiastical nobles, and anyone within the vision of Chindaswinth, never forgot his actions, or forgave him, and Eugenius II even wrote a mocking epitaph.⁴⁶

Chindaswinth was not only feared for this, but he was, as seen in Recceswinth's promulgation of the *Liber Iudiciorum* closing VIII Toledo, keen to use the money and resources taken from the people he killed to make his own family and personal estates larger. His regulations on moveable property (*res mobiles*) were also a way to increase his own authority. For example, he decreed that slaves could no longer be put to death without a public trial, thereby removing the owner's right of impunity, and decreasing his "manorial" power.⁴⁷ Re-locating such punishments into the public forum allowed Chindaswinth to display his power. Chindaswinth also gave the wives and daughters of the deceased to his supporters, and, in a move to limit the power of other nobles, forbade the transfer of patrimony between noble families, unless they had his explicit consent.⁴⁸

Furthermore, Chindaswinth increased royal authority in the ecclesiastical sphere, reducing episcopal power even further, and ended the practice of sanctuary for fugitives.⁴⁹ A recent analysis of Braulio's letter collection helps scholars further grasp the problems that Braulio and his network, and perhaps ecclesiastics more widely, had with Chindaswinth. The structure of the collection, and its chosen contents, shows the severe problems Braulio faced concerning Chindaswinth and his intensified interference with episcopal jurisdiction. The purpose of the letter collection, Ruth Miguel Franco has argued, was meant to subtly reveal this story of royal interference. The letters with Eugenius II, for example, and their potentially inverted chronological order, show Braulio's and Eugenius's shared opposition to the king.⁵⁰

The mood of terror, fear, distrust and general malaise left behind by his father was what Recceswinth entered into when he was raised as co-king in 649, and then which he had to reconcile once he became sole king in 653, after his father's death. In 646, Chindaswinth, echoing and citing the Bible (and, likely unwittingly, the Talmud), declared that "fear of God is the beginning of

---

45 Fred., *Chron.*, 4.82.
46 For the epitaph, see Chapter 1, note 97.
47 Thompson, *Goths*, 269.
48 García Moreno, "Building an Ethnic Identity," 276.
49 Fugitives were to be handed over for blinding, if not death (*LI*, 6.5.16).
50 Braulio manipulated the history of the letters in order to create a historical logic that presented his vision of the truth. On this, see Miguel Franco, "Braulio de Zaragoza," esp. 173ff.

wisdom" ("principium sapientiae timor Domini") and also that "fear of God is the beginning of religion" ("timor Domini principium religiositatis").[51] Chindaswinth adapted this godly model of authority in order to intimidate the elite of his kingdom into obedience. He attempted to centralize all forms of power and knowledge in Toledo, with the activities mentioned but also, for example, in ordering Eugenius II to redraft Dracontius, and in sending Taio to Rome to gather books for Toledo's library.[52] This authority was moderated by Recceswinth in the *LI*, which relies for it on the fear of law.[53] In the 670s, Julian abandoned this Isidore-Seville approach and tied the Visigothic monarchy directly to God.[54]

Although Recceswinth was joint king, and effectively the sole ruler, of the kingdom since 649, upon his father's death in 653 he faced a serious revolt in the Ebro valley by one Froia.[55] The antipathies against his father meant that Recceswinth had to pay a price for the support needed to defeat Froia. This price was, in part, the concessions made in the *LI* and at VIII Toledo, in which Recceswinth promised to act in *bonae voluntatis*. At the end of the council, Recceswinth gave a lengthy address in which he promulgated the new law-code. The purpose of the code, Recceswinth explained, was to restrain the powers of the king, ensure domestic tranquility, prevent abuses of power, preserve the property rights of individuals, and separate the king's private property and the property of the royal treasury. The pronouncement formally ended the council.[56]

Recceswinth's *LI*, some historians argue, was an explicit act of opposition against his deceased father, for example, in restoring the right of sanctuary with an *antiqua* law.[57] Despite such gestures, Recceswinth did not ease up on his father's drive to centralize power into the hands of the monarchy. The

---

51 In the *Cartula Donationis Quindasuinth Regis* of 18 October. For the edited text, see *Diplomática*, ed. Canellas López, no. 115. For the Biblical passages see Sirach 1:16; 25:11, and in the Talmud, Shabbat 31b in explaining the role of process of Torah study. Fear of God as the foundation of wisdom though can be found throughout the Biblical and Rabbinical texts.
52 See Tizzoni, "The Poems of Dracontius," 173–85, and, on Taio, see *Chron. 754*, 29–33.
53 For example, see *LI*, 1.2.5, but this logic is consistent throughout Recceswinth's *LI*.
54 See Gregorio García Herrero, "Julian de Toledo y la Realeza Visigoda," *Arte, sociedad, economía, y religíon durante el Bajo Imperio y la Antigüedad tardia. Antigüedad y Cristianismo,* 8, ed. José María Blázquez, Antonio Gonzáles Blanco, Javier Fernándex Nieto, and José Remesal Rodríguez (Murcia, 1991), 201–55.
55 On the revolt of Froia, see Taio of Zaragoza, *Epistola ad Quiricum*, Patrologia Latina 80, col. 727.
56 *CCH* 5 (1992), 460–86.
57 *LI*, 9.3.1. The inclusion of this law further shows that Recceswinth was the designer of the code, not his father. On the *LI* as an act of opposition, see Céline Martin, "*Liber Iudiciorum*."

creation of the *LI* afforded Recceswinth a perfect opportunity to make formal concessions, while both increasing the centrality of power in Toledo and destroying, through sublimation, the competitive dialectics of the schools and expressions of regional authority.[58]

4 The Structure of the *Liber Iudiciorum*, and Its Meaning

The Sixth Council of Toledo, led by Chintila in 638, spoke of rewarding fidelity to the king, to protect and promote the universal virtue of faithfulness, and to defend religious piety by "the people."[59] In an unapologetic and tactless move, Chindaswinth in his Seventh Council of Toledo in October of 646, several years after his initial slaughter of nobles, inaugurated the event by attacking traitors and deserters (those fleeing his persecutions). Chindaswinth went straight to the matter in the very first canon, *de refugis atque perfidis clericis sive laicis*, before any initial proclamations of faith, as was the standard performance. Recceswinth would also deal with the matter early in his first council, VIII Toledo, but not until after a lengthy proclamation of faith, hence the difference in approach, if not actually the policies, of the son from that of the father.[60] At VII Toledo, in contrast to VI Toledo, fidelity was established for the sake of the king's benefit, and not for the benefit of salvation. An explicit purpose of the *LI*, as laid out in VIII Toledo, was to return to the salvific path after the terrorizing reign of Chindaswinth which had established a fatal pattern of noble emigration out of the kingdom. To appease the émigrés, Recceswinth set out to limit the king's powers, ensure justice, protect property and return to this holy path. He chose to do this not by continuing to pass individual legislation or working through the conciliar legislation, as previous kings had done. Instead, he promulgated a smartly designed, well-constructed law-code, and this point alone is worthy of a pause for consideration. It was the first time any Catholic Visigothic king issued a law-code.

Recceswinth chose a different method to do what other Catholic kings had attempted, and he chose one, wisely, that spoke within the context of the literary style, historical rhetoric, and audience expectations, at the time.[61] He not only promulgated laws, he gave them meaning inside a constructed narrative

---

58 For recent research on the realities of central power, see Castellanos and Martín Viso, "the local articulation of central power," 1–42.

59 VI Toledo 13 and 16.

60 Recceswinth included a law in the *LI* based on VII Toledo 1 (*LI*, 2.1.6).

61 On the education of Recceswinth, see Pierre Riché, "L'enseignement et la culture des laïcs dans l'occident pré-carolingien," in *La scuola nell'occidente latino dell'alto medioevo*,

about the history of Visigothic law. He used the main form of political rhetoric in the period: historical narration. It is in relation to this form, not to any other forms of legal history, that the *LI* was instilled with contemporary meaning. Recceswinth issued laws after 654, but he never added them to the *LI*.[62] If Recceswinth saw the *LI* primarily as a book of laws meant for the courts, he would have updated it with the new laws at some point during the next eighteen years of his reign.

Recceswinth gave the laws a structure for their own origins story and promoted his dynasty as the "illustrious men" and heirs to if not authors of the Catholic conversion of the peninsula and the kingdom. To do so, he used the literary tropes and historical rhetoric common to the literature of the period, knitting together the past and present into a narrative about the law that legitimized his dynasty.[63] How Recceswinth did this is demonstrated here by eliciting from the text its historical narration, use of *damnationes memoriae* and directed memory, elevation of Recceswinth's dynasty as illustrious men, their role in the conversion of the kingdom, and the significance of the use of the number twelve.

What, then, is the historical narration of Recceswinth's *Liber Iudiciorum*? How does it play with the past to present a historically legitimized meaning in the present? As noted, the *LI* contains over five hundred laws. The majority of them have had the names of their promulgators erased from the record and are instead attributed to being ancient laws. The attribution *antiqua* was supposed to indicate that a law was derived from Arian kings, from the kings up to and including Liuvigild, a collective, un-nominated mass, unworthy of naming. That the so-called *antiqua* occasionally included, or in fact were, canons and laws from the Catholic kingdom helps to demonstrate their tropical function.[64] Except for a handful of laws in the final book, which at times travelled separately, the only names of legislators mentioned in the *LI* are Chindaswinth and Recceswinth. This was done not because kings in between them and Liuvigild did not legislate, but rather, the inclusion of them was meant as a rhetorical device serving to collectivize the unnamed as past as outside of the (significance of the) present.[65]

Settimane di Studio del Centro Italiano di Studi sull'Alto Medioevo 19 (Spoleto: Presso la sede del Centro, 1972), 231–53 (esp. 238).

62 See Collins, *Visigothic Spain*, 235, and especially, *Diplomática*, ed. Canellas López.
63 See Reydellet, *Sidoine Apollinaire*, 526–27.
64 For example, *LI*, 5.7.1, 5.7.9, and 10.3.5.
65 The two laws by Sisebut are *LI*, 12.2.13 and 14, and the three of Reccared are *LI*, 3.5.2, 12.1.2, and 12.2.12. Three of these five are listed together (*LI*, 12.2.12–14), with another very nearby. Outside of the twelfth book, the only law attributed to a king other than Chindaswinth

The entire first book of the *Liber Iudiciorum* is anonymous: none of the laws are attributed to any authors, neither Chindaswinth nor Recceswinth, and they are not even described as *antiqua*. This was a different type of universalization and removal from time than that of the *antiqua*, which were anonymous parts of totalized time, but not of the nominated and imagined present. The universal laws of the so-called Visigothic constitution, the first book of the *LI*, were to be self-evident. Recceswinth brilliantly removed them from the underlying historical narrative of the text and, in so doing, did not tie his historically and spiritually constructed legitimacy to the prescriptions of this constitution.[66] Moreover, any violation of them would not be an affront either to such legitimacy or to his dynasty, or a contradiction of his own word according to the law. The second book of the *LI*, which specifically lays out the rights and duties of the kings and judges, is almost completely constituted by laws of Chindaswinth and Recceswinth, in higher proportion than the laws of the other books.[67]

What this structure did was direct memory of the laws, and thus the present opinion about them, in such a way that Chindaswinth and Recceswinth were the Catholic legislators, the bringers of Catholic-approved law to the kingdom, for the first time. This model of tying Catholic justice to the history and present of Visigothic law, embodied in Recceswinth's family, promoted Recceswinth's legitimacy in the eyes of religious leaders and their local populaces, for whom the *LI* may have been translated.[68] It also served to restore the image of Chindaswinth, who had lived the last years of his life in penitence, presenting both Chindaswinth and Recceswinth as the kings who brought Christian-inspired justice to the kingdom. It was no coincidence that Recceswinth included slightly more laws by his father. This was not only a subtle subordination of the son to the father, but it also helped to create a positive image of Chindaswinth, whose legacy desperately needed a re-imagination to repair it. The *LI* re-crafted the history of the law to elevate the memory of Chindaswinth and legitimacy of Recceswinth, suggesting them as the unique defenders of justice and piety in the history of the Catholic kingdom. In creating a sort of mass

---

and Recceswinth is *LI*, 3.5.2, which was re-attributed to Recceswinth in later manuscripts, and so was not firmly associated with or attributed to Reccared.

66 For a recent discussion on the relationship between temporality and law, and the rise of interest in "time" in legal history since the spatial turn, see Andreas Thier, "Time, Law, and Legal History – Some Observations and Considerations," *Rechtsgeschichte* 25 (2017): 20–44.

67 The Recceswinth version opens with a law by him, while the version of Book 2 in Ervig's revision begins with a law by him. For further discussion on the differences between the versions and specifically on how Ervig's reframing of *LI* 2 affected the narrativity of the *LI* see Kelly, "The *Liber Iudiciorum*: A Visigothic Literary Guide."

68 *LI*, 2.1.9.

damnationes memoriae of the previous kings, the *LI* provided a historical lineage that favored Recceswinth's dynasty and cut others out of the historical record.[69] This basic method of historical narrative and rhetoric was used to write the *DVI*s, *Hispana*, origins stories and histories of Isidore-Seville discussed above in the other chapters.

In using historical rhetoric to present spiritually supported legitimacy for his reign, Recceswinth's *Liber Iudiciorum* promoted him and his father as the true converters of the kingdom, the fathers of justice, and the only rightful princes of the kingdom, as well as the first Catholic monarchs to give the kingdom law. It also suggested that Chindaswinth and Recceswinth were the direct line of authority from the conversion: it was they that represented the conversion of the kingdom from the *antiquae*, from Arianism. This would be a twist on other attempts by Toledo to tie their conversion firmly to Gregory and Reccared. The *LI* re-confirmed the king's rightful place as head of the kingdom, but also its Church. It may also have been an allusion to Chindaswinth and Recceswinth as temporal versions of God and Jesus, father and son (and simultaneously the prince) lawgivers, on Earth. Recceswinth could easily have erased his father's name from the laws, but he chose not to do so.

The *Liber Iudiciorum*, with this internal structure, was a clever way for Recceswinth to support reconciliatory acts, while maintaining the king's ultimate authority over ecclesiastical affairs (sublimating Isidore-Seville). By creating a narrative of historical legitimacy of the Catholic kings, of which Recceswinth was the ultimate embodiment, the *LI* gave legitimacy to laws of his dynasty, and so their legal position, which was, since Gundemar, also *de facto* head of the Church. This combination of reconciliation and proliferation of royal authority helps demonstrate how the *LI* was both the fulfillment of the Isidore-moment and also its closing off.

Finally, the use of the number twelve for the books and the religious laws may have further imbued the *Liber Iudiciorum* with an important sense of spirituality. Twelve was also important as it connected Recceswinth and Visigothic law with the Roman Empire, since, as Isidore relates, Roman law began with the Twelve Tables.[70] The fact that the eleventh book of the *LI* is a relatively hapless collection of constitutions, all of which could easily have been placed elsewhere, enhances the view that the authors of the *Liber Iudiciorum* ensured that it had exactly twelve books. The importance of twelve, and the conscious application of it to the structure of the *LI*, is confirmed by the fact that the

---

69 On the anonymity of the pre-Reccared laws in the *LI* as *damnationes memoriae* of the Arian Visigothic kings see Martin, "*Liber Iudiciorum*."
70 Isid., *Orig.*, 5.1.3.

council at which it was promulgated, VIII Toledo, had exactly twelve canons, which was almost unique in Visigothic conciliar history.

5   Constituent Influence of the School of Isidore-Seville

The general topography of the *Liber Iudiciorum* is quilted with influences from Isidore and his school. For example, the *LI* states that the law should be according to its historical context, "suitable according to its time and place, and the customs of the people."[71] The idea comes from Isidore, who states that the law should be just and honorable, agreeable to the customs of the local culture, and relevant to the specific settings. He also says it should be clear and for the common benefit of the people, which are all principles pronounced in the *LI*.[72] The influence of Isidore was, here and more widely, not a passive one, as is implied in historiography reliant on "renaissance" interpretations of the Isidorian impact in Visigothic Hispania. The examples of the application of principles, thoughts and texts of the school of Isidore-Seville, largely from Isidore himself, were, as everything else in the smartly crafted *LI*, carefully selected and served a specific purpose: the sublimation of potential opposition into the framework of Toledan authority. The few examples below are meant to provide a sampling of this phenomenon. Each represents a long development in Isidorian thought and issues that the school of Isidore-Seville had been dedicated to and trying to make function. This further illustrates how the *LI* represents not only the end of the historical moment, but also its pinnacle.

How does the contents argument buttress the structural one? The latter argues that the structure of the *Liber Iudiciorum* reveals its intention to elevate Recceswinth and his dynasty, to justify his reign spiritually and ecclesiastically, through historiography and historical fulfillment, to promote him as head of the Church, and to further centralize powers in Toledo. How does the content do this? It not only fulfills major aims and ideas of the Isidorian school, but it also selects ones from it that support the claims and associations made in the structure of the *LI*: issues of monarchy theory, territoriality and regionality, and Jewish-related legislation, were chosen specifically in order to block reactionary claims.

In appropriating the school of Isidore-Seville into the *Liber Iudiciorum*, and so into the power structure of Toledo, the school was effectively destroyed,

---

71 *LI*, 1.2.4: "[Lex] Erit secundum naturam, secundum consuetudinem civitatis, loco temporique conveniens [...]."

72 Isid., *Orig.*, 5.21, and *LI*, 1.2.4.

subsumed into the central authority, and made part of it, as opposed to being part of a competitive dialectics with Toledo-Agali. Incorporating so much of Isidore and the school into the *LI*, and even having Braulio, Taio and maybe Eugenius II edit and essentially draft the text, was a brilliant way to subordinate that contrary voice and the competitive dialectics in which it spoke.

5.1 Monarchy Theory

The most apparent incorporation of Isidorian thought into the *Liber Iudiciorum* is Isidore's and his school's work on the development of a theory of proper monarchy. The issue of Isidore's construction of a theory of monarchy is one that has been well traversed in the historiography and needs elaboration here only to the extent that the information helps illustrate Recceswinth's use of the theory for his aims in the *LI*.[73]

The Visigoths were the first post-Roman society to practice royal coronation and to celebrate the sanctity of the king, which began, it has been argued, with Reccared in 589.[74] However, a theory of proper kingship developed only later, with the work of Isidore and his school. Isidore began thinking theoretically about the role of a monarch in society, and his proper way of life and government, during or shortly after the traumatic reign of Gundemar. As explained in Chapter 4, in 610 Gundemar effectively decreed ecclesiastical authority to be that of the monarchy in Toledo, a move that was regretfully signed off by Isidore. The recognition of the powers that he had afforded to the monarch was, in retrospect, the event that drove Isidore to begin seriously considering the proper duties of the monarch and his relation to the wider Church, and to regional churches in the peninsula. Isidore began developing his model of

---

[73] For a review of Isidore's thoughts on monarchy and generally his political philosophy, see Cazier, *Isidore de Séville*, 64–67 and 245–50; Reydellet, *La royauté*, 505–97; Reydellet, "La conception du souverain chez Isidore de Séville," in *Isidoriana*, ed. Díaz y Díaz, 457–66; Pablo C. Díaz, "Rey y Poder en la Monarquía Visigoda," *Iberia* 1 (1998): 175–95; Pablo C. Díaz and María del Rosario Valverde Castro, "The theoretical strengths and practical weakness of the Visigothic monarchy of Toledo," in *Rituals of Power. From Late Antiquity to the Early Middle Ages*, ed. Janet L. Nelson and Frans Theuws (Boston and Leiden: Brill, 2000), 59–93; María del Roasario Valverde Castro, "Simbología del poder en la monarquía visigoda," *Studia Historica, Historia antiqua* 9 (1991): 139–48; and, Valverde Castro, *Ideología, simbolismo y ejercicio del poder real en la monarquía visigoda*.

[74] For discussion, short historiography and bibliography see Céline Martin, "L'innovation Politique dans le Royaume de Tolède: le Sacre du Souverain," in *Élections et pouvoirs politiques du VIIe siècle du VIIe au XVIIe siècle*, ed. Corinne Péneau (Paris: Bière, 2009), 281–300. According to King, the Visigothic king after 589 was a "divinely sanctioned head" of a *societas fidelium Christi* (for the evidence see Isid., *Sent.*, 3.49.3 and *LI*, 12.2.15, and for the citation King, *Law and Society*, 132).

kingship in his *Sententiae*, which he wrote between the years 612 and 615, just after the reign of Gundemar.[75] Although the *Sententiae* was already Isidore's tenth text, it was only in it that he began developing his theory of kingship.[76]

In the *Sententiae* Isidore argues that kings should set moral examples, thereby living by Christian mores.[77] This was an attempt to reclaim some authority from the monarchy since it was, naturally, the Church that would define Christian morality and customs. In the text, Isidore promotes the monarchy primarily for its salvific potential – a point Recceswinth made evident in his promulgation of the *LI* – and claims that royal power is effective only when subordinate to the higher authority.[78] Kings were accountable to God, but also, fundamentally, they were a punishment from God, in so far as their appointment to lead was based on humanity's original sin and the evil that unleashed.[79] Not only is this a less than glorious explanation for the origin of kingship, but it also highlights the other main function of kingship for Isidore: kingship as an office, a duty to be fulfilled.[80] The king's role is to mediate between men, and he should act accordingly. Isidore felt that a king should be a *rex* and should rule (*regere*) as a leader of the people, equal in the eyes of God.[81] The king was the servant of the people existing for the common good – an idea made explicit in the first book of the *LI* – not as the intermediary between God and

---

75 See Isid., *Sent.*, 3.47–3.51. On the dating of Isidore's *Sententiae* to between 612 and 615 see Aldama, "Indicaciones sobre la cronología," in *Miscellanea Isidoriana*, 87–88, and José Carlos Martín-Iglesias, "Une nouvelle édition critique de la *Vita Desiderii* de Sisebut, accompagnée de quelques réflexions concernant la date des *Sententiae* et du *De uiris illustribus* d'Isidore de Séville," *Hagiographica* 7 (2000), 127–80 (141–45). For a later dating, see Pierre Cazier, "Les *Sentences* d'Isidore de Séville et le IV Concile de Tolède. Réflexions sur les rapports entre l'Église et le pouvoir politique en Espagne autor des années 630," in *Los Visigodos. Historia Civilización: actas de la Semana Internacional de Estudios Visigóticos*, ed. Antonio González Blanco, Antigüedad y Cristianismo, Monografías Históricas sobre le Antigüedad Tardía 3 (Murcia: Universidad de Murcia, 1986), 379.

76 See Reydellet, "La Conception du Souverain," in *Isidoriana*, ed. by Díaz y Díaz, 457.

77 Isid., *Sent.*, 3.50.6, and 3.51.3: "vinculo tamen fidei tenentur adstricti, ut et fidem Christi suis legibus praedicent, et ipsam fidei praedicationem moribus bonis conseruent." For discussion, see Wood, *Politics and Identity*, 90, and Molina Gómez, "Las Coronas de donación regia del Tesoro Guarrazar," 471–72. Wallace-Hadrill argued that for Isidore, the king's *potestas* existed only in relation to ecclesiastical authority (Michael Wallace-Hadrill, *Early Germanic Kingship in England and on the Continent* [Oxford: Oxford University Press, 1971]), 53–54.

78 Isid., *Sent.*, 3.51.3: "Sub religionis disciplinam saeculi potestates subiectae sunt."

79 See Isid., *Sent.*, 3.51.6, and 3.47.1: "Propter peccatum primi hominis humano generi poena divinitus illata est servitutis […] Inde et in gentibus principes, regesque electi sunt, ut terrore suo populos a malo coercerent, atque ad recte vivendum legibus subderent."

80 Reydellet, "La Conception du Souverain," in *Isidoriana*, ed. Díaz y Díaz, 458.

81 Isid., *Sent.*, 3.48–49. King, *Law and Society*, 27–30.

the people, and certainly not between God and the bishops.[82] Kingship is supposed to be a public service, a care for the Christian *regnum*, not vice against or dictatorship over it.[83] Braulio and Eugenius II were loyal to Isidore's theory of monarchy, and their shared expression of the imagined ideal ruler.[84] In the *LI*, Recceswinth embraced the functions and roles of kingship following Isidore-Seville, using them to appease opposition and silence a competitive dialectic, but also to reinforce his dominant position.

Before Recceswinth, Sisebut had also attempted to manipulate this discourse in his favor by writing a text of apparent appeasement – his *Vita Desiderii* – but in reality, it was a reinforcement of his domineering position. Based on manuscript evidence, some scholars have argued that Sisebut wrote the *Vita Desiderii* (*VD*) before he became king, but it is commonly accepted that he was king while he wrote the entire text.[85] Regardless of whether he wrote the *VD* in anticipation of becoming king or while he was king it is clear that through it he tried to ease tensions created by Gundemar, and specifically to satisfy the kingdom's leading cleric, Isidore. The *VD* may have been a direct response to Isidore's *Sententiae*, a way for Sisebut to imply that he was not like Gundemar in terms of royal and ecclesiastical relations.[86]

Since the events of Gundemar's reign, Isidore was trying to create a relationship between the monarchy and Church, and between the center and

---

82   Isid., *Sent.*, 3.49.3: "dedit Deus principibus praesultatum pro regimine populorum," and Isid., *Sent.*, 3.51.3: "Sub religionis disciplinam saeculi potestates subiectae sunt."
83   Isid., *Sent.*, 3.48.2.
84   On Braulio and especially Eugenius II's ideas of kingship as extensions of Isidore's, see Elena Marey, "Образ правителя в стихах Евгения Толедского и его параллелис 'Книги приговоров' (*Liber Iudiciorum*)," *Bulletin of the Russian State University for the Humanities* (2012): 24–33.
85   The twelfth-century Oviedo manuscript of Sisebut's *VD*, which is now lost but described in the 1793 España Sagrada (vol. 38, 368ff.) by Ambrosio de Morales, says that the original title *Vita vel passio sancti Desiderii a Sisebuto rege composita* did not contain *rege*, suggesting that the *VD* was written by Sisebut before he was king. Krusch, however, demonstrated, on philological grounds, that the text must have been written while Sisebut was king, and this view has been widely accepted (see *Rer. Merov.* 3, ed. Krusch, 630; *Index Scriptorum*, ed. Díaz y Díaz, no. 86).
86   Sisebut was writing history as he thought "it should be read." (Fontaine, "Sisebut's *Vita Desiderii*," in *Visigothic Spain*, ed. James, 101). In condemning Theuderic and Brunhild, Sisebut used them as negative models for kingship, as examples on what a monarch ought not to do. This could have been Sisebut's way of pleasing, or appeasing, Isidore, by showing how Frankish monarchs rule incorrectly, and that Sisebut would rule differently. That the *VD* was a response to the *Sententiae*, see Stocking, *BCC*, 126 and n. 35; Martín-Iglesias, *Renotatio*, 78ff., notes 145, 146, and 149; and, Reydellet's chapter "Isidore of Seville, tradition and novelty" in his "La conception du souverain," in *Isidoriana*, ed. Díaz y Díaz.

provinces, that was mutually dependent: a partnership of semi-autonomous equals. In the *VD*, Sisebut suggests that he would act accordingly. The *VD* presents a traditional mirror image of kingship, one in which any monarch who deigned to act against the Church and its clergy would be roundly punished. This ran counter to the real actions of Sisebut who acted on his own will, above the Church, ordering the Church what to do.[87] One of Sisebut's first actions as king was to exercise his right to appoint bishops, and announce the names of judges, effectively merging, or at least blurring, the lines between secular and ecclesiastical, while maintaining the monarch's absolute right to decide on all matters involving both spheres.[88] The *LI* renews this call for centralization of authority.[89] Isidore had hoped to persuade Sisebut to embrace his theory of monarchy or constitutionally limited royal authority, but it was to little avail. It was finally embraced, in theory, only in the first two books of the *LI*.

In 633, Isidore led IV Toledo in the church that Sisebut built, St. Leocadia.[90] The council was not only led by Isidore, but also represented the transfer of the school of Isidore-Seville to Braulio, who is said to have "shone above the rest" during the event.[91] It was here in IV Toledo that the famous pronouncement on Visigothic governmentality as an inter-relationship between *rex, gens, et patria Gothorum* was formulated.[92] Moreover, the council's seventy-fifth canon re-confirmed much of the school's theory of monarchy, including especially

---

87   On the contrasting agendas of Isidore and Sisebut see Stocking, *BCC*, 120.
88   See the *Edictum Sisebut Regis*, from the beginning of Sisebut's reign some time earlier in 612. The record is extant in MS Reg. lat. 1024, and edited in *Diplomática*, ed. Canellas López, no. 97.
89   See *LI*, 1.2–6.
90   Isidore could have chosen St. Leocadia's as the site for the council as a way to elicit the memory of 619, when the church was built and also when Isidore wrote the *DVI* to promote Zaragoza. On the other hand, Sisenand could have chosen the location as a *damnatio memoriae* of sorts to Swinthila, as a way to jump over he and Riccimer's reigns. Between these options the latter seems to be the more likely scenario, since a Toledan passionary to St. Leocadia was also written about the same time, and it seems that it was in Toledo's interest to promote the saint at this point.
91   *Chron. 754*, 20.
92   IV Toledo 75. For discussion see Isabel Velázquez, "Pro patriae gentisque Gothorum statu," in *Regna and Gentes*, ed. Goetz et al., 196. The expressed concept of canon seventy-five may derive from Flavius Corippus's *In laudem Iustini August minoris Libri IV* where he says that Justin II was elected (in 565) unanimously by the senate, army, and people. It is possible that this was Isidore's source, since he mentioned Verecundus of Junca, one of the North Africans who went to Constantinople in the middle to late sixth century to fight monophysitism. That Isidore knew Verecundus's work is important here because the only extant version of it (the *Carmen de Satisfactione Paenitentiae*) is in a Spanish manuscript (Madrid BNE 10.029, or, the *Azgara codex*) that also contains the only extant version of Corippus's *In laudem Iustini*. This demonstrates a Spanish tradition of collecting these texts together, which could reach back to Isidore. For more on Corippus's text see

the salvific potentiality of shared power and the humility of the king, yet adds that a king should be elected.[93] Nevertheless, Sisenand, who had called and then oversaw the council, was himself a usurper and he had no qualms about maintaining and exercising royal supremacy over all matters, including internal church affairs. Bishops were appointed and ecclesiastical decisions continued to be made at the king's discretion; ultimately the election rule failed. Other legislation made in IV Toledo had failed before the council had even ended.[94]

During the following years, between 633 and 638, the potential constitution of the Visigothic monarchy evolved within conciliar law. Initiated by the prescriptions in Isidore's and Braulio's Fourth Council of Toledo, the Fifth and Sixth councils continued manipulating the conditions of monarchy. The final canon of the Fourth Council pronounced a canon setting out the structure for the legal succession of the king. Three years later at V Toledo, the rules of succession were bolstered, including the requirement of election, as well as descent from Visigothic nobility.[95] The Sixth Council of Toledo decreed that a legitimate king would be one that was born free, was not of a "foreign gens" (*extraneae gentis*), and who did not win the Crown through tyranny.[96] The following canon demanded that a new king should, if the previous king was murdered, avenge the killing of his predecessor as if the murdered king was his father. This intended circular logic was aimed at preventing usurpers from killing their predecessors.

Chindaswinth's apparent usurpation violated the prescriptions of the 630s, and his subsequent violent destruction of nobles, their families, and their properties, and other abuses were anathema to the theory of monarchy that had so far been voiced in the canon law and the thoughts and writings of the school of Isidore-Seville. The reaction against Chindaswinth was hard, with Eugenius II's epitaph likely expressing a collective anger at, and fear of, Chindaswinth. In it,

---

Flavius Cresconius Corippus, In laudem Iustini Augusti minoris Libri IV, ed. Averil Cameron (London: The Athlone Press, 1976).

93   IV Toledo 75: "et reges et populis, et populi in regibus, et Deus in utrisque laetetur." For discussion see Abilio Barbero de Aguilera, "El pensamiento político visigodo y las primeras unciones regias en la Europa Medieval," *Hispania, Revista Española de Historia* 115 (1970): 265–75, and Marcelo Vigil and Abilio Barbero, "Sucesión al trono y evolución social en el reino visigodo," *Hispania Antiqua* 4 (1974): 379–93 (387ff.).

94   See Chapter 4, § 4.

95   V Toledo 3: "Ut quisquis talia meditatus fuerit, quem nec electio omnium provehit nec Goticae gentis nobilitas ad hunc honoris apicem trahit [...]."

96   VI Toledo 17: "Rege vero defuncto nullus tyrannica praesumptione regnum assummat, nullus sub religionis habitu detonsus aut turpiter decalvatus aut servilem originem trahens vel extraneae gentis homo, nisi genere Gothus et moribus dignus provehatur ad apicem regni."

Eugenius lays out the faults of the previous king, painting a pretty nasty picture of him, in which we are told how "noxious" the king was, and how he tried to sow discord and create tensions, the very opposite that Recceswinth would be as king.[97] That Recceswinth allowed this epitaph says volumes about the reconciliatory tone at the promulgation of the LI. Through the open recognition and expression of the father's faults, a new spirit of cooperation with the son was possible. Recceswinth created by far the most extensive and transparent vision of the governmentality and theory of monarchy in the kingdom's history. In the LI, ecclesiastical ideas about the monarch deriving from the school of Isidore-Seville, from Isidore to Eugenius II, and recent, pre-Chindaswinth, canonical legislation are subsumed into the text, and eloquently elaborated, providing them ultimately with the framework to perform, or so such a fruition was the intended image.[98] The content of the LI fulfilled the growing desire for such a constitution and theory of monarchy,[99] while setting that constitution inside a structure that preserved the pre-existing powers of the monarch.[100]

An important subtlety in their theory of monarchy, Isidore and Braulio both explicitly advocated hereditary monarchy on multiple occasions.[101] For example, Braulio wrote to Chindaswinth suggesting Recceswinth be raised as co-king.[102] Isidore, for his part, had promoted the raising of Swinthila's son Riccimir as co-ruler. In both instances, there were political situations that influenced these expressions. In the former, Chindaswinth may have sought out support for raising his son to the throne. In the latter, Isidore may have made this suggestion to expand his subtle criticism of Sisebut, who did not raise his son Reccared II to co-rulership. Instead, Sisebut left his son to succeed

---

97 "Chindasuinthis ego noxarum semper amicus, patrator scelerum Chindasuinthus ego. Impius obscenus probrosus turpis iniquus, optima nulla volens, pessima cuncta valens, quidquid agit qui prava cupit, qui noxia quaerit, omnia commisi, peius et inde fui [...]." For discussion, see Thompson, *Goths*, 199.

98 The LI opens with ideas on monarchy taken from Isidore (compare LI, 1.2 and Isid., *Sent.* 3.50.6).

99 The canons of the Eighth Council largely mirrored the prescriptions on monarchy expressed in the first books of the LI, and demanded that the king's election be approved by the bishops.

100 Perhaps it should be noted that the words for monarch and monarchy are used only five times throughout the entire twelve books of the LI: *monachis, monachum, monaci, monacorum,* and *monacus*.

101 On hereditary succession, see Rafael Gibert, "La sucesión al trono en la monarquía española," *Recueils de la Société Jean Bodin* 21 (1969): 447–546, and García Moreno, "La sucesión al trono."

102 Braulio, *Ep.*, 37. There is some uncertainty, given Chindaswinth's overbearing kingship, about whether or not Braulio's suggestion reflected his true sentiments; that he made the suggestion is certain.

him after his death, and subsequently Reccared II only reigned for a few days.¹⁰³ Nevertheless, there are several instances of support for hereditary monarchy, and this seems to have been a fixture of the school of Isidore-Seville's thinking on monarchy. In seeming contrast to that school, various canons required royal election, but this should not be seen as necessarily anathema to hereditary monarchy. In VI Toledo, however, there is a canon more damning to hereditary monarchy: its seventh canon states that nobody should even suggest raising a new king while the current one was alive.¹⁰⁴ This was a clear prescription against co-rulership, preventing the preparation of an heir. Chindaswinth, and by default Recceswinth, ignored this legislation and reverted to the model of co-rulership, yet elective monarchy was re-confirmed in the tenth canon of VIII Toledo, showing that the concepts may not have been incompatible, or that Recceswinth was unable to gloss all contradictions.

In conclusion, the *Liber Iudiciorum* employs the ideas of Isidore-Seville to reinforce Recceswinth's dynastic position, despite potential challenges to it in the canonical legislation at VIII Toledo.¹⁰⁵ Recceswinth could use the words of Isidore and his school to defend a Toledan royal position; he could manipulate the memory especially of Isidore and Braulio, thereby neutralizing opposition from this network and, potentially, the larger ecclesiastical one. In the second canon of VIII Toledo, Recceswinth oversaw the explicit recognition of Isidore as Doctor of the Church, thereby granting him a formal status that he, and his school, previously had not had.¹⁰⁶ This was, however, not in earnest, but as a way to promote royal authority at the expense of the competing networks. It was an ingenious move by Recceswinth's court. In that same canon, Isidore's own words are used to defend a position of love over law, in the situation of oaths. This allowed mercy to be granted to Froia and his followers, despite oaths taken before, and a law issued by Chindaswinth not to allow mercy for

---

103 Isidore, in chapter 60 of his *De Origine Gothorum*, maintains that proper royal succession is not by election, but by hereditary succession, in imitation of God and Jesus. In chapter 65 of *De Origine Gothorum*, he suggests that the proper form of royal succession is for a king to appoint his son as co-ruler, as Swinthila did with Riccimir. In contrast to Swinthila, Sisebut left young Reccared II to succeed his father on the latter's death (Isid., *De Orig. Goth.*, 61).

104 VI Toledo 17.

105 Fredegar says that Chindaswinth was elected by nobles, but suggests that this was a select cadre of associates with him, likely around Pamplona.

106 Though Isidore had referred to Leander as doctor in his poem to him, "Non satis antiquis doctoribus impar haberis, Leander vates hoc tua dicta docent" (*Isidorus Hispalenis, Versus*, ed. José María Sánchez Martín, Corpus Christianorum Series Latina 113A [Turnhout: Brepols, 2000], 225).

rebels.[107] Recceswinth asked to be allowed to show mercy to Froia despite having taken the oath not to do so. Isidore and his school were rigidly formalist: the rule of law took precedence over Christian empathy and passion.[108] Moreover, good law made a good king: in *De Origine Gothorum* Isidore says that the virtues of royal greatness are "fides, prudentia, industria, in iudiciis examinatio strenua, in regendo regno cura praecipua, circa omnes munificentia [...]."[109] Recceswinth manipulated the memory of Isidore in order to promote a politically expedient Christian piety, playing on the monarchy theory of Isidore-Seville, the memory of the Doctor, and the emphatic Christian emotions of those at VIII Toledo. This must have seemed like a grand gesture of reconciliation. In actuality, by neutralizing the legalist, Isidore-Seville position, Recceswinth was blocking the possibility of future opposition based on his breaking of constitutional law. From this point on, he could revert to pleas of Christian compassion when the law did not suit his needs. It was no coincidence that Recceswinth was the longest reigning monarch in the history of the Visigothic kingdom of Toledo.

5.2   Territoriality and Provincial Authority

There is some argument amongst historians that territoriality in Visigothic law was based firmly in conciliar practice, and that the Fourth Council of Toledo was the platform for establishing its territoriality.[110] The second canon of IV Toledo clearly expresses the desire for liturgical uniformity based on boundaries of Hispania, not the kingdom as a whole. In the *Hispana*, which was constructed just after IV Toledo, Hispania is an ecclesiastical unit of its own: it is an integral, geographical unit, regardless of the political borders of the kingdom. For example, the *Hispana* includes the councils of Braga in 561 and 572, despite Braga being, at those times, in the Suevic kingdom. If this is the logic of territoriality, then it should be pointed out that it was under Gundemar, in his council, that Hispania was created as an integral unit, territorially, and geographically, since Narbonne was not considered to be part of the ecclesiastical provinces. In his *VD*, Sisebut mentions none of the names of peoples north of Pyrenees, despite the location of the narrative's actions.[111] In contrast, Braulio in his letter to Pope Honorius defending the kingdom's Church and criticizing the Pope's knowledge of Scripture, refers to "our territory" as Spania (Iberia)

---

107   See *LI*, 2.1.6 versus *LI*, 2.1.7.
108   See, for example, II Seville, 1, 3 and 8.
109   Isid., *De Orig. Goth.*, 64.
110   For example, see Stocking, *BCC*, 157 and 175.
111   Fontaine, "Sisebut's *Vita Desiderii*," in *Visigothic Spain*, ed. James, 124, n. 1.

and Gallia Narbonensis, suggesting that there was an internal discourse on these matters, as well as one used in external communication.[112]

Territoriality in the law is not a geographical concept, *per se*: it refers to law that is applied to all people within defined political boundaries, because they are within that territory and tied somehow to it. The conciliar and ecclesiastical legislation and discourses show that there was an evolving concept of territory and law, of the idea of Hispania and its jurisdictional boundaries. However, territoriality in Visigothic law did not derive from these discussions, it was integral to its law from the beginning of its legislative history.[113]

In contrast to territorial law is the concept of personal law, which refers to laws that apply to specific people within a territory because of their identities. For example, laws against Jews should be classified as personal laws, since they were a legally separate group of people from others living in the same communities. Another example would be laws meant only for Romans, or for Goths, such as the canonical legislation declaring that only Goths could become kings, or the laws from Liuvigild and Recceswinth allowing intermarriage between these groups. All of these laws are personal, in the sense that they are based on a person's identity and not exclusively on the territorial kingdom of which they are subject. The *LI* includes multiple laws such as these and could be considered a codification with personal law. Its tenth book is dedicated to boundaries, limits of land and partitions, yet it does not mention broader territory, and hints at the preservation of personal distinctions in the law.[114] However, as some historians have convincingly argued, the entire concept of personal law was a later development, one that began in the Carolingian Empire, and so the *Liber Iudiciorum* must have been territorial. Law as territorial was a tradition carried from Rome into the post-Roman, barbarian kingdoms. For example, in the sixth century, the Ostrogothic king Theoderic explicitly stated that all people should follow the same law, whether Roman or Gothic, and this seems to have been the situation in sixth- and seventh-century Hispania as well.[115]

---

112   Braulio, *Ep.*, 21.
113   See Chapter 5, note 117.
114   For example, *LI*, 10.1.8, 9 and 16 discuss land between Romans and Goths.
115   See Cass., *Var.*, 3.13.2 and 8.3.4. For secondary discussion, see Walter Pohl, "Introduction; Strategies of Distinction," in *Strategies of Distinction,* ed. Pohl and Reimitz, 1–16 (11), and, Brigitte Pohl-Resl, "Legal Practice and Ethnic Identity in Lombard Italy," in *Strategies of Distinction,* ed. Pohl and Reimitz, 205–19. For a historiography of the principle of personality of the law, see Simeon Guterman, *The Principle of Personality of Law in the Germanic kingdoms of Western Europe from the Fifth to the Eleventh Century* (New York: Peter Land, 1990). Carl von Savigny imagined a mutual dependency between the person and the law in the legacy of Roman law, implying, furthermore, the complexity of personality as an

Although the dichotomy of personal law versus territorial law may have been a feature of law after the demise of the Visigothic kingdom of Toledo, it has been common in the scholarship of early medieval law to classify entire codes of law as either territorial or personal. There are examples where such categorizing is suitable, but not necessarily with the *LI*, although it has often been labeled the first territorial law-code of the Visigoths.[116] This cannot be an accurate description if the dichotomy did not yet exist, but is, nevertheless, a strange label for a code that never once mentions the territory over which it has jurisdiction.[117] The first two books of the *LI* are an unprecedented discussion of the role of law in society, yet there is nothing about its territorial application. The law applied both to the people of the kingdom, as individuals with unique identities and social situations, and to the places in which they were, the definition of which was left vague to encourage use in the provinces and many regions of the kingdom. Therefore, the *LI* was not a radical break in thought, but rather it was the product of the evolving culture and dialectics of the Isidore-moment, in which shifting attitudes towards the role of law – from the Isidorian legalist and regional, to the Toledan passions of justice and central authority – and the place of the king within the kingdom were tantamount.

The discussions about territoriality in the conciliar records, from Gundemar to the Fourth Council of Toledo, concern a matter of territory that was somewhat different in character, and one that was pivotal in the dialectical struggle between Isidore-Seville and Toledo-Agali: namely, regionalism. Since the 610s, the former had been pushing for the powers of the provincial metropolitans

---

issue in the law (Carl F. von Savigny, *Jural Relations, or, The Roman Law of Persons as Subjects of Jural Relations*, trans. W. H. Rattigan, 2nd edn. [London: Wildy, 1884]).

116 On territoriality, Thompson, *Goths*, 212–15; King, *Law and Society*, 18; *Leges Visigothorum*, ed. Zeumer (1902), 82–83; and Vismara, "*Leges Visigothorum*," 1804.

117 The Recceswinth version of the *Liber Iudiciorum* never mentions Spain or Hispania, or at all the territory over which it is territorially authoritative. It was not until the 670s that such a reference arose, in legislation by Wamba, which first appears in a twelfth-century manuscript (MS Skokloster [Upsala], ms. 22, 1 E 8641). For the text of the Wamba law, see *Diplomática*, ed. Canellas López, no. 148. For a discussion of the Upsala manuscript and of the potential appearance of Wamba laws in the tenth century, see García López, *Lex Wisigothorum*, 41–47, and 135–37. On the personal and territorial labelling and some problems with them see defenses by King, *Law and Society*, 18ff.; King, "King Chindasvind and the First Territorial Law-code of the Visigothic kingdom," in *Visigothic Spain: New Approaches*, ed. Edward James (Oxford: Oxford University Press, 1980), 131–58; and, Alvaro d'Ors, *Estudios Visigóticos 2, El Codigo de Eurico*. Cuadernos del Instituto Jurídico Español 12 (Rome: Consejo Superior de Investigaciones Científicas, 1960). For a problematizing of territoriality see Guterman, *The Principle of the Personality of Law*, esp. 242ff. The discussion of Visigothic law as personal is a tradition reaching back at least to Montesquieu (*De l'Esprit des Lois*, lb. 28).

against the royal Church and the Crown. This struggle for devolution or decentralization was paramount to the competition between the schools; the desire to preserve provincial integrity is what drove these conciliar discussions, both in Seville and Toledo, and in the texts they produced. The *LI* was meant to solve this problem, to quell the disagreements, and come up with a solution that could satisfy both schools, for regional autonomy and for Toledo's central authority. The attempt was made at IV Toledo, in which it was stated that from then on provincial councils were to meet regularly, and were also meant to be local law courts administering secular justice. This maintained the integration of secular and ecclesiastical, vital for the monarch's claims for central authority, but also gave the metropolitans outside of Toledo a fair level of jurisdiction, relative to the bishop and king in Toledo. Ultimately, this plan failed to come to fruition, for various reasons, as the regions continued to function and use law in their own ways.[118] It is reasonable to believe that Recceswinth saw the potential merits of the general idea, and that the *LI* was promulgated at the end of VIII Toledo with this in mind. It is likely that the *LI* was meant to go out with the bishops for them to use in the provincial councils, or otherwise sold in the provinces for such purposes.[119]

5.3   Jewish Legislation

The Jewish community of late antique Hispania was well established, relatively extensive, and economically viable, owning estates, businesses and slaves, and holding high political positions, although it faced sporadic persecutions.[120] The situation was not wholly different in the Visigothic kingdom

---

[118]   For a historiography and discussion of the failure of the plan to make provincial councils courts of justice see Stocking, "Martianus, Aventius and Isidore: Provincial Councils," n. 80.

[119]   See the law on price, *LI*, 5.4.22, and for other evidence of regional use and intention see *LI*, 2.1.28. For an archaeologically supported discussion of the operation of regional and municipal structures in seventh-century Hispania, and their relation to the law, see Chris Wickham, *Framing the Early Middle Ages: Europe and the Mediterranean, 400–800* (Oxford: Oxford University Press, 2005), 665.

[120]   See Ross Kraemer, "Jewish Women's Resistance to Christianity in the Early Fifth Century, The Account of Severus, Bishop of Minorca," *Journal of Early Christian Studies* 17 (2009): 635–65, and, Scott Bradbury, Severus of Minorca, *Letter on the Conversion of the Jews* (Oxford: Clarendon Press, 1996). Jewish communities are mentioned in Iberia in the oldest extant conciliar record from Spain, reach backing to the time of the Emperor Diocletian (284–305). The community is mentioned in canons 49 and 50 of the Council of Eliberritanum (Granada), which seems to have been a plenary council, since there are representatives from across the peninsula, including Seville, Toledo, and Zaragoza (*CCH* 4 [1984], 233–68). Jewish communities maintained their presence and self-identities within Iberia throughout late antiquity and the early middle ages, and were not, by that time,

of the seventh-century, in which "the Jewish community was relatively large, economically important, and politically influential."[121] "Visigothic Jews were no marginalized minority, but part and parcel of society."[122] There remains sufficient evidence to demonstrate that Jews, as individual people, were as part of the everyday life of neighbors, friends and associates as anyone else in the diverse communities of seventh-century Hispania, as the laws of the *LI* reveal.[123] An extant, early seventh-century epistolary exchange between the count of Toledo, Froga, and the bishop of Toledo, Aurasius, revealing that both, especially Froga, were in regular communication with and perhaps assisted the head rabbi of Toledo, Levi Shmuel.[124] This shows relationships of partnership, trust and cooperation, as well as antagonism, based more on socio-economic than religious identity. Individual Jews held, in seventh-century Hispania, important political capital, and even in the late seventh century, during the reign of Wamba and beyond, there were Christians converting to Judaism, and tombstones erected bearing Jewish inscriptions.[125] Even the anti-Jewish Julian of Toledo had no qualms about entrusting a Jew, one Restitutus, with private documents and communication – including a copy of the *Prognosticum futuri saeculi* – between the bishop of Toledo and regional bishops.[126] The Jewish condition, it would seem, only partly reflected legislation.[127] That there was such a

---

new arrivals from the East. For a general survey see Aron C. Sterk, "Latino-Romaniotes: The Continuity of Jewish Communities in the Western Diaspora, 400–700 CE," *Melilah, Manchester Journal of Jewish Studies* (2012): 21–49.

121   Robert Chazan, *The Jews of Medieval Western Christendom: 1000–1500* (Cambridge: Cambridge University Press, 2006), 91.

122   Drews, *The Unknown Neighbour*, 32.

123   For example, Ervig's *LI*, 12.3.19–24, and see Drews, *The Unknown Neighbour*, 289ff.

124   *Mis. Wisig.*, XVIII, and *Ep. Wis.*, 20.

125   Heather, *Goths*, 290; Julian of Toledo, *Insultatio*, in *Historia Wambae*, ed. Levison, 245; and, with bibliography, Friedrich Lotter, "Zur sozialen Hierarchie der Judenheit in Spätantike und Frühmittelalter," *Aschkenas* 13 (2003): 341ff.

126   Julian sent Restitutus as a messenger to bishop Idalius of Barcelona. Idalius was not pleased with having a Jew carry their communication, and made this known to Julian (Idal., *Ep. Ad Iul.*, Patrologia Latina 96, col. 458, and *Epistulae Idalii Barcinonesis episcopi ad Iulianum Toletanae sedis espiscopum*, in *Sancta Iuliani Toletani sedis episcopi opera*, Corpus Christianorum Series Latina 115, ed. Jocelyn N. Hillgarth [Turnhout: Brepols, 1976], 4). For discussion, see Martínez Pizarro, *Wamba*, 64–65, and Solomon Katz, *Jews in the Visigothic and Frankish kingdoms of Spain and Gaul* (Cambridge: The Medieval Academy of America, 1937), 131. Restitutus may have been a recent convert to Christianity, but even if this was the case, "until 690–700 converted Jews were still considered part of the Jewish communities (Liubov Chernin, "*Quod fidei plenitudine fines semper Spaniae floruerunt*... Egica and the Jews," *Sefarad* 69 [2009]: 10)."

127   This is not to say that Jews, as a collective and politically conscious entity, lived untroubled. The anti-Jewish legislation and attempted forced conversions are well known in the

gap between the law and the reality of life on this issue should be no surprise given the argument presented for the rhetorical nature of Recceswinth's *LI*.[128]

Returning to the main question then, how did Recceswinth use, to his favor, Isidore and his school's views on Judaism and Jewish people in Hispania? One of the reasons Isidore was annoyed by Sisebut's forced conversions, in addition to it being incorrect theology, was that it ignored the long-standing practices of Roman legislation, not to mention Visigothic law.[129] To resolve the conflicting views and competing opinions, Recceswinth juxtaposed Isidore-Seville's legalist position, and stance against forced conversions, with the anti-Jewish pronouncements of Toledo. For the twelfth book of the *LI*, designed to be the only one dealing with matters of Judaism, Recceswinth made a general exception to the overall structure: he allowed the laws of kings other than Chindaswinth and Recceswinth to be nominated.[130] There are no laws from any other kings in the first eleven books of the *Liber Iudiciorum*, which makes up the vast bulk of the text.[131] Throughout the first eleven books there is also not a single mention of Judaism: the word Jew (*Judaeus*) is never used, nor is the word Hebrew (*Hebreaus*). In contrast to the first eleven books, the twelfth book is not only dedicated to Jewish affairs, but there are also no *antiqua*, which constitute the

---

historiography of the Catholic kingdom of the Visigoths, and the letter from rabbi Shmuel concerns Jews converted by the bishop of Toledo, and their death. It has been argued that the forced conversions were not an innovation of the Catholic kingdom, but that they also existed in the Arian kingdoms of the Visigoths in which Jewish life was also disturbed by the authorities. This was possible, considering the late Roman persecutions of Jews in Hispania. For the argument of Arian Visigothic kings continuing late Roman policies against Jews see Raúl González Salinero, "Los judíos en el reino visigodo de época arriana," in *Judaísmo Hispano: Estudios en memoria de José Luis Lacave Riaño*, ed. Elena Romero, 2 vols. (Madrid: Consejo Superior de Investigaciones Científicas, 2003), II, 399–408. In contrast to such a claim, see Hagith Sivan, "The Invisible Jews of Visigothic Spain," *Revue des Études Juives* 159 (2000): 369–85, and, M.C. Díaz y Díaz, *San Isidoro de Sevilla: Etimologías* (Madrid, 1982), 53.

128 Later versions of the *LI*, and laws pronounced against Jews by Ervig and Egica, raise historical questions of their own. On this, see Chernin, "*Quod fidei...*," 7–24, and Kelly, "The *Liber Iudiciorum*: A Visigothic Literary Guide to Institutional Authority and Self-Interest."

129 See Isid., *Sent.*, 3.51.5; Reydellet, *La Royauté*, 595; and, Bat-Sheva Albert, "Isidore of Seville: His attitude towards Judaism and His impact on Early Medieval Canon Law," *Jewish Quarterly Review* 80 (1990): 207–20.

130 In 681, Erwig created the section title "concerning the Jews," which was not in Recceswinth's version of the *LI* (see Chernin, "*Quod fidei...*," 8). For the Jewish position in Toledo, see also Ildefonsus's rhetorical attacks on an anonymous Jew (chs. 3–10), and those he borrowed from Jerome (ch. 2), in Ildefonsus, *De virginitate perpetua Sanctae Mariae. The Perpetual Virginity of the Holy Mary by Ildefonsus of Toledo*, intro. and trans. Malcom Drew Donalson (Lewiston, NY: Edwin Mellen Press, 2011).

131 As pointed out above, an exception is the questionable law of Reccared in the third book.

majority of laws throughout the rest of the books. Furthermore, whereas laws in the other books were composed, copied from, or influenced by those of other legal collections, from Byzantium and back to Baetica, the twelfth book also leans on biblical passages. These points suggest that the twelfth book was meant to serve a particularly rhetorical purpose of appeasement: to make transparent Recceswinth's concessions to Church authorities in Toledo, on the one hand, but to do so within a power structure solidifying royal authority. The twelfth book is, in a sense, a living being in itself, although it is integral to the *LI*, as the book designed to deal with Jewish affairs.[132] Recceswinth made a move against Isidore-Seville with the twelfth book, but he merged, or satisfied, the conflicting and competing discourses by giving way especially to the legalist position of that school: in putting the laws into a secular law-code that was categorically separate from the canonical legislation.

6   Conclusion

The *Liber Iudiciorum* was the first Visigothic law-code issued by a Catholic king, in a Catholic kingdom, at a Catholic council.[133] These features alone indicate the uniqueness of the event of the *LI* from that of the previous Visigothic law-codes.[134] However, historians have tended to lump them together as if there was an essentiality to Visigothic legal codification. The *Edictum Theodorici*, *Codex Euricianus*, *Lex Romana Visigothorum*, *Codex Revisus* and *Liber Iudiciorum* do not represent a linear history of writing and meaning: they did not function the same way in their historical contexts, and were not issued for the same reasons.[135] Some of them were immediate responses to situations

---

[132] See *LI*, 12.2.1.
[133] Reccared may have issued one as well, but it is not extant. If he did, it is likely that Recceswinth and other contemporaries were aware of it and built from this legacy.
[134] The *LI* is also the only Visigothic law-code in which old and new laws were explicitly collected together into a single text. For his *Breviary*, or *LRV*, Alaric II had jurists write new interpretations for the old laws, as a way to update and clarify their meaning. However, these were added as interpretations not new laws, and not ascribed to Alaric II or his father Euric, who also produced a law-code, the *Codex Euricianus*.
[135] The prevailing opinion is that the *Edictum Theoderici* is the work of the Ostrogothic king Theoderic, not the Visigothic Theoderic I or II. However, the evidence allows for other possibilities. For a discussion of the evidence, see Sean D. W. Lafferty, *Law and Society in the Age of Theoderic the Great: A Study of the "Edictum Theoderici"* (Cambridge: Cambridge University Press, 2013), and the review of Lafferty by Otávio Luiz Vieira Pinto in *Networks and Neighbours* 2, no. 2 (2014): 400–03. Furthermore, for the influence of the Theodosian corpus on the *Liber Iudiciorum*, see Esperanza Osaba García, "Influenza delle

on the ground, others well-planned formalizations of authority, and others deeply entangled within the competitive discourses and narrative frameworks of the time. As is often repeated, Visigothic law-codes arose at moments of crisis and political anxiety.[136] As a general statement this is true, but practically, many non-legal sources were also produced in response to significant events: for example, all of those produced around the time of the usurpation of Sisenand. Yet, in instances such as those, new legal codes were not the chosen form of literature used to alleviate political problems and anxieties. There must have been other reasons, purposes and meanings of, and for, the *LI*. The significance, function and practical voice of the *LI* were determined by the prevailing dialectics and literary modes, from the use of *damnationes memoriae*, to uses of the past, prevalent in its historical situation. Recceswinth's *LI* was not an isolated text in its time, and, if grasping its historical meaning is the aim, as it is here, it should not be read in comparison to the earlier Visigothic or other law-codes, but part and parcel of the writing and competitive dialectics of the period; it should be considered together with the writing of its time, not as a separate, floating signifier in a chain of legal history.[137] Conciliar canons functioned perfectly well without being codified into collections, even at times when they were not written down, as in the case of those passed at the Council of Huesca.[138] When they were brought together into smartly designed historical collections, they were imbued with additional, if not alternative, meaning. This act of re-signifying the laws and their pasts is what Recceswinth did: he historicized them and made them perform in a literary way. It is inappropriate, then, to argue whether the *LI* was functional or symbolic: it was law, but it was also historical narrative, and as such, performed in literary ways, as did the *DVI*, origin-stories, histories, chronicles, and *Hispana*.[139] The *LI* employed the

---

leggi costantiniane nella *Lex Visigothorum*', in *Diritto@Storia. Quaderni di Scienze Giuridiche e Tradizione Romana*, Anno II, Quaderno no. 2 (2003): np.

136 For a recent proliferation of the idea see Koon and Wood, "Unity from Disunity', 796, and before them, Collins, *Visigothic Spain*, 223–30

137 For further discussion, see Carlos Petit, *Iustitia Gothica: Historia social y teología del proceso en la "Lex Visigothorum"* (Huelva: Universidad de Huelva Press, 2001).

138 The proceedings of the Council of Huesca in 598 were first put into writing in 614, by those at the Council of Egara, yet Huesca's canons presumably functioned during the intervening sixteen years. For more, see Chapter 4, note 43.

139 On the historiographical dialectics that interprets the law-code as functional or symbolic see Thompson, *Goths*, 210ff., against Wallace-Hadrill, *Long-Haired Kings*, 179–81, and for a mediating position, Wormald, *Legal Culture*, 13. Wormald maintained that early medieval written legislation was primarily symbolic, or "ideological" (see Wormald, "*Lex scripta*"). Rosamond McKitterick, in dialogue with Wormald, argues that written early medieval legislation can only have had symbolic value if audiences understood and appreciated

tropes, forms, and historical, competitive dialectics of the historical situation, using them to sublimate the schools-competition. The *LI* represents the definitive poetics of the Isidore-moment in the form of a poetics of the law independent of its past.¹⁴⁰

---

the practical function of law, therefore a law-code could only have meaning if its practicality as legislation was expected (see Rosamond McKitterick, *The Carolingians and the Written Word* [Cambridge: Cambridge University Press, 1989], 23–66). The *LI* was a collection of valid laws, which were respected as such, but its meaning was determined not by this, but by its engagement with the literary and historical forms and expectations of the written word of politics in the middle of the seventh century.

140 An interpretive adaptation of Vico's poetics of theology (see Giambatista Vico, *The New Science*, trans. D. Marsh (New York: Penguin, 1999 [orig. 1744]).

Conclusion

"Always historicize!"
FREDRIC JAMESON

∴

Writers in seventh-century Hispania engaged events, discourses, people(s) and, in fact, time, as constitutional elements of narration about the "before now," as imagined pasts imbued with significance in the present and future. These authors employed a diverse range of historical methods and structures for their historiographies. These forms were chosen, and this plurality embraced, because they had meaning within the cultural life and political discourses specific and endemic to the Isidore-moment. The employment of these literary models and this vibrancy of historical narration, of historiography, in this historical situation, were the product of the struggles between various sites and networks of power in Hispania and the broader kingdom.

That these struggles took the form of a dialectical competition fought through history-writing and historiographies was due to a collection of reasons all pertinent to the specific historical moment. The training, education and individual abilities of Isidore certainly were a driving force behind the proliferation of historical forms and employments of the "before now" to construct power by means of imagined pasts. However, Isidore's brilliance was not in his ability to "shine above the rest," which he also did, but rather, to enlighten divergent persons, groups and communities. Isidore did not create, outside of a small network of students, new philosophies of history, for the majority of society, rather, he engaged the past as narrative in ways that made sense to his audiences on multiple levels.

Hispania in the earlier seventh century was a diverse society, but it was also one in which Christians increasingly became aware of and sensitive to historical consciousness, if not in terms of the world around them, then in terms of the world(s) to come. For them, the past and the future had become an intertwining of temporal and a-temporal, finite and infinite. In this culture, the past held tremendous spiritual, social and political power, and, as such, could also be a form of cultural capital able to be deployed, capitalized upon, for means other than expressions or confirmations of general human salvation and historiographically determined truth. Historiography became a means of fulfillment: writers in the Isidore-moment could write history to fulfill a host of desires, from spiritual salvation, to local autonomy, to the elevation of one's sister as a nun.

Authors, from Isidore to Ildefonsus, did precisely this, writing about the past in ways that promoted the aspirations of persons, networks and institutions above others in the kingdom. Historiography, as act and as product, experienced a relative renaissance in seventh-century Hispania because it was a superbly multifaceted and effective means of legitimation. A single text could deliver positive spiritual messages to, for example, Byzantine audiences in the south and local communities in Seville, while subtly advancing antagonistic opinions to nobles and church figures in Toledo. Moreover, another site of authority could adapt that same historical model or historiography to reverse the meaning of a text and fight back against the other author(s) and the networks and interests they represented. Isidore's and his school's commitment to writing was an important factor in the prolongation of this historiographical, historical moment, yet their very need to create this situation, as such, to find expression of power in this way, was the result of their growing political insignificance, which would be exposed between the 670s and 680s, by Julian of Toledo and Ervig.

The theory of the Isidore-moment helps us understand a lot of mysteries of the period, and ties together fragmented discourses about the fractured and antagonistic state of affairs of the period, suggesting for the first time the intimate relationship of this *convivencia* with the texts produced. We find out that many texts, recensions and redactions whose purposes were unclear, seem to have evident meaning as actual part of this schools rivalry. Moreover, we are able to reconsider the 630s and its exceptional literary-political events, such as the Fourth Council of Toledo and its placement within a narrative of historical fulfillment, the *Hispana*, by Isidore-Seville, not as terminal points in a (real or local) *longue durée*, or crucial moments in consensus-building and royal consolidation, but, rather, as a pivotal period of the Isidore-moment in which the schools-competition flourished and took on the next generation.

By exposing the schools and the Isidore-moment, it is possible to critically interrogate, and deconstruct, the texts of seventh-century Hispania in novel ways, revealing an historical situation of bitter rivalries, struggles and competitions between the same people that historiography has long figured to have been allies working towards unity. From eliciting the schools and the deeply sublimated competition between factions of Catholics in seventh-century Hispania, the research of this book allows important new conclusions about the texts and history of Visigothic Hispania. The first, shown especially in Chapters 2 and 3, is that the pervading historiographical narrative that the elite of seventh-century Hispania strove desperately for unity and consensus is less reflective of the historical situation than of a pointed rhetoric whose ultimate aims were somewhat contrary, and which were later uncritically adapted and developed into lasting historiographies, from at least the ninth century.

Second, as shown throughout the book, is the absolute centrality, in seventh-century Hispania, of history-writing, historical representation, and the drive for networks of authority to own and mediate the past, or rather, the "before now," a non-totalized imagination of past, for multi-layered purposes which this book uncovers. The presence of diverse and impressive methodologies for imagining, inventing, and presenting pasts for various purposes of power, is a paramount feature of writing in the period, and its methodological plurality also could serve as a model for self-reflection on modern historical writing.

Third, and this is what this book ultimately leads to, is that the contemporary meanings and functions of the famous mid-seventh-century Visigothic law-code known variously as the *Liber Iudiciorum*, *Lex Visigothorum* or *Forum Iudicum*, and which has even found its way into legal systems of America, can only be grasped by contextualizing the *Liber Iudiciorum* as a product of the literary culture and competitive dialectics of the moment, defined by invented narratives, *damnationes memoriae*, and expedient constructions of memory.[1] The LI's significance and ways of communicating were entangled within the competitive dialectics of the period, and the text should be interpreted through this prism. By grasping the historical and discursive world in which the LI "spoke" and the conditions out of which it was born, scholars can better understand the significance of this law-code in its historical place, without the need to rely on a-historical historiographies, and legal history, to interpret it. As the cultural theorist Fredric Jameson once declaimed, "always historicize!," the slogan, he argued, of "the one absolute and we may even say 'transhistorical' imperative of all dialectical thought."[2]

---

1 On the naming of the *Liber Iudiciorum*, see Chapter 5, § 2.3.
2 Fredric Jameson, *The Political Unconscious: Narrative as a Socially Symbolic Act* (Ithaca: Cornell University Press, 1981).

APPENDIX

Julian of Toledo Not an Agalian

The history of Julian's education makes it evident that Julian was not trained or raised at Agali, and that any affiliation to it was by secondary association. According to his second successor and biographer Felix, Julian was never an abbot at all, let alone abbot of Agali: Julian was a deacon, priest (presbyter), and then bishop.[1] Nevertheless, other records provide some curious clues as to Julian's career, including as abbot. For example, in the signatory list of the Eleventh Council of Toledo in 675, there are two abbots named Julian. One of them, whose signature is sixth in the list of abbots, is listed as the abbot of the church of the monastery of St. Michael's in Léon (San Miguel de Escalada). The other Julian is listed first, and the name of his monastery is not stated. Given that the bishops of Toledo were generally the primary signatories at Toledan councils, and Agali's primary position in Toledo, it is reasonable to assume, if one has not read the words of Julian and Felix about Julian's education and career, that this Julian was abbot of Agali. However, when Ildefonsus was abbot of Agali, he never signed councils of Toledo (VIII and IX Toledo) as primary abbot. Since lists of conciliar signatories were prone to heavy editing, it may be that Julian was simply added to the list of abbots later from the eighth century on and was listed first based on the association of the bishops of Toledo with Agali. It is uncertain, then, if this Julian was abbot at all, let alone of Agali, but also it is unclear whether he was even the same Julian that became the bishop of Toledo.[2]

The story of Julian's potential abbacy, despite his own remarks and those of his biographer, does have strange twists. For example, despite the strong contrary evidence, there is some case for Julian of 675 being abbot of Agali and the future bishop of Toledo. Julian the primary abbot at XI Toledo signs as "Iulianus indignus abba haec gesta synodica a nobis definite ss.," according to some manuscript traditions.[3] When he signed XII Toledo, he wrote "ego Iulianus indignus," suggesting that this was indeed the same Julian. Also, neither Julian ever appears again as abbot, and in the next council of Toledo the

---

1   Felix, *Vita Iuliani*, 4.
2   Paul Wengen argued that neither of the two Julians that signed as abbot in XI Toledo were the later bishop Julian. See Paul Wengen, *Julianus, Erzbischof von Toledo. Sein leben und seine Wirksamkeit unter den Königen Ervig und Egica* (St. Gallen: Zollikofer, 1891).
3   On this, see the contrasting editions, and related notes in the latter, of *Concilios Visigoticos*, ed. Vives, 368–69 and *CCH* 6 (2002), 131–33.

leading two signatories are both Julians: Julian of Toledo and Julian of Seville. It is possible that these two abbots became bishops. In his *Vita Iuliani*, Felix said that Julian had dreamed with a deacon Gudila to run off to monastic lives.[4] There seems to be merit to this story, since a deacon Gudila signed XI Toledo, after the signatures of both Julians. It could have been then that the Julians were similarly close, perhaps together with Gudila. If so, this could help explain why the other Julian was appointed by Ervig, upon Julian of Toledo's recommendation, as metropolitan of Baetica, and also signed XII Toledo as the lead signatory, as bishop of Seville. This could have been Toledo's most aggressive move ever to silence any competition from Seville.

Furthermore, when Julian revised the history of the church councils of Hispania, the *Hispana*, he cut from the record the Eleventh Council Toledo in 675, at which the mysterious Julian signed as abbot. There are a few reasons why he would have done so if he had been that abbot. One is that he was trying specifically to disassociate himself from the abbacy, Agali, and Wamba. The end of the reign of Wamba is clouded in mystery and legend, but it is certain that Julian was somehow party to the usurpation of the Crown from Wamba by Ervig. Julian could have cut XI Toledo to hide some corruption about which we no longer have any information.[5]

If Julian was abbot of Agali, the contemporary silence about this fact is remarkable. This is especially so considering the multiple contemporary references to other abbots of Agali who were notably less prolific, such as Helladius, Justus, Eugenius I, and also Rechila, who never became bishop. It is, moreover, strange that none of the near-contemporary sources that discuss in fair detail the life of Julian ever mention his time as abbot of Agali.[6] Even the ninth-century *Chronicle* of Alfonso III, full of true and fanciful stories, does not mention Julian as abbot of Agali.[7] The signature at the end of XI Toledo, a council left out of the *Hispana* by Julian of Toledo, is the only early medieval evidence of

---

4   Felix, *Vita Iuliani* 2–3. For more on this friendship, see also Stancati, intro. and trans., Julian of Toledo, *Prognosticum seculi futuri*, pp. 49–53. I would argue, in addition, that the friendship could also have been metaphorical. Gudila could have represented the Visigothic monarchy, which, as Felix predicts, dies in adolescence.
5   Julian may have cut XI Toledo to maintain silence about Cartagena in a way that defended his reintroduction of Cartagena into XII Toledo.
6   For example, see the *Chronicle of 754*, the letters between Idalius to Julian, and, most damning of all, the actual *Vita* to Julian, by his successor Felix.
7   There are two versions of the Chronicle of Alfonso III. For the one mentioning Julian, in its opening entry, see the *Cronica ad Sebastianum*. For an edited version, see *Crónicas asturianas*, ed. Juan Gil (Oviedo: Universidad Oviedo, 1985), 114–49.

Julian as abbot of Agali. Julian of Toledo may have earlier signed XI Toledo as abbot, yet it is uncertain whether he was abbot specifically of Agali. If he was, it was for a short period, and it is a point that he himself wanted to erase from the records, hardly indicating a deep affinity for Agali and its traditions.

Bibliography

Primary Sources

Anonymi Valesiani pars posterior. In *Chronica Minora Saeculi*, edited by Theodor Mommsen, 306–29. Monumenta Germaniae Historica, Auctorum Antiquissimorum 9. Berlin: Weidmann, 1894.

Braulio of Zaragoza. *Epistolae*. Editions: *San Braulio, Obispo de Zaragoza (631–651), Su Vida y sus Obras*. Edited by Charles H. Lynch and Pascual Galindo. Madrid: Instituto "Enrique Florez," 1950; *Braulio de Zaragoza: Epístolas*. Edited by Ruth Miguel Franco. Madrid: Ediciones Akal, S. A., 2015; *Braulionis Caesaraugustani Epistulae and Isidori Hispalensis Epistulae ad Braulionem*. Edited by Ruth Miguel Franco. Corpus Christianorum Series Latina 114B. Turnhout: Brepols, 2018. Translation: *Braulio of Zaragoza, Fructuosus of Braga*. Iberian Fathers 2. Translated by Claude W. Barlow. Washington, D.C.: Catholic University of America Press, 1969.

Braulio of Zaragoza. *Renotatio*. Edition: José Carlos Martín-Iglesias, *La "Renotatio Librorum Domini Isidori" de Braulio de Zaragoza*. Logroño: Fundación San Millán de la Cogolla, 2002.

Braulio of Zaragoza. *Vita Aemiliani*. Edition: *Vita Emiliani Sancti Braulionis Caesaraugustani Episcopi. Edición crítica*. Edited by Luis Vázquez de Parga. Madrid: Consejo Superior de Investigacions Científicas, 1943. Translation: *The Life of St. Aemelian the Confessor, called the hooded*, in *Lives of the Visigothic Fathers*, translated by Andy Fear, 15–44. Liverpool: Liverpool University Press, 1997.

Chronica Regum Visigothorum. Laterculus regum Visigothorum. In *Chronorum minorum*, edited by Theodor Mommsen, 461–68. Monumenta Germaniae Historica, Auctorum Antiquissimorum 13. Berlin: Weidemann, 1898.

Chronicle of 754. Editions: *Crónica mozárabe de 754: edición crítica y traducción*. Edited by José Eduardo López Pereira. Zaragoza: Anúbar, 1991; in *Chronica Minora*, edited by Theodor Mommsen, 334–60. Monumenta Germaniae Historica, Auctorum Antiquissimorum 11. Berlin: Weidmann, 1894. English translation in *Conquerors and Chroniclers of Early Medieval Spain*, edited by Kenneth Baxter Wolf, 111–60. Liverpool: Liverpool University Press, 1990.

Codex Theodosianus. Theodosiani libri XVI cum constitutionibus Sirmondianis et leges novella ad Theodosianum pertinentes. Edited by Theodor Mommsen and Paul M. Meyer. 2 volumes. Berlin: Weidmann, 1905.

La Colección Canónica Hispana. Edited by Gonzalo Martínez Díez and (from 1982 forward as co-editor) Félix Rodríguez, 6 vols. Madrid, 1966–2002. See also *Concilios Visigóticos e Hispano-Romanos*. Edited and translated by José Vives. Barcelona and

Madrid: Consejo Superior de Investigaciones Científicas, Instituto Enrique Flórez, 1963.

Corpus Nummorum Visigothorum Ca. 575–714: Leovigildus-Achila. Edited by Jesús Vico Monteoliva, María Cruz Cores Gomendio and Gonzalo Cores Uría. Madrid: Real Academia de la Historia, 2006.

Diplomática Hispano-Visigoda. Edited by Ángel Canellas López. Zaragoza: Institución Fernando el Católico, 1979.

El epítome hispánico, una colección canónica española del siglo VII. Edited by Gonzalo Martínez Díez. Comillas: Universidad Pontificia, 1961.

Epistolae Merovingici et Karolini aevi. Edited by Wilhem Gundlach, 658–90. Monumenta Germaniae Historica. Epistolarum III. Berlin: Weidmann, 1892.

Estoria de Espanna. Edited by Aengus Ward et al. Www.estoria.bham.ac.uk/blog/.

Eudocia. *Eudocia Augustae, Procli Lycii, Claudiani carminum graecorum reliquiae*. Edited by Arthur Ludwich. Leipzig: Teubner, 1897.

Eugenius. *Eugenius Toletani*. Edited by Paulo Farmhouse Alberto. Corpus Christianorum Series Latina 114. Turnhout: Brepols, 2005. For *Carmina* and *Epistulae*, see *Eugenii Toletani Episcopi Carmina et Epistulae*. Edited by Frideric Vollmer, Monumenta Germaniae Historica, Auctorum Antiquissimorum 14. Berlin, 1905.

Exemplar iudicii inter Martianum et Auentium episcopos. Editions: *España Sagrada*, 15. Edited by Enrique Flórez. Madrid, 1787; *Suplementos al Concilio Nacional Toledano VI*. Edited and translated (Sp.) by Fidel Fita y Colome. Madrid, 1881; and, *Die Könige der Germanen* 6, edited by Felix Dahn, 615–620, with commentary from 623 to 641. Leipzig, 1885.

Felix of Toledo. *Vita Iuliani*. Edition: *Vita sancti Juliani Toletani episcopi*, edited by Valeriano Yarza Urquiola, 9–14. Corpus Christianorum Series Latina 115B. Turnhout: Brepols, 2014; *España Sagrada. Theatro geographico-histórico de la Iglesia de España* V, edited by Henrique Florez. Madrid, 1747.

Flavius Cresconius Corippus, In laudem Iustini Augusti minoris Libri IV. Edited by Averil Cameron. London: The Athlone Press, 1976.

Formulae Wisigothicae. Las "Formulae Wisigothicae:" Aproximación a la práctica jurídica visigoda. Edited by Edorta Córcoles Olaitz. Lecce: Edizioni Grifio, 2010.

Hydatius. *Chronicles*. In *Hydatii Lemici continuatio chronicorum Hieronymianorum ad a. CCCCLXVIII*, in *Chronica Minora, saec. iv–vii*, edited by Theodor Mommsen, 13–36. Monumenta Germaniae Historica, Auctorum Antiquissimorum 11. Berlin: Weidmann, 1894; Richard W. Burgess, ed., *The Chronicle of Hydatius and the Consularia Constantinopolitana: Two Contemporary Accounts of the Final Years of the Roman Empire*. Oxford: Oxford University Press, 1993 [digitized 2017].

Idalius of Barcelona. *Epistulae Idalii Barcinonesis episcopi ad Iulianum Toletanae sedis espiscopum*, in *Sancta Iuliani Toletani sedis episcopi opera*, edited by Jocelyn N. Hillgarth, 3–7. Corpus Christianorum Series Latina 115. Turnhout: Brepols, 1976.

Ildefonsus of Toledo. *De virginitate perpetua Sanctae Mariae. The Perpetual Virginity of the Holy Mary by Ildefonsus of Toledo*. Introduced and translated by Malcom Drew Donalson. Lewiston, NY: Edwin Mellen Press, 2011.

Ildefonsus of Toledo. *De Viris Illustribus*. Edition: in *Ildefonsus Toletani, De virginitate Sanctae Mariae, De cognitione baptismi, De itinere deserti, De Viris Illustribus*, edited by Carmen Codoñer Merino, 483–616. Corpus Christianorum Series Latina 114A. Turnhout: Brepols, 2007. Codoñer Merino, Carmen. *El "De viris illustribus" de Ildefonso de Toledo. Estudio y edición crítica*. Salamanca: Universidad de Salamanca, 1972. Translation: *On the Lives of Famous Men*, in *Lives of the Visigothic Fathers*, translated by Andy Fear, 107–22. Liverpool: Liverpool University Press, 1997.

Index Scriptorum Latinorum Medii Aevi Hispanorum. Edited by Manuel C. Díaz y Díaz. Madrid: Consejo Superior de Investigaciones Científicas, 1959.

Inscripciones Cristianas de la España Romana y Visogoda (ICERV). Edited by José Vives. Barcelona: Instituto Erique Flórez, 1969.

Isidore of Seville. *Chronicles*. Editions: *Chronica*. Edited by José Carlos Martín-Iglesias. Corpus Christianorum Series Latina 112. Turnhout: Brepols, 2003; *chronica maiora* ed. *primum a* DCXV, *and chronicorum epitome ed. a* DCXXVII in *Chronica Minora, saec. Iv–vii*, edited by Theodor Mommsen, 391–488. Monumenta Germaniae Historica, Auctorum Antiquissimorum 11. Berlin: Weidman, 1894. Translation: *Conquerors and Chroniclers of Early Medieval Spain*, translated by Kenneth Baxter Wolf, 79–110. Liverpool: Liverpool University Press, 1990.

Isidore of Seville. *De Origine Gothorum*. Edition: *Las Historias de los Godos, los Vandalos y los suevos de Isidoro de Sevilla*, edited by Cristobal Rodríguez Alonso, 167–321. León: Centro de Estudios e Investigación "San Isidoro," 1975; *Historia Gothorum Vandalorum Sueborum* in *Chronica Minora, saec. Iv–vii*, edited by Theodor Mommsen, 267–303. Monumenta Germaniae Historica, Auctorum Antiquissimorum 11. Berlin: Weidmann, 1894. Translation: *History of the Kings of the Goths, Vandals, and Sueves*. Translated by Guido Donini and Gordon B. Ford, Jr. Boston and Leiden: Brill, 1966.

Isidore of Seville. *De Origine Officiorum*. Edition: *Sancti Isidori Episcopi Hispalensis, De Ecclesiasticis Officiis*. Edited by Christopher Lawson. Corpus Christianorum Series Latina 113. Turnhout: Brepols, 1989.

Isidore of Seville. *De Viris Illustribus*. Carmen Codoñer Merino. *El "De Viris Illustribus" de Isidoro de Sevilla: Estudio y Edición crítica*. Salamanca: Consejo Superior de Investigaciones Científicas, 1964.

Isidore of Seville. *Differentiae*. Editions: *Isidoro de Sevilla Diferencias Libro I*. Edited by Carmen Codoñer. Paris: Belles Lettres, 1992; *Liber Differentiarum*, edited by Faustino Arevalo, Patrologia Latina 83, columns 9–170; and, *Isidorus Hispalensis Liber Differentiarum* II. Edited by María Adelaida Andrés Sanz. Corpus Christianorum Series Latina 111A. Turnhout: Brepols, 2006. Translation: *Isidore of Seville's "Synonyms"*

(*"Lamentations of a Sinful Soul"*) *and "Differences."* Translated by Priscilla Throop. Charlotte, VT: Medieval MS, 2012.

Isidore of Seville. *Expositio in Vetus Testamentum: Genesis.* Edited and introduced by Martine Dulaey and Michael M. Gorman. Freiburg: Herder, 2008.

Isidore of Seville. *Liber numerorum.* Patrologia Latina 83, column 229; *Le livre des nombres = Liber numerorum, Isidore de Séville.* Edited and translated (Fr.) by Jean-Yves Guillaumin. Paris: Belles Lettres, 2006.

Isidore of Seville. *Origines,* or *Etymologies.* Edition: *Isidori Hispalensis Episcopi Etymologiarum sive Originum Libri XX.* Edited by W. M. Lindsay, Oxford, 1911; *Etymologies IX.* Edited by Marc Reydellet. Paris: Les Belles Lettres, 1984. Translation: *The "Etymologies" of Isidore of Seville.* Translated by Stephen A. Barney, W. J. Lewish, J. A Beach, and Oliver Berghof. Cambridge: Cambridge University Press, 2006.

Isidore of Seville. *Sententiae.* Edition: *Isidorus Hispalensis Sententiae.* Edited by Pierre Cazier. Corpus Christianorum Series Latina 111. Turnhout: Brepols, 1998.

Isidore of Seville. *Synonyma.* Editions: *Synonyma.* Edited by Jacques Elfassi. Corpus Christianorum Series Latina 111B. Turnhout: Brepols, 2009. *San Isidoro de Sevilla "Sinónimos."* Edited and translated (sp.) by Antonio Viñayo González. León: Universidad de León, 2001.

Jerome. *Hebraicae quaestiones in libro Geneseos; Liber interpretationis hebraicorum nominum.* Corpus Christianorum Series Latina 72. Edited by Paul de Lagarde, Germain Morin, and Marc Adriaen. Turnhout: Brepols, 1959.

John of Biclar, *Chronicles.* Editions: *Iohannes abbatis Biclarensis chronica a* DLXVII–DXC, in *Chronica Minora, saec. Iv–vii,* edited by Theodor Mommsen, 211–20. Monumenta Germaniae Historica, Auctorum Antiquissimorum, 11. Berlin: Weidmann, 1894; and, *Victoris Tunnunensis Chronicon cum reliquiis ex Consularibus Caesaraugustanis et Iohannis Biclarensis Chronicon,* edited by Carmen Cardelle de Hartmann and Roger Collins. Corpus Christianorum Series Latina 173A. Turnhout: Brepols, 2001. Translation: *Conquerors and Chroniclers of Early Medieval Spain,* translated Kenneth Baxter Wolf, 57–78. Liverpool: Liverpool University Press, 1990).

Jordanes. *Getica.* In *Jordanes: "Getica,"* edited by Antonio Grillone, 3–263. Auters Latins du Moyen Âge. Paris: Les Belles Lettres, 2017); *Romana et Getica,* edited by Theodor Mommsen, 53–138. Monumenta Germaniae Historica, Auctorum Antiquissimorum 5.1. Berlin: Weidemann, 1882; Translation: *The Gothic History of Jordanes: In English with an Introduction and a Commentary,* translated by Charles C. Mierow. Princeton: Princeton University Press, 1915.

Julian of Toledo. *Beati Hildefonsi Elogium.* Edited by Jacques-Paul Migne, cols. 43–44. Patrologia Latina 96.

Julian of Toledo. *Historia Wambae.* In *Historia Wambae regis, Epistula ad Modoenum,* edited by Wilhem Levison, 217–55. Corpus Christianorum Series Latina 115. Turnhout: Brepols, 1976; *The Story of Wamba: Julian of Toledo's "Historia Wambae regis."*

Introduced and translated by Joaquin Martínez Pizarro. Washington, D.C.: The Catholic University Press, 2005.

Julian of Toledo. *Prognosticum futuri saeculi*. In *Opera I: Prognosticum futuri saeculi libri tres, Apologeticum de tribus capitulis, De comprobatione sextae aetatis, Idalii Barcelonis Episcopi epistulae*, edited by Jocelyn N. Hillgarth, 11–126. Corpus Christianorum Series Latina 115. Turnhout: Brepols, 1976; *Prognosticum saeculi futuri: Foreknowledge of the world to come*, introduced and translated by Tommaso Stancati. Ancient Christian Writers 63. New York: Newman Press, 2010; and, Jocelyn N. Hillgarth, "A Critical Edition of the *Prognosticum* of Saint Julian of Toledo." Ph.D. diss., Cambridge University, 1956.

Laterculi Imperatorum Romanorum Codici Theodosiano Adiuncti. In *Chron. min.*, edited by Theodor Mommsen, 411–13. Monumenta Germaniae Historica, Auctorum Antiquissimorum 13. Berlin: Weidmann, 1898.

Leander of Seville. *Liber de Institutione Virginum*. Edition and translation: *Saint Leander, Archbishop of Seville: A Book on the Teaching of Nuns and a Homily in Praise of the Church*. Edited and translated by John C. Martyn. Lanham, MD: Lexington Books, 2009. Translation and study: *De la instrucción de las vírgenes y desprecio del mundo. Traducción, studio y notes*. Translated (Sp.) by Jaime Velázquez. Madrid: Fundación Unversitaria Española, 1979.

Liber Iudiciorum. Lex Visigothorum. In *Leges Visigothorum antiquiores*, edited by Karl Zeumer, 21–313 and 33–456. Monumenta Germaniae Historica, Legum. Hanover and Leipzig: Hahn, 1894 and 1902; Yolanda García López. *Estudios Críticos y Literarios de la "Lex Wisigothorum."* Alcalá: Universidad de Alcalá, 1996; Pierre Pithou. *Codicis legum Wisigothorum libri XII, Isidori Hispalensis Episcopi de Gothis Wandalis et Sueuis, Historia siue Chronicon*. Paris: Sébastien Nivelle, 1579; Spanish translation in *El Libro de los Juicios (Liber Iudiciorum)*. Edited by Rafael Ramis Barceló. Translated (Sp.) by Pedro Ramis Serra and Rafael Ramis Barceló, 41–877. Madrid: Agencia Estatal Boletín Oficial del Estado, 2015.

Paul the Deacon. *History of the Lombards*. Edition: *Pauli Historia Langobardorum*, edited by Ludwig Bethmann and Georg Waitz, 12–187. Monumenta Germaniae Historica, Scriptores Rerum Langobardicarum et Italicarum, saec. vi–ix. Hanover: Hahn, 1878.

Petronius. *Satyricon*. Edited and translated by Michael Heseltine and W. H. D. Rouse. Revised by Eric Herbet Warmington. Loeb Classical Library 15. Cambridge: Harvard University Press, 1913; *Petronius Satyricon Reliquiae*. Edited by Konrad Müller. Leipzig and Stuttgart: Tuebner, 1995.

Quiricius of Toledo. *Epistolae*. Edited by Jacques-Paul Migne, Patrologia Latina 96, cols. 193–94.

Sidonius Apollinaris. *Letters*. Edited and translated by William B. Anderson in *Sidonius: Poems and Letters*. 2 volumes. Loeb Classics. Cambridge: Harvard University Press, 1965.
Sisebut. *De Defectione Lunae*. In John R. C. Martyn, *King Sisebut and the Culture of Visigothic Spain*. 111–17. Lewiston, NY: The Edwin Mellen Press, 2008.
Sisebut. *Vita Desiderii*. *Vita Desiderii: Vita vel Passio Sancti Desiderii Episcopi Viennensis*, edited by Bruno Krusch, 630–37. Monumenta Germaniae Historica, Scriptores rerum Merovingicarum 3. Hanover and Leipzig: Hahn, 1896; José Carlos Martín-Iglesias, "Une nouvelle édition critique de la *Vita Desiderii* de Sisebut, accompagnée de quelques réflexions concernant la date des *Sententiae* et du *De viris illustribus* d'Isidore de Séville," *Hagiographica* 7 (2000): 127–80. Translation: *Life and Martyrdom of Saint Desiderius*, *Lives of the Visigothic Fathers*, translated by Andy Fear, 1–14. Liverpool: Liverpool University Press, 1997.
Suetonius. *De Vitis Caesarum*. J. C. Rolfe, trans., and K. R. Bradley, *Lives of the Caesars*. 2 volumes. Loeb Classical Library 31 and 38. Cambridge: Harvard University Press, 1914; Robert Kaster, ed., *C. Suetoni Tranquilli: De Vita Caesarum Libros VIII et De Grammaticis et Rhetoribus Librum*, Oxford Classical Texts (Oxford: Oxford University Press, 2016 [digitized, 2018]).
Taio of Zaragoza. *Epistolae*. Edited by Jacques-Paul Migne, Patrologia Latina 80, col. 723.
Taio of Zaragoza. *Sententiae*. Edited by Jacques-Paul Migne, Patrologia Latina 80, cols. 727–990.
Valerius of Bierzo. *De Coelesti Revelatione*. Edited by Jacques-Paul Migne, Patrologia Latina 87, cols. 435–36; Manuel C. Díaz y Díaz. *Valerio del Bierzo. Su persona. Su obra*. León: Centro de Estudios e Investigación San Isidoro, 2006.
Vita Fructuosi. Edition: *La Vida de San Fructuoso de Braga*. Edited by Manuel C. Díaz y Díaz. Braga: Diário do Minho, 1974. English translation in *The Life of St. Fructuosus of Braga*, *Lives of the Visigothic Fathers*, translated by Andy Fear, 123–44. Liverpool: Liverpool University Press, 1997.
Vita sancti Isidori. *Scripta medii aevi de vita Isidori Hispalensis episcopi*. Edited by José Carlos Martín-Iglesias. Corpus Christianorum Continuatio Mediaevalis 281. Turnhout: Brepols, 2016.
Vitas Patrum Emeritensium. Edition: *Vitas sanctorum patrum Emeritensium*, edited by Antonio Maya Sánchez, 3–102. Corpus Christianorum Series Latina 116. Turnhout: Brepols, 1992; English translation in *Lives of the Fathers of Mérida*, *Lives of the Visigothic Fathers*, translated by Andy Fear, 45–106. Liverpool: Liverpool University Press, 1997.
Vita vel Gesta Sancti Ildephonsi. Valeriano Yarza Urquiola. "La *Vita vel Gesta Sancti Ildephonsi, de ps. Eladio*: Estudio, Edición Crítica y Traducción." *Veleia* 23 (2006): 279–325.

Secondary Sources

Adams, James N. *The Regional Diversification of Latin 200BC–AD600*. Cambridge: Cambridge University Press, 2007.

Agamben, Giorgio. *State of Exception*. Translated by Kevin Attell. Chicago: University of Chicago Press, 2008.

Aguilar Miquel, Julia. "El *Epigramma operis subsequentis* de Tajón de Zaragoza en los mss. Aug. Perg. 255, Clm 14854 y Ott. lat. 2546." *Revista de Estudios Latinos* 18 (2018): 73–88.

Aguilar Miquel, Julia. "*Epistual ad Quiricum Barcinonensis antistitem y Epigramma operis subsequentis* de Tajón de Zaragoza. Estudio, edición crítica y traducción." *Euphrosyne, Revista de Filología Clássica, New Series* 46 (2018): 181–204.

Albert, Bat-Sheva. "Isidore of Seville: His attitude towards Judaism and His impact on Early Medieval Canon Law." *Jewish Quarterly Review* 80 (1990): 207–20.

Allen, Michael. "Universal History 300–1000: Origins and Western Developments." In *Historiography in the Middle Ages*, edited by Deborah Mauskopf Deliyannis, 17–42. Boston and Leiden: Brill, 2003.

Allies, Neil. "The Monastic Rules of Visigothic Iberia: A Study of Their Text and Language." Ph.D. diss, University of Birmingham, 2009.

Amorós Ruiz, Victoria, Julia Sarabia Bautista, Carolina Doménech Belda, and Sonia Gutiérrez Lloret. "The Buildings of the Visigothic Elite: Function and Material Culture in Spaces of Power." *Visigothic Symposia* 2 (2017): 34–59.

Arce, Javier. "The city of Mérida (Emerita) in the *Vitas Patrum Emeritensium* (VIth c. A.D.)." In *East and West: Modes of Communication*, edited by Evangelos K. Chrysos and Ian Wood, 1–14. Boston and Leiden: Brill, 1999.

Arce, Javier, and Xavier Barral i Altet, eds. *Art and Architecture of Spain*. Boston: Little, Brown, 1998.

Badiou, Alain. *Conditions*. Translated by Simon Corcoran. New York: Continuum, 2008, orig. 1992.

Badiou, Alain. *Theory of the Subject*. Translated by Bruno Bosteels. London: Continuum, 2009, orig. 1982.

Badiou, Alain. "The Subject Supposed to be a Christian: On Paul Ricœur's *Memory, History, Forgetting*." Translated by Natalie Doyle and Alberto Toscano. *The Bible and Critical Theory* 2, no. 3 (2006).

Badiou, Alain. *Wittgenstein's Anti-Philosophy*. Translated by Bruno Bosteels. New York: Verso, 2011.

Balmaseda, Luis J. "En busca de las iglesias toledanas de época visigoda." In *Hispania Gothorum: San Ildefonso y el reino visigodo de Toledo*, edited by Rafael García Serrano, 194–214. Toledo: Don Quijote, 2006.

Banniard, Michel. *Viva voce. Communication écrite et communication orale du IVe au IXe siècle en Occident latin*. Paris: Institut des Études Augustiniennes, 1992.

Barbero, Abilio, and María Isabel Loring. "The Catholic Visigothic Kingdom." In *The New Cambridge Medieval History, Vol. 1: c. 500-c.700*, edited by Paul Fouracre, 346–70. Cambridge: Cambridge University Press, 2008.

Barnish, Sam J. "Sacred Texts of the Secular: Writing, Hearing, and Reading Cassiodorus' *Variae*." *Studia Patristica* 38 (2001): 362–70.

Barnwell, Paul S. "Emperors, Jurists and Kings: Law and Custom in the Late Roman and Early Medieval West." *Past and Present* 168 (2000): 6–29.

Barroso Cabrera, Rafael. *De la provincia Celtiberia a la qūrā de Santabariyya: Arqueología de la Antigüedad tardía en la provincia de Cuenca (siglos v–viii d.C.)*. Oxford: Archaeopress, 2019.

Barroso Cabrera, Rafael, Jesús Carrobles Santos, Jorge Morín de Pablos, and Isabel Sánchez Ramos. "Ciudad y territorio toledano entre la Antigüedad tardía y el reino visigodo: la construcción de una *Civitas regia* (ss. iv–viii d.C.)." *Erytheia* 36 (2015): 9–61.

Barroso Cabrera, Rafael, Jesús Carrobles Santos, Jorge Morín de Pablos, and Isabel Sánchez Ramos. "El Paisaje Urbano de Toledo en la Antigüedad Tardía." *AnTard* 23 (2015): 55–78.

Bartlett, Peter, and Gonzalo Cores. "The Coinage of the Visigothic King Sisebut [612–621] from the Mint Barbi." *Gaceta numismática* 158 (2005): 13–22.

Bartlett, Peter, Andrew Oddy, and Cécile Morrisson. "The Byzantine gold coinage of Spania (Justinian I to Heraclius)." *Revue Numismatique* 167 (2011): 351–402.

Barton, Simon, and Richard Fletcher. *The World of El Cid: Chronicles of the Spanish Reconquest*. Manchester: Manchester University Press, 2000.

Basset, Paul Merritt. "The Use of History in the *Chronicon* of Isidorus of Seville." *History and Theory* 15 (1976): 278–92.

Bentham, Jeremy. *The Influence of Natural Religion on the Temporal Happiness of Mankind*. New York: Prometheus Books, 2003.

Bischoff, Bernard. "Die europäische Verbreitung der Werke Isidors von Sevilla." In *Isidoriana*, edited by Manuel C. Díaz y Díaz, 317–44. León: Centro de Estudios "San Isidoro," 1960.

Bjornlie, M. Shane. *Politics and Tradition Between Rome, Ravenna and Constantinople: A Study of Cassiodorus and the Variae, 527–554*. Cambridge: Cambridge University Press, 2013.

Bonch Reeves, Ksenia. *Visions of Unity after the Visigoths: Early Iberian Latin Chronicles and the Mediterranean World*. Turnhout: Brepols, 2016.

Breternitz, Patrick. "Was stand in Isidors Bibliothek? Zur Petronrezeption in den Etymologien Isidors von Sevilla." *Rheinisches Museum für Philologie* 159 (2016): 99–112.

Brown, Peter. *Religion and Society in the Age of Saint Augustine*. New York: Harper & Row, 1972.

Brown, Peter. *The Cult of the Saints: Its Rise and Function in Latin Christianity*. Chicago: University of Chicago, 1981.

Brown, Peter. *The Rise of Western Christendom: Triumph and Diversity*, AD 200–1000. Oxford: Blackwell, 1996.

Brown, Peter. *Through the Eye of a Needle: Wealth, the Fall of Rome, and the Making of Christianity in the West, 350–550 AD*. Princeton: Princeton University Press, 2012.

Buchberger, Erica. *Shifting Ethnic Identities in Spain and Gaul, 500–700*. Amsterdam: Amsterdam University Press, 2017.

Burrows, Michael, and Michael J. Kelly, eds. *Urban Interactions: Communication and Competition in Late Antiquity and the Early Middle Ages*. Binghamton: Gracchi Books, 2020.

Cameron, Averil. "Remaking the Past." In *Interpreting Late Antiquity*, edited by Glen W. Bowersock, Peter Brown, and Oleg Grabar, 1–20. Cambridge: Harvard University Press, 2001.

Cameron, Averil. "Writing about Procopius then and now." In *Procopius of Caesarea: Literary and Historical* Interpretations, edited by Christopher Lillington-Martin and Elodie Turquois, 13–25. New York: Routledge, 2018.

Cardelle de Hartmann, Carmen. "Wissenorganisation und Wissensvermittlung im ersten Teil von Isidors *Etymologiae* (Bücher I–X)." In *Exzerpieren – Kompilieren – Tradieren: Transformationen des Wissens zwischen Spätatike und Frühmittelalter. Millennium-Studien 64*, edited by Stephan Dusil, Gerald Schwedler, and Raphael Schwitter, 85–104. Berlin and Boston: De Gruyter, 2017.

Carley, James P. "A Glastonbury Translator at Work: Quedam Narracio de nobili rege Arthuro and *De Origine Gigantum* in their Earliest Manuscript Contexts." *Nottingham French Studies* 30, no. 2 (1991): 5–12.

Carley, James P., and Ann Dooley. "An Early Irish Fragment of Isidore of Seville's Etymologiae." In *The Archaeology and History of Glastonbury Abbey: essays in honour of the ninetieth birthday of C. A. Ralegh Radford*, edited by Lesley Abrams and James Carey, 135–61. Woodbridge: Boydell, 1991.

Carley, James P., and Julia Crick. "Constructing Albion's Past: An Annotated Edition of *De Origine Gigantum*." In *Arthurian Literature* 13, edited by James P. Carley and Felicity Riddy, 41–114. Cambridge: D. S. Brewer, 1995.

Castell Maiques, Vicente. *Proceso sobre la ordenación de la Iglesia Valentina (1238–1246)*. 2 volumes. Valencia: Corts Valencianes, 1996.

Castellanos, Santiago. *La Hagiografía Visigoda: Dominio Social y Proyección Cultural*. Logroño: Fundación San Millán de la Cogolla, 2004.

Castellanos, Santiago. *Poder social, aristócracias y "hombre santo" en la Hispania visigoda. La "Vita Aemiliani" de Braulio de Zaragoza*. Biblioteca de investigación 20. Logroño: Universidad de La Rioja, 1998.

Castellanos, Santiago. "The Political Nature of Taxation in Visigothic Spain." *Early Medieval Europe* 12 (2003): 201–28.

Castellanos, Santiago, and Iñaki Martín Viso. "The Local Articulation of Central Power in the North of the Iberian Peninsula (500–1000)." *Early Medieval Europe* 13 (2005): 1–42.

Castellanos, Santiago, and Santiago Fernández Ardanaz. *Hagiografía y sociedad en la Hispania visigoda. La "Vita Aemiliani" y el actual territorio riojano (siglo VI)*. Biblioteca de temas riojanos 103. Logroño: Instituto de Estudios Riojanos, 1999.

Castillo Maldonado, Pedro. *La Época Visigótica en Jaén (siglos VI y VII)*. Universidad de Jaén, 2006.

Castillo Maldonado, Pedro. "La Muerte de Isidoro de Sevilla: Apuntes de Crítica Histórico-hagiográfica." *Habis* 32 (2001): 577–96.

Castro, Ainoa. "The Reconstruction of Early Medieval Spanish Manuscript Sources." *Early Medieval Europe* 22 (2014): 69–87.

Castro, Américo. *The Spaniards: An Introduction to Their History*. Translated by Willard F. King and Selma Margaretten. Los Angeles: University of California Press, 1971.

Castro Priego, Manuel. "Absent Coinage: Archaeological Contexts and Tremisses on the Central Iberian Peninsula in the 7th and 8th Centuries AD." *Medieval Archaeology* 60, no. 1 (2016): 27–56.

Cau, Ettore. *Scrittura e cultura a Novara (secoli viii–x)*. Pavia: Università degli studi di Pavia, 1971–1974.

Cazier, Pierre. *Isidore de Séville et la Naissance de l'Espagne Catholique*. Collecion Théologie historique 96. Paris: Beauchesne, 1994.

Cazier, Pierre. "Les *Sentences* d'Isidore de Séville et le IV Concile de Tolède. Réflexions sur les rapports entre l'Église et le pouvoir politique en Espagne autor des années 630." In *Los Visigodos. Historia Civilización: actas de la Semana Internacional de Estudios Visigóticos*, edited Antonio González Blanco, 373–86. Antigüedad y Cristianismo, Monografías Históricas sobre le Antigüedad Tardía 3. Murcia: Universidad de Murcia, 1986.

Cazier, Pierre, and Jacques Fontaine. "Qui a chassé de Cathaginoise Severianus et les siens? Observations sur l'histoire familiale d'Isidore de Séville." In *Estudios de Homenaje a Don Claudio Sánchez Albornoz en sus 90 años*, vol. 1, 349–400. Ávila: Instituto de España, 1983.

Chance, Jane. *Medieval Mythography: From Roman North Africa to the School at Chartres, AD 433–1177*. Gainesville: University Press of Florida, 1994.

Chavarría Arnau, Alexandra. "Churches and aristocracies in seventh-century Spain: some thoughts on the debate on Visigothic churches." *Early Medieval Europe* 18 (2010): 160–74.

Chernin, Liubov. "*Quod fidei plenitudine fines semper Spaniae floruerunt...* Egica and the Jews." *Sefarad* 69, no. 1 (2009): 7–24.

Chernin, Liubov. "Visigothic Jewish Converts: A Life in Between." *Visigothic Symposia* 3 (2018): 1–18.

Christiansen, Arne Søby. *Cassiodorus, Jordanes and the History of the Goths. Studies in Migration Myth*. Copenhagen: Museum Tusculanum Press, 2002.

Christys, Ann. *Christians in Al-Andalus, 711–1000*. 2nd edition. New York: Routledge, 2010.

Chrysos, Evangelos K., and Ian Wood, eds. *East and West: Modes of Communication*. Boston and Leiden: Brill, 1999.

Clark, Elizabeth A. *History, Theory, Text: Historians and the Linguistic Turn*. Cambridge: Harvard University Press, 2004.

Claude, Dietrich. "Freedmen in the Visigothic kingdom." In *Visigothic Spain: New Approaches*, edited by Edward James, 159–88. Oxford: Oxford University Press, 1980.

Cochrane, Charles. *Christianity and Classical Culture: A Study of Thought and Action from Augustus to Augustine*. Oxford: Oxford University Press, 1940.

Codoñer Merino, Carmen. "*El libro de 'Viris Illustribus' de Ildefonsus de Toledo*." In *La Patrología Toledano-Visigoda*, edited by Joaquín Blázquez, 337–48. Madrid: Consejo Superior de Investigaciones Científicas, 1970.

Codoñer Merino, Carmen. "Los *De viris illustribus* de la Hispania visigótica. Entre la biografía y la hagiografía." In *Las biografías griega y Latina como género literario. De la Antigüedad al Renacimiento. Algunas calas*, edited by Vitalino Valcárcel Martínez, 239–55. Vitoria: Universidad del País Vasco, 2009.

Cohen, Rodrigo Laham, and Carolina Pecznik. "Iudaei et Iudaei baptizati en ley de los visigodos." *Anuario de Historia de la Universidad Nacional de Rosario* (2016): 141–69.

Collins, Roger. "Ambrosio de Morales, Bishop Pelayo of Oviedo and the Lost Manuscripts of Visigothic Spain." In *Wisigothica After M. C. Díaz y Díaz*, edited by Carmen Codoñer Merino and Paolo Farmhouse Alberto, 485–503. MediEVI 3. Florence: SISMEL – Edizioni del Galluzzo, 2014.

Collins, Roger. *Early Medieval Spain: Unity from Diversity, 400–1000*. London: Macmillan, 1983.

Collins, Roger. *Fredegar: Authors of the Middle Ages* 13. Brookfield: Variorum, 1996.

Collins, Roger. "Julian of Toledo and the Royal Succession in Late Seventh-Century Spain." In *Early Medieval Kingship*, edited by Peter H. Sawyer and Ian Wood, 30–49. Leeds: University of Leeds, 1977.

Collins, Roger. *Keepers of the Keys of Heaven*. Basic Books, 2009.

Collins, Roger. "Literacy and the laity in early medieval Spain." In *The Uses of Literacy in the Early Middle Ages*, edited by Rosamond McKitterick, 109–33. Cambridge: University of Cambridge Press, 1990.

Collins, Roger. "Mérida and Toledo: 550–585." In *Visigothic Spain. New Approaches*, edited by Edward James, 215–18. Oxford: Oxford University Press, 1980.

Collins, Roger. "*Sicut lex gothorum continet*: Law and Charters in Ninth and Tenth-century León and Castile." *English Historical Review* 100 (1985): 489–512.

Collins, Roger. "The Autobiographical Works of Valerius of Bierzo: their structure and purpose." In *Los Visigodos: Historia y Civilización* 3, 425–42. Murcia: Universidad de Murcia, 1985.

Collins, Roger. "Visigothic law and regional custom in disputes in early medieval Spain." In *The Settlement of Disputes in Early Medieval Europe*, edited by Wendy Davies and Paul Fouracre, 85–104. Cambridge: Cambridge University Press, 1986.

Collins, Roger. *Visigothic Spain: 409–711*. Malden: Blackwell Publishing, 2004.

Córcoles Olaitz, Edorta. "About the Origin of the *Formulae Wisigothicae*." *Anuario Facultad de Derecho, Universidade de Coruña* 12 (2008): 199–221.

Croke, Brian. "Jordanes and the Immediate Past." *Historia* 54 (2005): 473–94.

Crusafont, Miquel de, Jaume Benage, and Jaume Noguera. "Silver Visigothic Coinage." *Numismatic Chronicle* 176 (2016): 241–60.

Cuello, Christian. "Visigothic coins in the Gale collection of the Australian Centre for Ancient Numismatic Studies." *Journal of the Numismatic Association of Australia* 28 (2017): 19–33.

D'Abadal y de Vinyals, Ramón. *Del Reino de Tolosa al Reino de Toledo*. Madrid: Real Academia de la Historia, 1960.

De Aldama, José A. "Indicaciones sobre la cronología de las obras Isidorianas." In *Miscellanea Isidoriana*, 57–89. Rome: Typis Pontificiae Universitatis Gregorianae, 1936.

De Brestian, Scott. "Material Culture in the Etymologiae of Isidore of Seville." *Journal of Late Antiquity* 11, no. 1 (2018): 216–31.

De Certeau, Michel. *The Writing of History*. Translated by Tom Conley. New York: Columbia University Press, 1975.

Derrida, Jacques. *Of Grammatology*. Translated by Gayatri Chakravorty Spivak. Baltimore: The Johns Hopkins Press, 1997, orig. 1967.

Deswarte, Thomas. "Why a new edition of Isidore's *De Ecclesiasticis Officiis*: the 'De Acolythis' chapter and the three versions of the treatise." *Mittellateinisches Jahrbuch: international Zeitschrift für Mediävistik* 52, no. 3 (2017): 347–61.

Diarte-Blasco, Pilar. *Late Antique and Early Medieval Hispania*. Philadelphia: Oxbow Books, 2018.

Díaz y Díaz, Manuel C. *De Isidoro al siglo XI*. Barcelona: Ediciones El Albir, 1976.

Díaz y Díaz, Manuel C. ed. *Isidoriana*. León: Centro de Estudios 'San Isidoro', 1960.

Díaz y Díaz, Manuel C. "La transmisión textual del Biclarense." *Analecta Sacra Tarraconensia* 35 (1962): 57–76.

Díaz y Díaz, Manuel C. "Pequeñas aportaciones para el estudio de la 'Hispana'." *Revista Española de Derecho Canónica* 17 (1962): 373–90.

Díaz, Pablo C. "La diócesis de Osma en la Antigüedad." In *Arte e historia de la diócesis de Osma*, 215–25. El Burgo de Osma, 1998.

Díaz, Pablo C. "Rey y Poder en la Monarquía Visigoda." *Iberia* 1 (1998): 175–95.

Díaz, Pablo C. "Sociability and Sense of Belonging: Community Interaction in the World of Valerius of Bierzo." *Visigothic Symposia* 3 (2018): 112–29.

Díaz, Pablo C., and María del Rosario Valverde Castro. "Goths Confronting Goths: Ostrogothic Political Relations in Hispania." In *The Ostrogoths from the Migration Period to the Sixth Century: An Ethnographic Perspective*, edited by Sam J. Barnish and Federico Marazzi, 353–76. San Marino, 2007.

Díaz, Pablo C., and María del Rosario Valverde Castro. "The theoretical strengths and practical weakness of the Visigothic monarchy of Toledo." In *Rituals of Power. From Late Antiquity to the Early Middle Ages*, edited by Janet L. Nelson and Frans Theuws, 59–63. Boston and Leiden: Brill, 2000.

Domingo Magaña, Javier Á. "The use of marble in Hispanic Visigothic architectural decoration." In *Interdisciplinary Studies on Ancient Stone, ASMOSIA X*, edited by Patrizio Pensabene and Eleonora Gasparini, 527–36. Rome: L'Erma di Bretschneider, 2015.

Doran, Robert, ed. *Philosophy of History After Hayden White*. London: Bloomsbury, 2013.

D'Ors, Alvaro. *Estudios Visigóticos 2, El Codigo de Eurico*. Cuadernos del Instituto Jurídico Español 12. Rome: Consejo Superior de Investigaciones Científicas, 1960.

Dossey, Leslie. "Wife Beating and Masculinity in Late Antiquity." *Past and Present* 199 (2008): 3–40.

Drew, Katharine Fischer. "The Barbarian Kings as Lawgivers and Judges." In *Life and Thought in the Early Middle Ages*, edited by Robert S. Hoyt, 7–29. Minneapolis: University of Minnesota Press, 1967.

Drews, Wolfram. "Jews as Pagans? Polemical definitions of identity in Visigothic Spain." *Early Medieval Europe* 11 (2002): 189–207.

Drews, Wolfram. *The Unknown Neighbour: The Jew in the Thought of Isidore of Seville*. Boston and Leiden: Brill, 2006.

Duchesne, Louis. *L'Église au VIe siècle*. Paris: E. de Boccard, 1925.

Eagleton, Terry. *How to Read Literature*. New Haven: Yale University Press, 2014.

Evans, Ruth. "Gigantic Origins: An Annotated Translation of *De Origine Gigantum*." In *Arthurian Literature* 16, edited by J. P. Carley and Felicity Riddy, 197–217. Cambridge: D. S. Brewer, 1998.

Farmhouse Alberto, Paulo. "King Sisebut's *Carmen de luna* in the Carolingian school." In *Ways of Approaching Knowledge in Late Antiquity and the Early Middle Ages: Schools and Scholarship*, edited by Paulo Farmhouse Alberto and David Paniagua, 177–205. Nordhausen: Verlag Traugott Bautz, 2012.

Farmhouse Alberto, Paulo. "Three historical notes on Eugenius of Toledo's *Carmina*." In *Poesía Latina Medieval (Siglos V–XV). Actas del IV Congreso del 'Internationales Mittellateinerkomitee', Santiago de Compostela, 12–15 de septiembre de 2002*, edited by Manuel C. Díaz y Díaz and José Manuel Díaz de Bustamante, 109–22. Florence: SISMEL-Ed. del Galluzzo, 2005.

Faulkner, Thomas. "Carolingian kings and the *leges barbarorum*." *Historical Research* 86 (2013): 433–64.

Fernández, Damián. *Aristocrats and Statehood in Western Iberia, 300–600 C.E.* Philadelphia: University of Pennsylvania Press, 2017.

Fernández, Damián. "Property, Social Status, and Church Building in Visigothic Iberia." *Journal of Late Antiquity* 9, no. 2 (2016): 512–541.

Fernández, Damián. "Statehood, Taxation, and State Infrastructural Power in Visigothic Iberia." In *Ancient States and Infrastructural Power: Europe, Asia, and America*, edited by Clifford Ando and Seth Richardson, 243–71. Philadelphia: University of Pennsylvania Press, 2017.

Fernández Martínez, Concepción, and Joan Goméz Pallarès. "¿Hermenegildo, para siempre en Sevilla? Una nueva interpretación de *IHC*, n. 76 = *ILCV*, n. 50." *Gerión* 19 (2001): 629–58.

Ferreiro, Alberto. *Late Antique-Visigothic Gallia and Hispania: A Bibliography, 2016–2018*. Binghamton: Networks and Neighbours, 2019 [digital].

Ferreiro, Alberto. *The Visigoths in Gaul and Iberia: A Supplemental Bibliography, 1984–2003*. Boston and Leiden: Brill, 2006.

Ferreiro, Alberto, ed. *The Visigoths: Studies in Culture & Society*. Boston and Leiden: Brill, 1999.

Ferreiro, Alberto. *"Epistolae Plenae": The Correspondence of the Bishops of Hispania with the Bishops of Rome: Third through Seventh Centuries*. The Medieval and Early Modern Iberian World. Boston and Leiden: Brill, 2020.

Ferreiro, Alberto. "*Quia pax et caritas facta est*: Unity and Peace in Leander's Homily at the Third Council of Toledo (589)." *Annuarium Historiae Conciliorum* 48 (2016/2017): 87–108.

Ferreiro, Alberto. Review of Carmen Codoñer Merino and Paulo Farmhouse Alberto, eds., *Wisigothica after M. C. Díaz y Díaz* (MediEVI 3) Florence: SISMEL Edizione del Galluzzo, 2014. *Speculum* 9, no. 2 (2016): 477–79.

Ferreiro, Alberto. Review of Pedro Juan Galán Sánchez. *El género historiográfico de la "Chronica". Las crónicas hispanas de época visigoda*. Anuario de Estudios Filológicos (Anejo 12). Cáceres: Universidad de Extremadura, 1994. *Anuario de Historia de la Iglesia* 7 (1998): 496–97.

Ferreiro, Alberto. "Saint Martin of Braga and the Germanic Languages: An Addendum to Recent Research." *Perita* 6 (1987): 298–306.

Ferreiro, Alberto. "*Sanctissimus idem princeps sic venerandum concilium adloquitor dicens*: King Reccared's Discourses at the Third Council of Toledo (589)." *Annuarium Historiae Conciliorum* 46 (2014): 27–52.

Ferreiro, Alberto. "*Sufficit septem diebus*: Seven Days Mourning the Dead in the Letters of St. Braulio of Zaragoza." In *Studia Patristica* 97, edited by Markus Vinzent, 255–63. Leuven: Peeters, 2017.

Ferreiro, Alberto. "The Bishops of Hispania and Pope Innocent I (401–47)." *Visigothic Symposia* 3 (2018): 19–35.

Ferreiro, Alberto. "The See of Dumium/Braga before and under Visigothic Rule." *Euphrosyne, Revista de Filología Clássica, New Series* 45 (2017): 97–115.

Fontaine, Jacques. "Conversion et culture chez les Wisigoths d'Espagne." *Settimane di Studio* 14 (1967): 87–147.

Fontaine, Jacques. "Education and Learning." In *Cambridge Medieval History, 500–700*, I, edited by Paul Fouracre, 735–59. Cambridge: University of Cambridge Press, 2008.

Fontaine, Jacques. "El *De Viris Illustribus* de San Ildefonso de Toledo: Tradición y originalidad." *Anales Toledanos III: Estudios sobre la España visigoda*, 59–96. Toledo, 1971.

Fontaine, Jacques. *Isidore de Séville et la Culture Classique dans l'Espagne Wisigothique*, 2 vols. Paris: Études Augustiniennes, 1959.

Fontaine, Jacques. "King Sisebut's *Vita Desiderii* and the Political Function of Visigothic Hagiography." In *Visigothic Spain: New Approaches*, edited by Edward James, 93–129. Oxford: Clarendon Press, 1980.

Fontaine, Jacques. *L'art préroman hispanique* I. La Pierre-qui-Vire: Zodiaque, 1973.

Fontaine, Jacques. "Le culte des saints et ses implications sociologiques. Réflexion sur un récent essai de Peter Brown." *Analecta Bollandiana* 100 (1982): 17–41.

Fontaine, Jacques. "Les relations culturelles entre l'Italie byzantine et l'Espagne visigothique: La présence d'Eugippius dans la bibliothèque de Seville." In *Tradition et actualité chez Isidore de Séville*, edited by Jacques Fontaine, 9–26. London: Variorum, 1998.

Fontaine, Jacques. "Romanité et hispanité dans la littérature hispano-romaine des IVe et Ve siècles." In *Assimilation et résistance à la culture gréco-romaine dans le monde ancien. Actes du VIe Congrès, International d'Études Classiques*, edited by Dionis M. Pippidi, 301–22. Paris: Société d'édition "Les Belles Lettres," 1976.

Fontaine, Jacques. "Un manifeste politique et culturel: Le *De Laude Spaniae* d'Isidore de Séville." In *Le discours d'éloge entre Antiquité et Moyen Age*, edited by Lionel Mary and Michel Sot, 61–68. Paris: Éditions Picard, 2001.

Foucault, Michel. *Foucault Live (Interviews, 1961–1984)*. Edited by Sylvère Lotringer. Translated by Lysa Hochroth and John Johnston. New York: Semiotext(e), 1996.

Foucault, Michel. *Les Mots et les Choses*. Paris: Gallimard, 1966.

Franck, Bernard. "Recherches sur le manuscript de l'Hispana de l'évêque Rachio." *Archives de l'église d'Alsace, new series* 7 (1956): 67–82.

Frighetto, Renan. "Las dificultades de la unidad política en la Hispania Visigoda: Las controversias entre la Realeza y la Nobleza en la siglo VII." *Revista de Historia* 16 (2006): 11–19.

Frighetto, Renan. "Memória, história e identidades: considerações a partir da historia Wamba Juliano de Toledo (século VII)." *Revista de História Comparada* 5 (2011): 50–73.

Frighetto, Renan. "O problema da legitimidade e a limitação do poder régio na Hispania Visigoda: o reinado de Ervigio (680–687)." *Gerión* 22 (2004): 421–35.

Frighetto, Renan. "When confrontation generates collaboration: Goths, Romans and the emergence of the Hispano-Visigothic Kingdom of Toledo (5th–6th centuries)." *Vínculos de Historia* 7 (2018): 157–72.

Furtado, Rodrigo. "Isidore's *Histories* in the Mozarabic scholarship of the eight and early ninth centuries." In *Ways of Approaching Knowledge in Late Antiquity and the Early Middle Ages: Schools and Scholarship*, edited by Paulo Farmhouse Alberto and David Paniagua, 264–83. Nordhausen: Verlag Traugott Bautz, 2012.

Galán Sánchez, Pedro Juan. "El *De viris illustribus* de Ildefonso de Toledo o la modificación del género." *Anuario de estudios filológicos* 15 (1992): 69–80.

Galán Sánchez, Pedro Juan. *El género historiográfico de la "Chronica". Las crónicas hispanas de época visigoda.* Anuario de Estudios Filológicos (Anejo 12). Cáceres: Universidad de Extremadura, 1994.

García López, Yolanda. *Estudios Críticos y Literarios de la "Lex Wisigothorum."* Alcalá: Universidad de Alcalá, 1996.

García Moreno, Luis A. "Building an Ethnic Identity for a New Gothic and Roman nobility: Córdoba, 615 AD." In *Romans, Barbarians, and the Transformation of the Roman World*, edited by Ralph W. Mathisen and Danuta Shanzer, 271–82. Burlington: Ashgate, 2011.

García Moreno, Luis A, ed. *Prosopografía del Reino Visigoda de Toledo*. Salamanca: Universidad de Salamanca, 1974.

García Moreno, Luis A. "Expectatives milenaristas y escatolólogicas en la España tardoantigua (ss. v–viii)." In *Spania. Estudis d'Antiguitat Tardana oferts en homenatge al professor Pere de Palol i Salellas*, 103–09. Barcelona: Publicacions de l'Abadia de Montserrat, 1996.

García Moreno, Luis A. "La sucesión al trono en el Reino Godo: La perspectiva prosopográfica." In *Doctrina a magistro discipulis tradita. Estudios en homenaje al Prof. Dr. Luis García Iglesias*, edited by Adolfo Jerónimo Domínguez Monedero and Gloria Mora Rodríguez, 395–410. Madrid: Ediciones de la Universidad Autónoma de Madrid, 2010.

García Moreno, Luis A. "Los monjes y monasterios en las cuidades de las Españas Tardorromanas y visigodas." *Habis* 24 (1993): 179–92.

García Moreno, Luis A. "Los orígenes de la Carpetania visigoda." In *Toledo y Carpetania en la Edad antiqua: simposio celebrado en el Colegio Universitario de Toledo 6 al 8 noviembre 1986)*, edited by Jaime Alvar and Carmen Blánquez, 229–49. Toledo: Colegio Universitario, 1990.

García Moreno, Luis A. "Prosopography and Onomastic: the Case of the Goths." In *Prosopography Approaches and Application: A Handbook*, edited by Katharine Keats-Rohan, 337–50. Oxford: Unit for Prosopographical Research, University of Oxford, 2007.

García Moreno, Luis A. "Spanish Gothic Consciousness among the Mozarabs in al-Andalus." In *The Visigoths: Studies in Culture & Society*, edited by Alberto Ferreiro, 303–24. Boston and Leiden: Brill, 1999.

Garai-Oraun, Augustín Azkárate. "El País Vasco en los siglos inmediatos a la desparación del Impero Romano." In *Historia del País Vasco*, edited by Pedro Barruso and José Ángel Lema Pueyo, 23–50. San Sebastian: Hiria, 2004.

Geary, Patrick. *Myth of Nations: The Medieval Origins of Europe*. Princeton: Princeton University Press, 2002.

Geary, Patrick. *Phantoms of Remembrance: Memory and Oblivion at the End of the First Millennium*. Princeton: Princeton University Press, 1994.

Gil, Juan, ed. *Miscellanea Wisigothica*. Seville: Universidad de Sevilla, 1972.

Goffart, Walter A. *Barbarian Tides: The Migration Age and the Later Roman Empire*. Philadelphia: University of Pennsylvania Press, 2006.

Goffart, Walter A., ed. *Rome's Fall and After*. London: Hambledon Press, 1989.

Goffart, Walter A. *The Narrators of Barbarian History (AD 550–800): Jordanes, Gregory of Tours, Bede and Paul the Deacon*. Princeton: Princeton University Press, 1988.

González Blanco, Antonio. "El decreto de Gundemaro y la historia del siglo VII." In *Los Visigodos. Historia y civilización, Antiqüedad y Christianismo III*, 159–69. Murcia: Universidad de Murcia, 1985.

González Blanco, Antonio. "La historia del S. E. peninsula entre los siglos III–VIII d.C. (Fuentes literarias, problemas y sugerencias)." *Antiqüedad y Christianismo* 23 (2006): 53–79.

González Ruiz, Ramón. "Agali: Historia del Monasterio de San Ildefonso," *Toletum: boletín de la Real Academia de Bellas Artes y Ciencias Históricas de Toledo* (2007): 99–145.

Ghosh, Sam. "The Barbarian Past in the Early Middle Ages." Ph.D. diss., University of Toronto, 2009.

González Salinero, Raúl. "Los judíos en el reino visigodo de época arriana." In *Judaísmo Hispano: Estudios en memoria de José Luis Lacave Riaño*, edited by Elena Romero, volume 2, 399–408. Madrid: Consejo Superior de Investigaciones Científicas, 2003.

Grayzel, Solomon. "The Papal Bull *Sicut Judeis*." In *Studies in Essays in Honor of Abraham A. Neuman*, edited by Meir Ben-Horin, Bernard D. Weinryb, and Solomon Zeitlin, 243–80. Boston and Leiden: Brill, 1962.

Gruber, Henry. "Indirect Evidence for the Social Impact of the Justinianic Pandemic: Episcopal Burial and Conciliar Legislation in Visigothic Hispania." *Journal of Late Antiquity* 11, no. 1 (2018): 193–215.

Guiance, Ariel. "*Dormavit Beatus Isidorus*: Variaciones hagiográficas en torno e la muerte de Isidoro de Sevilla." *Edad Media* 6 (2003): 33–59.

Gutiérrez Lloret, Sonia, Lorenzo Abad Casal, and Blanca Gamo Parras. "La Iglesia Visigoda de el Tolmo de Minateda (Hellín, Albacete)' in *Sacralidad y Arqueología: homenaje al Prof. Thilo Ulbert al cumplir 65 años, Antigüedad y cristianismo* 21, edited by Thilo Ulbert, José María Blázquez, and Antonino González Blanco, 137–69. Murcia: Universidad de Murcia, 2004.

Halfond, Gregory I. *The Archaeology of Frankish Church Councils, AD 511–768*. Boston and Leiden: Brill, 2010.

Hanaoka, Mimi. *Authority and Identity in Medieval Islamic Historiography: Persian Histories from the Peripheries.* Cambridge: Cambridge University Press, 2016.

Handley, Mark. *Death, Society and Culture: Inscriptions and Epitaphs in Gaul and Spain, AD 300–750.* Oxford: BAR Series, 2003.

Harper, Kyle. *The Fate of Rome: Climate, Disease, and the End of an Empire.* Princeton: Princeton University Press, 2017.

Harries, Jill, ed. *Law and Empire in Late Antiquity.* Cambridge: Cambridge University Press, 1999.

Heather, Peter, ed. *The Visigoths from the Migration Period to the Seventh Century: An Ethnographic Perspective.* Woodbridge: Boydell Press, 2003.

Heather, Peter. "The Creation of the Visigoths." In *The Visigoths from the Migration Age to the Seventh Century: An Ethnographic Perspective*, edited by Peter Heather, 43–68. Woodbridge: Boydell Press, 1999.

Heather, Peter. *The Goths.* Oxford: Oxford University Press, 1996.

Hefele, Charles J. *A History of the Councils of the Church from the Original Documents.* Translated by Henry Nutcombe Oxenham. Edinburgh: T&T Clark, 1896.

Hegel, Georg Wilhem Friedrich. *Phenomenology of Spirit.* Translated by Arnold V. Miller. Oxford: Oxford University Press, 1976, orig. 1807.

Hegel, Georg Wilhem Friedrich. *Philosophy of History.* Translated by J. Sibree. Mineola: Dover Publications, 2014, orig. 1837.

Heidegger, Martin. *Being and Time.* Translated by John Macquarrie and Edward Robinson. New York: Harper Collins, 2008, orig. 1927.

Hen, Yitzhak. "A Visigothic king in search of an identity – *Sisebutus Gothorum gloriossimus princeps.*" In *Ego Trouble: Authors and Their Identities in the Early Middle Ages*, edited by Richard Corradini, Matthew Gillis, Rosamond McKitterick, and Irene van Renswoude, 89–99. Vienna: Österreichische Akademie der Wissenschaften, 2010.

Hen, Yitzhak. *Roman Barbarians: The Royal Court and Culture in the Early Medieval West.* New York: Palgrave MacMillan, 2007.

Henderson, John. *The Medieval World of Isidore of Seville.* Cambridge: Cambridge University Press, 2007.

Hernández Mártin, Ramón. "La España visigoda frente al problema de los judíos." *La Ciencia Tomista* 94 (1967): 627–71.

Hijano, Manuel. "Monumento inacabado: la Estoria de España de Alfonso VII a Fernando III." *Cahiers d'études hispaniques médiévales* 37, no. 1 (2014): 13–44.

Hillgarth, Jocelyn N. "Coins and Chronicles: Propaganda in Sixth-Century Spain and the Byzantine Background." *Historia: Zeitschrift für Alte Geschichte* 15 (1966): 483–508.

Hillgarth, Jocelyn N. "Review, *Isidore de Séville et la Culture Classique dans l'Espagne Wisigothique*, vols. I, II: Paris: Études Augustiniennes, 1959." *Journal of Roman Studies* 51 (1961): 273–75.

Hillgarth, Jocelyn N. "Spanish Historiography and Iberian Reality." *History and Theory* 24 (1985): 23–43.

Hillgarth, Jocelyn N. *The Visigoths in History and Legend*. Toronto: PIMS, 2009.

Hodgkin, Thomas. *Italy and Her Invaders*. Oxford: Oxford University Press, 1880–1889.

Hodgkin, Thomas. "Visigothic Spain." *The English Historical Review* 2 (1887): 209–34.

Ihnat, Kati. "Liturgy against apostasy: Marian commemoration and the Jews in Visigothic Iberia." *Early Medieval Europe* 25, no. 4 (2017): 443–65.

Jameson, Fredric. *Late Marxism: Adorno or the Persistence of the Dialectic*. London: Verso, 2007, orig. 1990.

Jameson, Fredric. *The Hegel Variations*. London: Verso, 2010.

Jameson, Fredric. *The Political Unconscious: Narrative as a Social Symbolic Act*. Ithaca: Cornell University Press, 1981.

Jameson, Fredric. *The Prison-House of Language: A Critical Account of Structuralism and Russian Formalism*. Princeton: Princeton University Press, 1972.

Johannesson, Kurt. *The Renaissance of the Goths in Sixteenth-Century Sweden: Johannes and Olaus Magnus as Politicians and Historians*. Berkeley: University of California Press, 1991.

Johnston, David. *Roman Law in Context*. Cambridge: Cambridge University Press, 2004.

Jolowicz, Herbert F., and Barry Nicholas. *A Historical Introduction to the Study of Roman Law*. Cambridge: Cambridge University Press, 2008, orig. 1972.

Kampers, Gerd. "Exemplarisches Sterben. Der '*Obitus Beatissimi Hispalensis Isidori episcopi*', Klerikers Redemptus." In *Nomen et Fraternitas. Festschrift für Dieter Geuenich zum 65 Geburtstag*, edited by Uwe Ludwig and Thomas Schilp, 235–48. Berlin: De Gruyter, 2008.

Kampers, Gerd. "Isidor von Sevilla und seine Familie. Überlegungen zu 'De institutione virginum et de contemptu mundi' c. 31." *Frühmittelalterliche Studien* 52 (2018): 43–58.

Kelly, Michael J. *Alain Badiou: A Graphic Guide*. London: Icon Books, 2014.

Kelly, Michael J. "From Rhetoric to Dialectic: the Becoming 'Germanic' of Visigothic (Legal-) Literature, and (Postulating) the End of a 'Truth'." In *Interrogating the 'Germanic': A Category and its Use in Late Antiquity and the Early Middle Ages*, Ergänzungsbände zum Reallexikon der Germanischen Altertumskunde 123, edited by Matthias Friedrich and James M. Harland, 127–143. Berlin: De Gruyter, 2020.

Kelly, Michael J. "Gundemar the Ghost, Isidore the Historian: Rethinking Visigothic History from the Whispers of its Literature." In *Creative Selection: Emending and Forming Medieval Memory*, edited by Sebastian Scholz and Gerald Schwedler. Berlin: De Gruyter, in press (2020).

Kelly, Michael J. Review of Paul Taylor, *Žižek and the Media*. Cambridge: Polity, 2012. *Continuum: Journal of Media and Cultural Studies, 26.1* (2013): 183–86.

Kelly, Michael J. "The *Liber Iudiciorum*: A Visigothic Literary Guide to Institutional Authority and Self-Interest." In *The Visigothic Kingdom of Toledo: Concepts and Forms of Power*, edited by Paulo Pachá and Sabine Panzram, 258–72. Amsterdam: Amsterdam University Press, 2020.

Kelly, Michael J. "The Politics of History Writing: Problematizing the Historiographical Origins of Isidore of Seville in Early Medieval Hispania." In *Isidore of Seville and His Reception in the Early Middle Ages: Transmitting and Transforming Knowledge*, edited by Andy Fear and Jamie Wood, 93–110. Amsterdam: Amsterdam University Press, 2016.

Kelly, Michael J., and Arthur Rose, eds. *Theories of History: History Read Across the Humanities*. New York and London: Bloomsbury, 2018.

Kelly, Michael J., Javier Martínez Jiménez et al., eds. *The Prosopography of the Visigothic Period in Gaul and Iberia, c. 400–750*. Binghamton: Gracchi Books, forthcoming 2021.

Kersken, Norbert "High and Late Medieval National Historiography." In *Historiography in the Middle Ages*, edited by Deborah Mauskopf Deliyannis, 181–216. Boston and Leiden: Brill, 2003.

Kéry, Lotte. *Canonical Collections of the Early Middle Ages (ca. 400–1140). A bibliographical guide to the manuscripts and literature, History of Medieval Canon Law*. Washington, D.C.: The Catholic University of America Press, 1999.

King, Paul D. *Law and Society in the Visigothic kingdom*. Cambridge: Cambridge University Press, 1972.

Koch, Manuel. *Ethnische Identität im Entstehungsprozess des spanischen Westgotenreiches*. Berlin and Boston: De Gruyter, 2011.

Kojève, Alexandre. *Introduction to the Reading of Hegel: Lectures on the Phenomenology of Spirit*. Translated by James H. Nichols, Jr. Ithaca: Cornell University Press, 1980.

Kolozova, Katerina. *Cut of the Real: Subjectivity in Poststructuralist Philosophy*. New York: Columbia University Press, 2014.

Kulikowski, Michael. *Late Roman Spain and Its Cities*. Baltimore: The Johns Hopkins University Press, 2004.

Kulikowski, Michael. "Plague in Spanish Late Antiquity." In *Plague and the End of Antiquity*, edited by Lester K. Little, 150–70. Cambridge: Cambridge University Press, 2007.

Kurt, Andrew. "Lay Piety in Visigothic Iberia: liturgical and paraliturgical forms." *Journal of Medieval Iberian Studies* (2015): 1–38.

Kurt, Andrew. *Minting, State and Economy in the Visigothic Kingdom: From Settlement in Aquitaine through the First Decade of the Muslim Conquest of Spain*. Amsterdam: Amsterdam University Press, 2020.

Lacan, Jacques. *Écrits*. Translated by Bruce Fink. New York: W. W. Norton, 2006.

LaCapra, Dominick. *History & Criticism*. Ithaca: Cornell University Press, 1985.

LaCapra, Dominick. *Writing History, Writing Trauma*. Baltimore: Johns Hopkins University Press, 2000.

Lafferty, Sean D. W. *Law and Society in the Age of Theoderic the Great: A Study of the "Edictum Theoderici."* Cambridge: Cambridge University Press, 2013.

Lambertini, Renzo. *La codificazione di Alarico II*. Turin: Giapichelli, 1990.

Laruelle, François. *Principles of Non-Philosophy*. Translated by A. P. Smith (London: Bloomsbury, 2013).

Lear, Floyd S. "The Public Law of the Visigothic Code." *Speculum* 26 (1951): 1–24.

Ledesma, Juan Pablo. *El "De Itinere Deserti" de San Ildefonso de Toledo*. Toledo: Instituto Teológico San Ildefonso, 2005.

Levy, Ernst. *West Roman Vulgar Law: The Law of Property*. Philadelphia: American Philosophical Society, 1952.

Licht, Tino. *Schriftkultur im Zeitalter der ersten lateinischen Minuskel (III.-IX. Jahrhundert)* (*Quellen und Untersuchungen zur lateinischen Philologie des Mittelalters* 20). Stuttgart: Anton Hiersemann, 2018.

Lillington-Martin, Christopher, and Elodie Turquois, eds. *Procopius of Caesarea: Literary and Historical Interpretations*. New York: Routledge, 2018.

Linehan, Peter. *History and the Historians of Medieval Spain*. Oxford: Oxford University Press, 1993.

Lomas Salmonte, Javier. "Análisis Funcionalidad de la *Vita Aemiliani* (*BHL* 100)." *Studia Historica. Historia Antigua* 16 (1998): 247–66.

López-Costas, Olalla, and Gundula Müldner. "Fringes of the Empire: Diet and cultural change at the Roman to post-Roman transition in NW Iberia." *American Journal of Physical Anthropology* 161, no. 1 (2016): 141–54.

Lotter, Friedrich. "Zur sozialen Hierarchie der Judenheit in Spätantike und Frühmittelalter." *Aschkenas* 13 (2003): 333–59.

Lukács, Georg. *The Young Hegel: Studies in the Relations between Dialectics and Economics*. Translated by Rodney Livingston. Cambridge: MIT Press, 1975.

Lynch, Charles H. *Saint Braulio, Bishop of Saragossa [631–651]: His Life and Writings*. Washington, D.C.: The Catholic University of America, 1938.

Manuel Pérez-Prendes y Muñoz-Arraco, José. "Historia de la legislación visigótica." In *San Isidoro Doctor Hispaniae*, 51–67. Seville: Centro Cultural El Monte, 2002.

Marey, Elena. "Образ правителя в стихах Евгения Толедского и его параллелис 'Книги приговоров' (*Liber Iudiciorum*)." *Bulletin of the Russian State University for the Humanities* (2012): 24–33.

Marfil, Pedro. "La sede episcopal cordobesa en época bizantina: evidencia arqueológia." In *V Reunió d'arqueologia cristiana hispànica*, edited by Josep M. Gurt and Núria Tena, 157–75. Barcelona: Institut d'Estudis Catalans, 2000.

Marone, Paola. *Donatism. Online Dynamic Bibliography*. Rome: Sapienza, Università di Roma, 2018.

Marrou, Henri-Irénée. *St. Augustin et la fin de la culture antique*. Paris: E. Boccard, 1958.
Martin, Céline. "Las Cartas de Montano y la autonomia episcopal de la Hispania septentrional en el siglo VI." *Hispania Antiqua* 22 (1998): 403–26.
Martin, Céline. "Le *Liber Iudiciorum* et ses différentes versions." *Mélanges de la Casa de Velázquez, Nouvelle série* 41 (2011): 17–34.
Martin, Céline. "L'innovation Politique dans le Royaume de Tolède: le Sacre du Souverain." In *Élections et pouvoirs politiques du VIIe siècle du VIIe au XVIIe siècle*, edited by Corinne Péneau, 281–300. Paris: Bière, 2009.
Martin, Céline. "The Asturia of Valerius: Bierzo at the End of the Seventh Century." *Visigothic Symposia* 2 (2017): 60–78.
Martindale, John R., ed. *The Prosopography of the Later Roman Empire*. 3 volumes. Cambridge: Cambridge University Press, 1992.
Martínez Díez, Gonzalo. "Concilios españoles anteriores a Trento." In *Repertorio de Historia de las Ciencias Eclesiasticas en España, vol. 5, Siglos i–xvi*, 299–350. Salamanca: Universidad Pontificia, 1976.
Martínez Díez, Gonzalo. "Dos nuevos firmantes del Concilio III de Toledo." *Anuario de Historia del Derecho español* 42 (1972): 637–42.
Martínez Díez, Gonzalo. "La colección del ms. de Novara." *Anuario de Historia del Derecho español* 33 (1963): 391–538.
Martín-Iglesias, José Carlos. "El corpus hagiográfico latino en torno a la figura de Isidoro de Sevilla en la Hispania tardoantigua y medieval (ss. vii–xiii)." *Veleia* 22 (2005): 187–228.
Martín-Iglesias, José Carlos. "El *Epitaphium Leandri, Isidori et Florentinae* (*ICERV* 272) o la compleja transmisión manuscrita de un texto epigráfico. Nuevo edición y studio." *Euphrosyne: Revista de Filología Clássica, New Series* 38 (2010): 139–63.
Martínez Jiménez, Javier. "Aqueducts and Water Supply in the Towns of Post-Roman Spain (AD 400–1000), Volume I." Ph.D. diss., Oxford University, 2014.
Martínez Jiménez, Javier. "Engineering, Aqueducts, and the Rupture of Knowledge Transmission in the Visigothic Period." *Visigothic Symposia* 3 (2018): 37–57.
Martínez Jiménez, Javier. "Reccopolitani and Other Town Dwellers in the Southern Meseta during the Visigothic Period of State Formation." In *Urban Interactions: Communication and Competition in Late Antiquity and the Early Middle Ages*, edited by Michael Burrows and Michael J. Kelly, 183–224. Binghamton: Gracchi Books, 2020.
Martínez Jiménez, Javier. "The Rural hinterland of the Visigothic capitals of Toledo and Reccopolis, between the years 400–800 CE." In *Authority and Control in the Countryside: Continuity and Change in the Mediterranean, 6th–10th century CE*, edited by Alain Delattre, Marie Legendre and Petra Sijpesteijn, 97–127. Boston and Leiden: Brill, 2018.

Martínez Jiménez, Javier, and José María Moreno Narganes. "*Nunc autem a Gothis subversa*: the province of Alicante and the Spanish Mediterranean towns between the Byzantine and Visigothic periods." *Early Medieval Europe* 23, no. 3 (2015): 263–89.

Martínez Pizarro, Joaquin. "Ethnic and National History ca. 500–1000." In *Historiography in the Middle Ages*, edited by Deborah Mauskopf Deliyannis, 43–87. Boston and Leiden: Brill, 2003.

Marx, Karl. *The 18th Brumaire of Napoleon Bonaparte*. Translated by D. D. L. Rockville: Serenity Publishers, 2009, orig. 1851–52.

Mazal, Otto, ed. *Weiner Hispana-Handschrift: Vollständige Faksimile-Ausgabe im Originalformat des Codex Vindobonensis 411*. Codices selecti phototypice impressi 41 (Graz: Akademische Druck-und Verlagsanstalt, 1974).

McKitterick, Rosamond, ed. *The Uses of Literacy in the Early Middle Ages*. Cambridge: University of Cambridge Press, 1990.

McKitterick, Rosamond. *History and Memory in the Carolingian World*. Cambridge: Cambridge University Press, 2004.

McKitterick, Rosamond. *Perceptions of the Past in the Early Middle Ages*. Notre Dame: University of Notre Dame Press, 2006.

McKitterick, Rosamond. "Some Carolingian Law-Books and Their Function." In *Authority and Power: Studies on Medieval Law and Government Presented to Walter Ullmann on his seventieth birthday*, edited by Brian Tierney and Peter Linehan, 13–27. Cambridge: Cambridge, University Press, 1980.

McKitterick, Rosamond. "The audience for Latin historiography in the early Middle Ages: texts transmission and manuscript dissemination." In *Historiographie im frühen Mittelalter* (Veröffentlichungen des Instituts fur Österreichische Geschichtsforschung 32), edited by Anton Scharer and Georg Scheibelreiter, 96–114. Vienna: R. Oldenbourg Verlag, 1994.

McKitterick, Rosamond. *The Carolingians and the Written Word*. Cambridge: Cambridge University Press, 1989.

Meillassoux, Quentin. *After Finitude: An Essay on the Necessity of Contingency*. Translated by Ray Brassier. London: Bloomsbury, 2012.

Merrills, Andrew H. *History and Geography in Late Antiquity*. Cambridge: Cambridge University Press, 2005.

Merrills, Andrew H., and Richard Miles. *The Vandals*. New York: Wiley-Blackwell, 2010.

Miguel Franco, Ruth. "Braulio de Zaragoza, el rey Chindasvinto y Eugenio de Toledo: imagen y opinión en el *Epistularium* de Braulio de Zaragoza." *Emerita, Revista de Lingüística y Filología Clásica* 79 (2011): 155–76.

Miguel Franco, Ruth. "Braulio de Zaragoza y la corrección del Fuero Juzgo." *Helmantica* 57 (2006): 67–89.

Miguel Franco, Ruth. "*Sub Titulis Misi, in Libros Diuisi*: Braulio of Zaragoza and His Arrangement of Materials." *Visigothic Symposia* 1 (2017): 131–49.

Miles, Richard. *Constructing Identity in Late Antiquity*. London: Routledge, 1999.
Mirabile, Andrea. "Allegory, Pathos, and Irony: The Resistance to Benjamin in Paul de Man." *German Studies Review* 35 (2012): 319–33.
Molina Gómez, José Antonio. "Las coronas de donación regia del tesoro de Guarrazar: la religiosidad en la monarquía visigoda y el uso de modelos bizantinos'." *Antigüedad y Christianismo* 21 (2004): 459–72.
Momigliano, Arnaldo. "Pagan and Christian Historiography in the Fourth Century AD." In *The Conflict between Paganism and Christianity in the Fourth Century*, edited by Arnaldo Momigliano, 79–100. Oxford: Oxford University Press, 1963.
Momigliano, Arnaldo. "The Origins of Universal History." In *On Pagans, Jews and Christians*, edited by Arnaldo Momigliano, 31–57. Middletown: Wesleyan University Press, 1987.
Moreno Martín, Francisco J. "Visigoths, Crowns, Crosses, and the Construction of Spain." *Memoirs of the American Academy of Rome* 62 (2017): 41–64.
Nehlsen, Hermann. "*Lex Visigothorum*." In *Handwörterbuch zur deutschen Rechtsgeschichte*, 1966–79. Volume 2. Berlin: E. Schmidt, 1978.
Nelson, Janet. "Gender and Genre in Women Historians of the Early Middle Ages." In *L'Historiographie médiévale en Europe*, Jean-Philippe Genet, 149–63. Paris: Éditions du CNRS, 1991.
Nelson, Janet, and Alice Rio. "Women and Laws in Early Medieval Europe." In *The Oxford Handbook of Women and Gender in Medieval Europe*, edited by Judith Bennett and Ruth Karras, 1–18. Oxford: Oxford University Press, 2013.
Noble, Thomas F. X. *From Roman Provinces to Medieval kingdoms*. London: Routledge, 2003.
Nongbri, Brent. *God's Library: The Archaeology of the Earliest Christian Manuscripts*. New Haven: Yale University Press, 2018.
O'Brien O'Keffe, Katherine, and Andy Orchard, eds. *Latin Learning and English Lore: Studies in Anglo-Saxon Literature for Michael Lapidge*. Toronto: University of Toronto Press, 2005.
O'Donnell, James. *Cassiodorus*. Berkeley: University of California Press, 1979.
O'Donnell, James. "The Aims of Jordanes." *Historia* 31 (1982): 233–40.
Olmo Enciso, Lauro. "El Reino visigoda de Toledo y los territorios bizantinos. Datos sobre la heterogeneidad de la peninsula ibérica en época visigoda." In *Coloquio Hispano-Italiano de Arqueología Medieval*, Publicaciones del Patronato de la Alhambra, 185–98. Granada: Patronato de la Alhambra y Generalife, 1992.
Orlandis, José. *Die Synoden auf der Iberischen Halbinsel bis zum Einbruch des Islam*. Paderborn: Ferdinand Schöningh, 1981.
Orlandis, José. *La Iglesia en la España visigótica y medieval*. Pamplona: Ediciones de la Universidad Navarra, 1976.

Orlandis, José, and Domingo Ramos-Lissón. *Historia de los concilios de España romana y visigoda*. Pamplona: Universidad de Navarra, 1986.

Orlowski, Sabrina. "La inestabilidad política de los reyes visigodos de Toledo (s. vi–viii): balance historiográfico y nueva propuesta de análisis." *Trabajos y comunicaciones* 38 (2012): 227–46.

Osaba García, Esperanza. "Influenza delle leggi costantiniane nella *Lex Visigothorum*." In *Diritto@Storia. Quaderni di Scienze Giuridiche e Tradizione Romana*, Anno II, Quaderno no. 2 (2003): np.

Osland, Daniel. "Urban Change in Late Antique Hispania: The Case of Augusta Emerita." Ph.D. diss., University of Cincinnati, 2011.

Perea, Alicia, ed. *El Tesoro Visigodo de Guarrazar*. Madrid: Consejo Superior de Investigaciones Científicas, 2001.

Pérez Martínez, Meritxell. *Tarraco en la Antigüedad tardía. Cristianización y organización eclesiática (III a VIII siglos)*. Tarragona: Arola Editors, 2012.

Pérez Vejo, Tomás. *España imaginada. Historia de la invención de una nación*. Barcelona: Galaxia Gutenberg, 2015.

Pino Abada, Miguel. "El Papel de los concilios visigodos en la defense de los intereses nobiliarios frente al rey." *Hispania Sacra* 68 (2016): 119–26.

Pick, Lucy. *Conflict and Coexistence: Archbishop Rodrigo and the Muslims and Jews of Medieval Spain*. Ann Arbor: University of Michigan Press, 2007.

Pliego, Ruth. "A Hoard of Late Roman and Visigothic Gold." In *The Numismatic Chronicle* 176 Offprint, 377–86 (plus plates). London: The Royal Numismatic Society, 2016.

Pliego, Ruth., ed. *La Moneda Visigoda: Historia Monetaria del Reino Visigodo de Toledo* (c. 569–711). 2 volumes. Seville: Universidad de Sevilla, 2009.

Pliego, Ruth. "Kings' Names on Visigothic Coins: A New Minimus from Ispali in the Name of Leovigild." *American Journal of Numismatics, Second Series* 30 (2018): 245–57.

Pliego, Ruth. "La falsificación de la moneda visigoda." In *Falsificació i manipulació de la moneda: XIV Curs d'Història monetaria d'Hispania*, edited by Marta Campo, 81–102. Barcelona: Museu Nacional d'Art de Catalunya, Gabinet Numismàtic de Catalunya, 2010.

Pliego, Ruth. "La Moneda Visigoda, Anexo I." *SPAL: Revista de prehistoria y archaeología de la Universidad de Sevilla* 21 (2012): 209–32.

Pliego, Ruth. "The Circulation of Copper Coins in the Iberian Peninsula during the Visigothic Period: New Approaches." *Journal of Archaeological Numismatics* 5, no. 6 (2016): 125–60.

Pohl, Walter, Helmut Reimitz, and Ian Wood, eds. *The Transformation of Frontiers from Late Antiquity to the Carolingians*. Boston and Leiden: Brill, 2000.

Quesnay Adams, Jeremy du. "The Political Grammar of Julian of Toledo." In *Minorities and Barbarians in Medieval Life and Thought*, edited by Susan J. Ridyard and Robert G. Benson, 179–95. Sewanee: University of the South Press, 1996.

Quirós Castillo, Juan Antonio. "Early medieval landscapes in north-west Spain: local powers and communities, fifth-tenth centuries." *Early Medieval Europe* 19 (2011): 285–311.

Ramallo Asensio, Sebastián. "Aproximación al urbanismo de Carthago Nova entre los siglos iv–vii D.C." In *Spania: Estudis d'antiguitat tardana oferts en homenatge al profesor Pere de Palol i Salellas*, 201–08. Barcelona: Publicacions de l'Abadia de Montserrat, 1996.

Ramallo Asensio, Sebastián, and Elena Ruiz Vaderas. "Cartagena en la arqueología bizantina en Hispania: estado de la cuestión." In *V Reunió d'arqueologia cristiana hispànica*, edited by Josep M. Gurt and Núria Tena, 305–22. Barcelona: Institut d'Estudis Catalans, 2000.

Rapp, Claudia. *Holy Bishop in Late Antiquity: The Nature of Christian Leadership in the Age of Transition*. Berkeley: University of California Press, 2005.

Reimitz, Helmut. "The Historian as Cultural Broker in the Late and Post-Roman West." In *Western Perspectives on the Mediterranean: Cultural Transfer in Late Antiquity and the Early Middle Ages, 400–800 AD*, edited by Andres Fischer and Ian Wood, 41–54. New York and London: Bloomsbury, 2014.

Reydellet, Marc. "La diffusion des *Origines* d'Isidore de Séville au haut moyen âge." *Mélange d'Archéologie et d'Histoire de l'École Française de Rome* 78 (1966): 383–437.

Reydellet, Marc. *La Royauté dans la littérature latine de Sidoine Apollinaire à Isidore de Séville*. Rome: École Française de Rome, 1981.

Reydellet, Marc. "La signification du Livre IX des Etymologies: érudition et actualité." In *Los Visigodos, Historia y Civilización, Actas de la Semana Internacional de Estudios Visigóticos, Antigüedad y cristianismo* 3, 337–50. Murcia: Universidad de Murcia, 1986.

Reydellet, Marc. "Les intentions idéologiques dans la 'Chronique' d'Isidore de Séville." *Mélanges d'archéologie et d'histoire* 82 (1970): 363–400.

Reynolds, Paul. *Hispania and the Roman Mediterranean, AD 100–700: Ceramics and Trade*. London: Duckworth, 2010.

Riché, Pierre. *Éducation et culture dans l'occident barbare, VIe-VIIIe siècle*. Paris: Éditions du Seuil, 1962.

Riché, Pierre. *Henri Irénée Marrou, historien engagé*. Paris: Les Éditions du Cerf, 2003.

Riché, Pierre. "La pastorale populaire en Occident, VIe-XIe siècles." In *Histoire vécue du peuple chrétien*, ed. Jean Delumeau, 195–221. Toulouse: Privat, 1979.

Riché, Pierre. "L'enseignement et la culture des laïcs dans l'occident pré-carolingien." In *La scuola nell'occidente latino dell'alto medioevo*, 231–53. Settimane di Studio del Centro Italiano di Studi sull'Alto Medioevo 19 (Spoleto: Presso la sede del Centro, 1972).

Riché, Pierre. "Les écoles, l'église et l'état en Occident du Ve au XIe siècle." In *Église et enseignement. Actes du Colloque du Xe anniversaire de l'Institut d'Histoire du Christianisme de l'Université Libre de Bruxelles*, 33–45. Brussels: Editions de l'Université de Bruxelles, 1977.

Ricoeur, Paul. *History and Truth.* Translated by Charles A. Kelby. Evanston: Northwestern University Press, 1965.

Ricoeur, Paul. *Memory, History and Forgetting.* Translated by Kathlee Blamey and David Pellauer. Chicago: University of Chicago Press, 2004.

Rio, Alice. *Legal Practice and the Written Word in the Early Middle Ages: Frankish Formulae c. 500–1000.* Cambridge: Cambridge University Press, 2009.

Ripoll López, Gisela. "On the Supposed Frontier between the Regnum Visigothorum and Byzantine Hispania." In *The Transformation of Frontiers from Late Antiquity to the Carolingians,* edited by Walter Pohl, Ian Wood, and Helmut Reimitz, 95–115. Boston and Leiden: Brill, 2000.

Ripoll López, Gisela. "The archaeological characterisation of the Visigothic kingdom of Toledo: the question of the Visigothic cemeteries." In *Völker, Reiche und Namen im frühen Mittelalter, 65 Geburtstag Prof. Dr. Jörg Jarnut (Mittelalter Studien 22),* edited by Matthias Becher and Stefanie Dick, 161–80. Munich: W. Fink, 2010.

Ripoll López, Gisela. "The Arrival of the Visigoths in Hispania: Population Problems and the Process of Acculturation." In *Strategies of Distinction: the Construction of Ethnic Communities, 300–800,* edited by Walter Pohl and Helmut Reimitz, 153–87. Boston and Leiden: Brill, 1998.

Robles Carcedo, Laureano. "Tajón de Zaragoza, continuador de Isidoro." *Saitabi* 21 (1971): 19–25.

Rodríguez, Félix. "Los antiguos concilios españoles y la edición crítica de la colección canónica *Hispana.*" In *Monumenta Iuris Canonici, Vol. 6, Proceedings of the Fifth International Congress of Medieval Canon Law,* edited by Stephen Kuttner and Kenneth Pennington, 3–13. Vatican: Biblioteca Apostolica Vaticana, 1980.

Rodríguez, Félix. *Observaciones y sugerencias sobre algunos manuscritos de la Colección Canónica Hispana,* 139–42. Burgos: Facultad Teológica del Norte de España, 1975.

Rodríguez Martorell, Francesc, and Josep M. Macias Solé. "Buscando el siglo VIII en el Puerto de Tarracona: entre la residualidad y el desconocimiento." In *Cerámicas Altomedievales en Hispania y su entorno (siglos v–viii d.C.),* edited by Iñaki Martín Viso, Patricia Fuentes Melgar, José Carlos Sastre Blanco, and Raúl Catalán Ramos, 573–89. Valladolid: Glyphos, 2018.

Rodríguez Morales, Jesús. "¿Petronio en la Biblioteca de Isidoro de Seville?" *Helmantica: Revista de filología clásica y hebrea* 43 (1992): 69–77.

Sánchez-Albornoz, Claudio. *El aula regia y las asambleas políticas de los godos.* Cuadernos de historia de España 5. Buenos Aires: Facultad de filosofía y letras, 1946.

Sánchez Lopéz, Elena, and Javier Martínez Jiménez. *Los acueductos de Hispania: construcción y abandono. Colección Juanelo Turriano de Historia de la Ingeniería.* Madrid: Fundación Juanelo Turriano, 2016.

Sánchez Ramos, Isabel. "The understanding of the late urban landscape in Hispania from a material perspective." In *Cities, Lands and Ports in Late Antiquity and the*

Early Middle Ages: Archaeologies of Change, edited by Pilar Diarte-Blasco, 9–22. Rome: Bradypus Books, 2017.

Sánchez Velasco, Jerónimo. *The Christianization of Western Baetica: Architecture, Power, and Religion in the Late Antique Landscape*. Amsterdam: Amsterdam University Press, 2018.

Saragoça, Patrícia, et al. "Stable isotope and multi-analytical investigation of Monte da Cegonha: A Late Antiquity population in southern Portugal." *Journal of Archaeological Science: Reports* 9 (2016): 728–42.

Scherer, Cornelia. "Forschen ohne historisch-kritische Textgrundlage: der Dekretalenteil der *Collectio Hispana*." *Zeitschrift für Rechtsgeschichte, Kanonistische Abteilung* 102 (2016): 1–22.

Schiffman, Zachary Sayre. *The Birth of the Past*. Baltimore: The Johns Hopkins University Press, 2011.

Schmitt, Carl. *Political Theology: Four Chapters on the Concept of Sovereignty*. Translated by George D. Schwab. Cambridge: MIT Press, 1985.

Schwitter, Raphael. "Letters, Writing Conventions, and Reading Practices in the Late Roman World. Analysing Literary Reception in Late Antiquity and Beyond." *Linguarum Varietas* 6 (2017): 61–78.

Séjourné, Paul. *Le dernier père de l'église, S. Isidore de Seville*. Paris, 1936.

Shanzer, Danuta. "Augustine's Disciplines: *Silent diutius Musae Varronis*?" In *Augustine and the Disciplines: from the Cassiciacum to Confession*, edited by Karla Pollman and Mark Vessey, 69–112. Oxford: Oxford University Press, 2005.

Shippey, Tom. "The Merov(ich)ingian again: *damnatio memoriae* and the *usus scholarum*." In *Latin Learning and English Lore: Studies in Anglo-Saxon Literature for Michael Lapidge*, edited by Katherine O'Brien O'Keffe, and Andy Orchard, volume 1, 389–406. Toronto: University of Toronto Press, 2005.

Sirks, Adriaan J. B. "Shifting Frontiers in the Law: Romans, Provincial and Barbarians." In *Shifting Frontiers in Late Antiquity*, edited by Ralph W. Mathisen and Hagith Sivan, 146–57. Brookfield: Variorum, 1996.

Smith, Shawn. "The Insertion of the *Filioque* into the Nicene Creed and a Letter of Isidore of Seville." *Journal of Early Christian Studies* 22 (2014): 265–69.

Smyth, Marina. "The Seventh-Century Hiberno-Latin Treatise *Liber de ordine creaturarum*: a translation." *The Journal of Medieval Latin* 21 (2011): 137–222.

Sotomayor, Manuel. "Las Relaciones Iglesia Urbana-Iglesia Rural en los Concilios Hispano-Romanos y Visigodos. In *Sacralidad y Arqueología: homenaje al Prof. Thilo Ulbert al cumplir 65 años, Antigüedad y cristianismo*, 21, edited by Thilo Ulbert, José María Blázquez, and Antonino González Blanco, 525–39. Murcia: Universidad de Murcia, 2004.

Steinová, Evina. "The Materiality of Innovation: Formats and Dimensions of the *Etymologiae* of Isidore of Seville in the Early Middle Ages." In *Entangled Manuscripts*,

c. 600–1100, edited by Anna Dorofeeva and Michael J. Kelly. Binghamton: Gracchi Books, forthcoming 2021.

Steinová, Evina. "The Oldest Manuscript Tradition of the *Etymologiae* (Eighty Years after A. E. Anspach)," *Visigothic Symposia* 4 (2020): 100–143.

Sterk, Aron C. "Latino-Romaniotes: The Continuity of Jewish Communities in the Western Diaspora, 400–700 CE." *Melilah, Manchester Journal of Jewish Studies* (2012): 21–49.

Stewart, Peter. "The Destruction of Statues in Late Antiquity." In *Constructing Identity in Late Antiquity*, edited by Richard Miles, 159–89. London: Routledge, 1999.

Stocking, Rachel. *Bishops, Councils and Consensus in the Visigothic kingdom*. Ann Arbor: University of Michigan Press, 2000.

Stocking, Rachel. "Martianus, Aventius and Isidore: Provincial Councils in Seventh-Century Spain." *Early Medieval Europe* 6 (1997): 168–92.

Thier, Andreas. "Time, Law, and Legal History – Some Observations and Considerations." *Rechtsgeschichte* 25 (2017): 20–44.

Thompson, Edward A. *Goths in Spain*. Oxford: Oxford University Press, 1969.

Tizzoni, Mark. "The Poems of Dracontius in Their Vandalic and Visigothic Contexts." Ph.D. diss., University of Leeds, 2012.

Tomás-Faci, Guillermo, and José Carlos Martín-Iglesias. "Cuatro documentos inéditos del monasterio visigodo de San Martín de Asán (522–586)." *Mittellateinisches Jahrbuch* 52 (2017): 261–86.

Toso, Alice, and Michelle Alexander. "Paleodietary reconstruction (Visigothic Setubal, Portugal)." *Setúbal Arqueológica* 17 (2018): 203–06.

Tovar, Antonio. "Un obispo con nombre británico y los orígenes de la diócesis de Mondoñedo." *Habis* 3 (1972): 155–58.

Tuori, Kaius. "Legal Pluralism and the Roman Empire." In *Beyond Dogmatics: Law and Society in the Roman World*, edited by John W. Cairns and Paul J. du Plessis, 39–52. Edinburgh: Edinburgh University Press, 2007.

Ubl, Karl. "Eine Verdichtung der *Lex Salica*. Die *Septinas septem* der Handschrift Paris, BN lat. 4411." In *Exzerpieren – Kompilieren – Tradieren: Transformationen des Wissens zwischen Spätatike und Frühmittelalter. Millennium-Studien 64*, edited by Stephan Dusil, Gerald Schwedler, and Raphael Schwitter, 223–44. Berlin and Boston: De Gruyter, 2017.

Ungvary, David. "The voice of the dead king Chindasuinth: poetry, politics, and the discourse of penance in Visigothic Spain." *Early Medieval Europe* 26, no. 3 (2018): 327–54.

Valcárcel Martínez, Vitalino. "Sobre el origen geográfico de la familia de Braulio, obispo de Zaragoza." In *Mnemosynum C. Codoñer a discipulis oblatum*, edited by Augustín Ramos Guerreira, 333–40. Salamanca: Universidad de Salamanca, 1991.

Valente, Cynthia María. "As Relações Políticas entre o Império Bizantino e o Reino Visigodo de Toledo durante o século VI." *Revista Mosaico* 11 (2018): 123–30.

Valverde Castro, María del Rosario. *Ideología, simbolismo y ejercicio del poder real en la monarquía visigoda: un proceso de cambio.* Salamanca: Universidad de Salamanca, 2000.

Valverde Castro, María del Rosario. "Simbología del poder en la monarquía visigoda." *Studia Historica, Historia antiqua* 9 (1991): 139–48.

Vallejo Girvés, Margarita. *Bizancio y la España tardoantigua (ss. v–viii): un capítulo de historia mediterránea.* Alcalá de Henares: Universidad de Alcalá, 1993.

Valverde Castro, María del Rosario. "El sistema viario peninsular en los límites de la provincia bizantina de Spania." In *Camineria hispánica: actas del II Congreso Internacional de Caminería Hispánica*, edited by Manuel Criado de Val, 95–108. Madrid: AACHE Ediciones, 1987.

Van Parys, Michel Jan. "The Historical Evidence on the Council of Chalcedon: the Council of Chalcedon as Historical Event." *Ecumenical Review* 22 (1970): 305–20.

Varela Rodríguez, Joel. "Las *Sententiae* de Tajón de Zaragoza. Sus modelos literarios y su aproximación a la teología de Gregorio Magno." *e-Spania* (2018): 1–15.

Varner, Eric R. *Mutilation and Transformation: "Damnatio Memoriae" and Roman Imperial Portraiture.* Boston and Leiden: Brill, 2004.

Velázquez Soriano, Isabel. *La Literatura Hagiográfica: Presupuestos Básicos y Aproximación a sus Manifestaciones en La Hispania Visigoda.* Libros Singulares 17. Burgos: Fundación Instituto Castellano y Leonés de la Lengua, 2007.

Velázquez Soriano, Isabel. *Las Pizarras Visigodas: Entre el latín y su disgregación. La lengua hablada en Hispania, siglos vi–viii.* Madrid: Real Academia Española, 2004.

Velázquez Soriano, Isabel. "*Pro patriae gentisque Gothorum statu* (4th Council of Toledo, Canon 75, A. 633)." In *Regna and Gentes. The Relationship between Late Antique and Early Medieval Peoples and kingdoms in the Transformation of the Roman World*, edited Hans-Werner Goetz, Jörg Jarnut, and Walter Pohl, 161–218. Boston and Leiden: Brill, 2003.

Velázquez Soriano, Isabel, and Gisela Ripoll López. "*Toletum*, la construcción de una *urbs regia*." In *Sedes Regiae (ann. 400–800)*, edited by Gisela Ripoll, Josep María Gurt, and Alexandra Chavarría Arnau, 521–71. Barcelona: Reial Acadèmia de Bones Lletres, 2000.

Vessey, Mark. "The Demise of the Christian Writer and the Remaking of 'Late Antiquity'." *Journal of Early Christian Studies* 6 (1998): 377–411.

Vessey, Mark, and Karla Pollman. *Augustine and the Disciplines: from the Cassiciacum to Confession.* Oxford: Oxford University Press, 2005.

Vieira Pinto, Otávio Luiz. "O Mais Belo Ornamento de Roma." M.A. thesis, Universidade Federal do Paraná, 2012.

Vieira Pinto, Otávio Luiz. Review of Sean D. W Lafferty, *Law and Society in the Age of Theoderic the Great: A Study of the "Edictum Theoderici"* (Cambridge: Cambridge University Press, 2013). *Networks and Neighbours* 2, no. 2 (2014): 400–03.

Vilella Masana, Josep. "Los obispos y presbíteros del supuesto concilio de Elvira." In *El obispo en la Antigüedad tardía. Homenaje a Ramón Teja*, ed. Silvia Acerbi, Mar Marcos, and Juana Torres, 335–54. Madrid: Editorial Trotta, 2016.

Vizcaíno, Jaime. *La presencia bizantina en Hispania (siglos vi–viii)*. 2nd edition. Murcia: Universidad de Murcia Press, 2009.

Vismara, Guilio. *Edictum Theoderici*. Ius romanum medii aevi. Volume 1.2b aa. Milan: Giuffrè, 1967.

Vismara, Guilio. "*Leges Visigothorum*." In *Lexikon des Mittelalters* 5, 1804–05. Munich and Zurich: Artemis Verlag, 1991.

Wallace-Hadrill, John Michael. *Early Germanic Kingship in England and on the Continent*. Oxford: Oxford University Press, 1971.

Wallace-Hadrill, John Michael. *The Barbarian West, 400–1000*. 3rd edition. London: Hutchison, 1967.

Walsby, Malcolm, and Natasha Constantinidou, eds. *Documenting the Early Modern Book World: Inventories and Catalogues in Manuscript and Printing*. Boston and Leiden: Brill, 2013.

Warntjes, Immo. "The Continuation of the Alexandrian Easter table in Seventh-Century Iberia and its Transmission to Ninth-Century Francia (Isidore, *Etymologies* 6.17)." *Revue d'Histoire des Textes* (2018): 185–94.

Werner, Karl-Ferdinand. "Gott, Herrscher und Historiograph. Der Geschichtschreiber als Interpret des Wirken Gottes in der Welt und Ratgeber der Könige." In *"Deus qui mutat tempora." Menschen und Institutionen im Wandel des Mittelalters. Festschrift für Alfons Becker*, edited by Ernst Dieter Hehl, Hubert Seibert, and Franz Staab, 1–31. Sigmaringen: Thorbecke, 1987.

White, Hayden. "Historicism, History, and the Figurative Imagination." *History and Theory* 14 (1975): 48–67.

White, Hayden. *Metahistory: The Historical Imagination in Nineteenth-Century Europe*. Baltimore: The Johns Hopkins University Press, 1975.

White, Hayden. "The Value of Narrativity in the Representation of Reality." In Hayden White, *The Content of Form*, 1–25. Baltimore: The Johns Hopkins University Press, 1987.

Wickham, Chris. *Framing the Early Middle Ages: Europe and the Mediterranean, 400–800*. Oxford: Oxford University Press, 2005.

Wickham, Chris, and James Fentress. *Social Memory*. Oxford: Oxford University Press, 1992.

Wolf, Kenneth Baxter. Review of Ksenia Bonch Reeves, *Visions of Unity after the Visigoths: Early Iberian Latin Chronicles and the Mediterranean World* (Cursor Mundi 26). Turnhout: Brepols, 2016. *Speculum* 93, no. 3 (2018): 801–02.

Wood, Ian. Review of Søby Christiansen, *Cassiodorus, Jordanes and the History of the Goths. Studies in Migration Myth* (Copenhagen: Museum Tusculanum Press, 2002). *Historisk Tidsskrift* 103 (2003): 465–84.

Wood, Ian. "Social Relations in the Visigothic kingdom from the Fifth to the Seventh Century: The Example of Mérida." In *The Visigoths from the Migration Period to the Seventh Century: An Ethnographic Perspective*, edited by Peter Heather, 191–208. Woodbridge: Boydell Press, 2003.

Wood, Ian. "The Bloodfeud of the Franks: A Historiographical Legend." *Early Medieval Europe* 14 (2006): 489–504.

Wood, Ian. *The Merovingian kingdoms 450–751*. New York: Longman, 1994.

Wood, Ian. *The Modern Origins of the Early Middle Ages*. Oxford: Oxford University Press, 2013.

Wood, Jamie. "Defending Byzantine Spain: frontiers and diplomacy." *Early Medieval Europe* 18 (2010): 292–319.

Wood, Jamie. "Playing the Fame Game: Bibliography, Celebrity, and Primacy." *Journal of Early Christian Studies* 20 (2012): 613–40.

Wood, Jamie. *The Politics of Identity in Visigothic Spain: Religion and Power in the Histories of Isidore of Seville*. Boston and Leiden: Brill, 2012.

Wood, Jamie, and Javier Martínez Jiménez. "New Directions in the Study of Visigothic Spain." *History Compass* 14, no. 1 (2016): 29–38.

Wood, Jamie, and Sam Koon. "Unity from disunity: law, rhetoric and power in the Visigothic kingdom." *European Review of History* 16 (2009): 793–808.

Wormald, Patrick. "*Lex Scripta* and *Verbum Regis*: Legislation and Germanic Kingship from Euric to Cnut." In *Legal Culture in the Early Medieval West: Text, Image and Experience*, 1–43. London: The Hambledon Press, 1999.

Wormald, Patrick. *The Making of English Law*. Oxford: Oxford University Press, 1999.

Wreglesworth, John. "The Chronicle of Alfonso III and its Significance for the Historiography of the Asturian kingdom 718–910 AD." Ph.D. diss., University of Leeds, 1995.

Young, Simon. "The Bishops of the Early Medieval Spanish Diocese of Britonia." *Cambrian Medieval Celtic Studies* 45 (2003): 1–19.

Žižek, Slavoj. *First as Tragedy, Then as Farce*. New York: Verso, 2009.

Žižek, Slavoj. *For They Know Not What They Do*. New York: Verso, 2002.

Žižek, Slavoj. *Less Than Nothing: Hegel and the Shadow of Dialectical Materialism*. New York: Verso, 2012.

Žižek, Slavoj, and John Milbank. *The Monstrosity of Christ: Paradox or Dialectic?* Cambridge: MIT Press, 2009.

Žižek, Slavoj, and Simon Critchley. *How to Read Lacan* (How to Read). New York: W.W. Norton, 2007.

Index

Agali monastery 97, 114, 117, 140, 145, 149, 184
   Helladius and 30, 35, 37–39, 145
   Julian of Toledo and 213–215
   Toledo-Agali, School of 18–19, 22–23, 27–43, 50, 53–54, 65, 69, 75, 118, 121, 129–130, 137, 146, 158–169, 171, 175, 182, 193, 202
Agila, Visigothic king 4, 52, 100–104, 110
Arianism/Arians 2, 24, 33, 55, 95, 102–103, 106, 142, 145, 147, 189, 191, 205
Athanagild, Visigothic king 4, 52, 103–104, 110

Badiou, Alain 66, 87, 90, 105
Baetica 1–2, 22–23, 26–27, 37, 53, 94, 98, 100, 124, 126, 148, 155, 157, 161–162, 171–172, 206, 214
Barcelona 3–4, 22, 57, 104, 145, 154, 182, 204
   Council of (599) 132
Braulio of Zaragoza 24, 27–35, 39, 44–50, 52–53, 60, 62, 72–74, 82–83, 85, 87, 124, 128, 130, 133, 151, 155–157, 175, 195, 198–199
   Epistolae 46, 161–166, 170, 173, 186
   Etymologies (Origines) 73–74, 113
   Fourth Council of Toledo 28, 132, 197
   Fifth Council of Toledo 150
   Chronicle of 754 149–150
   Isidore of Seville, relationship with 23, 27, 148
   Isidore-Seville, School 23, 147, 196
   Letter from/to Pope Honorius 170, 200
   Liber Iudiciorum 28, 181–182, 185, 193
   Renotatio 46–47, 77–78, 82, 109, 118
   Vita Aemeliani 28

Carpetania 1, 5, 52, 70, 138, 142–143, 145, 155
Cartagena 22–25, 118, 125, 138, 140–142, 144, 152–157, 214
Carthaginensis 1, 26, 36–38, 52–53, 118, 138–145, 150
Catholicism 2, 10, 24–25, 51–52, 66, 101, 103, 105–106, 124, 142, 184
Chindaswinth, Visigothic king 14, 28–29, 31–32, 39–41, 53, 55, 183–191, 197–199, 205
Convivencia 67, 97, 118, 210

Córdoba 9, 22, 44, 47, 79, 100, 103–104, 109, 125, 128, 133, 172, 178–179
Councils of the Visigothic Church
   Conciliar collections
     Hispana 18, 26, 28, 42, 48, 68, 76, 114, 119–174, 178, 182, 191, 200, 210, 214
     Catalonian/Pyrennean 123
     Epitome Hispana 132
     Novara collection 121–122, 173
     St. Maur 121, 123
   III Braga 31
   Egara 132, 207
   Huesca 131–132, 207
   Narbonne 131
   II Seville 2, 13, 47–48, 58–59, 68, 118, 125, 139, 153, 157, 164, 166, 172, 182, 184, 200
   III Seville 48–49, 104, 122, 130–132, 144, 147, 150–151, 153, 157, 159–160, 162–174
   III Toledo 2, 24–25, 33, 51–52, 56, 58, 121–122, 132, 138, 140, 142, 145, 155
   IV Toledo 13, 26–28, 33, 38, 41, 48, 68, 77, 123–126, 128, 130, 132, 138, 147, 149–150, 160–161, 167–169, 171, 173, 182, 184–185, 197, 200, 202–203, 210
   V Toledo 33, 124, 138, 150, 167, 182, 197
   VI Toledo 52, 122, 148, 150, 159, 161–163, 167–173, 188, 197, 199
   VII Toledo 31, 35, 56–57, 123, 182, 188
   VIII Toledo 2, 32, 40, 45, 54–59, 63, 134, 157, 159, 173, 175, 177–178, 182–183, 185–188, 192, 198–200, 203
   II Zaragoza 123, 131–132

Duero plateau 135

Eugenius I, bishop of Toledo 33, 39, 169, 171, 214
Eugenius II, bishop of Toledo 23, 28–32, 35–36, 39, 41, 47, 52–53, 57, 59, 186–187, 193, 197
   Liber Iudiciorum 22, 157, 182, 193, 195, 198
Euric, Visigothic king 3

INDEX

Fontaine, Jacques   1, 7, 11, 23, 25, 44, 46–47, 56, 68, 73, 77, 82, 86, 91, 94, 97, 116, 127, 136, 145, 180–181, 191, 195, 200
   Isidorian Renaissance   15–17, 20–21, 67, 181
Forum Iudicum   167, 179, 211
Froia, rebel/attempted usurper   57, 187, 199–200
Fronimian   28–30, 46, 133
Fructuosus   27, 33–35, 37, 39, 46, 148, 169
   Vita Fructuosi   13, 33–34, 37, 59
Formulae Wisigothicae   13, 109
Fuero Juzgo   179, 181

Galicia   1, 22, 27, 34, 129, 167
Gallia Narbonensis/Septimania   1, 34, 125, 138, 149, 201
Gerontius, ecclesiastical usurper   31, 39–40, 149, 162, 173
God   59, 80, 95, 111–112, 186–187, 191, 194–195, 199
   Augustine, City of God   46
   See also Jesus Christ

Gothstalgie   20, 63
Gregory of Tours, Bishop   10, 19, 68
Gregory the Great, Pope   11, 25, 48, 51, 57, 59, 61–62, 67, 106, 140, 154, 191
Gog/magog   106–113
Gundemar, Visigothic king   31, 37–40, 42, 47–49, 52, 56, 84, 97, 102, 117–120, 125, 127, 129–161, 165, 174, 177, 184, 191, 193–195, 200, 202

Hegel, G. W. F.   19, 158
Helladius, bishop of Toledo   30, 35, 37–39, 62, 111, 128, 145, 149, 173, 214

Ildefonsus, bishop of Toledo   33, 35–37, 39–40, 44–45, 49–54, 60, 63, 72, 91, 109, 110–11, 149, 175, 205, 210, 213
Isidore of Seville, bishop
   Gundemar and   47, 49, 97, 102, 117–118, 136–161, 193–195
   Helladius and   37–38, 173
   Historiography of   43–63
   Philosphy of History of   87–96
   Sisebut and   25–26, 28, 59, 69–73, 75, 84, 90, 100, 102–103, 118, 145–148, 157, 160, 198–199, 205
   Writings
     Chronicles   47, 66, 68–73, 76, 78, 81, 85, 93, 134, 136, 176, 181, 207
     De Origine Officiorum (*De Ecclesiasticis Officiis*)   47, 49, 66, 71–72, 76, 82, 92, 153, 179
     De Origine Gothorum (*Historia Gothorum*)   3, 9, 47, 55, 66, 68–69, 75–86, 90, 92–93, 98–116, 126–128, 136, 146, 152, 158, 160, 199–200
     De Viris Illustribus   13, 44–54, 68, 113, 123, 153, 155, 196, 207
     Etymologies (*Origines*)   28, 35, 47, 68–75, 83, 85, 89, 92–93, 95, 102, 111, 113, 115, 127–128, 137, 154, 157, 166, 181
     Sententiae   29–30, 56–58, 84, 87, 94, 127–128, 146, 194–195
     See also Jews and Judaism; Isidore-Seville; Isidore-moment; Fontaine-Isidorian Renaissance
Isidore-moment   14–42, 48, 51, 63–65, 70, 75, 79–80, 83, 96–97, 118–119, 158, 160, 174–177, 202, 208–210
Isidore-Seville, School of   18–19, 22–23, 27–43, 50, 53–54, 65, 69, 75, 118, 120, 123–124, 129–130, 137, 146, 158–169, 171, 175, 182, 193, 202
Iudila, rebel/attempted usurper   52, 126, 148–149

Jesus Christ   19, 181, 191, 199
   See also God
Jews and Judaism   5–6, 27, 41, 107, 111, 114, 152, 160, 163, 170, 176, 183, 201, 203–206
   Rabbinical   107, 187, 204–205
   Talmud   107, 111, 186–187
   See also God; Isidore of Seville; Levi Shmuel; *Liber Iudiciorum*; Sisebut
John, Bishop of Zaragoza, brother of Braulio   53, 155–156
John of Biclar   9, 25, 62, 69–70, 101, 104, 154
Justus, Bishop of Toledo   38–40, 149, 162, 173, 214
Justinian, Roman emperor   6, 84, 119, 142, 182–183

Leander of Seville, Bishop and brother of
    Isidore   11, 23–25, 51–52, 59, 70,
    124, 132, 153–154, 157, 199
  Gregory the Great and   48
  Homily   24
  Third Council of Toledo   24–25, 142
Levi Shmuel, Rabbi of Toledo   204–205
Liber Iudiciorum (*Visigothic Code*)   12–18, 22,
    28, 31–32, 40, 54, 58, 63, 73, 76,
    116, 120, 133–136, 157, 159, 167,
    173, 175–207, 211
Liuvigild, Visigothic king   2, 4, 8, 24, 55–56,
    61, 104, 126–127, 140, 144, 154,
    189, 201
Liuva, Visigothic king   102
Lusitania   1, 22–23, 126, 138

Masona, Bishop of Mérida   52–53, 102, 126,
    138, 142, 144
Mérida   4, 9, 20, 22, 52–53, 56, 103, 105, 124,
    126–128, 138, 148, 152
  See also *Vitas Patrum Emeretensium*

Narbonne   22, 33, 39, 48, 92, 120–121, 123, 131,
    138, 148, 169, 200

Pagans/paganism   5, 93, 95, 102–103, 107,
    110, 130

Reccared, Visigothic king   2, 24, 55–56, 64,
    102, 134, 138, 140, 142, 183–184,
    189–191, 193, 205–206
Reccared II, Visigothic king   38, 198–199
Recceswinth, Visigothic king   6–7, 14, 31–32,
    34–35, 40–41, 55–57, 66, 169–170,
    175, 177–178, 180–195, 198–207
Reccopolis   8–9, 36

Saint Leocadia, church of   118, 128, 134, 169,
    196
  Passio S. Leucadiae   128

Sisebut, Visigothic king   25–26, 28, 37–38,
    50, 55, 59, 61, 68–69, 73, 75, 84,
    90, 94, 97, 100, 102–103, 117–118,
    128, 133–134, 136, 141, 145–146,
    148, 157, 160, 183, 189, 194–196,
    198–200, 205
Sisenand, Visigothic king   31, 33, 35, 38–40,
    74, 77–79, 104, 125–127, 148–151,
    165, 169, 185, 196–197, 207
Sueves/Suevic kingdom   4, 7, 75, 77, 79–81,
    83–84, 93, 95, 100, 106, 200
Swinthila, Visigothic king   8, 38, 49–50,
    75, 78, 84, 100, 125–126, 148–149,
    161, 164, 166, 169, 182, 196,
    198–199

Taio of Zaragoza   29–30, 57, 182, 187, 193
Tarraconensis   1, 27, 143, 148
Tarragona   4, 9, 22, 27, 29, 122–124, 128, 132,
    145, 173
Theudisculus, Visigothic king   3, 101–103, 110

Vitas Patrum Emeretensium   52, 126–128,
    152
  See also Mérida

Visigothic law
  Breviarium Alarici (*Lex Romana
      Visigothorum*)   139, 162, 169,
      182, 206
  Codex Euricianus   182, 206
  Codex Revisus   206
  See also *Liber Iudiciorum*

Witteric, Visigothic king   102, 125, 141

Zaragoza   22, 27–31, 36, 46–48, 86, 99, 101,
    105, 112–113, 123–125, 128
  See also Braulio of Zaragoza; John, Bishop
      of Zaragoza
Žižek, Slavoj   18–19, 105, 158

Printed in the United States
By Bookmasters